DONALD HORNE

A Life in the Lucky Country

RYAN CROPP

LA TROBE
UNIVERSITY PRESS

IN CONJUNCTION WITH BLACK INC.

Published by La Trobe University Press in conjunction with Black Inc.
Wurundjeri Country
22–24 Northumberland Street
Collingwood VIC 3066, Australia
enquiries@blackincbooks.com
www.blackincbooks.com
www.latrobeuniversitypress.com.au

La Trobe University plays an integral role in Australia's public intellectual life, and is recognised globally for its research excellence and commitment to ideas and debate. La Trobe University Press publishes books of high intellectual quality, aimed at general readers. Titles range across the humanities and sciences, and are written by distinguished and innovative scholars. La Trobe University Press books are produced in conjunction with Black Inc., an independent Australian publishing house. The members of the LTUP Editorial Board are Vice-Chancellor's Fellows Emeritus Professor Robert Manne and Dr Elizabeth Finkel, and Morry Schwartz and Chris Feik of Black Inc.

9781760641375 (paperback)
9781743823248 (ebook)

A catalogue record for this book is available from the National Library of Australia

Cover design by Akiko Chan
Text design and typesetting by Beau Lowenstern
Cover photo of Donald Horne in 1984 © News Ltd / Newspix
Index by Belinda Nemec

For Deirdre

The unexamined nation is not worth living in.

—Donald Horne, June 1973

CONTENTS

Contents

ABBREVIATIONS

The following abbreviations appear in the text and footnotes:

ABC	Australian Broadcasting Corporation
ACP	Australian Consolidated Press
AACF	Australian Association for Cultural Freedom (1957–82)
ACCF	Australian Committee for Cultural Freedom (1954–57)
ASIO	Australian Security Intelligence Organisation
CCF	Congress for Cultural Freedom
CIA	Central Intelligence Agency
EEC	European Economic Community
NLA	National Library of Australia
SLNSW	State Library of New South Wales

INTRODUCTION

Late spring, 1968. A swarm of pedestrians make their way across a busy intersection in Sydney's CBD. As they approach the footpath and begin to go in separate directions, a short, serious-looking man in thick-rimmed black spectacles emerges from the throng. He is dressed neatly in a grey suit and tie. He walks purposefully, if a little stiffly: he is being filmed by ABC television for a special episode of *Four Corners*. He waves goodbye to a friend, strides confidently across the frame and steps onto a waiting bus.

On board, he takes a seat three rows from the back. He appears in profile, thin-lipped and sharp-nosed, his waft of white hair combed front to back. He peers out the window, seemingly absorbed in thought. His expression is inscrutable. As the vehicle begins to move, the camera starts toggling between his face and the things he observes: a busy road, a row of shops, a petrol station. Each image is framed twice: first by the bus window, then by the camera itself. It has a doubling effect: the man is both there and not, fully present in the scene yet somehow detached from it, the watcher and the watched.

His voice sounds over the montage, from above, as if he is reviewing his own performance. A few years earlier, he says, he wrote a book called *The Lucky Country*. It was an experience that taught him many new things, both about the country and about himself. The most fundamental, he thinks, was the need to abandon much of what he had been taught about Australia. While writing the book, he had tried to unlearn the artificial ways that the country had previously been analysed and interpreted. Doing so had forced him to see the world anew, in the way he had as a boy, taking things as they came.

The man providing this public self-analysis, Donald Horne, was no ordinary Australian talking head. He was, by vocation, a social critic, someone who trafficked in serious ideas and arguments, famous for thinking rather than doing. He was, in effect, an intellectual celebrity. For such a figure, an appearance on *Four Corners* was not simply an opportunity to burnish his reputation with a few self-serving anecdotes. Instead, it was a platform for further explication of his vision of Australian society, another place to mine the story of his own life for what it might reveal about the world around him. In one scene, for example, he stands on the verandah of his childhood home in Muswellbrook and declares the sight of his father's dead rose garden to be a reminder of the inevitability of change. In another, he leans on the gate of Muswellbrook's Anglican church and reflects on the history of Australian religious sectarianism. On a boat on Sydney Harbour, framed by the city's changing skyline, he expounds assuredly on topics such as suburbia, the convict inheritance and the nature of 'the Australian condition'.[1]

As a writer and critic, Horne had a natural inclination to draw meaning from the personal and the everyday, to make sense of the meaninglessness of existence. He was always taking a look around, always peering out the bus window and thinking carefully about what he saw. He was constantly absorbed in and fascinated by the world, forever seeking out new ideas and images for analysis, interrogation, categorisation. He was interested in anything and everything, untroubled by constraints of discipline or expertise. His friends sometimes described him as a bowerbird: a collector and an arranger of ideas and events, relentlessly trying to make new patterns out of the increasing complexity of postwar society.

Horne was not easily typed. He was at times a journalist, a magazine editor, an academic and an arts bureaucrat, though none of these professional labels ever really served as an adequate description of the role he played in Australian public life. He operated, for the most part, as a kind of public explainer, a crystalliser and a clarifier, a taker of the cultural and political temperature. His finger was always on the pulse, or close to it. As the critic Mark Thomas once put it, Horne's talent was for distillation, for 'saying cleverly things which other people have already known'.[2] He could capture more in a single sentence or phrase than others could in entire books.

For Horne, memorable phrases were masterpieces. They were not invented every week. They were necessary simplifications, bringing coherence to the muddle of reality and order to the discussion of contemporary events. The best of them gave shape to ideas that already existed, nebulously, in people's minds. Their coinage often had an element of serendipity, requiring both a shift in the zeitgeist – some imperceptible change in the political and cultural winds – and a writer able to identify, distil and popularise it: Henry Fairlie and 'the Establishment', Walter Lippmann and 'the Cold War'. But most importantly, Horne thought, by attempting to make sense of the present, those who invented memorable phrases provided a framework for action and a new sense of the possible. With just a few short words, reality could be redefined.[3]

Few Australian phrases are as memorable – or have redefined reality as successfully – as 'the lucky country'. In the six decades since Horne coined it, it has invaded the language, contorting and evolving with each new use. It is deployed freely and interchangeably, either as a celebration of Australia's unique virtues, a criticism of its unique vices, or – most often – simply as a glib synonym for the nation itself. Rarely do more than a few months go by without a fresh reference to it in Australian public life. It is the name of a podcast, a bus company and a brand of liquorice. It is the template for a small production line of introspective books: *The Adolescent Country*, *The Golden Country*, *The Lucky Culture*. In a suburb in Western Sydney, there is a Greek restaurant called 'Souvlucky Country'.

Horne lived in the shadow of the phrase for much of his life. *Four Corners*, for example, called its Horne profile 'Son of the Lucky Country'. Within months of the book's publication, the phrase was being used in slogans and advertisements: 'Australia truly is a lucky country for surfboards', went one.[4] In certain moods Horne would decry its existence and insist he was sick of being asked about it.[5] More often, though, he was ambivalent about its long afterlife. It was, in the end, a source of authority and prestige, the platform from which he launched his long and incredibly productive career as a writer and public figure.

He was never idle, unhappy without a project. Over four fruitful decades, he published thirty book-length works of social and political analysis, cultural commentary, history, fiction, biography and auto-biography, at a rate of almost one per year, as well as many hundreds of columns and essays, television and radio appearances, lectures and public addresses. He led campaigns against communism, censorship and the dismissal of the Whitlam government. He was a passionate advocate for the arts. He sat on countless committees and boards. For the majority of that time he was also Australia's leading republican, having almost single-handedly invented the idea as a modern polit-ical issue in the early 1960s. Geoffrey Blainey once compared him to a bee, always buzzing, occasionally stinging, before happily flying off to the next enthusiasm when the time came.[6]

His intellectual journey, though, was unorthodox. In the three decades between the end of World War II and the fall of the Whitlam government, he reversed the standard assumptions about the effects of ageing on one's political disposition, starting out somewhere on the political right and ending up as an icon of a new political centre-left. This slow and sometimes agonising personal transformation goes right to the heart of Horne's significance as both a social critic and a subject of biography. His was not a sudden switch of political alle-giance, but a long and considered process, forged in the productive tension between his periodic bouts of intense self-questioning, his open-minded curiosity about the social and political changes of the 1960s, and his relentless desire to make sense of those changes. Horne emerged from this chrysalis with a new and more progressive vision of the country, one coloured by a belief that with good leadership, Australia could and should be a much better place.

In 1979, while working in the political science school at the University of New South Wales, Horne published a study of Billy Hughes, the Australian prime minister during World War I and its aftermath and one of the most influential political figures of the post-Federation period. Hughes, too, had been on a political and intellectual odyssey – he had represented three different parties dur-ing his eight-year term as prime minister – and the book charted his journey from socialism and the trade union movement to his eventual leadership of a patriotic anti-Labor coalition of conservatives and liberals.

Horne insisted, however, that his book on Hughes was not a biography in any conventional sense. Nor, he added, was it 'Billy Hughes – the man behind the politician', and it was definitely not 'The love life of Billy Hughes'. Instead, he suggested, it was a personal and social portrait constructed entirely from Hughes' own words and images. Horne's Hughes was a wholly public animal, a political illusionist, mythmaker and a summoner of 'magical shapes'. He was, in Horne's view, an artist. But most importantly, he wrote, in the images 'cast up' by Hughes it was possible to see 'some of the roads by which Australia became what it is'.[7]

When he wrote *Billy Hughes* in the late 1970s, Horne was looking back nearly sixty years, to the early decades of Federation, and to a master rhetorician whose words reshaped Australian political culture in deep, enduring ways. It is in a similar spirit that this book – written from an almost identical distance – looks back at Horne himself, one of the master image-makers of postwar Australia. Throughout the second half of the twentieth century, Horne sketched out first drafts of many of the distinctive shapes of our modern political culture: the shifting boundaries of left and right, progressive and conservative; the dilemmas of Australia's British and American connections, of Asia, of national identity and the republic; and the effects of affluence, technology and generational change on Australian politics. It is my hope that in a critical account of the images that Horne 'cast up', it will once again be possible to see some of the roads by which Australia became what it is.

I.

WILD YOUNG SAVAGE

A new record had been set. According to the editorial team behind *Honi Soit*, the University of Sydney's student newspaper, more correspondence had flooded into the paper's tiny mailbox in the first week of October 1941 than at any other time in its short history. So overwhelming was this epistolary deluge that the *Honi* staff decided to give it front-page treatment. The nature of these impassioned epistles, they reported, differed widely. Some offered enthusiastic support for the paper's editorial line. Others tended towards outrage. The majority of the animus, though, was directed at the paper's controversial young editor, Donald Horne. 'Purge the moron!' wrote one irate reader. 'Resign!' demanded another. How much longer, they howled, would students have to endure the 'sneering, contemptuous' attitudes of this 'ill-educated youth'?[1]

In late 1941, a little over two years into Australia's participation in yet another catastrophic European war, there was no shortage of topics on which a mass of excitable university students could have found a way to furiously disagree. But the incendiary issue with which this student journalist had managed to divide his peers had very little to do with the conflict itself. Horne's subject was censorship, and in particular the censorship of 'indecent' literature, an issue ignited by the federal government's decision to reinstate a ban on James Joyce's 1922 novel *Ulysses*.[2] Horne's offending editorial 'SEX! – isn't it dreadful' had taken aim at what he saw as the government's latest absurd, neo-Victorian failure to acknowledge the 'actual existence of sex'. Australians, he alleged, could get 'more "filth" in an hour's stroll around public lavatories' than they would ever get from reading *Ulysses*. The best thing the university could do to combat such nonsense, he proposed, would be to offer 'a couple of frank lectures upon the sexual act itself'.[3]

In subsequent days, the hostility between Horne and his readers escalated rapidly. For this irascible young editor, nothing was more indicative of the weakness of Australian society than its failure to treat this 'modest' problem 'scientifically'.[4] The only outcome of sex censorship, he thought, was superstition and ignorance.[5] By mid-October, two weeks into the controversy, his vituperative arguments had metastasised into a full-blown attack on the nation. Australia, he believed, had become 'tired and wrinkled with waste and dust'. Its citizens clung 'pitifully close to the coastal fringe, ignoring the problems of its very earth'. In their small-minded materialism they were little more than 'spiritual evacuees in their own land', with their eyes fixed across the ocean at 'the Old World and its annexe America'. Horne's contempt for ordinary Australians was palpable. They were quiescent, escapist and mindlessly patriotic. They cared only for horse races, cinemas and 'horse-trough beer swilling'. Among their political representatives, too few possessed great minds. 'If we are to stave off perdition,' he warned, 'we must cease to ignore the facts.'[6]

Horne's pessimistic assessment of the Australian situation, though exaggerated almost to the point of hysteria, was not entirely baseless. In its official guises, at least, the society he harangued in 1941 was a conservative and parochial one. The newly established Australian Broadcasting Corporation (ABC) was formally prohibited from broadcasting controversial opinions, and its presenters self-consciously imitated the clipped tones of their British counterparts at the British Broadcasting Corporation (BBC). Commercially, almost all Australian trade was with other Commonwealth countries. When Britain declared war on Germany in September 1939, then prime minister Robert Menzies announced in a radio broadcast that 'as a result, Australia is also at war'. This intense sense of Britishness pervaded almost all aspects of Australian life. Cultural authority, too, came from abroad: if not from Britain, then from the popular films and music of the United States (though censorship and immigration law kept a lock on any unwanted foreign incursions). In the early years of World War II, Australia might not have been 'tired and wrinkled with waste and dust', as the nineteen-year-old *Honi* editor saw it, but it did have provincialism in its bones.[7]

◆ ◆ ◆

Such pessimism would have come as a surprise to those who knew Horne as a boy. By most accounts, he had been a cheerful child, eager, talkative and – owing to a lack of siblings – comfortable conversing with adults. It was from his mother's family that he derived his earliest feelings of belonging. Like characters out of an English novel, he joked, they would regularly go through genealogical recitations, amusing themselves by claiming to be a part of an old family. His grandmother Laura could allegedly trace her lineage back to an eighteenth-century French surgeon, who had fled France during the revolution and settled in Australia in 1797.[8] His father's family, by contrast, had shallower Australian roots. John and Grace Horne had migrated to Australia from Scotland in the late nineteenth century and settled in Wallsend, then a small mining town west of Newcastle, where Horne's father, David, was raised as one of nine children. The family were deeply affected by World War I, when five Horne brothers enlisted to fight but

Donald Horne as a schoolboy

only four returned. David, who served in the Australian Light Horse in the Middle East, made it back in 1919 and settled in Sydney, where he met Florence Carpenter and found work as a schoolteacher. They married in 1921, and Donald, their only son, was born later that year.[9]

In Sydney, the Hornes had lived a nomadic existence, moving around as David searched for work. By the time of his sixteenth birthday, Donald and his family had lived in ten different homes.[10] His earliest memories were of his maternal grandparents' house, 'Denbigh', in the southern Sydney suburb of Kogarah. He remembered this modest dwelling as an Australian version of Marcel Proust's Combray, a happy, boisterous place crammed with aunts, uncles, cousins, second cousins, neighbours, friends and pets. His mother's father, Ed Carpenter, was a railway sleeping car conductor, who had once run away from his family as a teenager to go droving. For Donald, he was the embodiment of a certain Australian ideal: proud and unpretentious, democratic and sceptical, stoical, convivial and – most importantly – contemptuous of humbug. At Denbigh, Donald later wrote, what was most important was to 'be yourself'.[11]

In 1927, David took a job at a school in Muswellbrook, a small town in the Hunter Valley region of New South Wales. For the next six years, their family of three occupied the same tin-roofed weatherboard bungalow and lived a life of lower-middle-class respectability. Their stay in the Hunter overlapped with the worst of the Depression, a time of immense social and political unrest, particularly further down the valley at Newcastle, where several shanty towns sprang up on the city's fringes to accommodate the unemployed. In Muswellbrook, the hardship had been less immediately visible, though Donald could remember striking miners marching down the main street and 'swaggies' knocking on the door looking for food. Like most Australians, the Hornes could not escape the impacts of the economic downturn, but with David's school teaching salary, they were spared the worst of it.[12]

Donald remembered his time in the Hunter as the happiest period of his life. He was enrolled in the Muswellbrook Rural District School, where he was consistently one of the top students in his class. His parents enjoyed a vibrant social life, and their house was always busy with the coming and going of friends. David played golf and

Florence tennis. Together, they all played bridge. Each summer, they went back to Sydney, where they would spend several weeks in the Carpenters' 'weekender' at Yowie Bay, swimming, fishing and lying on the sand. Life, as Donald had first experienced it in these years, had seemed to be one big fun fair. As far as he could tell, the point of all human destiny had been 'to have a good time'.[13]

The feeling was not to last. In 1933, David Horne abruptly accepted a transfer to a school in Westmead in Sydney's western suburbs. Donald, who had been boarding at a high school in Maitland, said goodbye to his new friends, and the Hornes said goodbye to Muswellbrook. As he later recalled, it was here that the innocent and optimistic outlook of his boyhood had begun to come apart. He was enrolled as a second-year student at Parramatta High School. From his new classmates he learned a kind of worldly teenage cynicism, rebellious and ironical, a lot of which he chose to direct at the unsophisticated and rote educational practices that students were forced to endure in those years. Bored and alienated, he developed an interest in news and current affairs, particularly those discussed in the pages of Sydney's *Daily Telegraph*. Both *The Daily Telegraph* and the family's new wireless radio opened up a world beyond the one he previously knew: political ineptitude, economic malaise and European fascism, among other things, suddenly became a part of his daily existence.[14]

He had, by his own account, a troubled adolescence. In 1932, before they left Muswellbrook, the family had briefly decamped to Bondi for six weeks so that David could receive treatment for a nervous condition they suspected might have been related to his war service. As Donald recalled, his father had always been a serious man with a 'systematic view of life', but after this episode he had become 'tense' and 'difficult to get on with'. In David's anxious presence, their home life became increasingly difficult. When Florence gave birth to a second child, Janet, in 1936, a teenaged Donald took an interest in childrearing that was perhaps uncharacteristic of high-school boys his age, reading up on the risks and rewards of different parenting strategies and offering advice to his mother.[15]

Other disillusionments followed. His grandfather, Ed Carpenter, died in 1936. In mid-1937, the family moved to Sandringham, a nascent suburb adjoining Botany Bay in southern Sydney, and Donald was forced to change schools again. For the final two years of his secondary education, he was enrolled at Canterbury Boys High School, to which he travelled, alone, by a bus and two trains. One day, he arrived home to find that his dog, Zac, had been killed by poison that their neighbours threw over the fence to stop him barking.[16]

Of all the events that combined to shatter Donald's childhood optimism, however, none had a greater impact on him than the collapse of David Horne's mental health. Despite his stern and serious demeanour, Donald recalled, his father had always been someone who felt it was important to be funny and to make 'wise cracks'. By the early 1930s, this aspect of his personality had disappeared. A few years after the move to Westmead, David was accused of sexual misconduct by a student and removed from his job. Not long after, he was declared to have had a mental breakdown and was admitted to a 'lunatic asylum' at Callan Park in Sydney. When he returned home with a pension from the Repatriation Department, he became little more than an absent presence in their life, an 'empty shell'. 'That was the end of that, from there, with regard to fathers', as Donald put it in an interview more than half a century later.[17]

From the moment Horne burst onto the university scene in 1939, he seemed hell-bent on finding new and affronting ways to express his disappointment with the general state of things. As a graduate of a state school, he had earned himself a free place at the university. This development, he thought, put him at odds with most of his more well-connected, private-school-educated peers, many of whom he believed were only there by virtue of their parents' bank accounts. For the recalcitrant young Donald, no attempt to undercut the prevailing rules and social orthodoxies was too petty. Without a living allowance, he took a Teachers' College stipend worth £40 a year, then deliberately flouted practically every requirement of the scholarship, such as the mandatory weekly physical training on the College grounds. When war broke out in September 1939, he and a few young friends ambled down to Central Station to fill out National Register cards under 'spurious names'. Learning to kowtow to authority, he decreed, was the opposite of an education.[18]

At the University of Sydney in the early 1940s, Horne's relentless prodding of the most exaggerated manifestations of this second-rate culture earned him considerable notoriety among students. He was, for a time, a minor campus celebrity, well known as an enfant terrible of the highest and most disreputable calibre. Sharp-tongued, voluble and quick-witted, he sought out verbal conflict wherever he could get it. Few who quarrelled with him emerged unscathed. Under Horne, remembered one former *Honi* staff writer, the prevailing atmosphere in the paper's offices was invariably one of 'contempt (of anything and everybody)'. 'It was the most unfriendly place imaginable,' she reported. Or as the Labor prime minister John Curtin once said of a political rival: 'He would rather make a point than make a friend.'[19]

With such insubordinate inclinations, it was only a matter of time before Horne stumbled into the path of the university's most famous and influential rebel, John Anderson. He was not alone. Between the 1930s and 1950s, hundreds of noncompliant Sydney undergraduates were drawn to this tall moustachioed professor and his exhilaratingly anti-authoritarian ideas. Born in Scotland and educated at the University of Glasgow, Anderson had migrated to Australia in 1927 to assume Sydney's Chair of Philosophy. Working mostly independently

John Anderson, c. 1926

of philosophical debates in Europe and elsewhere, he developed a school of philosophy called 'Australian Realism', known colloquially among students as 'Freethought'. With the aid of rigorous logical argument and a complicated theory of aesthetics, he aimed to understand the objective reality of things.[20]

Anderson had a deep impact on the undergraduates who fell under his spell. The campus was often abuzz with celebrated examples of his iconoclasm (the philosopher David Armstrong once likened it to Socrates' popularity among the youth of Athens).[21] In one tale, the Scot thumbed his nose at the university's conservative establishment, striding nonchalantly across the Quadrangle during the daily broadcast of 'God Save the King'. In another, he was the bane of Sydney society, twice censured by the NSW parliament as a corrupter of young minds, a 'Socratic gadfly stinging the bourgeoisie'. One legend even circulated that he was one of only three men who understood Einstein. For several generations of future writers, poets, critics, philosophers, bureaucrats, diplomats and politicians, wrote Clive James in 2005, Anderson left 'a heritage of scepticism' that helped 'set limits' to the influence of fashionable leftist theorising.[22]

A deep understanding of the substance and detail of Anderson's philosophical ideas was not common among his many student followers. Membership of the Sydney University Freethought Society, the student organisation set up in his image, instead required four simple commitments: to the primacy of secularism and scientific observation, to the extension of knowledge in all fields, to the elimination of censorship and to the 'emancipation' of knowledge from 'superstition' and 'government interference'.[23] For many Freethinkers, most of whom did not go on to study philosophy, Anderson's influence was largely attitudinal. Bill Pritchett – one of Horne's closest university friends – attributed the professor's impact to the rebellious culture that surrounded him. Neither he nor Horne were 'strict Andersonians', he recalled, but they were both completely under his influence. 'To have a figure of that establishment supporting us ... reinforced our anti-establishment beliefs'.[24]

Of particular attraction to young know-alls like Horne and Pritchett was Freethought's posture of detachment from the petty squabbles of politics. From Anderson, they learned that society was 'pluralist'; that there was no single thing called 'Australia' or 'the national interest' but rather a variety of competing 'ways of life'; that politics was an 'unceasing conflict', a largely meaningless battle for power between competing interest groups. In the 1930s Anderson had been a communist sympathiser, but by the 1940s he had begun to criticise the prevailing Marxist faith in historical progress. He argued that historical development – the improvement of humanity and the march of civilisation – was not inevitable, nor linear, but cyclical. In Anderson's view, struggle was the 'doctrine of history'.[25] Horne quickly internalised this rather bleak realism. 'Every period of history,' he later parroted in *Honi Soit*, provided examples of 'conflict between social forces', a conflict as irreconcilable as it was unavoidable.[26]

In the late 1930s and early 1940s, as Australia moved onto a war footing, the debate over the expansion of the federal government's social and economic powers formed the principal ideological fault line among university students. On the back of this ongoing dispute, the Freethought Society – opposed as it was to any form of censorship or 'government interference' – became a kind of campus political faction, armed chiefly against what they saw as the authoritarian instincts of the Labor Club and, to a lesser extent, fascist sympathisers and religious groups. The ascension of John Curtin's Labor government in October 1941 fanned these flames, as did Nazi Germany's 1941 invasion of Russia and the subsequent Allied support for Stalin's Soviet Union. As this disagreement played out in various campus elections, it ushered in something of a golden age for the Freethinkers, who took control of student organisations and publications, such as the Students' Representative Council (SRC), *Honi Soit*, *ARNA* and *Hermes*.[27]

Beyond this basic ideological contest, though, Anderson's chief allure – for Horne at least – was the special role he reserved for critics. The professor maintained, in the Socratic tradition, that the freedom to pursue knowledge through rational and logical argument was a fundamental political virtue, one that was essential to the proper functioning of free societies. It was thus the social, moral and philosophical duty of Freethinkers to engage in a process of relentless critical enquiry into the myths, illusions and 'phantasies' that governed human behaviour (even if, in practice, this often manifested as little more than a heightened form of undergraduate contrarianism). Nothing was sacred: tradition, morality, socialism, religion. John Anderson had an answer to every conceivable question', as one former student remembered. 'It was "No".'[28]

◆ ◆ ◆

Literature, too, felt the impact of Andersonianism. Over the summer of 1939–40, Horne forced himself onto the fringes of a disconnected circle of campus poets that included James ('Jimmy') McAuley, Harold Stewart, Alec 'A.D.' Hope, Joan Fraser (later known as Amy Witting) and Alan Crawford. The group published their poems in the university literary magazine *Hermes* (which McAuley had edited in 1937) and the arts faculty magazine *ARNA*. It was rare to find this older set in the Quadrangle, however. They preferred to congregate in pubs and sly parlours: either the Park View Hotel on Myrtle Street or a bar in the Sydney CBD called Ushers. They smoked cigarettes and dressed in the 'intellectual fashion'. They were, to Horne's eyes, a picture of maturity and sophistication, 'the finest flowering of European civilisation'.[29]

Of this crowd, it was Jimmy McAuley who truly mesmerised Horne. In 1940, McAuley was a serious-minded twenty-three-year-old student writing a Masters thesis on symbolist poetry. Charismatic and good-looking, with a legendary talent for jazz piano, he possessed an immense personal magnetism that attracted both men and women. He had an uncanny ability to dominate a room upon entry, his dazzled and awestruck followers hanging on his every word.[30] For the eighteen-year-old Donald, he was Christ returned. McAuley, he recalled, was 'a genius whose brilliance shone for me like the sun'. After befriending him over the 1940 summer holidays, Horne even started to imitate some of his enigmatic 'literary' mannerisms. He learned the effectiveness of the cutting remark and the casual dismissal and tried to speak in wisecracks and mumbled witticisms. He also intuited that it was important to cultivate a sense of personal mystery, to give an impression of the inexpressibly deep and serious thoughts going on beneath the surface.[31]

Ingratiating himself with 'the Sydney poets' as best he could, Horne installed himself as a subeditor and frequent contributor to *Hermes*. Among this very male-dominated literary milieu, he became known as 'Young Donald', and under their influence he enjoyed a haphazard, informal introduction to modern poetry and prose. Joyce, Eliot, Pound and E.E Cummings were all brief fascinations, as were the nineteenth-century French symbolists Baudelaire, Mallarmé and Laforgue.[32] He quickly came to see poetry as the ideal literary form, the one that came closest to the truth of existence. Good art, he believed, had to 'reveal something of the nature of things'. It had to say something new, to accurately portray a 'mental situation' or a 'causal connection'. Above all else, it had to be grounded in the *real*. 'My friends, the Sydney poets, are attempting to overcome this difficulty,' he bragged. They had given up 'obsessions of novelty' and were working hard as 'apprentices in the world's second-oldest trade'.[33]

To Horne's enthusiastic mind, artists were engaged in the same probing quest for truth as the Freethinkers. In September 1941, for example, both the poet McAuley and the philosopher Anderson wrote to *Honi Soit* to express their outrage at the *Ulysses* ban, and the latter was also an influential force in the University Literary Society. For Horne, the professor's idiosyncratic brand of anti-materialist libertarianism provided a bridge between politics and literature. Great art, in Horne's view, combined the critic's 'spirit of inquiry' with the artist's 'love of beauty'. Its subject matter was the exposure of the 'many problems ... involved in living'. In pluralist societies, he declared, special responsibilities were conferred on artists – just as they were on critics – who 'must of necessity come into conflict with other forces in society'[34]:

> Poets are among the great discoverers ... True poetry feels towards things, imperfectly perhaps, but for the first time. If this conception is granted, poetry's position in the intellectual hierarchy can go unchallenged.[35]

Horne's own creative output in these years suggests that for a time he, too, fostered a serious commitment to the craft. Close to one hundred poems, drafts and fragments survive from his three years at the university. One agonising effort was composed during a solitary night spent observing drifters and eccentrics from a cafe in Sydney's Central Station. It was written 'For Stephen Daedalus', the literary alter ego of James Joyce and the protagonist of his novel *A Portrait of an Artist as a Young Man*. In his neat, scratchy handwriting, Horne turned repeatedly to Joycean themes of separateness, isolation and social alienation. In cryptic and overwrought verse, he struggled to describe the soul of man in the modern world: 'The whole is an all awful hole / That impregnates the cosmic soul'; 'And men live sick, disconsolate and bare.'[36]

Sex also featured heavily. In Horne's undergraduate verse, women had 'phantasticke breasts' and were in their 'sultry prime'. Others were 'whores' or 'harlots'. Love was unrequited or remembered: 'you had a lover and it was not I'; 'I wandered lost, and pined for you'; 'This girl you know … Whose limbs are at the service of your mind.'[37] Female memories of the time were much less romantic. Amy Witting, the lone woman of their group, remembered it as an age of deep male chauvinism. Women, she said, were 'sex objects'. If you were not a sex object, you were not accepted. If a woman wanted to be a writer, she had to be 'a George [or] a Henry'. 'It was an extremely sexist society.'[38]

Whatever you thought of Horne, though, there was no doubt that he put on a good show. As a furious *Honi Soit* reader complained, he was an unrepentant 'exhibitionist'. In 1940, for example, he became part of campus folklore when he filled an entire edition of *Hermes* with his own verse. When the young soldier Peter Ryan encountered him in Canberra, he could barely keep up. The talk was 'stratospherically' over his head. 'I watched Horne and marvelled – my first acquaintance with a human word factory was in full blast, and no "OFF" button to be found.' Pat Donovan, the editor of the University of Queensland's *Semper Floreat*, met him at a debating tournament, where he, too, found himself 'the victim of a fifteen-minute tirade' by 'Sydney's wild young savage'. Others were simply mesmerised by his fabled meanness. He was equal parts 'clever, cynical and egotistical,' recalled Bruce Miller – *Honi Soit* editor in 1943 – sometimes 'personally obnoxious' but nevertheless a young man of 'outstanding brilliance.'[39]

Despite being surrounded by this self-selected elite of Sydney poetry and freethinking, it was not until early 1941 that Horne found his true intellectual lodestar. When *Honi Soit* got into a spat with the *The Daily Telegraph* over student exemptions from war service, he was dispatched to the *Telegraph* offices on Park Street to argue the students' case. Anticipating a hostile verbal joust, he instead found himself on the receiving end of an apology from the paper's fearsome editor, Brian Penton, who appreciated his chutzpah so much he offered him a job on the spot. Starting immediately, Horne would – when required – be the *The Daily Telegraph*'s official university correspondent.

By 1941, Penton was already a semi-legendary figure in Australian newspapers, as notorious for his love of food, wine and extramarital affairs as he was for his muckraking journalism. Having started as a copy boy at *The Brisbane Courier*, he had worked his way to the top, building his reputation lampooning politicians in his 'From the gallery' and 'Sydney spy' columns, writing speeches for Billy Hughes and cavorting with literary figures such as Norman Lindsay and Henry Handel Richardson. After a five-year sojourn in London attempting to publish a novel, he had returned to Sydney to work on *The Daily Telegraph*. Under his editorship the paper was known for its irreverent approach, its fierce opposition to censorship and 'red tape', and its criticism of the complacency and mediocrity of Australian public life.[40]

Penton made an immediate impression on Horne. Here was a character who had no time for distracting trivialities or political weasel words. His only interest was in the identification and fearless exposure of objective, journalistic facts. In the exercise of this honourable duty, he appeared to wield an impressive influence over political affairs. In his columns and editorials, he transformed a Freethinker's disdain for outdated traditions and moral codes into aggressive and stylish verbal tirades. Horne was thrilled. Back in the *Honi Soit* office, he confessed to then editor Pritchett that he wanted to be a journalist. 'I staggered back in horror,' Pritchett remembered. 'Journalists weren't something one respected.' But in the formidable newspaperman, Horne had found an ideal model.[41]

Despite his reputation as a stirrer, Penton saw himself as the inheritor of two distinct intellectual traditions: one, the classical English liberalism of John Locke; the other, the sensual individualism of his literary hero D.H. Lawrence. He was a self-described 'realist', albeit of a more prosaic, journalistic kind than Anderson. In 1941, he published an incendiary book-cum-political pamphlet titled *Think – or Be Damned*, which he envisioned as an all-out assault on 'national pride, patriotism and other forms of respectable ostracism practised in Australia'. The book was widely read and reprinted three times before the end of the war. Its purpose, he admitted, was to provide an approach to the simmering national malaise rather than to offer any concrete solutions. It was, in effect, a polemic: an 'ill-mannered, cantankerous, unpatriotic, subversive and destructive' diatribe against muddy thinking, narrow-minded policymaking and misleading and emotional political language.[42]

Brian Penton, c. 1931

Horne found much to admire in Penton's inflammatory style. Politeness, it seemed, was just another way of obscuring the facts. Provocation was instead a moral duty, and offence was the price paid for truth. And so, after seizing the editorship of *Honi Soit* from Pritchett,

Horne set about offending as many groups as he could. 'You are such a dull lot,' he wrote of his fellow undergraduates, 'you do so little that is worth reporting.' Since so few students possessed a 'critical spirit', he suggested they 'go on growing like unhealthy little mushrooms in a cosy tunnel'. In homage to his new journalistic hero, he titled his diatribe 'Grin or Be Damned'.[43]

Horne revelled in this new Penton-like persona: the campus rabble-rouser, exhibitionist and uncompromising truth-teller. When he represented the university in a national debating tournament in Canberra, he was described in the program – very likely by himself – as an 'enfant terrible', someone who 'began as a precocious genius, developed an impenetrable hide, a pontifical delivery, and a mastery of provocative epigram'.[44] In a report to the student council on *Honi Soit*, he described his chosen editorial style as 'critical satirical reformist'. Under his supervision, he wrote, *Honi Soit* articles would be 'provocative and/or informative' and 'preferably attack something'.[45]

In his furious book, Penton had depicted the muddying of arguments and the obfuscation of meaning as some of the most egregious political crimes known to man. Language, in the hands of politicians and bureaucrats, was used not to solve problems but to obscure them. In his first chapter, 'Words and Blah-Blah', he wrote of the need to 'expunge from our national vocabulary every word, slogan or inflating poetic dictum which cannot be proved to have a meaning'. In his view, Australian political discourse was riddled with 'resounding abstractions' and 'poppycock-encrusted catchcries'. Words, properly used, should instead be 'unambiguous' and 'tied to observable facts'. Only if these abstractions – words and phrases such as 'democracy', 'civil rights and liberties' and 'freedom of thought and expression' – were purged from the national debate would Australia 'have the remotest hope of travelling anywhere but in a big circle'.[46]

In Penton's dark prophecy, Australia's failure to think clearly about its problems would bring dire consequences. It was obvious to him that 'no more politically muddled people exist on the face of the globe'. Australians, he thought, were more concerned with short-term policies than they were with working out a 'system of social cooperation'. As a result, he wrote, he was 'full of forebodings' and felt an 'acute expectation of consequences yet unreaped'. The 'darker Age of Confusion' was, in his mind, always imminent. Penton's was an apocalyptic worldview; there was every possibility that Australian civilisation would soon come to an end. The alternative to 'extinction', he thundered, 'is an effort *here* and *now*'; the only guides to Australia's urgent problems – finite raw materials, the future of White Australia and the tariff system, the choice between Britain or America, the need to establish a relationship with 'our immediate neighbours' – were 'the relevant facts'.[47]

Penton was not alone in his estimation of the many new and urgent dilemmas facing the nation. The shocks and realignments of a catastrophic global war – many of which were happening in Australia's backyard – prompted much soul-searching among the nation's political and intellectual elite. As Prime Minister Robert Menzies put it: 'What Great Britain calls the Far East is to us the near north.'[48] In late 1940, Penton's newest acolyte, Donald Horne – the veteran of hundreds of unresolved undergraduate arguments – happily joined this anxious chorus. In fact, his infamous 'Let us Rejoice' editorial in *Honi Soit* read like a parody of Penton's *Think – or Be Damned*. Australia's 'superstitious' and 'quiescent' patriotism, Horne warned, was a threat to national survival: 'A fool's paradise is notoriously short-lived.'[49]

This last *Honi* outburst was an early rehearsal of Horne's critical style and pet themes, encapsulating some of the tenor of his critical response to Australia's problems in the decades to come. A concern with the myriad dilemmas created by the wartime reordering of the world would never leave him. Australia would remain at a crossroads: in one direction, complacency, fear, mediocrity, decay; in the other, intelligence, culture, leadership. As did Penton, he presented these options in stark, unambiguous terms. There is a preference for striking images, telling metaphors and clever phraseology over a more systematic presentation of argument and evidence. A specific plan of action is generally absent. Ahead lies the possibility of a brighter future, but the way forward remains unclear.

Horne would find no better model for this critical style than Penton. The *Daily Telegraph* man presented an exciting alternative to the complicated philosophy of John Anderson. For all his relentless deconstruction of Australian life, in effect Anderson remained distant from it, mostly lecturing to students, arguing with colleagues and publishing in academic journals. He was a critic in exile. But Horne would never be satisfied with complete intellectual detachment. He yearned to bloody his hands in political battle. Though he might spend the morning inquiring into the nature of reality with the Freethinkers, in the afternoon he would be manoeuvring to seize the editorship of *Honi Soit* or getting himself elected as president of the Literary Society. In contrast with Anderson, Penton sent his critical missives into the political arena itself, into the offices of politicians and businessmen and the living rooms of ordinary Australians. It was one thing to know the relevant facts. It was another to make them known.

◆ ◆ ◆

In the summer of 1941–42, Horne was struck down with chickenpox. Confined to his family home in Sandringham, he spent four days in bed internalising Fyodor Dostoyevsky's novels of spiritual crisis and social alienation. Like many angry young men experiencing *The Brothers Karamazov* or *Notes from Underground* for the first time, he was troubled by the existential questions they posed.[50] In his three years at Sydney University, Horne had tried on several personas – the good-natured boy from the suburbs; the libertarian philosopher; the rampaging, freethinking debater and critic; the sad, soft-spoken poet; the enfant terrible journalist and shit-stirring newspaper editor – but none seemed to stick.

Horne's bedroom self-questioning in late 1941 was the culmination of an extended period of disillusionment and self-doubt. During his time as an undergraduate, he penned several searching poems and essays on these themes. One, for example, was titled 'Poem Commemorating the Development of a Soul through the Conflict of Social Forces and Other Types of Strange Disturbance'.[51] He believed that his mind, like society, was nothing but a battleground of identities and passions, at war with itself. In another scrap, grandly titled 'Manifesto', he imitated Dostoevskian notions of the splintered self.

The characters – all named 'Don' – appear to represent different types of people, or conflicting parts of a singular man: the man of action, the man of words, the man of spiritual searching. In the end, Horne's fractured narrator confesses that he is left 'with the emptiness of one who has nothing to hide ... dressed in rags but clothing himself in others' dreams of life'.[52] In another confessional fragment, titled 'In Search of My Self', he went even further:

> I have known the fullness of actual attention, but the most persistent memory is that of a grand emptiness through which I may walk for hours like a clumsy doll mouthing silly sentences, earning the scorn of friend and enemy alike, conscious of this fact, but my mind so emptied that I can do nothing except to present the merest scraps thrown from the life of others.[53]

In his poetry, too, language and images of fraudulence appeared repeatedly: 'mask', 'pose', 'decorate', 'doubt'. There seemed no way out of this maze of false identities, this 'noisy menstruation of the mind'.[54] 'What is this being I call myself?' he worried. This seemed to be the question of questions, the great puzzle of life, the scrambled knot at the heart of existence. It was the most important theme of literature, art and philosophy. And it perplexed him. He had no answer. Was he a poet or a critic? An activist or an observer? Was he the sum of his outward appearances, or were they a veil for something more inward and intangible? In the depths of his adolescent solipsism, he could offer only a tepid non-answer: there was no self. At the heart of the thing people called their 'selves' there was a 'grand emptiness'. 'The gods of the self', he wrote, 'are dead.'[55]

Donald Horne reached this nihilistic conclusion at the age of nineteen. He worried that three years of tertiary education had amounted to little more than a series of hollow and unconvincing performances. The amorphous existential doubts he had periodically entertained in his adolescence had, by university training, been given shape and form. The intellectual values he had learned to cultivate – observation, inquiry, scepticism – seemed to bring him to a dead end. Turned inward, his insatiable curiosity was a debility. 'Introspection,' he lamented, 'is a pig rooting for potatoes when his very feet are made of potato.'[56]

There was a world outside of his mind, however, and the dramatic global events of late 1941 and early 1942 called an abrupt halt to this personal crisis. Horne emerged from his convalescence to discover he had been fired from *The Daily Telegraph*. A major university story had broken during his illness and the paper had been scooped by *The Herald*. When backroom scheming forced a vote on his *Honi Soit* editorship, he suddenly found himself involuntarily relieved of all journalistic duties.[57] Smarting from these twin humiliations, and with almost all male students now being strongly encouraged to join the armed forces as part of an intensive national mobilisation effort, Horne – using his real name this time – enlisted to become a soldier.[58]

His timing was apposite. Just over a week later, Japanese bombers mounted a devastating surprise attack on the American naval base at Pearl Harbor, forcing the United States into the war. For Australia, too, it was a dramatic shock. When war had first been declared in Europe in September 1939, it had seemed a remote, British affair fought in distant lands. But now, with the Japanese advancing southward and Britain preoccupied with an existential threat of its own, many Australians foresaw disaster. In the frantic early months of 1942, the country was gripped with a sense of overwhelming existential peril. In a New Year's message, the prime minister, John Curtin, made a famous appeal for American support, 'free of any pangs as to our traditional links or kinship to the United Kingdom.'[59] The following months saw the catastrophic collapse of the British military base on Singapore Island, the imprisonment of over 100,000 Allied troops, frequent air raids on Northern Australian cities and ports, the partial Japanese conquest of Papua New Guinea, submarine attacks on Sydney Harbour and an epic naval battle off the coast of Queensland.[60]

This crisis came as a particular shock to older Australians; for most of them, the drama of international conflict had always occurred at a safe distance. Outside of war service, few Australians had travelled overseas, and by the early 1940s only 14 per cent of the population were foreign-born – most of those in Great Britain. For these older generations, Australia's isolation from global affairs was taken almost as an article of faith. However, for their children – many of whom had no memory of World War I – the experience of early 1942 had a formative impact on their lives: the streets and bars teemed with American soldiers, northern cities were under direct threat from the Japanese, and thousands of Australians fought in what Curtin dubbed the 'Battle for Australia'. Those coming of age in these years found the Australian continent much closer to the centre of world events – and would continue to do so long after the war had ended. Australia might still have been no more than a footnote in the broader scheme of things, but in these anxious months, wrote the historian Geoffrey Bolton, the nation's traditional sense of insularity from the world was 'abruptly and permanently shattered'.[61]

The emergency came hot on the heels of Horne's apocalyptic 'Let us Rejoice' editorial, his Brian Penton–inspired prophecy of impending Australian 'perdition'.[62] The irony, though, was that his personal experience of the crisis months of 1942 was one of great tedium. After enlisting, he endured a few desolate months training as an infantryman, first at Ingleburn in far western Sydney, then in an empty paddock at Mullet Creek, a few kilometres south of Wollongong. When his university regiment was disbanded in February, he transferred to artillery and moved to a camp outside Newcastle, which he hoped might launch him, somehow, into a more interesting army career. Nearly everyone he had befriended at university seemed to be on the up and up: Jim Plimsoll had a job in 'army research'; Bruce Miller, his protégé from *Honi Soit*, was working at the ABC, and Doug McCallum, another *Honi Soit* alumnus, had – before it was evacuated in early 1942 – been involved in Australian operations in Malaya. Somehow, only McAuley had missed out, and Horne saw him irregularly in Newcastle, where McAuley had a job as a high-school teacher.[63]

Despite its incredible distance from anything of consequence, in Newcastle Horne managed to have his own brush with death. In May 1942, as he and a small group of artillerymen from the 1st Field Regiment were hurtling along a narrow Hunter Valley bush track in an army truck, another vehicle appeared up ahead. When the driver of the truck swerved to avoid collision, Gunner Horne, stationed in the rear, was struck violently in the face by an overhanging tree branch. The blow broke his eye socket, ripped open his cheek and slashed his eyelid. Thrown across the vehicle, he slammed the back of his head on a pick and was knocked unconscious. Awaking in a pool of his own blood, barely cognisant of his injuries, he was put in an ambulance and rushed to an army hospital, where he was pronounced 'seriously ill' and committed to three months' bed rest.[64]

For the entirety of that fateful year, and some of the next, Horne languished in his various rural purgatories: after Wollongong and Newcastle came army hospitals in the NSW country towns of Greta and Tamworth, followed by a long stay in a 'dismal, haunted' retraining centre in Albury.[65] Life in these dusty outback camps, he discovered, was a kind of endless exile, punctuated by farcical mishaps, absurd officiousness and pointless exercises and drills. His only respite came in the form of intermittent leave, a gluttonous diet of books and the relentless dispatch of letters.[66]

War service had not fully severed his ties with *Honi Soit*, and with another Andersonian ally, Peter Gibbons, now at the helm, Horne continued to provoke controversy wherever he could.[67] For example, when that year's Henry Lawson Prize for Poetry was awarded to one of his antagonists in the *Ulysses* debate, he sent an abusive letter to the student newspaper, detailing the many failings of this 'worthless and unimportant' poet, triggering another round of outrage and complaints.[68] For three weeks he was chided by the poet's friends for his 'petulant outburst'. One noted that Horne's own publishing record could be boiled down to 'one or two very obscure and very minor pieces of verse'.[69] Another chafed at his unrepentant meanness: 'What type of a spirit has he who immediately attacks the prize work of a contemporary?'[70] Humiliatingly, though, it was one of his allies and idols, the 'Sydney poet' A.D. Hope, who delivered the most cutting blow. Despite agreeing with Horne's judgement of the poem, Hope thought his 'virulent abuse' was exaggerated and adolescent. Both the shoddy poet and her obnoxious critic, he wrote, simply needed to grow up.[71]

In June 1943, eighteen featureless months after he first enlisted, Horne was sent with the rest of his regiment on a twelve-day overland journey to Darwin, via Adelaide and Alice Springs.[72] When the Japanese had first bombed the city in February 1942, its defence capabilities had been almost non-existent. Despite Darwin's proximity to the conflict in South-East Asia, the city had boasted just one aircraft radar, and even that was reportedly out of action when the Japanese planes first appeared on the horizon. In the wake of this devastating first attack – seen by some as 'Australia's Pearl Harbor' – Darwin had been abandoned as a port and civilian centre and transformed instead into an ad hoc collection of tents and army vehicles surrounding four large Allied airfields.[73]

As fully fledged anti-aircraft artillerymen, Horne's regiment were expecting to be stationed at gun posts and tasked with covering Allied fighter planes during air raids, of which there had been over fifty in the area since February 1942. By the time they arrived, however, the region's defence was being handled with relative comfort by RAAF aircraft, and by November 1943 the air raids had ceased completely. If it were not for the remote possibility of enemy attack, life in this supposed combat zone seemed to differ little from the petty tediums and discomforts of the training camps in New South Wales. Gunners in

Donald Horne reading to a group of soldiers

isolated areas around Darwin, chained to their posts for days at a time, had it particularly bad. In his official history of the Australian artillery, the military historian David Horner described their service as 'not glamorous or, except in a few instances, exciting'.[74] For those, like Horne, who arrived in the twilight of the conflict in Northern Australia, the biggest enemy was the climate. Oppressive heat, dry dust, torrential rain, thousands of biting insects and the near impossibility of gaining leave all made life in these far-flung encampments characteristic of a tropical gulag.[75] When the rain came, wrote Horne to his mother in November, 'the bottom suddenly drops out of the sky ... It is like the emptying of some celestial bath tub'.[76]

Cast into this indefinite exile, Horne determined to turn his uneventful army life into an intellectual exercise of its own, reading widely and carefully and 'straightening out a few attitudes and thoughts'.[77] His fellow gunners must have considered him a bit of a queer fellow, he thought, a 'cynical' chap who 'used to read a lot of books and write long letters'.[78] Shortly after arriving in Darwin, he corralled some reluctant fellow soldiers into a short-lived discussion group on 'The Australian Political Scene'.[79] He also acquired for himself the somewhat aspirational post of 'librarian', assuming responsibility for the two hundred or so books that were circulating around the regiment.[80] All the while, he implored his family and friends to send him reading material – particularly newspapers, novels and current-affairs journals – and notepads, 'for various purposes, mainly intellectual rather than military'.[81]

Horne was, by nature, an autodidact, possessed of a near-insatiable appetite for knowledge. He had been a prolific reader from a young age. His great boyhood desire, he said, had been to 'know everything'.[82] In primary school, he remembered, this had seemed to set him apart from the other children. From his household encyclopedia, he had accumulated facts like stamps. When he was in Second Grade, a teacher had pulled him out of his classroom and made him demonstrate his reading talents to a group of Fifth Grade delinquents. As an adolescent, he had kept up a relentless reading program, stalking the stacks of the Sydney Municipal Library: Carlyle's *The French Revolution*; the poetry of T.S. Eliot and Ezra Pound; the novels of Dickens,

Wells, Hardy and Conrad. At university he expanded his palette: Joyce, Proust and Flaubert, Liddell Hart's *A History of the First World War* and Freud's *The Psychopathology of Everyday Life*.[83]

In wartime Darwin, without the obligations of lectures and examinations, Gunner Horne recommenced this ramshackle literary, political, historical and philosophical reading program. He read anything he could get his hands on: Shakespeare's *Henry IV*, the collected essays of Bertrand Russell, the novels of Evelyn Waugh and Christopher Isherwood, Epictetus' *Moral Discourses*, Thorstein Veblen's *The Theory of the Leisure Class*, Sydney's daily newspapers and British newspapers and magazines, such as *Tribune, Scrutiny*, the *New Statesman, The Standard* and the *Times Literary Supplement*.[84]

When he wasn't reading, he was writing. He dispatched long letters to as many as twelve regular correspondents. From his flyblown hut he wrote several droll prose sketches of army life, which were published in *ARNA*, of which he was so pleased he fantasised about selling them as a full series – titled 'Through the Menagerie' – to a famous literary journal such as *Horizon*.[85] This soon morphed into plans for a book about the war, 'Sounds of Battle', that would detail his strange journey 'from private to gunner'.[86] 'It's not going to make very nice reading,' he warned. 'But then this is a notoriously nasty world.'[87]

Sometime between his departure from university and his arrival in Darwin, it seemed, Horne had shifted his allegiances from poetry to prose. His literary diet, he informed Miller, had taken on 'more of an historical than an aesthetic bent'.[88] While recovering from his accident in Newcastle, he had read Leo Tolstoy's epic novel *War and Peace*, and discovered in its long treatise on history a kind of philosophy of life. Most historical narratives, Tolstoy argued, were no more than gross simplifications of impossibly complex and random events. Military battles were given meanings by commanders, politicians and historians that rarely had any relation to the chaotic reality of what had occurred. To write truthfully about war, and indeed about life itself, was instead to come to terms with how little control humans had over events. The most any politician or military commander could ever do – whether John Curtin or Napoleon – was 'preside over' the accidents of history and 'give meaning to confusion'.[89]

Reading Tolstoy in his hospital bed limbo, Donald had decided – somewhat fatalistically – that no political philosophy or military strategy could ever fully account for the essential randomness of events, of the ever-present possibility of death-by-tree. What was the point of anything – of participating in politics, producing art, pursuing a career or even fighting in a war – if life could end so suddenly and farcically? At a time when the Nazis had conquered Paris and the Japanese most of South-East Asia, to have been maimed and almost killed by something so innocuous as a tree, thousands of miles from the real fighting, was perfectly ridiculous, proof of the essential meaninglessness of life.[90]

Horne's cynical appraisal of his experience in the army 'menagerie', meanwhile, is difficult to disentangle from the influence on his young mind of another fatalistic war novel, E.E. Cummings' *The Enormous Room*. A military camp, in Cummings' telling, was a kind of ridiculous human zoo, peopled by a random and bizarre cast of characters, all tyrannised by a set of arbitrarily enforced rules. Having read it only a few weeks before enlisting, the jaded and disobedient Gunner Horne – forced to march around empty cow paddocks for no obvious reason – now seemed determined to see army life through its lens. Darwin, he wrote, was 'exile'.[91] Trapped in the middle of nowhere, he felt 'shiftless' and 'irresponsible', his talents unappreciated by those who mattered. War was not an exciting adventure but a dull purgatory, a prison for the mind. Real life was elsewhere. 'I find life very tedious,' he wrote to Bruce Miller in August 1943. 'Don't you ever get frightfully bored with the utter inadequacies of things?'[92]

As his Darwin 'exile' passed from weeks to months, Horne drifted into a state of bitter, romantic nihilism, and experienced a revival of the existential jitters that had plagued him just under two years earlier. 'Neither you, nor anyone else, could cure my soul,' he moaned melodramatically to Miller. 'I have killed my God and planted his bones in a vacant lot.'[93] His correspondent, who by this time was fielding as many as three histrionic letters a week from Horne, expressed concern about what he saw as 'great strain' and a 'general feeling of hopelessness' in his dispatches. In reply, Horne suggested that his own pessimism, though

unpleasant, amounted to a kind of political wisdom. 'The ideal attitude'
was that of 'scepticism straight':

> I am a somewhat carping critic, distrusting ecstasies of joy or pain. It
> has always seemed to me that out of all emotional colourings, hate is
> perhaps the most satisfactory, provided it is not self-righteous or self-
> abnegatory hate – a good general all round hatred is a good framework
> to begin with.[94]

As ever, he found the best outlet for this anti-philosophy to be the letters page of *Honi Soit*. In September 1943, he appeared again with a
brutal attack on the poetry of Harry Hooton, a peripheral member of
McAuley's circle. Hooton, wrote Horne, was 'a merchant in birdlime',
'a bag of wind' and a 'crank'. His poetry was 'overdone, undermeant'
and 'too sticky with mysticism'.[95] A month later he tried a different
subject, attacking the 'inverted religious maniacs' of the campus Labor
Club for their defence of Stalin. It was 'schoolboy stuff,' he wrote.
'Petit-bourgeois youth clutching at substitute fanaticisms as the edifice collapses. The yawp and yatter of little, empty souls. A facade of
intellectuality hastily erected by near-ignorance.'[96]

Questions of politics were still far from Horne's 'monologue of
an existence' in Darwin, and he longed for a lucky break. '[I am in
search of] pleasant occupations with which to distract my fretful
mind,' he wrote. Back at home many of his contemporaries were
already on the path to promising postwar careers. Hugh Gilchrist, a
former editor of *Honi Soit*, was working in army education and sub-
editing the army magazine *Salt*. Horne responded with dismay and
jealousy. 'What the hell am I going to do?' he complained to Miller.
'Any ideas?'[97]

His options were limited. After attending two battery school
educational courses outside Darwin, he considered a return to university study, hoping to make his continuing self-education more
'systematised'. Meanwhile, he informed Miller of his plans to write a
'documentary observation of Australian life and ways'. He also made
a few discreet entreaties to Alf Conlon – a well-connected university acquaintance who had recently snapped up McAuley for his

ambiguously defined army 'Directorate of Research' in Melbourne –
all of which were ignored.[98]

It was almost out of desperation, then, that Horne sent off an
application for the Department of External Affairs' new diplomatic
cadetship program. When he had joined the army in late 1941, he could
never have envisaged that he would attempt to leave it just over two
years later for a career in foreign affairs. A newspaperman, perhaps, but
not a public servant. The cadetship was also an incredible long shot:
of the 1,500 applications received in 1943, only twelve were selected for
the program.[99]

After sending off his expression of interest, Horne endured a roll-
ercoaster few months. In January 1944, by virtue of his military service,
he progressed straight to the written examination, which he thought
was 'quite easy'. 'I don't expect my application to be successful,' he
assured his mother (and himself). 'To be among the outstanding hundred in such an exam is mainly a lottery.' Selection for the second
round, though, gave him cause for hope, and he was granted leave in
March to travel to Townsville for interviews. In April, back in Sydney
for a few weeks, he awaited the results, but heard nothing. To his dismay, his leave expired and the situation did not change. 'Fuck it fuck
it fuck it,' he wrote to Miller. 'Feelings indescribable.' More despondent than ever, he set sail for a second exile in Darwin, but it was not to
last. In May, he was selected for the program, along with eight other
servicemen. By the end of the month, he was in Canberra, ready to
embark on his new career.[100]

2.

———

THE GOLDEN AGE

Visitors to Canberra in the 1940s were routinely underwhelmed. Close to three decades after the American architect Walter Burley Griffin first submitted his plans for a splendid new city on the banks of the Molonglo River, Australia's bush capital had barely 12,000 residents. Far from the rural Arcadia of its founder's visions, it instead had the appearance of a rather self-important country town. Its sparse, neatly organised civic infrastructure was erected beside cow pastures and bushland. Those arriving from the noise and activity of the wartime coastal metropolises were often spooked by the emptiness and the silence of the place. The winters were brutally cold, the summers scorching and flyblown. And facilities were shabby. Train travellers from Sydney disembarked at an old goods shed at the railway terminus and were herded the rest of the way in buses. With office space at a premium, many government departments operated out of hotels. Parliament House, locals joked, spoiled what was otherwise one of Australia's best sheep stations. The city, wrote the historian W.K. Hancock in 1930, was no less than a 'document of Australian immaturity'.[1]

When the twenty-three-year-old Donald Horne arrived by overnight train on a freezing Canberra morning in early May 1944, he saw little to contradict this unflattering picture. His allotted place of residence – a gloomy, concrete-floored hostel named Brassey House – fronted onto a large empty paddock. Situated about a kilometre south of Parliament House (and five long kilometres from Canberra University College), the building was enveloped in what he described as an atmosphere of 'faded gentility'.[2] His assigned room, to be shared with another recent arrival, was furnished with the bare essentials: two beds, two desks and a radiator to see out the winter.[3]

However, as in most Canberra boarding houses, very little could be done about the cold. When the lights went out at midnight, recalled one former resident, the place became a 'howling wilderness'. This cheerlessness extended to social life, and with few outside dining options, meals were shared three times a day in the hostel's large dining room. Many Canberrans got around on bicycles; the future governor-general Paul Hasluck, who joined the public service in 1941, commuted by horse. For most unmarried government recruits to the city, noted one historian of the period, it was a 'monastic existence'.[4]

As the reason for Horne's arrival attested, Canberra was not all misery and boredom. By 1944, the city's bureaucratic machinery was quietly abuzz with all kinds of ambitious new government activity. In the previous few years, the demands of organising a wartime economy had thrust unprecedented political responsibility and control into the hands of a small army of Canberra-based politicians and public servants. With the shape of the postwar world in the balance, many talented and intellectually inclined young men and women were enticed to public sector jobs in the remote bush capital, hoping to play their part in the making of a new Australia.[5]

The branch of government that Horne had been handpicked to join – External Affairs – was at the very centre of this shake-up. As late as 1935, Australia's international relations had been the responsibility of the prime minister's office, but even after it had gained independence from these constraints, the newly formed department had struggled to assert itself. Since World War I, Australian governments had instead favoured a foreign affairs policy of imperial defence, seeking shelter beneath the British global military umbrella. When war broke out in 1939, Australia's budding diplomatic service was – by Horne's estimation – still emerging from its 'long babyhood', concerned mainly with a handful of 'tiddly-wink international questions'.[6] It was only in the aftermath of the British capitulation in South-East Asia in the early months of 1942 that the impetus for real change finally arrived, and under Labor's energetic new minister, H.V. Evatt, the department had begun to broaden the horizons of Australia's foreign affairs outlook, and to professionalise its ranks.[7]

Such changes were not welcomed by all. In the early 1940s, a culture of amateurism pervaded much of the public service, a lot of which was staffed by career civil servants without university degrees. External Affairs was something of an exception to this rule, and its preference to recruit directly from universities throughout the mid-to-late 1930s had earned it a reputation for elitism.[8] Evatt's Diplomatic Cadet Scheme – inaugurated in 1943 and targeted explicitly at young men and women who had had their university studies cut short by the war – would only have confirmed such criticisms. Bringing in twelve new cadets each year, the program was developed to create an elite cohort of professional diplomats to staff a radically expanded Australian diplomatic footprint in the postwar years.[9] In 1944, neither Horne nor his fellow cadets could have entertained any doubts about the important role they had been earmarked to play in the making of postwar Australia.

Horne's cohort was indeed a brilliant one, many of whom eventually did go on to influential postwar positions.[10] Among the precocious young men reporting daily for lectures and tutorials were Gordon Jockel, Horne's colleague at *Honi Soit* in 1941, who later held several important diplomatic posts in South-East Asia; Brian Hill, who would have a similar trajectory (and also play a minor role in the Petrov espionage scandal in the 1950s); John Rowland and James Cumes, who would both work mostly in Europe; John Petherbridge in Asia; and David Anderson, whose long career would include a posting to Vietnam in the mid-1960s. Bill Pritchett, another university chum and a future Secretary of the Department of Defence, arrived in the 1945 intake. A few others in Horne's year went on to distinguished careers in academia: Brian Beddie in political science and Bill Morrison in law.[11] Like Horne's poetry circle at university, though, it was an almost exclusively masculine world. Despite Evatt's decree that three of every twelve cadetships should be reserved for women, only one – Kathy Jones – was included in Horne's intake.[12]

This select group of bright, expectant youngsters arrived in Canberra in 1944 looking to make their mark. Though they all chafed at the city's remoteness, the group nevertheless benefited from a decision made in late 1943 to transfer the course from its original location at the University of Sydney to the fledgling Canberra University College, where they were instructed by some of the leading intellectuals of the day, including the political scientist Leslie Crisp, the legal scholar Kenneth Bailey, the economists Peter Karmel and Fred Wheeler, the writer and literary anthologist Tom Inglis Moore and the historian Laurie Fitzhardinge.[13] Despite the many hardships it presented, Canberra offered them better access to the city's many men of influence. With social facilities severely lacking, it was not uncommon for the cadets to be invited to dinner parties in the homes of department bigwigs.[14] Some – such as the eminent diplomat and lawyer Frederic Eggleston – were even drafted in to the official program to dole out practical advice and present guest lectures.[15]

The course was generalist in nature, organised around such broad topics as Australian history, economics, Pacific studies, international relations, 'The Political Thought of the Western World' and 'The History of Western World Since 1815'. Recommended reading ran the gamut from Homer to Hobbes, Plato to Rousseau and everything in between.[16] On top of this formal training, cadets were expected to stay abreast of current affairs and regularly read several international magazines (including the British *Spectator*, the *New Statesman* and the American journal *Foreign Affairs*).[17] The entrance exam, too, required familiarity with many of the central issues of the day: 'how to enforce the peace', the future of the British Empire, the pursuit of the 'Four Freedoms' and the prickly problem of postwar migration (one essay prompt read: 'Australia will have to convince the rest of the world that she is entitled to preserve a high standard of living and a high degree of racial purity in her people').[18] On a personal level, meanwhile, the cadets were expected to show 'personality and character', 'tact', 'initiative' and, above all else, 'intellectual excellence'.[19]

By all accounts, Horne appears initially to have enjoyed his return to formal study. The course's generalist flavour, touching on a wide variety of topics and disciplines in a relatively short amount of time, seemed perfectly tailored to his own broad tastes. In the first few weeks, he was put to work on essays concerning Herodotus and 'Locke or Hume or something'.[20] Of all the subjects on offer, it was history that most captured his attention. In 1944, both history subjects were taught by the Director of the School, Laurie Fitzhardinge, whom

Horne later praised as an eccentric, broad-minded scholar of 'gentle temperament'. Under the instruction of this genial, sociable teacher he did some of his most diligent work, including an entertaining essay on 'The Rise of Nationalism in Australian Literature'.[21] When Fitzhardinge fell ill later in the year, Horne despaired, predicting he would be replaced by 'some awful bastard'.[22]

Once the thrill of these initial intellectual excitements wore off, however, Horne aligned with most of the other cadets in expressing his general disappointment with the program. Even after the shift from Sydney, much of the course's organisation remained haphazard, the subjects incoherent and the teaching uninspired and rote.[23] The most common complaint – and one that particularly rankled Horne – was the poor pay and conditions. Forced to live in barrack-like hostels where the only social opportunities came over dreary meals and in crowded buses, Horne thought the city to be thoroughly antithetical to 'adult intellectual interests'.[24] On his paltry salary, he often wondered where he would find the money to buy an adequate wardrobe if he ever received a diplomatic appointment. At other times, he would find himself 'fingering his sixpences' trying to rustle up enough money to buy a round of drinks for Canberra figures he desperately wanted to meet.[25]

In his diplomatic studies essays, Horne often displayed the same prodding, colourful and highly opinionated style he had deployed in his polemical writing in *Honi Soit*. As one marker observed, his were 'journalist's notes rather than an essay! – but enjoyable and easy to read'.[26] It was a shrewd observation: for all his many wartime preoccupations, Horne never quite shook off the journalistic bug he had caught during his time as editor of *Honi* in 1941. Shortly after arriving in Canberra, he had informed his fellow cadets of his intention to personally revive the university's student newspaper, *Prometheus*, which had ceased publication in 1941. A chance encounter with the veteran press gallery reporter Massey Stanley in the Hotel Canberra further encouraged Horne's journalistic curiosity. From his far-flung army camps in 1942 and 1943, he had maintained regular correspondence with his editorial successors at *Honi*, frequently imparting advice and remaining on the lookout for new opportunities to stoke public controversy.[27] Horne's characterisation of the fifth-century Greek statesman Alcibiades in a diplomatic studies essay, meanwhile, sounded suspiciously like self-portrait:

> A devilish fascination in speech, of precocious, hasty and masterful youth, of a many-sided personality, of easy insolence towards his fellows and impatient contempt for their traditions and beliefs, of sudden generosities and extreme cruelties – as well as those episodes of sexual licenses, riotous conduct and excessive drinking that seem to get mixed up in the lives of many young men who have a liking for critical argument and a fondness for dialectic debate. He was the type that proves an irritant to any society.[28]

In fact, in late 1944, a mere six months into his diplomatic training, journalism presented itself as a serious alternative career. Earlier that year, he had befriended Cyril Pearl – one of Stanley's senior colleagues at *The Daily Telegraph* – at a protest in Sydney over the government's wartime censorship of newspapers.[29] In December, when he departed Canberra for the summer holidays, Horne sent a letter to Pearl looking for a temporary job to subsidise his meagre cadet income. After a successful meeting, Horne was granted another interview with the paper's editor, Brian Penton, who immediately recognised him as the cocky young student journalist who had stormed into his office back in 1941, and offered him three days a week work as a casual reporter.[30]

For two months in early 1945, while still officially employed as a trainee diplomat, Horne moonlighted as a professional journalist of the lowest rank. Alongside a handful of other young stringers – including Murray Sayle, his editorial successor at *Honi Soit*, and Harry Hooton, the poet he had insulted in that same publication less than twelve months prior – Horne was given his first taste of life in the newsroom of a large metropolitan daily. In contrast with his miserable Canberra existence, this temporary life as a Sydney journalist – researching stories, learning the intricacies of the paper's style, drinking in nearby bars and even catching the odd glimpse of the God-like Penton – was a world of excitement, even if most of his duties were rather humdrum. As junior casuals, he and Sayle were fed the journalistic scraps, left to write bits and pieces about the weather or, at a stretch, to report on the wartime shortage of meat.[31]

Given the insignificance of much of his work, it was likely the urbanity and bohemianism of many of his fellow newspapermen and women that so strongly attracted Horne to the profession. In January 1945, he became infatuated with an older, British-born court reporter named Elisabeth Lambert. Attractive, intelligent and six years his senior, she was a published poet, a peripheral member of several Sydney literary circles, a war widow (her Australian husband had died a few years earlier in the Battle of Britain) – and the first serious romantic interest of his life.[32]

Horne quickly took up residence in Lambert's small furnished flat and ingratiated himself as best he could with her artistic friends.[33] For the twenty-three-year-old Horne, who had spent much of the previous three years in outback army camps and bleak Canberra boarding houses, hers was a life of unimagined sophistication and maturity, the closest thing to literary bohemia as could be found in an Australian city. When his studies resumed in March, the allure of this lifestyle, the demands of his love affair and his ongoing

Elisabeth Lambert, 20 November 1947

flirtations with journalism all combined to get him into the time-honoured Canberra habit of heading back to Sydney on weekends.[34]

After this golden summer, Horne's Canberra existence appeared more dismal than ever, a kind of 'semi-Siberian exile' in an Australian 'frontier settlement', where he plodded away at a career he could not stomach. The nights at Brassey House were 'dreary' and 'desolate', social life 'submerged and secretive'.[35] As if to add insult to injury, his favourite teacher, Laurie Fitzhardinge, left for a job in Sydney. In the subsequent months, he grew less and less interested in his studies, extending his weekends in the harbour city to such absurd length that he sometimes spent as little as one day a week in Canberra. The surviving letters from Lambert, beginning in April of that year, show Horne to have been in a state of continuing crisis over his future. Was he going to be a 'Press Gent' or a 'Diplomatic Gent', she wondered: 'I rather gather you incline towards the big newspaper world.'[36] In July, barely twelve months into his studies, Horne decided that this was indeed the case, and resigned his position in the cadet program. In August, not long after his army discharge, *The Daily Telegraph* agreed to put him on its permanent staff. In September, he was transferred to a regional bureau. Its location: Parliament House, Canberra.[37]

◆ ◆ ◆

Horne filed his first story as a parliamentary reporter on 13 September 1945, just over a month after the detonation of atomic bombs over the Japanese cities of Hiroshima and Nagasaki.[38] Over the previous five years, war had wrought vast and irreversible changes to the world he had known as a boy. The United States, having played a decisive role in the war, was now unquestionably the dominant force in world affairs. Across the Atlantic, the Soviet Union, though weakened in its struggle with Nazi Germany, appeared to hold the ascendancy across Eastern Europe. By contrast, the international influence of the devastated European imperial powers was under threat, and independence movements were gathering momentum in both Africa and Asia. Across the globe, long-awaited plans for a more stable and cooperative postwar world were about to be put to the test. It was the dawn of a new political epoch, and for many Australians – particularly those of Horne's generation – it was a moment of both hope and uncertainty.

Optimistic sentiments about the nature of the postwar world had emerged almost from the moment the conflict commenced. In 1941, a joint Anglo-American statement of war aims – known as the Atlantic Charter – had provided a vague assurance that in the future, 'all the men in all the lands may live out their lives in freedom from fear and want.'[39] In Australia, the Labor Party's ascension to power in October of that year and its resounding federal election victory in August 1943 had given much encouragement to those who saw the war as an opportunity to plan the peace along these lines. Both John Curtin and his closest colleague, Ben Chifley, had had their political imaginations shaped by World War I's failed settlement and the deep global Depression that was its legacy; they were determined not to see a repeat of past mistakes.[40]

In the Australian public service in the early to mid-1940s, these optimistic ambitions had combined with wartime necessity to transform the culture of policymaking. In the crisis months of early 1942, Curtin had further extended the federal government's already significant economic powers, enforcing controls over prices, manufacturing output, the distribution of labour and the rationing of food. Not long after, with the Japanese threat receding, he had announced the creation of a Department of Post-War Reconstruction to design and coordinate Labor's large-scale social and economic reform program.

This new organisation was staffed by an outstanding group of young, mostly university-educated men. Almost all possessed some form of training in economics, a sympathy for the American New Deal project and a knowledge of the ideas of the Cambridge economist John Maynard Keynes. Crucially, though, these men brought a belief in the power of governments to direct capitalist societies towards more efficient and equitable outcomes. As H.C. 'Nugget' Coombs, the department's highly influential director-general, wrote in 1981, they had a conviction that 'human communities could, by corporate action, shape the context in which the lives of their members were to be lived'. In the hands of this new policy elite, postwar Australia was not going to be left at the mercy of market forces. Like Canberra, it would be planned.[41]

For Australians, the abrupt transition from war to peace coincided with the death of the Labor prime minister John Curtin, who had spent close to three years presenting the conflict's many hardships as a necessary sacrifice for the peaceful and prosperous new world that was to come in its wake. When *The Daily Telegraph*'s newest political correspondent first took his seat in the Parliamentary Press Gallery, it was not Curtin but his treasurer, Ben Chifley, who sat in the prime minister's chair, tasked with turning these ambitious plans into reality. Chifley had served as the original Minister for Post-War Reconstruction, and though different to Curtin in style and personality, was no less committed to his vision of state-led economic and social renewal. With the conflict at an end, however, and the federal government's emergency defence powers soon to be extinguished, Labor was now faced with the task of selling its comprehensive reconstruction program to an electorate weary from six years of war.[42]

The government's predicament elicited little sympathy from Horne. His reading throughout 1943 and 1944 had instead instilled in him a kind of philosophical anarchism, opposed to any substantial form of state intervention, left or right. During his army service in Darwin, he had copied out instructive quotations from the nineteenth-century Russian radical Mikhail Bakunin, exchanged letters with friends about Oscar Wilde's essay 'The Soul of Man under Socialism' and devoured several popular jeremiads about the evils of bureaucracy, including Robert A. Brady's *Business as a System of Power* and James Burnham's 1941 bestseller *The Managerial Revolution*. Burnham's thesis – that power in modern capitalist societies, whether fascist, socialist or liberal democratic, was increasingly concentrated in the hands of a compliant bureaucratic elite – sharpened Horne's already instinctive libertarianism.[43]

The essence of his opposition to planning, however, came from two radical liberals. The first was his university professor John Anderson, whose influential 1943 essay 'The Servile State' had found its way to Horne's Darwin army encampment. Anderson contended that the planners' pursuit of economic security and sufficiency would bring about a lifeless, quasi-military culture of 'servility' and 'regimentation'.

Under conditions of true freedom, he argued, no single group could be allowed to impose order over the social turmoil, or to 'plan' society. Planning brought authoritarianism, and authoritarianism extinguished the invigorating, productive flame of freedom.[44] As Horne explained a few years later, Anderson was a 'realist': he rejected the 'dogma of "progress"' and he denied that societies could be 'adapted to man's requirements, or that man has any reason to expect satisfaction'.[45] No human could know the future, nor could they control it; planning was a fool's errand.

The most prominent international proponent of such a view – and the other great influence on Horne's mind in this period – was the London-based economist Friedrich Hayek, whose 1944 broadside *The Road to Serfdom* contended that economic controls of the kind proposed by many Western governments would lead inevitably to totalitarianism. Written in the context of similar British debates over postwar reconstruction, Hayek argued that since planning put responsibility for the distribution of scarce economic resources into the hands of bureaucrats, the ultimate realisation of such ideals would always be 'tyranny'. For the Canberra-based Horne, exposed daily to planning's more enthusiastic and high-minded advocates, Hayek and Anderson spoke essential truths, and he learned passages from both texts by heart.[46] This unprecedented concentration of government power in the hands of a small group of unelected experts, he concluded, signalled the beginning of the end for political liberty.

In Australia, Anderson was by no means alone in his hostility towards the more ambitious elements of Labor's reconstruction agenda. Indeed, his dissenting idea – that planning amounted to a kind of creeping authoritarianism – was a popular line of argument among conservatives on the Opposition benches in the latter years of the war.[47] A few months after Horne's initial arrival in Canberra, it had become a central plank of the successful 'No' case in the government's 'Fourteen Powers' referendum, held in August 1944. After their big election victory in 1943, the Labor Party had sought – in the interests of 'economic security and social justice' – to extend some of the federal government's wartime powers beyond the declaration of peace.[48] Robert Menzies, newly re-established as leader of the opposition

United Australia Party, had framed it as a brazen attempt to enshrine Labor's platform in the constitution, and to erode the liberties of citizens. Harold Holt, too, channelling Anderson, had declared that the people did not want 'a regimented Australia, a drab grey world in which every human being is pushed around'.[49] In October 1944, when the key political leaders of this broad coalition of dissent had met at two large conferences – one of which was held in Canberra – the result was the formation of a new consolidated organisation to represent the conservative side of politics: the Liberal Party of Australia.

Horne was a keen local witness to these early debates over planning throughout 1944 and 1945, but as a trainee diplomat and then as a very junior reporter he remained more of an interested observer than a participant. What feelings he did have on the subject at the time had instead made their way into his diplomatic studies essays and private notes. Planning, he argued in one particularly forthright effort, was simply a more respectable version of socialism, mostly 'pie in the sky theorising', in practice little more than a means of enforcing 'social discipline'. Like Anderson, he saw the planners' interventionist enthusiasm as an extension of the 'flight from responsibility into paternalism that has been growing so steadily since the regimentations of World War One'. And as he believed – following Hayek's cynical reasoning – that the management of an economy on such quasi-socialist principles would inevitably lead to 'dictatorship, not of but over the proletariat', he concluded that a 'socialist democracy' would be even more of a 'sham' than a 'capitalist' one.[50]

He made similar claims in drafts of a proposed (and later abandoned) book about Australia. Canberra, he wrote, was a 'monument to small jealousy and twopenny national pride'. Parliament, too, was a 'living exhibition of semi-literates going through the gestures of debate', while planning – the biggest folly of all – was to be given an entire chapter, titled 'Your Masters, the Public Servants'.[51] In a review article in *The Daily Telegraph*, he also spruiked the classically liberal ideas put forward by the Austrian economist Ludwig von Mises in his 1944 book, *Bureaucracy*. The 'main concern' of staff in a bureaucracy, echoed Horne, was to 'comply with the formalities necessary for their own promotion'. Destroying the profit motive and replacing private enterprise with government control, he added, 'destroys initiative' and 'endangers human progress and welfare'.[52]

Part of what goaded arch-libertarians like Horne to such rhetorical extremes was the sense of bipartisanship that had formed around planning over the previous decade. By the end of World War II, both sides of Australian politics – with different degrees of public enthusiasm – had broadly committed themselves to policies of full employment and social security.[53] Even Menzies, otherwise a staunch anti-socialist, had admitted that in the postwar period there would be a need for 'more law, not less; more control, not less'.[54] By the war's end, the Department of Post-War Reconstruction had spawned four large new agencies (rural industry, secondary industry, housing and training), and in the twelve months following the end of the war, it succeeded in putting close to 600,000 Australian soldiers back to work. In the coming years, it seemed, an expanded and more interventionist state was almost an inevitability – no matter who was in charge.[55]

After parliament adjourned in October 1945, Horne was temporarily dispatched back to Sydney, where – after his relationship with Lambert fell apart – he spent almost the entire summer living out of a series of bed-and-breakfasts near Kings Cross and working on 'general reporting'. When he returned to Canberra a few months later, he took up residence in a similarly austere two-person room in the Hotel Civic. It was barely an improvement on his previous Canberra lodgings, but with a substantially increased salary – nearly twice what he had earned as a diplomatic cadet – he could now largely avoid money worries.[56] For the first half of 1946, he put most of it to use in bars with fellow Canberra journalists, old university friends, the remaining trainee diplomats and – occasionally – politicians (such as Arthur Fadden, the leader of the Country Party, who informed him that his newspaper was 'the arsehole of Australia').[57]

Despite his strong opinions on almost all topics, Horne did not have any great influence on Australian public discourse during his stint in the Canberra Press Gallery. Unlike his experiences of student journalism, he was given very few opportunities to speak his mind. As a junior reporter, the work was mostly menial – so much so that he sometimes filed up to eight stories a day. In his first twelve months as a full-time journalist, he was more like a cipher, filtering the daily trivia of politics and current affairs through the flat, 'objective' lens of newspaper style. His contribution to the debate over changes to Australia's immigration laws, for example, was the prosaic 'Quota Migration System Urged: Replacement of White Australia Policy Suggested'. A trip north to report on striking Hunter Valley coalminers yielded 'Miners Settle in Xmas Camps: Canvas Towns Spring Up On Lake Macquarie'.[58] He was present, but he was not a player.

His first break came in August 1946 when he wrote a disparaging article about the grim conditions endured by his friends in the diplomatic cadet program. Penton, it seemed, was pleased with it, and arranged for him to be transferred back to Sydney and put on the paper's features staff. Horne – at that point enduring his third Canberra winter – was more than happy to oblige. And his escape from the city was not the only cause for optimism: in features, he would be given more licence to express his opinion – sometimes even on subjects that interested him.[59] This, though, depended on the news cycle: features were always constructed around a 'news tie-in', which Horne thought gave them an element of 'literary contrivance'.[60] Nevertheless, the contrast with his previous drudge work was immense.

Though professionally he seemed to be on an upward trajectory, Horne's position at *The Daily Telegraph* was never quite secure. At times, he was a pawn in the power games of Penton and the other company executives. For unexplained reasons he was put back on 'general reporting' in November 1946, then moved to *The Sunday Telegraph* in February 1947, where he spent several listless months reporting on the paper's 'Beach Girl Contest'. At one point, he was even briefly sacked (and quickly reinstated) after charging a large taxi expense to the company.[61]

In 1946, Horne moved into a small flat in Kings Cross with the *Telegraph* foreign affairs reporter Sam White, from which he began pretending to the kind of cosmopolitan urban existence he had idealised from his various rural exiles over the previous half decade. With its cramped terrace houses, modern apartment complexes and lively strip of cafes, restaurants and bars – often operated by recently arrived

European migrants – Kings Cross could seem to Horne like a little pocket of London or Paris, hidden away from the overwhelming dullness of the Sydney suburbs. At the *Telegraph*, too, he was drawn to those who had spent time overseas: either war correspondents, such as White, Ronald Monson, Ian Fitchett, Rita Dunstan and Ronald McKie, or émigré intellectuals, such as George Molnar and Emery Barcs. When White succumbed once again to the everlasting allure of Europe, Horne's friend and colleague Adrian Deamer moved in, and along with other ambitious young reporters, including Murray Sayle and Peter Hastings, they began to contemplate their own overseas futures.[62]

At a small gathering at the flat in early 1947, Horne met Ethel Deyns, an attractive Englishwoman who had only recently divorced her Australian husband and was now working as a hospital almoner. The two of them sat up all night talking. Ethel, in her educated upper-middle-class accent, regaled Donald with stories of her upbringing in a small English village. As she lived nearby, they began venturing out on long walks through the surrounding suburbs. Before long, they were a couple, and when Deamer moved out in mid-1947, Ethel moved in. Within a year, they were married.[63]

◆ ◆ ◆

When Brian Penton finally allowed Horne to resume writing occasional *Daily Telegraph* features in the winter of 1947, it was in a political climate much more receptive to his hitherto rather unfashionable point of view. When he had first joined the profession two years earlier, residual wartime solidarity and a widespread anticipation of the good times to come had tended to drown out liberal warnings of government overreach. But now, just twelve months on from Labor's sweeping victory at the 1946 federal election – where it had won control of both houses of parliament for the first time since 1913 – the consensus over government controls had begun to fray. Ongoing austerity measures fuelled a submerged but growing sense of discontent among an electorate impatient to escape the privations of war, while the renewed threat of communist subversion was emerging as a source of significant international anxiety. This mood, coupled with several prominent High Court

Donald and Ethel Horne with Janet, Donald's sister

challenges to key parts of Labor's legislative program, provided fertile ground for those liberals predicting future socialist tyranny.

In August, one such constitutional wrangle emerged as the lightning rod for this kind of criticism. With consumer demand running hot, inflation a consistent threat and the memory of the Depression ever-present, Chifley had placed a high priority on the maintenance of economic stability. His government's (somewhat reluctant) decision to enter Australia into the new international economic arrangements agreed at Bretton Woods, however, came with the risk of exposure to the kind of international money power that had once hamstrung Australian governments during the Depression. As such, Chifley had moved to reform the Australian banking system – principally through the establishment of a central bank. The High Court, though, stood in the way, and on 16 August, after it had rejected part of Labor's new banking legislation, Chifley abruptly announced that his government would nationalise the entire banking sector.[64]

For those who saw every one of Labor's new policies as another step along the road to totalitarian rule, the banking controversy was God's gift. Menzies called it a 'new war' and likened it to Nazi attacks on civil liberties. The banks themselves launched a coordinated and expensive anti-nationalisation campaign.[65] And less than a week after Chifley's announcement, Horne, too, delivered his own public denunciation of the policy. Recycling the argument of James Burnham's latest book – 1943's *The Machiavellians* – he accused Chifley of nothing less than 'Bonapartism'. Progressive leftist movements, he argued, always acted as if 'in some mystical way they were the embodiment of the people's will'. But if Labor truly was the sole agent of the people, he warned, then it had 'an open season ticket to play havoc with their liberties':

> Now that the government wants to nationalise the banks, the imagination blackens at what it may later do to some of the long-cherished freedoms, particularly when these freedoms become hamstrung by over-extending economic controls.[66]

On this matter, certain journalists had good reason to mistrust Labor. During the war, both the *Telegraph* and *The Sydney Morning Herald* had fought fierce campaigns against government attempts to muzzle the press. These resentments were not quickly forgotten. In early 1947, Brian Penton – who had been editor of the *Telegraph* at the time – published a book called *Censored!*, which he dubbed 'a true account of a notable fight for your right to read and know, with some comment upon the plague of censorship in general'.[67] In July, Horne followed suit, delivering his own Andersonian-inflected defence of press freedoms in a lecture at the University of Sydney. By campaigning for control of the press, Horne argued, progressives stripped socialism of its 'liberal element and its final anarchist goals'. Justifications for press control on the grounds of a 'common good', he added (per Anderson), ignored the fact that 'there is no common good … only different sections of society attempting to maintain or strengthen the rights to different ways of life'. Rather than being a tool of the capitalist class, he concluded, newspapers – with their long-established traditions of 'objectiveness and disinterestedness' – stood as 'one of the few safeguards against complete government tyranny'.[68]

As the banking issue dragged on, first in parliament and then in an inevitable High Court challenge, public opposition mounted. In August 1948, six months after High Court proceedings began, the banking legislation was ruled unconstitutional. Not to be deterred, Labor took the matter to the Privy Council in London, Australia's highest court of appeal at the time, where it continued until June 1949, before it was defeated again. For Horne, it was confirmation of all of his most conspiratorial ideas about the government's authoritarian intent. His brief experience of both Canberra bureaucracy and wartime newspaper censorship loomed large in his political imagination, and in his apocalyptic moods he was prone to conflate them with the kind of totalitarian horrors depicted in the popular dystopian books of the period, such as George Orwell's *Animal Farm* (1945) and Arthur Koestler's *Darkness at Noon* (1940).[69] The Labor Party would perpetrate as many 'evils' in the name of the 'common good,' he thought, as they had during the war in the name of 'public morale'.[70]

Beginning in April 1948, Horne produced a torrent of articles attacking Chifley, the Labor government, socialism, communism, nationalisation, bureaucracy, foreign policy and everything in between.[71] It was here that he perfected the art of the news tie-in: in Horne's hands, almost anything could be spun into a Hayekian argument about the erosion of the sacred freedoms of the people. The proposed National University, he argued, would be hampered by 'bureaucratic strangulation'; likewise the government habit of issuing important information via press release was 'a form of silent censorship'; electricity rationing inspections were an assault on 'personal liberties'; and the public service was 'paternalistic and parasitic'.[72] And in addition to these frontal assaults, he also wrote profiles of prominent anti-nationalisation figures, including the NSW Labor politician Francis Joseph Finnan, the Sydney University academic Francis Bland, and his more prominent colleague and 'Stubborn No-man' John Anderson.[73]

Like many liberal critics, Horne would often frame policy questions as a crude choice between free markets and socialism. Since discovering *The Economist* as a soldier, he had thought of himself as a kind of hard-headed economic realist, with an unsentimental commitment to economic data and statistics.[74] In 1948, he read and reviewed Douglas Copland's critique of reconstruction planning, *Back to Earth in Economics*. Copland, a pioneer of the economics profession in Australia, took issue with the ascendancy of the new Coombs-led, Keynes-inspired generation of Australian public administrators, for whom full employment and economic 'stability' – the deliberate flattening out of boom-and-bust cycles – were important and achievable policy goals. Copland thought that this 'obsession with stability' was the result of 'depression psychology' and that the key to unlocking true growth was a loosening of government controls to allow investment in essential industries. In his view, whatever postwar prosperity Australia had so far enjoyed was largely 'artificial', the result of high export prices – or, in other words, luck. Coombs later described Copland as a 'somewhat pedestrian economist'. Horne, though, approved of his appeal to the language of laissez-faire, to economic openness and the Australian 'pioneering spirit'. Like *The Economist*, he thought, Copland had delivered a 'blast of common sense'.[75]

Not for the first time, Horne's critique was rather cynical and shallow, a lively collection of journalistic quips seemingly constructed for the purpose of irritation rather than insight. But as the historian Jo-Anne Pemberton has observed, Horne was not unique in this regard. In these years, such 'acid remarks' were a common feature of the liberal opposition to reconstruction planning. In the face of the 'righteousness' and 'calm confidence' of planning's devotees, notes Pemberton, critics harangued what they saw as the widespread and near-religious belief in the malleability of the social universe. The fight over planning was – to some extent – a war of words, a battle over the excesses of rhetoric rather than the details of policy.[76]

But even if such criticism hewed closely to the popular conservative line in the debate over government controls, it still oversimplified the complex economic and geopolitical predicament facing Australia in the late 1940s. To simultaneously promote growth, control inflation and avoid the disasters of the past, Australian governments needed to strike a delicate balance between encouraging international investment and regulating its power. Finding buyers for Australian exports, too, was contingent on widespread international cooperation, stability and prosperity – something that was by no means guaranteed in these years. In Europe, relations between the American-aligned West and the Soviet-controlled East were rapidly deteriorating, with a battered Germany emerging as the hostile dividing line. Britain, Australia's biggest trading partner, was crippled by war debts and facing a balance of payments crisis. Across Australia's own region, meanwhile, there were questions over the future of a demilitarised Japan, the possibility of a communist-controlled China, the administration of Australia's newly mandated territory of New Guinea and – immediately to the north – an ongoing conflict between Indonesian nationalists and Dutch colonists.

Horne's interest in these kinds of big international questions had long outlasted his time in External Affairs, and he stayed abreast of the latest developments through magazines and old diplomatic friends.[77] Since Labor had come to power in 1941, its External Affairs minister, H.V. Evatt, had put an end to the party's traditional isolationism and instigated a turn towards a policy of liberal internationalism, whereby Australia would pursue its foreign policy ambitions through the framework of international law. Rather than sheltering behind great powers, Australia would instead attempt to seek its security collectively – an idea that had its greatest expression in 1948 when Evatt served as president of the United Nations General Assembly. Horne – unsurprisingly – disapproved, and between May and August 1948 offered several stinging criticisms of Labor's reliance on the United Nations and what he saw as its dangerous neglect of Australia's great-power relationships:

> The Government's foreign policy seems to stake everything on the final ability of the United Nations to build one, big happy world. Members of the Government speak as if the days of power politics were really over, as if the United Nations had already established world goodwill.[78]

As he had in his *Honi* editorials, Horne prophesied disaster for Australia. He thought the communist attack on the British colony of Malaya was the 'first step in the general plan to Sovietise Asia', and that the peninsular now constituted 'Australia's front line in an increasingly hostile East'. Australia's neglect of New Guinea, meanwhile, was nothing less than 'an invitation to the land-hungry millions of Asia'. In late August, in a contribution to a panicked *Telegraph* series titled 'Asia, Achilles Heel of the West', Horne sounded an even more pessimistic note, suggesting that if communists were to set up 'strong regimes' in Asia – which he thought looked likely – 'Australians might as well migrate to the US'.[79]

This growing public anxiety about the spread of communism, stoked and prodded by prominent conservatives and large sections of the press, provided both the domestic and international backdrop for the federal opposition's ongoing assault on Labor's banking policy. Throughout the latter part of 1948 and most of the election year of 1949, Horne more than played his part in this scare campaign. In July 1948, seizing on a remark of Chifley's that Labor would bring about a 'Golden Age' of happiness and prosperity, he began a series of satirical dispatches from this imagined future utopia which attempted to show socialist overreach at its most absurd. In one, the party's 'Conciliation Commissioner to conciliate Conciliation Commissioners' abolishes privately owned buttons as a 'relic of the long-discredited system of private enterprise'.[80] In another, happy citizens march at a government parade bearing placards such as 'Long Live the Latest Sewage Disposal Plan' and 'All Strength to the Regional Cultural Facilities Committees'.[81] Typically, though, the chief antagonist of Horne's satirical nightmares was not so much socialism as it was bureaucracy, and this anti-bureaucratic animus had its most concise expression in one memorable Golden Age maxim: 'There can be no improvement in social well-being without an increase in administrators.'[82]

Horne's 'Golden Age' series displayed the obvious talent for provocation that he had first honed as a student journalist. It is significant, then, that as his star rose – or fell, depending on whom you asked – he managed to strike up a tentative friendship with his long-time model for such a style, Brian Penton. Soon they were on social terms. Abrasive, needling and sarcastic, Penton was an outspoken critic of anything that stunk of mediocrity, complacency or muddy thinking. His biographer, Patrick Buckridge, observed that when it came to politics, Penton was 'less a fully-fledged individual ... than a series of masks – the shameless gossip, the serious intellectual, the patient reasoner, the languid aesthete, the moral radical, the tough reporter, the even tougher editor'.[83] On one memorable occasion, Penton barged into a dinner party hosted by Donald and Ethel and set about attacking the political opinions of their only other guest. When his interlocutor left in a rage, he poured himself another drink and – job done – sat back to enjoy the evening.[84]

Horne – the one-time 'wild young savage' of Sydney University – was clearly cut from the same cloth as his confrontational editor: he was sceptical, liberal, egotistical, sharp-tongued, literary-minded and committed to upsetting as many people as possible. He shared Penton's method of destructive analysis, his desire to make people think, to force them to face up to facts, to jolt them into self-awareness with insults and hyperbole.[85] 'Insofar as I imagined a model reader for what I was writing,' Horne recalled, 'it was most likely to be someone whom it would enrage.'[86]

Like Penton's, Horne's relentless assaults on the Chifley government earned him considerable notoriety, even among old friends – some of whom began to think of him as a journalistic mercenary whose opinions were not far enough removed from those of his boss, Frank Packer. Bruce Miller, unable to countenance Horne's willingness to attack Labor, returned all the letters Horne had sent him during the war.[87] Horne, though, did not doubt what he was writing. Like Anderson and Hayek, he forecasted a future of servility and regimentation. Like Burnham, he feared the stupefying power of state bureaucracies. And like Penton, he thought that one of the only effective bulwarks against the bureaucratic beast was the democratic right of the press to state uncomfortable facts. By saying all this publicly, he thought himself a fearless truth-teller. In his view, Freethought was a kind of moral crusade, a heroic refusal to be silenced by the fashionable groupthink of the progressive crowd.

Ultimately, for the young Horne, the central political and economic question of the postwar years – to plan or not to plan – stood in for two competing views of life. On one side were those who believed in the capacity of humans to control their own destinies, to mould societies to their needs and shape the direction of the future. On the other side were the realists: those who saw life as a series of random events, who knew that the path of history was violent and crooked, and that the good intentions of men and women spilled out into a mess of unintended consequences. Things happened, they reasoned, and the best one could do was to accept this inevitable fact and adapt as best one could.

The 1940s were the decade in which Horne convinced himself of this latter perspective. Educated during World War II by men disillusioned by the outcomes of World War I, he was animated not by political hope and idealism but by scepticism and fear of the destruction that such ideals could reap.[88] It was an understanding of life shaped as much by literature as by political pamphlets and philosophical treatises. The novelists who had spoken most deeply to him – Waugh, Tolstoy, Dickens – shared a kind of fatalism: that things rarely turned out as planned, life was often absurd, most things happened by chance, history was essentially meaningless. For Horne, this was not simply an inarticulable gut-feeling that unconsciously guided his thoughts and behaviour: by the late 1940s, he believed it consciously and explicitly:

> If history can be spoken of as having 'lessons', one of its lessons is the futility of human schemings. Historical situations arise from other factors than, and often in spite of the desires and intentions of men. Plans do not operate in a vacuum. They act on AND ARE ACTED ON BY other factors that are not conscious demands at all. Plans cannot be, as the planners believe, the controlling agent of social history. There is no such thing.[89]

Not long after they were married, Donald and Ethel made a plan of their own. Ever restless, Horne had reached what seemed to be yet another career impasse. Journalism, while offering some satisfaction, was ultimately not the kind of writing he wanted to do. With his twenty-eighth birthday approaching, he still had never travelled further than Darwin. Early in 1949, they decided that if they could find the money they would move to England, where they could live rent-free on Ethel's family's small farm in rural Buckinghamshire while Donald attempted to write a novel. In February, when he was asked to ghostwrite several 'statesman-like' (and very well-paid) opinion pieces for the Liberal Party president and aspiring MP Richard Casey, Horne quietly put aside his high-minded claims to press independence and took the job.[90] Six months later, with the money earned from these articles, they booked a passage and left.

3.

—

THE GREY CLIFFS OF DOVER

To many Australians raised in the interwar years, the prospect of living an artistic and spiritually fulfilling life in the land of their birth would have seemed a preposterous notion. Australians, they had been taught, were uniquely materialistic and anti-intellectual. Most were of the thought that locally produced art – if it was produced at all – was thin and insubstantial, second-rate knock-offs of the real European thing, or else parochial odes to kookaburras, bushrangers and gum trees. In all things of any import – poetry, manners, clothing, architecture, schooling, trees, wine – the colonial version was patently inferior. For those trained to recognise such stifling second-rateness, the traditional remedy was thought to be a ticket to London.[1]

In the summer of 1950, a little-known Melbourne critic made this problem real by giving it a name. Writing in *Meanjin*, A.A. Phillips, a schoolteacher at Melbourne's Wesley College, coined the term 'the cultural cringe' to describe the tendency for all serious art produced in Australia to be evaluated in direct comparison with foreign equivalents – most commonly, English ones. This 'disease of the Australian mind', he lamented, would not be easily overcome: unlike other colonial peoples, Australian writers were not able to take refuge in a different language, nor could they draw upon a distinctive and long-established cultural tradition of their own. Australians could not escape their Englishness, even if they wanted to. In literature, such derivativeness was a trap, and to simply replace the nightingale with the galah, as many Australian poets did, only drew attention to the problem. The result, wrote Phillips, was the 'estrangement of the Australian intellectual', the colonial writer's instinctive rejection of the 'dismaying crudity' of his or her own culture. Not surprisingly, many simply packed up and left.[2]

Twelve months earlier, when Donald Horne boarded the London-bound *Moreton Bay* at Circular Quay, dressed neatly in suit and tie alongside his new English wife, there could have been little doubt where he stood on such matters. Australia, he then believed, had had a 'protracted adolescence', oscillating between the 'feebly academic' and the 'crudely provincial'. Culturally, it had produced nothing of significance, barely 'a couple of dozen competent writers, and few notable painters'.[3] Instead, lining the leather suitcase he had borrowed from his father for the journey were what he believed to be the most serious and important works of literature: Dostoyevsky, Tolstoy, Mann, Flaubert, Stendhal, Proust, Joyce.[4] The European greats were his touchstones, the standard-bearers of the form. By his estimation, no Australians had ever made the grade; in all likelihood they never would. As he waved goodbye to the large crowd of friends and family who had come to see them off, he hoped that the dull Australian chapter of his life had finally come to an end. Never again would he have its second-rate dust on his heels.[5]

Australia's leading exports, went the old joke, were wool and brains. In his yearning for Europe, Horne was only the latest in the long line of creatively minded Australians to have succumbed to what Phillips described as the 'centrifugal pull' of the great cultural metropolises.[6] Generations of Australia's best and brightest had journeyed to the imperial metropole in search of recognition: writers, painters, poets, musicians, journalists and other lost souls, convinced that real life began the moment they stepped onto European soil. 'To stay at home was to condemn yourself to nonentity,' recalled Alan Moorehead. 'Success depended on an imprimatur from London.'[7]

Horne was no different, though it was as a novelist, not a journalist, that this provincial nonentity sought his English imprimatur. At sea, when he and Ethel weren't lazing about on deckchairs or half-heartedly socialising, he hoped to practise his developing talent for social observation. He planned to use his six weeks on the *Moreton Bay* to get started on his first book, a preposterous journey into the thickets of bureaucracy partly drawn from his own ongoing struggles with the government over his half-finished university scholarship. But even in his traveller's scraps, notebooks and – most revealingly – in copious letters to his mother, Horne continued to scratch his eternal itch: the need to transform his experiences into words.

The *Moreton Bay* followed the old empire trading route, as if completing a checklist of British colonial cities: Melbourne, Colombo, Aden, Gibraltar. Aware that his letters would be read aloud to his twelve-year-old sister at the dinner table, Horne peppered them with amusing observations of life in the colonies. The port city of Aden was 'a kind of dirty and more crowded Canberra'. In Melbourne the 'wharfies' provided 'a wonderful exhibition of laziness, malingering, drunkenness and inefficiency'. Amid the poverty of Ceylon, 'flags of Burma were flying in the breeze, horns honked and everything was very gay'.[8]

Horne was the first in his family to go abroad since World War I. To this bookish young Australian, 'overseas' was a dreamland, the subject of stories. London was an imaginary place that until now had only existed in novels – particularly those of Waugh and Dickens. When he finally arrived there, in early December 1949, it did not fail to have an effect on him. Writing home a few days later, he remembered his awe at its 'extraordinary hugeness'. It seemed as if there were 'no end to the place'. Here was his literary world made real. 'Everything was just as one imagined it,' he wrote. 'Grey mists, the Thames stretching into them on either side, the Houses of Parliament towering upwards, the people hurrying past.'[9]

London, however, was only a pitstop. Their destination was Bow Brickhill, a small village on the outskirts of Bletchley, 50 miles northwest of the capital. The house – part of a minor country estate known as the Old Rectory Farm – had belonged to Ethel's family for generations, however it had since fallen into disrepair. In this most stereotypically English of settings, they planned to share a roof with Ethel's mother, Constance, and her two elderly aunts, Lily and Rose.[10]

As his primary residence for much of the next four years, the Old Rectory Farm and Bow Brickhill formed an enduring image in Horne's mind of the charms and absurdities of English country life, and indeed England itself. He was, he later admitted, going through an 'anglophile stage' – 'I wanted to believe that somehow England had made me,' he wrote.[11] In these first few weeks, Horne dove headfirst into his new life as a country gentleman, hatching vague plans to grow vegetables and raise animals, and 'sitting in the front garden working and reading'. Like so many Australian expatriates before him, he was enchanted by the English countryside, as if finally seeing things as they were meant to be.[12] This produced a vertiginous effect – walking around Bow Brickhill, he wrote, was like walking through 'stage scenery'. Even the colours seemed more vibrant:

> Everything dark green, even the boughs and trunks of the trees, which are covered in moss. Even at this time of year the country looks most attractive. Most of the trees are bare of course, but everything else is very green – and a more green green than we get in Australia.[13]

This romantic vision of English country life did not last long. Horne soon found the attractions of pastoral England to be spoiled by the 'sullen conservatism' of those who lived there. He thought most of his fellow villagers to be complacently ignorant and small-minded. Some, he wrote to his mother, even thought that Australia was still a colony and that Sydney was 'a kind of large town'. He bristled at his regular dismissal as a 'colonial'. His go-to sources for examples of English snobbery and obliviousness were Ethel's aunts, 'two fat old toads' who 'still live back in another world'. The 'dowagers', as Ethel called them, were 'an awful pain in the neck', and by bringing Donald there she felt somewhat responsible for the tedium of their daily company. Her husband, she wrote, 'deserved a better fate than handing round cups of tea, putting up with the most idiotic twaddle … and meeting a lot of very dull people'.[14]

Farming conservatives, wrote George Eliot some eighty years earlier, are prone to believe that whatever is, is bad, and any change is likely to be worse. So when a British general election was called for the end of February, Horne found himself further disenchanted by what he saw as the almost complete absence of political debate in his English village. In Bow Brickhill, it seemed, political opinions were reserved only for trivialities such as campaigning against the installation of streetlights or sewage systems. As an Australian 'used to arguing his head off about politics in general', he wrote, this was 'rather depressing'. Faced with such stolid resistance to even the most minor of modern conveniences, Horne found himself cast in the 'uncomfortable new role of hot-headed progressive', trying to convince geriatric farmers that streetlights would not bring crime and that sewage and running water might even improve their lives.[15]

Nevertheless, from the moment Horne arrived in England, he became a determined opponent of Clement Attlee's Labour government. He and Ethel spent the night of the British election at a neighbour's house listening with 'great excitement' to the big gains made by the Tories: 'I got so excited that my pen was covered in jam as I jotted the results down,' he wrote. Horne saw himself as a liberal conservative and a 'Tory democrat', albeit of a more enlightened sort than some of his imbecilic neighbours.[16] Yet even the villagers, for all their intransigence, shared something of his worldview: during his foray into the streetlights issue, for example, a local man told him that 'every change isn't necessarily a step forward'. As Horne was forced to admit, 'no one could agree with this statement more thoroughly than I.'[17]

It was otherwise a quiet winter, with little to do, but as the weather improved so did their social life. In February, Doug and Ann McCallum arrived in England, and Donald and Ethel started visiting them regularly in Oxford, where Doug was beginning a philosophy degree. When spring came they took a trip to Cambridge, spent a fortnight in London and entertained more recently arrived Sydney friends, including Adrian Deamer and Gwen Tanner at Bow Brickhill, playing 'ironic' games of croquet on their newly reclaimed lawns.[18]

In June they set off on a driving tour of the West Country with the Australian journalist Lachlan Beaton and his wife, Coral, visiting popular tourist locations such as Bath and Stonehenge. One spot, however – the village of Polperro on the Cornwall coast – Horne enjoyed so much that he and Ethel determined to move there during the winter months, when it was less crowded. This small fishing village, he told his mother, was 'much frequented by artists' – George Orwell had spent his summers there as a boy, and it was the current home of Daphne du Maurier. Literature was certainly on his mind. His novel, now finished and titled 'The Richmond Affair', had been placed with a

Donald Horne [left] at Stonehenge

'very reputable firm of literary agents' in London, though no one had yet offered to publish it. With luck, he hoped, he and Ethel might be able to live off his pen and he could avoid journalism entirely. 'I don't expect the novel … to be a bestseller,' he wrote to his mother, '[but] I should like to make sufficient money out of it to keep going.'[19]

Picturesque, dowager-free Polperro was Horne's best attempt to live what he imagined was the life of a literary man. In October, on money borrowed against Ethel's inheritance, they set themselves up 'inexpensively and quietly' in a small cottage, 'up on a hill above the village, looking out to sea'. Donald brought his books with him and placed them next to his writing desk for inspiration. During the day he wrote, while Ethel went into town to buy cheap fish for dinner. In the afternoons, they went for walks along the cliffs or inland to look for old churches. Visiting friends, meanwhile, would bring news of the outside world: Doug McCallum had already begun teaching at Oxford. Adrian Deamer and Gwen Tanner were now married, and he and Beaton had both found jobs on Fleet Street. Back in Australia, James McAuley, of all people, had converted to Catholicism and settled down in the Sydney suburbs, while Bill Pritchett and Gordon Jockel had both begun careers in the diplomatic service. If he was ever going to make it as a novelist, it had to be now.[20]

In his seaside cottage, Horne started on his second work of fiction, a dry, satirical account of life in an English village that borrowed heavily from his recent experience of Bow Brickhill. As always, he wrote quickly. By January he had a finished manuscript, a dramatisation of the petty gossip and stubborn rituals of the petit bourgeois rural English called 'One Can Always Tell a Gentleman'.[21] In the story, a married couple – an American, John Thrumm, and his English wife, Elsa – arrive in the fictional town of Rottenham to inherit the estate of John's great-uncle, only to discover that in the preceding decades the property had been neglected and mismanaged, mainly due to the complacency and ignorance of the ageing landlord and his deceitful staff.[22]

Horne peopled his English village novel with the same kinds of backwoods conservatives who saw attempts to install streetlights and sewage as a threat to the divine order of things. He drew liberally from his own experiences: his sensible female protagonist was named after his and Ethel's only intelligent friend in the village, Elsa Macpherson, while the busybody Mrs Blair-Jones and her quiet husband were modelled on Ethel's aunts, Rose and Lily. The village's prevailing political ethos – a mix of pragmatic rural individualism and a rigid and self-serving belief in the rituals and traditions of a moribund social order – drives Thrumm mad, as it did Horne. Early in the novel, for example, Thrumm is lectured by the estate's caretaker, Grey, on the eternal truths of English life:

Well, that's the way we does things 'ere at Rottenham, sir, and it's all simple enough to us as 'ave grown up with it. Old Mr Thrumm [the great uncle], 'e never used to interfere, sir, or complain, or worry, 'e just used to say, 'You go ahead, Grey, and make the best arrangements you can.' Just like any gentleman would.[23]

In this environment of perpetual stasis, Thrumm, like Horne, is cast as the village radical. The village – and by extension, England – is presented as a place in thrall with its past, unable to confront or even recognise the problems and possibilities of modernity. 'God knows what's happened to the English,' says Thrumm, 'some kind of dry rot seems to have gotten into the middle classes.' England, Horne's book implied, needed to cure itself of its delusional obsession with its own history, or better yet, rediscover some of the imagination and creativity it had displayed during its golden age. As Thrumm proclaims:

> I come from a country that pioneered its own path, and hasn't forgotten it yet. Well, England pioneered its way, too … It was the greatest pioneering country of all time. It pioneered the whole world and that's the spirit it must recapture to-day, with its own traditional refinements, of course … The wide world was England's Wild West once.[24]

Though he might not have known it, Horne's book was of a piece with a new type of English fiction that had emerged since the war, some of which was being referred to, however speciously, as the 'provincial novel'. Within a few years, English critics were crediting two books – Angus Wilson's short-story collection *Such Darling Dodos* and William Cooper's novel *Scenes from Provincial Life*, both published in the first half of 1950 – as marking a thematic and stylistic break from the high modernism of Joyce, Forster, Eliot and Woolf, which had largely characterised the literature of the interwar period.[25]

Horne had long since renounced such Bloomsbury-era stylistic self-indulgence as 'heavily affected' and 'spurious'.[26] Writers, he thought, should project outwards, not inwards. The provincial novel, as it was later defined, rejected verbosity and formal experimentation in favour of plain-spoken, unsentimental, almost journalistic prose. As J.D. Scott argued in *The Spectator* in 1954, it was in some ways a return to the social realist style of the Victorian era, an attempt to depict modern social realities, such as the labour movement, bureaucracy and the welfare state. Wilson's and Cooper's protagonists were both lower-middle-class outsiders, and both writers were openly critical of the snobbery, hypocrisy and selfishness of the British upper classes.[27]

'One Can Always Tell a Gentleman' fit broadly into this tradition. Horne's protagonist is an intelligent, well-meaning provincial who succumbs to the absurd and irrational inefficiencies of a hegemonic social order. His novel was a thinly veiled comment on the backwardness and mediocrity of the popular idealised image of English rural life, and skewered those like Thrumm who fell victim to such images. England, in Thrumm's experience, was not all it was cracked up to be. Horne's own rapidly dawning disappointment with the 'reality' of the motherland was right there in the titles of the book's first three chapters: 'Coming Home', 'Finding Out', 'Full Details'.[28]

◆ ◆ ◆

Until at least the 1960s, if an Australian journalist spoke of 'home', it was entirely possible that they were not referring to the town in which they grew up, nor even to the place where they lived and worked, but to a mean, crooked stretch of road on the other side of the globe. For successive waves of ambitious Australian newspapermen and women, trying one's hand on Fleet Street, the historic home of the British newspaper industry, was something of a rite of passage. To make your name at a London newspaper was seen as the pinnacle of the profession. It was a fiercely competitive world for a foreigner, with a high risk of failure. But as most journalists would rather die than sit still, many an expatriate settled for a measly job in London over a decent one back home. Or, as the down-and-out Australian journalist Florence James quipped in 1928, 'the crumbs are better than a feast elsewhere.'[29]

Not long after he first arrived in England, Horne ventured down to London with three letters of introduction signed by Frank Packer.[30] Five years earlier, when Horne was still a cadet reporter in Packer's organisation, its editor-in-chief had been Clarrie McNulty, a progressive and liberal-minded veteran of the paper's 1930s golden age and a contemporary of legendary Australian journalists Syd Deamer – father of Horne's friend Adrian – and Cyril Pearl. McNulty had since been put in charge of *The Daily Telegraph*'s London bureau, and in early 1950 he agreed to throw Horne some crumbs.[31] Throughout that first year, however, this amounted to a grand total of four articles.[32] By 1951, with their savings almost exhausted and Horne's novel finished and awaiting the verdict of the publishers, he and Ethel needed something more substantial.

In February, their luck briefly turned when McNulty offered Horne a trip to West Germany to report on the reconstruction of cities destroyed during the war. Only very recently divided up by the conquerors, Germany had become one of the frontlines in the escalating diplomatic conflict between the US-led liberal democracies of the West and the Soviet socialist republics of the East. In 1948, the Soviets had blockaded West Berlin, cutting it off from the Western world and forcing the Americans to deliver supplies to the area by air for almost a year. The result, in 1949, was the creation of two Germanys: the Western-aligned Federal Republic and the communist-controlled Democratic Republic. In England, newspapers painted a picture of a world in a state of high tension. A brutal proxy war was underway in Korea, communist forces had taken power in China, and the Soviets had just produced an atomic bomb. Horne's job in West Germany, said McNulty, was to give a sense of the political struggles with the East and, if possible, find evidence of an impending war.[33]

When he arrived in West Germany in early March, Horne set to work looking for signs of World War III, wandering the ruins of Frankfurt, Cologne and Bonn, speaking to officials, diplomats and ordinary Germans, visiting Beethoven's childhood home, strolling along the banks of the Rhine and attending a chamber music recital. Despite these outward signs of normality, he reported, Germany was an 'explosive country right at the centre of most of the world's worries'. West Germans were in a 'highly hysterical, irresponsible state' and America and Britain were doing 'almost nothing' to counter phoney communist promises of 'peace and national unity'. With great urgency, he told *Telegraph* readers of the communist propaganda pouring over the border from East Germany, 'articles stressing what a nice old chap Stalin is … [and] photos of happy, fun-loving communists leading the good life in houses of Soviet culture.'[34]

Despite many German 'wiseacres' forecasting war and inevitable communist takeover, Horne found that the most serious threat to order in West Germany was not communism but the escalating European refugee crisis. In the wake of the war, millions of Germans had either fled or were expelled from countries such as Poland, Czechoslovakia and Hungary. By 1950, it was estimated that over eight million

Germans had been forced out of Eastern Europe, almost all of whom ended up living hand-to-mouth on the outskirts of destroyed German cities. This great underclass, wrote Horne, provided 'wonderful material' for 'unscrupulous mob orators'. Badly housed, without hope and fostering 'deep social inferiority complexes', they seemed more likely to be attracted to the promises of the extreme right than to the communists: 'They provide more potentially combustible material even than Hitler worked on so successfully.'[35]

Back in England after such excitements, Horne's life seemed especially drab. 'I have at last seen the rather greyish white cliffs of Dover,' he wrote to his mother. The future looked bleak. With the lease on their Polperro home due to end in early April and their money all but gone, he and Ethel were forced to return to Bow Brickhill, as if walking straight back into the ridiculous world of his own novel. To make matters worse, eight different publishers had rejected 'The Richmond Affair', and there was no word yet on 'One Can Always Tell a Gentleman'.[36] He entered a period of listlessness and depression of a kind he hadn't experienced since being marooned in wartime Darwin, stranded in the great waste of inactivity. Indeed, he recalled feeling so bored and sorry for himself in this period that he 'might have been a child, face to face for the first time with the prospect of meaninglessness'.[37]

Lack of direction increased his melancholy. He trialled several new ways of making money. Lachlan Beaton tried to get him a job as a press officer at Qantas. He had a go at freelancing, receiving wave after wave of rejection letters from magazines, including *Punch* and *John Bull*. He entered an *Observer* short-story competition but lost to a then unknown Muriel Spark. He and Ethel even tried their hand at farming, reconstructing the pigsty and determining to supplement their meagre income by keeping animals and vegetables. In September, as if in admission of defeat, they spent the last of Ethel's money on a two-week trip to Paris, where Donald delighted in its European sophistication: pavement cafes, 'civilised amenities' and the 'excellence' of the food and drink. Predictably, when they returned to England it was 'wrapped in autumnal mists and fog'.[38]

In Britain, and indeed most of Western Europe, the end of the war had simply marked the official end of the fighting. The 'age of austerity' had only just begun, and for most ordinary people the hardship had continued unabated. With many key industries crippled, food and other necessities were still scarce. For tired and hungry Britons, the promised postwar good times must have seemed a distant dream. Inheriting this exhausted economy, the Attlee Labour government had extended wartime economic controls and embarked on a policy of nationalisation, bringing the Bank of England, the mines, railways, docks, and gas and electricity industries under government supervision. Yet by 1951, many English were still unable to access even the most basic goods: meat, cheese, fats, sugar and tea all remained rationed.[39] At Christmas 1950, the Hornes received an aid package from Australia: cigarettes and shirts for Donald, stockings for Ethel and as much food as his mother could fit in the box.[40]

Britain's slow recovery under Labour only confirmed Horne's conviction of the futility of government planning. In October 1951, Attlee called another British general election, less than two years after the last. Horne, unemployed but politically energised, got himself elected chairman of the newly formed Bow Brickhill Conservative Committee, and set about educating his neighbours on the virtues of laissez-faire economics. Applied in the twentieth century, he wrote in the *Telegraph*, nationalisation had been a 'washout'. Nationalised industries were too 'huge and centralised'. They lacked the energy, vitality and competitiveness of private enterprise. They were 'rigid', 'unimaginative' and 'helpless in the face of difficulties'. A vote for the conservatives, he seemed to imply, was a vote for progress.[41]

In the lead-up to the election, Horne presented himself as the village's conservative revolutionary, overhauling the party's campaign in the district with his trademark principles of practicality and calm rationality. He instituted a survey of local voters, discarding any potential Labour supporters and ardently persuading any undecideds. On election day he manned the polling booth, marking off likely Conservative votes as they came in. After the Conservatives triumphed – due in no small measure to his enthusiastic corralling of support – Horne increased his involvement, officially joining the party, re-establishing the local branch, founding a newsletter and planning a village fete.[42] If he did not make it as a novelist, he speculated, perhaps he might become a politician?

During these lean years, Horne also formed a brief friendship with the Australian writer George Johnston, who had recently moved to England to take charge of Associated Newspapers' London office. Johnston was everything Horne aspired to – a working provincial journalist who had transformed himself into a successful novelist. By 1951, the former war correspondent had already published three works of fiction, and in Australia he and his wife, Charmian Clift, also a writer, had become a fashionable and somewhat infamous literary couple.[43]

Both Johnston and Clift came to stay with the Hornes at Bow Brickhill and both read and made comments on his unpublished novel. Even after several revisions, though, he was unable to find an interested publisher. The manuscript had spent a lot of the previous year in New York under the title 'Bow Brickhill Revisited', where a friend had shopped it around several American publishing houses. The response was troubling. 'It is not the kind of thing the author could fix up with a few suggestions,' wrote one reader. 'He just hasn't enough artistic skill, I fear.'[44]

A lack of artistic skill was precisely what much of the London intellectual world was then worrying itself over. Since the war, establishment names, such as Cyril Connolly, Philip Toynbee and J.B. Priestley had lamented that much of the energy and vibrancy of the English literary scene had disappeared, perhaps forever. Many of its leading lights – figures as diverse as Orwell, Joyce, Wells, Auden and Woolf – had either died or moved away. By 1950, significant literary periodicals, such as *Penguin New Writing, Horizon, Polemic* and *New English Review* had all ceased publication.[45] 'It is closing time in the gardens of the West,' wrote Connolly in the final issue of *Horizon*. 'From now on an artist will be judged only by the resonance of his solitude or the quality of his despair.'[46]

Younger, less pessimistic critics, however, were inclined to see a literary revival in a new anti-modernist generation of lower-middle-class British poets and provincial novelists. This cohort of 'outsider' writers and 'kitchen sink realists' – Philip Larkin, Kingsley Amis,

John Wain and John Osborne, among others – were all either publishing or working on their first major works by the early 1950s. In 1956, after the wild success of Colin Wilson's critical study of alienation in literature, *The Outsider*, and Osborne's equivalent play, *Look Back in Anger*, this loose conglomeration of writers was given a name: the 'Angry Young Men'.[47]

Horne was, in spirit, one of England's Angry Young Men. Floating about London in the early 1950s, he had no connection to the upper reaches of English literary life, and he had no time for modernist style. His days were spent brooding over publishers' rejection letters, commuting from Bletchley to meet an Australian friend for lunch or, more often, wandering alone among the paintings in the National Gallery or hunched in the darkness of the newsreel theatres. He thought the English people ridiculous, or else wilfully oblivious to contemporary political problems.[48] 'Here was poor old Britain tottering nearer and nearer to catastrophe,' he wrote, while British elites remained 'infected with the belief that things are not as bad as they are', an idea that had also possessed the minds of ordinary people 'like some hideous disease'.[49]

To his dismay, the drudgery of regular employment seemed to be working well for almost all of his expatriate Australian friends. On his trips to London, Horne often stayed with the Deamers in their Paddington flat. Earlier that year Gwen Deamer had given birth to a daughter; the McCallums, too, were also expecting their first child. He and Ethel, meanwhile, were almost broke, and Donald was engaged in a desperate search for work. Ethel was playing the football pools in the hope of striking it lucky, they ate mostly from their own vegetable garden and they were even forced to sell the pigs to make ends meet. Concerned letters poured in from Australia. Surely something must show up for him, wrote his mother. Bits and pieces of journalism kept them going. McNulty was sympathetic to Horne's thwarted literary ambitions and sent him north to report on the English exploits of the Australian golfer Norman von Nida.[50] 'Has literature finally won you from its drudge sister called journalism?' he gibed.[51] Australians in London, Horne recalled decades later, were like 'lost Russian intellectuals in the nineteenth century'.[52]

Donald Horne [right] in England

Finally, in the late months of 1952, after nearly three years of financial precarity, Horne lucked his way into full-time work. When Adrian Deamer ran into an Australian friend on the bus who worked at the tabloid *Weekly Overseas Mail*, he suggested Horne as someone who could write the lighthearted, mostly fabricated news stories they were looking for. Horne, the lost Russian intellectual, set to work on articles including 'Women Who Murdered for Love' and 'I Changed My Sex and Married'.[53] This new work arrangement disrupted his and Ethel's quiet rural existence. To avoid the long daily commute, they often spent entire weeks sleeping on Adrian and Gwen Deamer's couch in London. In the evenings, Donald toiled on rewrites of his novels. He was 'just about washed up by the weekends,' wrote Ethel, when they travelled back to Bow Brickhill to look after the garden.[54]

By November, when their exhausting new routine started to wear thin, they decided to find their own place in London. The Old Rectory Farm, which had long since become a prison to Horne, would now become their 'country house'. Though his professional work was increasingly frivolous, he hoped this new set-up would have its own sophistication: 'to have a flat in town and a house in the country,' he reassured his mother, 'is an ideal that several million Londoners never achieve, so that is quite something.'[55] The Hornes found a cheap flat near Bloomsbury and split the rent with Brian Beddie, a fellow Andersonian, army gunner and diplomatic cadet, who had moved to

London to study philosophy under Michael Oakeshott. Beddie, like McCallum, was writing a thesis on Max Weber, and made for great intellectual company – a considerable upgrade from the dowagers.[56]

London life suited Donald more than Ethel. At the end of 1952, they celebrated Christmas at the farm with the Beatons and the Johnstons, but when Monday came, wrote Ethel, Donald took off back to the city, 'leaving me like an old dish rag.'[57] Indeed, every so often there were signs that their marriage might have been under some strain. Donald, understandably, left few clues in his letters home, and he was only marginally more forthcoming in his autobiography of the period. In Paris, they had bickered and fought over trivialities. On the farm, they were playing at being small rural landholders, while in Polperro they had entertained ideas of running a guesthouse. Both these dreams of 'petit bourgeouis enterprise,' Horne later recalled, were really Ethel's. 'I was not emotionally ready to buy a house.'[58]

These disputes, however, probably had more to do with Horne's own continuing sense of self-doubt than they were an unwanted imposition of Ethel's bourgeois values. He had come to England enthusiastically, and both Polperro and the overhaul of the Old Rectory Farm were as much his dream as they were his wife's. If his English activities later seemed ridiculous, a bump in the road on his journey to personal enlightenment, or a fraudulent mask he had tried on for size, neither he nor Ethel could have fully grasped this at the time. All the remaining evidence suggests they were a perfectly amiable and contented couple. The few scribbled letters from Ethel to Donald that survive, mostly written while he was in Germany in 1951, are littered with affectionate, perhaps even ironic, private pet names: 'Take care of yourself little petal pie', 'Love Ethel Pot', 'Dear Petal Honey', 'Love Potethel', 'Dear Pan', 'Love from PoT.'[59]

After nearly six months fabricating nonsense for the *Weekly Overseas Mail*, Horne jumped at an offer from George Johnston to join the London office of the Sydney *Sun*, where he hoped to write features. His beat, however, barely changed. At *The Sun* he became the go-to writer of the same droll colour stories he had perfected at his previous job, many of which stemmed from his existing observational interest in English manners and social mores. In one such piece, he examined English terms of endearment, a nod to his and Ethel's private jokes. English men, wrote Horne, greeted their wives with expressions such as 'Hello, Parsley-Pants', 'Good evening, Paraffin-Oil-Face' and 'How is my little Lady Frog'. This was the kind of behavioural idiosyncrasy he might have tried to put into a novel twelve months earlier. Now they mostly just made for good gags:

> A Doncaster wife reported that her husband had these twelve pet names
> for her: Land Crab, Short Size, Bloater Face, Sweetie Pie, Pet Pippin,
> Pieface, Diddles, Squeeze, Skipper, Button Nose, Nut Brain, Sticko.[60]

Barely had Horne settled into this new job when he was on the move again. In September, he got wind that *The Sun* would be sold to *The Sydney Morning Herald* and, sensing this might not work out well for him, tapped McNulty for a job at the *Telegraph*. 'Three changes of employment in a year,' wrote Ethel. 'It's enough to go on with.' The move looked to be a good one: on a staff of thirteen, he wrote proudly to his mother, he was now third in command. Frank Packer, he announced, had personally accepted his new financial 'terms'. For now, it seemed, journalism – the 'drudge sister' of literature – had won.[61]

◆ ◆ ◆

For a moment following the victory of the Conservative Party in the 1951 British elections – accompanied as it was by the second coming of its heroic wartime leader and patriot-in-chief, Winston Churchill, and the coronation the following year of a youthful new monarch, Elizabeth II – it might have been possible for some optimistic Britons to indulge in fantasies of a 'new Elizabethan age' and a restoration of the simple and reassuring certainties of the prewar world. For well over a century the British had boasted a vast colonial empire, one on which sun never set, from whose resources, both human and material, they had constructed their global dominance.

In the years since the war, however, it had become increasingly obvious to those with an eye on reality that such hopes were unfounded: new demands – economic, military and moral – had hastened the decline of all the European colonial empires, while ideological conflict and the invention of the atomic bomb had reordered the world under the competing umbrellas of the two new superpowers, the United States and the Soviet Union. By the mid-1950s, the British had reluctantly, and often violently, ceded power to the newly independent states of India, Pakistan, Burma, Sri Lanka, Ghana and Nigeria. Without a consistent colonial policy, conflicts continued to rage in British Guiana, Malaya, Cyprus and, most brutally, in Kenya.[62]

In early 1954, the *Telegraph* sent their man in London, Donald Horne, to Kenya to report on the rapidly escalating conflict there between British settler farmers and insurgent independence forces. Throughout decades of colonial rule, white settler expansion had increasingly marginalised Kenya's largest ethnic group, the Kikuyu. In 1952, the Mau Mau, also known as the Kenya Land and Freedom Army (KLFA), emerged as a militant splinter group of the existing Kenya African Union, a more reformist organisation, which was attempting to secure political rights and land reforms from the British government. Mau Mau fighters began raiding settler farms, sometimes violently, and destroying livestock, leading the British to declare a state of emergency and begin counterinsurgency operations. It is now remembered as one of the bloodiest conflicts in the history of the British Empire, resulting in the deaths of up to 20,000 rebels, and just thirty-two settlers.[63]

In Germany, Horne had seen the Cold War up close. Now here was a chance to see the world's other great conflict, between the old European empires and their long-oppressed subjects. Maybe he would become a famous foreign correspondent, he imagined, 'Horne of Africa'.[64] In February 1954, he flew by plane – still a considerable, somewhat dangerous novelty – to Nairobi, Kenya's capital. As his plane descended on the colonial metropolis, he wrote, it seemed 'just as it used to be – a white man's luxury city in a dark man's continent'. Though it was, without a doubt, the most exotic place he had ever been, he also found it strangely familiar. With its dry, empty landscapes and grand colonial architecture, it looked eerily like Australia, so much so that he half 'expected to see some old friend come strolling down the street'.[65]

Horne holed up with the rest of the press at the New Stanley Hotel, an old, white-walled colonial relic that had previously played host to visiting royals, movie stars and, at one point, Ernest Hemingway. The European Quarter of the city, he found, was 'a kind of living museum of the good old days … when the lower classes knew their place and gentlemen were gentlemen'. Like he had in Germany, Horne spent a lot of time visiting British officials and dignitaries at 'sundowner parties', where respectable Kenyan colonists gossiped and sipped on cocktails. 'All that spoiled the picture,' he quipped, 'is the back pocket bulge that indicates a loaded pistol.'[66]

Horne found the colonists in Nairobi and its rural surrounds to be in a state of high, almost homicidal, tension – a mood that far exceeded that which he had found in Cologne and Bonn a few years earlier. Locals regaled him with stories of grisly murders, beheadings and other unprintable atrocities, which he exaggerated at every opportunity for *Telegraph* readers: British settlers lived in constant fear that they may be 'slashed to ribbons' by the 'deadly jungle knives' of the rebels. The Mau Mau were 'terrorists', 'brutes' and 'black monsters', 'filled with an animal-like bloodlust that nothing can control'.[67] In Horne's dispatches, it was certainly not made clear that almost all the murdering in Kenya – including official public hangings and more clandestine vigilante violence – was being done by the whites.

In England, the 'Kenya Emergency' was a topic of fierce debate. For Horne, this firsthand experience of the brutal realities and impossible dilemmas of colonial politics was formative. Informed as it was by the fear and hysteria of the English settlers with whom he spent most of his time, it made him intensely, almost blindly, critical of bleeding-heart attitudes toward decolonisation. In the *Telegraph*, he reported an argument he had had in the New Stanley with a freshly arrived English liberal, 'a mild-mannered visitor from England's pleasant welfare state', who was infuriated at the way Kenyan settlers went around 'armed to the teeth'. A few days later, after the man's car had broken down in the middle of Mau Mau territory, Horne noticed this same 'pacifist' now sported his own back pocket bulge. Even the softest of liberals, he implied, would be radicalised by the bitter realities of racial fear and violence. Horne suggested the colony might even need a 'strong man', as the Kenyan whites were caught in a 'hopeless dilemma' not dissimilar to Australia's:

> Like our own pioneers, they are genuine settlers who have staked themselves and their families to Kenya's future. They have given England away. Kenya is their homeland ... [but] some powers also have to go the way of the coloured man. Although most settlers accept this in theory, they cannot stomach it in practice, for belief in the superiority of the white races is still strong in Kenya.[68]

Horne's Kenya articles got 'a very good run in the Tele', Ethel proudly informed him upon his return. Packer was said to be very pleased with his work, particularly as he had got the world scoop on the British capture of 'General China', the leader of the Mau Mau forces. 'I think he would like to go away somewhere else,' wrote Ethel to Florence, 'it's more interesting than staying in the office!'[69] Indeed, in April, he did manage to wrangle another foreign assignment, a shorter and decidedly less dangerous trip to Finland to report on the expulsion of Australian diplomats from Russia following the dramatic defection of a Soviet agent back in Australia – his second personal experience of East–West conflict since arriving in England.[70] As the Australians' train pulled into Helsinki, wrote Donald, 'enthusiastic crowds sang "Waltzing Matilda"', as if greeting soldiers returning from war. That day, he and the expelled Australian chargé d'affaires, Brian Hill, breakfasted in the glass-walled Palace Hotel. It was the only interview he gave, and it was Horne's second big front-page story of the year.[71]

Though Horne's professional life was erratic, he was now earning a decent wage, and he and Ethel appeared to be looking to the future. Indeed, despite the petty gripes and bickering common to many domestic arrangements, it is difficult to find evidence to suggest that they were considering anything other than a life together. With their new financial resources, they were planning extensive renovations on the farm, building, decorating and furnishing to the tune of £300. Donald had begun converting the barn into a den, with floor-to-ceiling bookshelves. A year earlier he had taken responsibility for a dog, Rufus, and a cat, Kitten. With the lease on their London flat due to expire in June, they had also decided to move back to Bow Brickhill full-time. This, Donald calculated, would save them £5 a week. His mother was even sending over the rest of his books from Sydney. 'It doesn't look as if we shall be getting back for a while yet,' wrote Ethel. 'And he missed them so.'[72]

The other indicator that Horne was settling in for the long haul was his increasing involvement in local Conservative Party politics. Since the 1951 election he had been promoted to the district executive, had continued his overhaul of the local branch, and had been invited to share his political wisdom at the meetings of several nearby branches. In December 1953, he received a letter from the Buckingham Conservative Association: the current member would not be standing at the next election – did Horne know any interested candidates? Ever practical, Horne played a decisive role in subsequent factional manoeuverings. And as he later recalled, it was then made clear to him that he might very soon become a Tory MP in the House of Commons, 'an enlightened conservative making intelligent speeches.'[73]

Given the direction his life later took, this anointment as the rising star of Conservative Party politics in Buckinghamshire appears like a monumental fork in Horne's road, a point at which he might have been thrust in an entirely different direction. He was, he later admitted, 'more Whig than Tory', but the Conservative Party was a broad church, and he had long been an enthusiastic foot soldier in the battle of ideas. In parliament, he might have played the role of Tory revolutionary, he thought, discarding the reactionary elements of the party platform and reforming it from within.[74]

It seems unlikely, however, that Horne could ever really have sustained the mask of a professional politician, particularly at this moment in his life. He was a sceptic almost by reflex and, as his English experience had made evident, profoundly restless. Likewise, politics would never have satisfied his insatiable intellectual energy and curiosity, nor would it have fully allowed for the irony and amused indifference that seemed to him the only intelligent approach to life. Like a good novelist, Horne preferred the world at a distance, as the author of the story rather than one of its characters. This role – the amused observer, the mimic, mumbler of witticisms, anecdotes and drolleries – was, in effect, his true character. Though he was clearly a very practical person, with an activist streak and strong reforming impulse, he was no politician or country squire. Rather, he was most often himself in conversation, with kindred spirits Deamer, McCallum and his new friend at the *Telegraph*, Patricia Rolfe, wisecracking over lunch, observing life's absurdities.

This choice – between the detachment and independence of the novelist and the activism and discipline of the politician – went right to the heart of Horne's troubles, though he still could not see the distinction with such clarity. The bitterness and dissatisfaction that had dogged him throughout his time in England, and that had been with him since university, stemmed directly from the seeming irreconcilability of these two approaches to life. The question of politics versus literature pointed to a much more profound unease at the centre of his being, one that saw a deep contrast between the lofty realms of the artist and the grubby world of real life, between blind faith and crippling doubt, and between an optimistic, hopeful view of the world and a pessimistic, fearful one.

Ethel Horne

It is possible, then, that in 1953 and 1954, journalism acted not only as a necessary financial salve for Donald and Ethel, but also as a solution to his eternal dilemma. Journalism allowed, to some extent, for both detached observation and passionate advocacy. He could write with equal parts humour and seriousness, and he could maintain his sophisticated sense of ambivalence: one day he might chase a story, the next he might let one come to him. Of course, he knew he could not spend the rest of his career writing about the 'Woman Who Murdered for Love' or the eating habits of the royal family. Practised over an extended period of time, this kind of journalism would only increase his bitterness and sense of failure. But his professional life at least appeared to be on an upward trajectory, from the frivolity of the *Weekly Overseas Mail* to the tabloid sensations of *The Sun,* to third-in-command in the London *Telegraph* office. For all its shortcomings, journalism suited Horne perfectly, and during these restive years, he came closer than ever before to accepting where his talents lay.

By 1954, these talents had finally been noticed by Frank Packer, and in July that year, yearning for another foreign adventure, Horne boldly and somewhat capriciously accepted an offer to temporarily move back to Sydney and edit Packer's new, top-secret Australian version of the tabloid *Weekly Mail.* For all the spontaneity of this strange, sudden and seemingly regressive career move, it was not without considerable irony. Australia – the dull, second-rate place he had longed to escape four and half years earlier – now appeared, out of nowhere, as an exciting temptation, a daring six-month campaign on a significantly increased salary.[75] It was as if, in the mad rush to repack his father's old suitcase, Horne accidentally left his whole English life behind, like a half-finished book: the Old Rectory Farm, his collection of Great Literature, his political career, his home renovations, his handful of friends, his cat and dog, his two unpublished novels – and Ethel herself.

4.

BLIND MAN'S BLUFF

By the mid-1950s, the Sydney offices of Frank Packer's sprawling media empire, Consolidated Press, had grown so large they spread across an entire city block. After several decades of property acquisitions, renovations and extensions, this jumbled, rat-infested conglomeration of buildings on the border of Park and Elizabeth Streets resembled a city within a city, like a small medieval town rising out of the Hyde Park commons. It possessed its own political factions and social groupings, its own internal economy, and its own behaviours and rituals. From his executive suite at the top of the *Telegraph* building, Packer ruled over it all like a mad king, prone to acts of great benevolence and cruelty.[1]

At the age of thirty-two, Horne – still somewhat directionless and intellectually unsatisfied – could at least now boast of his newly acquired position of influence within this Australian newspaper kingdom. Having started at the bottom as a student journalist in the early 1940s, writing the odd story as the *Telegraph*'s university correspondent, he now found himself bumping shoulders with Packer's network of executives and editors, directly beholden to the whims, eccentricities and personal vendettas of the all-powerful boss himself.

In later years, Horne often likened his life as an executive at Consolidated Press to being a low-ranking member of a feudal court. Packer, he recalled, was most often encountered sitting behind his 'dictator-sized' desk, from which he cultivated a permanent 'atmosphere of potential terror'. Fierce rivalries and fragile alliances were maintained among the various courtiers, all of whom sought – usually at each other's expense – the approval and patronage of this 'cantankerous, bullying master of surprise and dominance'.[2]

Beginning in the mid-1950s, as the upstart editor of Packer's newest tabloid, Horne began to school himself in the dark arts of manipulating the boss's influence and authority for his own ends. Succeeding at such a game, he found, required the protection of great and powerful friends or, when all else failed, submission to the cruel hand of fate itself. Like life, working for Packer could be a merciless game of chance, and given the opportunity, it was best to stack the odds in your favour.

Indeed, there seemed to be a considerable element of serendipity in the nature and timing of Horne's four-and-a-half-year absence from his native land. In 1949, he and Ethel had left for England on a cruise ship, as Australians had for over a century, tracing the slow and familiar nautical route through the British colonies. But in the intervening years – undoubtedly the most intense of the still-developing Cold War – Horne had watched on, often with his own eyes, as this old world order was slowly and irreversibly up-ended. The United States had emerged as the new global superpower. Its ideological rival, the Soviet Union, had acquired atomic weapons and consolidated control over Eastern Europe, Britain's grip over its empire had become increasingly questionable, and proxy wars between East and West had been fought in Korea and Vietnam. In July 1954, like a head of state signalling a symbolic change in national outlook, Horne – free of any pangs as to his traditional links or kinship with the United Kingdom – had directed his airplane journey home via America.[3]

During this parade of international crises and geopolitical realignments, the nation to which he returned had proven itself no less sensitive than its European and American allies to the impending communist threat, and in the years of his absence, this 'great world struggle' had loomed large in the Australian political imagination.[4] A poll conducted in the late 1940s, for example, had found that one in three Australians thought peace could not last beyond 1953.[5] Since taking power in 1949, Robert Menzies' Liberal–National Coalition had signed a defence treaty with the United States (known as ANZUS), opened up remote outback regions for British nuclear testing, unsuccessfully attempted to ban the Communist Party of Australia and won a closely fought election on the back of sensational allegations of high-level Soviet espionage. In April 1954, the American president, Dwight Eisenhower, publicly put forward his 'domino theory' of the Asia-Pacific, which held that if one nation in the region came under the influence of communism, surrounding ones were sure to follow. In September of that year, he signed on to SEATO, a collective defence treaty aimed at seeing off communist influence in South-East Asia. It was a period, historians now tend to agree, in which for many people the outbreak of a third world war seemed a genuine possibility.[6]

By the time Horne arrived back in Australia on 18 July 1954, the likelihood of a widespread 'hot' war in the region was beginning to fade, and such antipodean geopolitical concerns, if they had registered at all during his time abroad, were nevertheless completely peripheral to his new existence.[7] According to his deal with Packer, he would only need to be in the country for six months, on an inflated salary, with his time devoted entirely to his smash-and-grab tabloid magazine operation. He did not even need to look for private accommodation. Shortly after arriving, the company set him up with a room at the Australia Hotel on Castlereagh Street – at that time one of Sydney's premier addresses – where the ageing newspaper baron kept several rooms for company business and, Horne learned, 'liaisons'. To outsiders and younger journalists, reports of Horne's accommodation seemed unlikely. Packer was notoriously stingy and looked for ways to cut costs at every opportunity. Horne's stay at the opulent hotel – 'on Packer's dime' – later grew into a Sydney journalistic legend. Horne, went the myth, was getting 'lashings of dough', and spent much of his time drinking champagne and getting weekly manicures.[8]

Horne's main correspondent in the months following his return to Australia was Howard French, a dandyish Fleet Street character who had been a colleague of Horne's at Associated Newspapers in London in 1953. French was something of a tabloid expert. Since starting out in journalism in the mid-1930s, he had worked exclusively on trashy publications such as the *Sunday Dispatch* and the *Daily Sketch*, and now served as editor of the British *Weekend Mail*. Given Packer had set up his new Australian tabloid magazine as a joint operation with the *Weekend Mail*, syndicating content and standardising layouts, French became Horne's man in London.[9]

In mid-August, French flew out to Australia to oversee the launch of the magazine, which they decided to call *Weekend*. David McNicoll, one of Packer's closest executives, had already hired a small team of reporters, and Horne and French set about the task of building a magazine from scratch. On 28 August, after a chaotic few weeks, the first issue of *Weekend* hit newsstands, describing itself as 'Australia's Brightest Newspaper'. It featured a swimsuit-clad blonde reclining across the front page. 'The sweetest Swede we've ever come across,' *Weekend* declared, with a wink. Other outlandish stories included 'I Married the World's Strongest Woman' and 'Bushranger Cut Off Their Heads'.[10]

At first glance, Horne's editorship of such a frivolous publication seems a strange blip, a few lost years between his abortive attempt to become a novelist and his more successful attempt to become a journalist-intellectual. How else to explain why this young man, who ten years earlier had been selected as one of the twelve brightest young minds in the country, was now slumming it (and living it up) as the editor of its 'brightest' newspaper? In later years, some of his friends and acquaintances expressed bemusement at the incongruity of someone like Horne devoting himself to a rag like *Weekend*. Robert Hughes called it a 'Packer tit-and-bum sheet', while Frank Moorhouse thought it 'sexually retarded'. Horne settled more politely on 'extreme lowbrow general magazine'. 'It was the equivalent of deliberately making a bad movie,' he told an interviewer in 1973.[11]

In his positive moments, Horne rationalised his new life as a daring escapade and a bold experiment, a bit of action after years of treading water, and indeed some part of him must have believed in *Weekend*. 'You couldn't work there without somehow believing in it,' recalled Ross Poole, who worked briefly as a writer on Horne's magazine. 'Donald believed in it, and he took it seriously.' Of course, this was precisely Horne's problem, because he also saw the magazine as a waste of time, pure tabloid rubbish with zero journalistic value.[12]

However, Horne had an undeniable talent for this kind of breezy, humorous writing, and in this regard he was a victim of his own success. The fourth issue of the magazine sold nearly 450,000 copies and unleashed the activist in him, the same way his takeover of the local

Conservative Party branch had back in England. There would be more reforms, more revolutions. He was a man on a mission: 'Everyone is astounded that *Weekend* is so successful, except me,' he told French. 'I want to see that half-million.'[13] Horne quickly became something of a magazine-launching machine. In October, Packer ordered him and Peter Hastings to start a new children's newspaper, the *Junior Telegraph*, which debuted disastrously a month later and was wound up by the following March. It did not matter: *Weekend*'s huge sales had lifted Horne up the company pecking order. He soon found himself one of Packer's most promising young executives. The *Junior Telegraph* would not be the last of the boss's thought bubbles he would be ordered to execute.[14]

Horne's increasingly good relationship with Frank Packer in the early years of *Weekend* might never have come to anything had he not chanced on the patronage and protection of the boss's eldest son, Clyde. Like Donald, the then nineteen-year-old heir apparent had started out in a lowly position at the *Telegraph* and had only just returned from London, where he had been sent by his father to get experience working on the *Daily Mail*. Crucially, though, wrote Horne much later, he was by disposition not a true Packer, and was instead 'touched by a gentleness he could not express'.[15] Clyde quickly became Horne's greatest and most powerful friend within the organisation, and when the young Packer was given responsibility for *Weekend*, became its most influential supporter, sharing ideas, offering criticisms and shielding Horne from Frank Packer's wrath.[16]

What Horne did outside the office is a mystery. In his papers at the State Library of New South Wales, there is almost no surviving personal correspondence from the *Weekend* years. The material that does exist is mostly mundane communication with Packer and French, practical memos to his staff and reams of budgets, marketing plans and administrative files. It is easy to imagine that all Horne did during this period was sit at his desk, besuited in a cloud of cigarette smoke, writing memos. Such a life could not have been further from his quiet Polperro existence just three years prior, writing novels by the seaside, or even his quasi-bohemian London world, lunching with friends and wandering the halls of the National Gallery.[17]

The makeup of the written material that survived the jagged course of Horne's early life seems wholly arbitrary. As he switched continents and careers, many notes, scribblings and even his precious books either disappeared or were discarded without a thought. He had so far never managed to keep a diary for more than a month, and his professional work was certainly not conducted with posterity in mind. Nevertheless, it is difficult to believe that Horne simply stopped writing personal correspondence once he arrived back in Sydney. Both his wife and two of his closest friends, Doug and Ann McCallum, remained in England. Even during his busiest periods on Fleet Street, he had still found time for the occasional dispatch.[18]

In September 1954, in a cryptic letter from London, Howard French informed Horne that he had recently spoken to Ethel. He reported that she was in 'very good form' and was 'looking forward to going out to join you'. She was also, he wrote, 'very glad to hear how well things had gone with you', which suggests that the two had not yet been in contact, well over two months after they had parted at London Airport.[19] When pressed to speak about this confusing moment in his marriage, Horne always remained conspicuously vague, consigning his departure to a single line in his memoirs: 'Ethel, standing at the gate that separates those who stay from those who depart.'[20] In 1992, he told an interviewer that this reticence was deliberate and he had intended for his retelling to 'have certain enigmatic qualities about it':

[I had] built up a whole life that seemed to have nothing whatsoever to do with what had preceded it … Why did that happen? … I think people can be over clever about giving reasons for why this, that or anything happened … Why this happened, I don't know. It was quite amazing, and when I wrote [the memoir] I just hoped people would be amazed by that and, like me, wonder why that happened, and then not know about it … I just got carried on by [my life in England] without intending that at all.[21]

Horne's move back to Australia was not intended to be permanent. When he left England it was with the stated plan of returning in six months. Shortly after he arrived in Sydney, however, he began an extramarital relationship, one that he later described in his memoirs (with literary flourish) as an '*affaire*'.[22] It was likely this infidelity that ended the marriage. By the end of 1954, with the perspective afforded by distance and time, his marriage to Ethel now appeared to him as a central part of the more generalised disappointment of his whole experience in England. In his eagerness for yet another fresh start, both were conveniently relegated to the past. When the six-month deadline rolled around, Horne appeared happy to leave the decision on his professional future in the hands of Frank Packer: 'I really would like to know what you want me to do after January 18,' Horne wrote to his boss.

> [That would be] six months after I left London with some empty layout sheets in my pocket. Then – if you would like me to stay – I can go ahead and plan for the future; or if I am to hand over to someone else I can start doing that in an organised way. Would you let me know what you think about this?[23]

Packer's response is unknown, but the outcome was clear: Horne remained in Australia, alone, for the duration of 1955. In January, he moved into more permanent accommodation, in an office flat in the fifteen-storey Marton Hall building on Margaret Street in the Sydney CBD.

The other great legend that grew around Horne during this period was his reputation as a fiery and intimidating editor, 'the Packer Group's next biggest sacker after Frank himself'.[24] The most popular anecdote, oft-repeated down the years, referred to the time when, in a fit of rage, Horne ripped up a young journalist's copy and threw it out the window, only to realise that he had torn up the wrong article and had to send a staff member down to the street to pick up the pieces. This story, noted his friend Frank Moorhouse many years later, has been told about every magazine Horne ever edited. Another widespread rumour was that Horne's bullying of younger journalists was so bad he could not enter a bar without having a beer thrown at him. Once again, the tale took on a life of its own, with every second journalist in Sydney soon claiming they had tipped a beer over the head of

Donald Horne. Donald, wrote Moorhouse, instead assured him that there were 'only three beers in all ever thrown at him'.[25] According to Graeme Eggins, a junior member of *Weekend* in these years, flying beers were the least of Horne's worries:

> One morning I witnessed Clyde Packer throw a small firecracker over the partition into Donald's office, where it exploded with a satisfying bang. Donald shot out of his office, his face diffused with anger, undoubtedly ready to instantly sack the perpetrator. But when he saw a grinning Clyde surrounded by even more grinning staff, Donald stopped dead and produced the weakest smile I've ever seen in my life. He couldn't sack the proprietor's son, at that time the heir apparent.[26]

Stories such as these would not have had any currency among journalists had they not possessed some kernel of truth. Horne clearly lorded it over many of his staff, a lot of whom disliked and feared him – a fact he never denied.[27] He himself recalled the emergence of an 'anti-Horne cult' in certain circles of Sydney journalists during the *Weekend* years. But it was not all fire and brimstone: Eggins also admitted that Horne would be very quick to give praise for good writing, and when the young staffer left for England in 1958, it was with an effusive letter of introduction written by his cantankerous boss.[28]

Outside of the office, drinking and socialising formed a central part of Horne's new existence. His principal companions in such exploits were two senior members of his staff, Larry Boys and Jim Murrant, with whom he sometimes snuck off during the day for a 'quiet' beverage. Alcohol-fuelled parties also became an important part of life at *Weekend*. Some of these gatherings appear to have been quite wild. One featured a drinking relay race and a woman jumping out of a pie. Another, allegedly, required the intervention of the fire brigade. Parties also complemented the blokey business dealings of the time. When the firm in charge of the magazine's advertising, Jackson Wain, raised questions about *Weekend*'s image, for example, Horne suggested a boozy get-together to placate them. But more than anything, it was through drinking, remembered

Horne, that he and his closest colleagues 'sought relief from life's desperate dilemmas'.[29]

When he was not at the office or the pub, Horne continued his own literary self-education, consuming important books with the same energy and diligence with which he had done as an adolescent. Having already read his way through the canon of nineteenth-century European literature, he now either re-read favourites or tried out more modern classics. In the early months of 1955, for example, he knocked off the entirety of Graham Greene's works, 'one after the other, like someone chain smoking'. Of other modern literary offerings, he judged the best to be Anthony Powell's *Dance to the Music of Time* series, Robert Musil's *The Man Without Qualities*, Joyce Cary's *Mister Johnson* and Bertolt Brecht's *Threepenny Novel*.[30]

Horne was attracted to unsentimental writers who depicted life as absurd and somewhat meaningless, and interior states as unknowable, random or simply irrelevant. Brecht, he wrote just three years later, 'explained why things happened in the wicked kind of way they so often do'.[31] Powell showed that 'the journey of life is itself discursive, accidental, largely mysterious, a game of blind man's bluff' – something he had known to be true since reading *War and Peace* in an army hospital fifteen years earlier.[32] Such an outlook, he continued to believe, was the very essence of history, and indeed of life. With this idea once again front of mind, Horne picked up the habit of reading biographies of 'great men', such as A.J.P. Taylor's life of Bismarck and Isaac Deutscher's of Trotsky.[33] Was there any real difference between Powell's fictionalisation of his own life and Deutscher's more scholarly telling of Trotsky's? Both suffered from the same blind spots and explanatory dilemmas. Both ran up against the same mysteries of the human mind. This was certainly true of his own life: Horne could barely explain to himself why he had come to Australia to edit a tabloid rag – how could any biographer tell him otherwise?

◆ ◆ ◆

In his rush to get home from England in July 1954, Horne had made a short three-day stopover in New York City, where he spent most of his time collecting photographs and clippings for Packer's new magazine. But like so many of his movements in the 1950s, the timing of this brief visit to the United States held considerable portents. Without prior intention, or indeed any special interest in the matter, he had happened to arrive in America at the moment when popular opinion was very publicly turning against the demagogic anti-communist senator Joe McCarthy, whose relentless, high-profile and often unsubstantiated pursuit of communist spy cells had become a global *cause célèbre*. Less than a month before Horne arrived in New York, McCarthy had been put on trial in a series of publicly broadcast Senate hearings, and later that year was officially censured by the US Senate. McCarthy's 'red scare', rather than exposing any kind of organised fifth column within the US government, had instead had the undesired effect of further discrediting anti-communism itself, especially among intellectuals already sympathetic to the Soviet 'anti-anti-communist' line. To be vocally anti-communist in these early years of the Cold War, as Horne so often was, was thus to expose yourself to automatic accusations of McCarthyism, regardless of the substance of your criticism. The final legacy of Joe McCarthy, Horne wrote a few years later, was to make it 'more difficult to be seriously anti-Communist'.[34]

When he arrived back in Australia, Horne's most important outlet for such thoughts was his old university friend James McAuley, who was now a published poet. Horne's journeys west to McAuley's house in Ryde in the 1950s functioned as brief escapes from his unserious professional life, a time to joust over intellectual matters and test out the usefulness of his latest reading. In these years, recalled Horne two decades later, 'there was no one I enjoyed having a talk with more than Jim McAuley'. When his old friend discussed liberalism, wrote Horne, it was like watching someone slowly blowing up a balloon, then suddenly and softly popping it with a needle. The two of them would 'thunder away all night', drinking brandy and waxing poetic about the state of the novel or the gathering storms of Asian communism, pausing briefly while McAuley's children joined them for a family breakfast, 'then do a bit more talking'.[35]

In the early 1955, McAuley was contacted by the secretary of an organisation calling itself the Australian Committee for Cultural

Donald Horne, early 1950s

Freedom (ACCF), who wanted to know if he was interested in editing a new literary magazine, one they hoped would help fight the cultural cold war and fill the void left by a purported leftist orthodoxy in Australian intellectual life. The ACCF had been established twelve months earlier by a motley group of lawyers, academics, Eastern European émigrés and right-wing unionists eager to act as the Australian branch of another recently formed network of anti-communist writers and intellectuals, headquartered in Paris and calling itself the Congress for Cultural Freedom (CCF). In that short period, these international connections had already started to pay dividends, with the ACCF sponsoring several lecture tours of Australia by prominent British and American anti-communist intellectuals and dissenters from Eastern European communist states.[36]

The international Congress for Cultural Freedom was a decidedly Eurocentric organisation that had grown out of the very particular political concerns of that continent in the wake of World War II. In those years, the radicalism and anti-Americanism of a small but influential set of politically 'committed' French intellectuals – among them Jean-Paul Sartre, Simone de Beauvoir, Maurice Merleau-Ponty and Paul Éluard – had typified the continuing attachment of many postwar European writers and thinkers to the communist cause, as well as their almost wilful blindness to the crimes being committed in its name by the Soviet Union. It was in this climate that a rather heterogeneous collection of dissenting

European and American liberals – most of whom had at some point in their lives identified with the left – had met in Berlin in 1950 to inaugurate an organisation that would defend 'culture' from its overt subordination to political ends. And though the CCF came together under the patronage of respectable names, such as Bertrand Russell, Benedetto Croce and Karl Jaspers, its heterodox intellectual energy came from a younger generation of disillusioned European writers, among them Arthur Koestler, A.J. Ayer, Raymond Aron and Stephen Spender, all of whom wanted to distance themselves from communist crimes in Eastern Europe without sacrificing their progressive credentials or exposing themselves to accusations of either reactionary conservatism or – in the hyperbolic communist lexicon – 'fascism'.[37]

In Australia, this intra-left civil war over communism continued to stifle the electoral prospects of progressives. In March 1955, the Labor Party officially split over the issue at its federal conference in Hobart, resulting in the formation of a new, breakaway and explicitly anti-communist political party, the ALP (Anti-Communist), which later became the Democratic Labor Party (DLP). In a snap election six months later, the Liberal–Country Party coalition inflicted even more pain on Labor, increasing its majority on the back of DLP preferences. In June the following year, reports appeared of a speech given by Nikita Khrushchev, leader of the Soviet Union, denouncing the purges and state violence under Stalin. A few months later the Soviets invaded Hungary, violently suppressing a revolt against its unpopular communist government. In Australia, and across the Western world, the organised left was devastated by these revelations of communist tyranny. For the newly formed ACCF, however, the time was ripe.[38]

What Horne made of these developments we can only guess. In the two years after he arrived back in Australia, he did not publish a single piece of serious political writing, being preoccupied instead with stories such as 'What Men Say about Women behind Their Backs: The Truth at Last!'[39] In March 1956, McAuley was confirmed as the editor of the ACCF's new literary magazine, soon to be named *Quadrant*. The dissemination of cultural periodicals was core Congress policy, and the organisation underwrote at least a dozen magazines in the 1950s, including *Preuves* in France, *Tempo Presente* in Italy and *Der Monat* in Germany. But the most successful Congress publication – and the model for McAuley's new magazine – was *Encounter*, published in Britain under the editorship of Spender and the American journalist Irving Kristol.[40]

For Horne, the discovery of *Encounter* was a revelation. Within the pages of this urbane magazine, written in a sceptical and sophisticated style, were famous literary names, including Nabokov, Amis and Auden, the philosophers and critics Bertrand Russell, Lionel Trilling, Stuart Hampshire and C.P. Snow, anti-communist Labour intellectuals Hugh Gaitskell and Anthony Crosland, as well as American liberals, such as Melvin Lasky, Arthur Schlesinger Jr and John Kenneth Galbraith. In the 1950s, *Encounter* published Nancy Mitford's famous critique of English social mores and Isaiah Berlin's essays on Russian literature. When he picked up *Encounter*, Horne recalled, he felt part of an intellectual community, a 'communion of those who could use the modes of common intellectual discourse to discuss *anything*'.[41]

Encounter also refocused Horne's attention on the big issues in global politics in a slightly different manner to that of his other international magazine of choice, *The Economist*. Its contributors produced robust and stylish critiques of world historical trends, for instance, the problems and possibilities of Keynesianism and the 'mixed economy', the decline of the European empires, the state of the colonial world – particularly Africa and Asia-Pacific – and the threat of communist influence in these newly independent states. Most importantly, *Encounter* promoted itself as a broad church in the classical liberal tradition, operating as a public forum by which writers and intellectuals who saw themselves as both progressive and anti-communist could reach an educated, non-specialist audience.

At times, however, anti-communism was just about all these writers had in common. As the historian Tony Judt has argued, the CCF was often an 'unholy alliance', its membership running the gamut from Trotskyists to neo-fascists. In the mid-1950s they generally fell into two broad camps. On one side were the liberal progressives, committed to cultural freedom and the arts but deeply uncomfortable with the various forms of overt political activism and lack of 'civility' promoted by the most prominent anti-communists – Joe McCarthy chief among them. On the other were those who saw the world in more Manichean terms, between the enlightened civilisations of the liberal West and the dark totalitarian armies of the communist bloc, and who viewed all political issues through this prism. In these early years, argues the intellectual historian Stefan Collini, the division was not yet terminal, but this latter crowd were becoming increasingly vocal, and *Encounter* gave off a 'distinct whiff of Cold War polemicising'.[42]

Horne, ever doubtful, found himself caught between these two positions, which he dramatised as a contest between his two most serious intellectual companions of the time, Jim McAuley and Doug McCallum. In their drinking sessions, McAuley revealed himself to be steadfastly in the Manichean camp, suspicious of communist activities to the point of paranoia, and, as a Catholic convert, lamenting what he saw as a decline in moral standards brought about by the excesses of liberalism. He determined that under his leadership, *Quadrant* would not promote the 'completely colourless, odourless, tasteless, inert and neutral mind on all fundamental issues which some people mistake for liberalism'. Instead, McAuley's magazine would strengthen 'the forces of mind in the nation which are threatened with totalitarianism', which in his view – guided as it was by his job at the Australian School of Pacific Administration – remained a 'terrible external threat'.[43]

McCallum, meanwhile, was a purer liberal, who espoused an updated variant of the philosophical anarchism and libertarianism they had all learned from John Anderson at Sydney University. In 1956, he and Ann had moved back to Australia (with two children) and bought a house in Cammeray on Sydney's North Shore. Not long after, when Horne decamped from Marton Hall to a new flat in Kirribilli, he began making the short journey up the hill to the McCallums' to 'talk the open language of liberalism' over Sunday lunch. McCallum was no Laborite, but nor could he stomach the doomsday prophecies of the group slowly coalescing around *Quadrant*. He allegedly referred to them as the 'Australian Committee for Cultural Arseholes'. Instead, he aligned himself with the younger, more radical liberal nonconformists operating under the umbrella label 'The Push'.[44]

As he travelled between Ryde and Cammeray, Horne switched back and forth between these two positions. McAuley's worldview was decidedly less generous, tarring all left fellow travellers with the same communist brush, but its muscularity and pragmatism were well suited to Horne's sense of himself as an enlightened conservative. McCallum's dance with anarchism, by contrast, seemed naive, but at the same time it appealed to the radical liberal in him, the campus rabble-rouser who had long opposed censorship and bourgeois moralism in all its forms. For years, vague formulations of this insoluble dilemma had plagued his political imagination, mysterious and unresolved. For now, however, Horne simply wore both hats: one for Cammeray and one for Ryde.[45]

Horne's other great unresolved question of these years, of course, was Ethel. In early July 1956, after two years in Australia, he finally returned to England in a long-overdue effort to salvage what remained of their broken marriage. The trip was clearly a disaster; however, all we know of their six weeks together is the rather bleak account given in Horne's memoirs. His estranged wife was now making her solitary living renting out the rooms of a house she had bought in London. Reconciliation was impossible, and their attempt to remain 'civilised' left them with little to say to each other. When they did finally address the situation, it resulted in a furious argument, during which Ethel slapped him in the face, then slept in a separate bed for the rest of the trip.[46]

Horne returned from England at a crossroads. He was, by most criteria, a successful man. *Weekend* was thriving, having reached record weekly sales of over 460,000. He had the respect and patronage of Frank Packer, the most powerful media baron in the country. A promotion to one of the organisation's more notable publications was not out of the question. Yet the price of his professional success had been the near destruction of his marriage. To make matters worse, none of this had resolved his ongoing crisis of identity. He still saw himself as an intellectual who, for want of a better option, was temporarily playing the role of a company man. His prolonged attempt to become a serious writer had so far come to nothing. His plan to edit *Weekend* for six months had stretched out to nearly three years. It was as a writer and an intellectual, not a middle manager and a peddler of tabloid dross, that Horne sought recognition. At some point, the wrong ambition had won.[47]

It was amid this cloud of despondency that the first issue of *Quadrant*, McAuley's right-wing alternative to *Meanjin*, finally arrived in December 1956. It featured poetry by A.D. Hope, Judith Wright and Vincent Buckley, as well as several perceptive pieces of literary criticism. But it was McAuley's editorial that set the tone of its political coverage, lamenting the 'advance to world domination of Communism' and the 'intellectual bastardry' of liberal intellectuals. The Melbourne journalist and foreign correspondent Denis Warner followed suit with a ten-page feature on the 'Communist Conspiracy in Asia'. Understandably, the magazine drew a hostile response from many in the literary establishment. Writing in the journal *Westerly*, the critic Max Harris called *Quadrant* 'arrogant, intolerant and aggressive'.[48]

Hiding unnoticed near the back of the inaugural issue was Horne's first serious piece of writing in years, a short and wholly unremarkable review of J.F.C. Fuller's *The Decisive Battles of the Western World: Volume 3*. For the frustrated editor of *Weekend*, it was charged with significance. The very existence of such a publication would have been inconceivable even two years earlier. With his return to England now off the table, both the discovery of *Encounter* and the arrival of *Quadrant* presented the possibility that an intellectual life sympathetic to his own political inclinations might be lived right here in Australia. Almost overnight, an entirely new and unforeseen version of his future opened up before him.[49]

In this unexpected atmosphere of excitement and enthusiasm, barely a month after his article in *Quadrant*, Horne approached Frank Packer with a daring proposal. Three years earlier, he alleged, before the first issue of *Weekend* had come out, Packer had told him that if it was a success, he might give him 'an intellectual weekly like *The New Statesman*'.[50] Now, in February, when *Weekend* had cracked the magical circulation of 500,000 for the first time, Horne suggested to his boss that he honour this promise.[51] It was a long shot: Packer was a decidedly unintellectual figure, and lived as much for the thrill of power as he did for the dollar. To Horne's surprise, however, Packer assented. Perhaps he was in a good mood? Perhaps Clyde had mentioned how depressed Horne was editing *Weekend*? The magazine's excellent performance can't have hurt, nor Horne's steady navigation of budget cuts, circulation-crippling labour strikes and several other minor crises.[52] It was all the same to Horne – the game of blind man's bluff had finally thrown one his way.

◆ ◆ ◆

In May 1957, just under three years after he had arrived back in Australia to launch a new magazine, Horne started preparing to repeat the process. This time, though, it would be a labour of love. Under the terms of his deal with Packer, he was to remain editor of *Weekend*, which would still require almost all of his professional time. His new magazine, by contrast, was more like a hobby, bringing him little prestige and no money. In an early costing report, he estimated that it would sell, at best, around 10,000 copies.[53] In July, as if in acknowledgement of this, he delegated most of the work of setting it up to two company men. Alan Ratcliffe, the son of Packer's tax accountant, would manage practical and administrative concerns, including budgets and printing, while editorial matters would be handled by an Oxford graduate named George Baker, whom Horne later claimed he hired because he 'seemed to know a little about a lot' and had 'something of an Evelyn Waugh eccentricity about him'.[54]

Over several long lunches at Adams Hotel on Pitt Street, Horne and Baker nutted out the shape of the new magazine.[55] It would be called *Observer*. In its style and presentation (though not its politics), it would be modelled on the British *New Statesman*. Both agreed that it would need to have a distinctive character. Politically, it would be a 'right-wing' alternative to the left-leaning publications *Overland* and *Meanjin*. Their conservatism, however, would be cloaked in urbanity and sophistication, and only revealed when 'confronted with policies that would weaken the whole fabric of capitalist organisation'.[56] On communism itself, they hoped to exercise 'deliberate restraint': they would let the facts speak for themselves. The tone, too, would be 'moderate to the point of coldness'; feeling was to be expressed 'only by irony'. There would be sections on books, arts, business and economics, along with an 'Every Man's Guide to a Sociology of Australia'. As Horne recalled a few years later, they were 'prepared to be interested in anything'.[57] Their readers, they surmised, would be a growing class of urban professionals, bankers, lawyers and white-collar workers, whom they described as the 'New Men':

> an educated but classless group found in Universities, in the Public Service, and in all kinds of niches in the private firms who do not really know what they think, who they are, or where they are going. We should tell them. For the moment they have nothing to guide them but the kind of cynicism which is all that is left over from the leftist enthusiasms of the 1930's and the authoritarian postwar reconstruction spirit of the 1940's.[58]

Lifestyle issues, Horne speculated, were more important to this new group than class struggle. A letter from Baker to Horne in October further crystallised their sense of this 'non-political' moment.[59] These 'New Men', he wrote, were representative of an end-of-ideology politics:

> Certainly the heat seems to have gone out of Australian politics. People will vote for one party or the other after a reasonable calculation of which will butter their bread more thickly. They no longer suffer from a sense of grievance which they hope to see righted by political action; and they do not expect political parties to usher in a golden age.[60]

From the beginning, Horne intended his magazine to express a sense of modernity, to describe and critique the society that had emerged from the war. But underlining this political and sociological objective, and in some ways giving *Observer* its sense of purpose, was his overwhelming anxiety about the economic and strategic consequences of what they termed the 'decline of Britain'.[61] Events in recent years had clearly dampened British hopes of a new Elizabethan age of international prestige. In March 1956, a Franco-British attempt to regain control of the Suez Canal from the Egyptian government had resulted in widespread international condemnation and a serious reassessment of British global influence. The establishment of an exclusive European Customs Union in March 1957, meanwhile, posed an equally significant challenge to Britain's system of preferential trade with Commonwealth countries. The economic and strategic certainties that had long underpinned the British world, it seemed, were under threat.[62]

Observer's foreign policy attitudes, Horne and Baker thus agreed, would always be 'judged in relation to Australia, and not to Great Britain'.[63] In Australia's own region, the emergence of new, explicitly anti-colonial independent nation-states had created unique foreign policy dilemmas, as had the ever-present threat of communist influence in these same states. In April 1955, several South-East Asian leaders attended a conference in the Indonesian city of Bandung in April 1955 to voice their opposition to colonialism, neo-colonialism and racism. Meanwhile, Australia's nearest neighbor, Indonesia, continued to make claims on the Dutch-controlled territory of West Papua. In this environment, friendly relations with stable South-East Asian states were seen as an important bulwark against possible Chinese communist expansionism in the region. In such an unpredictable climate, the *Observer* editors worried, changes to Australia's 'economic, foreign and defence' policies were happening 'neither quickly nor radically enough'.[64]

Near the end of 1957, Horne's burgeoning intellectual subdominion grew by two. The first new addition was Peter Coleman, a twenty-eight-year-old philosophy student who, like Brian Beddie, had spent time in London studying under Michael Oakeshott, and, like Horne, had been to colonial Africa, working in the Sudan as a teacher. Coleman also possessed the necessary Andersonian credentials and had been teaching at the newly established Australian National University (ANU) with the philosophers Eugene Kamenka and John Passmore. The other was Michael Baume, a twenty-seven-year-old reporter from *The Sydney Morning Herald*, who had a background in economics and political science. Both, Horne would later write, were 'to the left of me', though Baume was 'not as pure *Observer* as Coleman'. Along with Ratcliffe and Baker, they made up the magazine's entire staff. Horne, still heavily preoccupied by his *Weekend* commitments, became a kind of editorial overseer, his directions often handed out over lunch.[65]

In late September, however, *Weekend* was subject to a series of crises, and Horne was forced to indefinitely postpone *Observer*'s proposed 14 November launch date. First, *The Sydney Morning Herald* launched a prurient new magazine called *Crowd* in an attempt to undercut *Weekend*. Horne and his staff went into campaign mode. Cables were sent to Packer in London requesting an advertising war chest, spies were sent to the *Herald* offices and the front cover of *Weekend* got a makeover. When *Crowd* eventually launched to disappointing sales, Horne declared victory.[66]

The triumph was short-lived, though, when in a wave of moral panic, both *Weekend* and *Crowd* were attacked by a number of Catholic newspapers. These 'impure publications', wrote Melbourne's *Advocate*, 'destroyed moral standards and bred effeminate boys and masculine girls'. The influential Melbourne archbishop Daniel Mannix called the two newspapers a 'disgrace to Australia', while another priest urged every Catholic to support a campaign against their 'corrupting influence'. Even more worryingly, the Queensland Literature Board of Review used this criticism as an opportunity to restore a ban on the sale of *Weekend* in that state. The board alleged that a 'tendency to over emphasise sex' took advantage of a 'culturally sick and weak community'. Both actions threatened to severely affect circulation. It was likely that if *Weekend* took a significant hit on the newsstands, Packer would be inclined to lose interest in the *Observer* experiment. When the *Australian Women's Weekly*, one of Packer's flagship publications, started receiving letters threatening to discontinue subscriptions, the issue became urgent.[67]

Horne spent most of November and December petitioning prominent Catholics in Sydney and Melbourne to retract statements made against the magazine. *Weekend*, he wrote to the editor of *The Catholic Weekly*, is a 'happy paper which instructs as it entertains, not an exposé magazine'. Met with resistance, Horne became more aggressive in his defence of the magazine, thinking it an important liberal crusade – in the spirit of John Anderson – against the stifling moral puritanism of Australian society. Coleman, remembering Horne's 'quiet fury', admitted that it was hard to feel strongly about the *Weekend* campaign from a liberal perspective: it 'seemed an unlikely ally of James Joyce or Vladimir Nabokov'. Eventually, the Catholics relented, with *The Catholic Weekly* issuing a retraction and Mannix admitting he had never even seen a copy of *Weekend*. The Queensland censorship issue dragged on longer and required the flexing of Packer muscle. The prominent lawyer Sir Garfield Barwick was brought in and eventually secured an injunction against the ban. *Weekend* was saved, and, finally, *Observer* could begin.[68]

Horne welcomed the New Year period alone on a holiday cruise to New Caledonia, drinking French wine and 'thinking of nothing'. Having defused the crisis at *Weekend*, he planned to relax before the rescheduled launch of his new magazine. He would finally have an outlet for the kind of intellectual activity he craved. Yet, in a final, absurd twist, he discovered on his arrival back in Sydney that George Baker had conspired with Clyde Packer to replace him as editor of *Observer*. Furious, Horne spent twenty-four hours weighing up his options before announcing his resignation from *Weekend* and demanding a ticket back to London. In a panic, Clyde cabled his father in London, and within ten minutes Horne had been reappointed. Baker's coup had failed.[69]

An irreconcilable rift formed between the two men. Within a few weeks of *Observer*'s launch, Baker was gone. Horne insists that he fired his disloyal deputy after discovering he had been doing a lot less work than he claimed. Coleman merely remembers him leaving after his 'supporters abandoned him'. Either way, both Horne and Coleman have since been at pains to depict him as an incompetent, pompous fool. For Coleman he was 'an obese, tense homosexual' with an 'obviously tortured temperament', whose contributions to the magazine included a 'preposterous editorial' and a 'silly blast' about racketeering at universities. Horne never forgave Baker, even several decades later, writing of lunches at which he and his colleague Peter Hastings imagined Baker's 'lonely room filled with Heath Robinsonish devices for masturbation'.[70] Baker, so central to the creation of *Observer*, was ridiculed in Horne's first memoir of the period, and scrubbed from the second.

In February 1958, just over twenty years after he had first delighted in *The Daily Telegraph*'s enlightened rationalism as a teenager, Horne made a trip to the printers to get his hands on the first copy of *Observer*. It would be a moment to savour: the very first copy of his own intellectual periodical. But there had been a mistake. To his horror and amusement, all the copies had come out backwards. For Horne, it was a characteristically droll punchline to what was otherwise an incredibly important moment in his life: intellectually, professionally and personally. When *Observer* eventually rolled off the presses in the right order, he could finally let himself believe that he had arrived. He now had a platform for the kind of serious writing he had always wanted to do.[71]

5.
—

GATECRASHING

In early 1958, Horne migrated his growing personal stable of magazines to new headquarters on the third floor of the old building at 181 Elizabeth Street, a short walk down the road from the main Consolidated Press offices. Conditions at the original *Weekend* allotment had been notoriously spartan: reporters were forced to share cramped desks and typewriters, and Horne, despite being editor, worked in the same area among them. The new digs, while modest, were nonetheless a considerable upgrade for him and his staff. As if in return for his three and a half years of toil on *Weekend*, he was awarded his own private office, down the corridor from his reporters, in which he stationed himself behind a massive triangular, glass-topped desk – inherited from Packer's old business partner, E.G. Theodore – supervising his corner of the empire.[1]

Observer, though, did not share in these spoils. The fledgling magazine was run from a single room, one floor below *Weekend*. Its first issue, published on 14 February, was almost entirely produced by the three men squeezed in there – Coleman, Baume and Baker – with additional contributions from Horne himself. Its first cover story, titled 'Who Are the Managers?', revisited the thesis of James Burnham's *The Managerial Revolution* – a book that had shaped Horne's political imagination in the 1940s – and attempted to show 'the origins and education of Australian business executives and senior officials'. It also included an effusive review of Patrick White's 1957 novel *Voss*, banking and finance commentary, foreign affairs stories on Antarctica and the Sudan and a lifestyle column titled 'Consumption Observed'.[2]

To Horne's immense satisfaction, a small intellectual milieu began to coalesce around the new magazine almost from the moment of its conception. From his perspective, it was a completely 'ad hoc' group of writers, with no specific attachments. In the early weeks, names new and old drifted into *Observer*'s pages: Clyde Packer, Donald's friends Doug and Ann McCallum, British expat Charles Higham, German-born academic and *Dunera* veteran Henry Mayer, cartoonist Les Tanner, journalist Bob Raymond and a young art critic named Robert Hughes. From the very beginning, food, wine and argument kept the whole show on the road. *Observer*'s skeleton crew – Horne, Coleman and Baume (Baker having since departed) – lunched relentlessly, alternating between the New Hellas restaurant just down from the office on Elizabeth Street, and The Ada, a Polish eatery in Kings Cross. Dinner parties and office drinks, too, became an essential feature of *Observer* life. Arguments with strangers at parties, Horne later wrote, provided a chance 'to find out what you might imagine you believed'.[3]

What did Horne believe? The last time he had attempted serious journalism in Australia had been in the late 1940s, a time, he recalled, of shrill debates over 'free enterprise-versus-socialism'. In those years, the Cold War had not yet split the world along ideological lines, and for many liberal progressives of that era the Soviet Union remained a beacon of hope, a place of actually existing socialism. In politics, the Australian Labor Party (ALP) had then enjoyed its longest ever period of government, prolonging wartime controls over all areas of public life, expanding the public service and directly managing the economy. As if to compound this tragedy, the ALP's dominance of federal politics in that decade had had its analogue in literature. In the 1940s, much of the poetry and prose published in Clem Christesen's influential periodical *Meanjin* came under the umbrella of what Tim Rowse has since called 'Left-Australianism', repopularising the old collectivist tropes of the 1890s – mateship, egalitarianism and the bush – and positioning them at the heart of the Australian character.[4]

Now, ten years later, Horne's default intellectual posture – that of the singularly clear-minded, sharp-tongued outsider writing against the self-delusions of the establishment – continued to be shaped by the progressive ascendancy in those years. Australian intellectuals, he thought, had refused to move on from the political idealism and 'leftist enthusiasms' of the immediate pre- and postwar years. Intellectual life in Australia instead remained nothing but a back-slapping dinner party run by fellow-travelling liberals and out-of-touch university dons. Invitation to the party, he thought, was still contingent on a blind devotion to the unchallengeable virtues of the common man, worship at the altar of Henry Lawson and Banjo Paterson, and a deeply provincial attitude towards everything else. In such a climate, he sincerely believed, to be critical of progressive orthodoxies – regardless of the parlous state of progressivism in 1958 – was to condemn yourself to intellectual persecution and outsiderdom.[5]

Nowhere was this progressive orthodoxy more pronounced, he thought, than in literature. Like his ideological allies at *Quadrant*, Horne was profoundly sceptical of the radical-democratic hold over the Australian literary imagination, and this quickly became one of his magazine's most persistent themes, almost its raison d'être. In a typically pugnacious review of A.A. Phillips' *The Australian Tradition*, published less than three months after *Observer*'s launch, Horne alleged that the veneration of Lawson, Paterson and the 'legend of the nineties' was no less than a 'full-scale literary fraud' that had bred an army of 'imposter-novelists'. A work of fiction, he quipped, could not be considered 'good' by Australian standards unless it 'slobbers about the Common Man':

> The works of these authors are never evaluated as all other literary works are evaluated; they get in under the escape clause of being 'Australian'. If this escape clause did not exist they could be discussed as what they are: incompetent writers … you can get away with murder as a literary critic if you discuss the Australian holy books.[6]

For the *Observer* writers, literature was instead to be judged by more universal, cosmopolitan standards – what they referred to in the first issue as 'the sophistications of human nature'. This so-called 'anti-nationalism', wrote Horne, simply insisted that 'cultural activity should be judged as good or bad, and not just patted on the back because it is labelled "cultural activity"'. One Australian work that met such criteria was *Voss*, the Patrick White novel to which *Observer* had devoted a long unsigned review in its first issue. White's book, they argued, was not merely a fictional retelling of the explorer Ludwig Leichhardt's 'lunatic expedition' to the Australian interior, but an attempt to 'get beneath the superficialities of human behaviour into the madnesses that whistle and bubble below'. It was, they thought, a brilliant example of the kind of native literature that went beyond dull collectivist tropes and bushwhackery to explore the timeless, universal themes expected of great novels.[7]

In *Observer*, Horne repeatedly used arguments about literary standards to pit his enlightened liberal worldview against the socialist fantasies of the Australian literary left. He was continually and deliberately drawn to books about the lives and personalities of 'great men' – never 'common' ones – and reviewed biographies of William the Conqueror, Joseph Goebbels, Lord Beaverbrook and Napoleon, among others.[8] Powerful people, by Horne's calculation, were the great mavericks of history and the principal source of vitality in modern liberal societies, continually taking risks and trying new things. Rarely, he thought, did biographers comprehend the invigorating social function of such figures:

It is not their personal characteristics that should be attacked but the kind of enterprise that they – or history – create. To pick away at powerful people in the Lytton Strachey way not only displays a disappointed romanticism (great people should not really be human at all); it also sets too great a standard on politeness and conformity.[9]

Behind such arguments were shades of the same basic libertarian line that Horne had taken since the late 1940s, when he had regularly conflated rhetorical commitments to equality and human brotherhood with the promotion of mediocrity and the stifling of human enterprise. Ten years on, at the height of the Cold War, he continued to fight these battles. Socialist societies, he believed, were lifeless and mediocre. They did not value excellence nor venerate those who set themselves apart. On this account, he concluded, most biographers were 'anemic failures' because they failed to realise 'the great sense of fun that power can provide'.[10]

In other book reviews, meanwhile, Horne displayed the eclectic variety of his interests – and hatreds. He railed against the pointless impenetrability of the American novelist William Faulkner, the 'anxious footnotes' in academic writing and the poor treatment of sex in contemporary fiction.[11] Though his reading habits were omnivorous, Horne's early *Observer* reviews were always of the carnivorous variety. Fence-sitting was never an option; arguments were to be ruthlessly prosecuted; a book was there to be condemned or praised. Sometimes he seemed only to read books in order to reject them, reproachfully reeling off examples of the author's idiocy. Typically, he would state the book's crime in the first few paragraphs, before holding its follies up for forensic analysis. Then, in the final paragraph, the author would be nailed to the wall with a couple of swift aphoristic blows. 'It is only by unpicking the evidence – tediously and carefully – that one sees how little there is in it.'[12]

Coleman remembered Horne reading 'widely and savagely' in this period, 'not like the common reader, more like an artist seizing on bits and pieces that helped him at the moment'.[13] Thus Boris Pasternak's novel *Doctor Zhivago* was, for the noisily anti-communist Horne, 'a useful guide to what may happen to the rest of us'. Anyone who did not read it, he wrote, 'should never have been taught how to read'.[14] Like the skilful university debater he once was, he happily turned arguments inside out to expose their conceptual flaws and general stupidity. A sly 'leftist' advocate of nuclear disarmament, for example,

> points to the possibility of human suffering, then puts forward a policy that will allegedly relieve suffering, then assumes that if you reject his policy you favour human suffering.[15]

Horne saw this same 'humbug' about human brotherhood reflected in attitudes to Australian foreign affairs, a field that – like literature – he believed to be overrun with the naive humanist fantasies of liberal progressives. From the moment of its conception by Baker and Horne in 1957, *Observer* was self-consciously international in its outlook, seeing knowledge of international affairs and the internal workings of foreign countries as essential to Australia's very survival in a rapidly changing region.[16]

In May 1958, Horne penned his first major essay on the topic, a fiercely pessimistic piece titled 'Has Australia Got a Chance?'. In it, he prophesied disaster: since the war, he argued, the British Empire had disappeared and Australia's region had become a 'free-for-all' between anti-Western and communist forces. But it was a mistake, he thought, to believe that the United States would simply replace Britain as an imperial protector. Long insulated from world affairs, 'Australia was about to have its history'. To the immediate north, Sukarno's Indonesia continued to covet the Dutch-controlled territory of West Papua, 'the Alsace-Lorraine of the South Pacific'. Worse still, he thought, Australia's leaders did not share his alarm. Instead, Australia acted like 'a pleasant little domestic dog, cheerful, brave, capable of going hunting with its master but pathetically unprepared for solitary life in the jungle of wild beasts, full of tricks and very hungry'. 'If the worst happened,' he worried, 'we might very well be done for.'[17]

Horne had issued similarly dire warnings as far back as the early 1940s, when, as an undergraduate, he had been mesmerised by Brian Penton's equally pessimistic diatribes in *The Daily Telegraph*. But in this student journalism, mostly written before the outbreak of the Pacific War, he had predominantly laid the blame for the coming Australian 'perdition' at the feet of its cultural inertia, railing against things such as materialism, petit-bourgeois mindlessness and 'the inanities of our national escapism'.[18] For the young Horne, Asia – though presumably the ultimate source of such anxieties – had remained little more than a shadowy presence: unmentioned, undifferentiated and poorly understood.

It was only after Horne's drift into the AACF and *Quadrant* circle in the mid-to-late 1950s that he began to cultivate a serious interest in Australia's near north, and as such, his apocalypticism became increasingly coloured by Cold War paranoia and a more widespread sense that Australia was about to be engulfed by hordes of Asians. During the intellectually barren early *Weekend* years, conversations with James McAuley had trained Horne's eye on the communist threat in the region, as had the journalist Denis Warner's more recent writing about

Asian communism in *Quadrant*.[19] Though Horne had little experience of foreign affairs and had not set foot in an Asian country since his boat journey to England in 1949, he quickly repositioned himself as a prominent voice in the debate over the future of Australia's regional relations. And even when he was forced to cede the bulk of the day-to-day *Observer* editorial work to Coleman and Baume on account of his *Weekend* responsibilities, he made one notable exception:

> Any material at all covering either Indonesia or New Guinea should be referred to me. It doesn't matter whether it's a printed document, or a contribution, or whatever it might be. I want to receive all this material so that I can myself estimate public opinion.[20]

One reason for this move – aside from Horne's enthusiastic interest in such matters – was the appearance of a rival magazine.[21] In September 1958, six months after *Observer*'s first issue, the *Herald* financial journalist Tom Fitzgerald launched *Nation*, a fortnightly journal of opinion that had a similar appearance and sensibility to Horne's magazine. Ostensibly fighting over the same turf, the two periodicals immediately established a fierce rivalry (one that was further compounded by the defection of Robert Hughes twelve months later).[22] The hostility was to a large degree a product of the narcissism of small differences: *Nation* – which Fitzgerald had personally financed by taking out a mortgage on his own house, giving it bona fide 'independent' status – was mostly of a piece with *Observer*, taking a liberal line on social issues, including divorce, homosexuality and Indigenous affairs and showing a deliberate interest in modern topics, such as consumer affairs, mass culture and lifestyles.[23]

Where the two fortnightlies differed originally was on foreign affairs. In particular, *Nation* advocated for a relaxation of Australia's racially restrictive immigration policy and a more liberal internationalist approach to foreign diplomacy.[24] In response, Horne published a series of essays on the topic, the most substantial of which – February 1959's 'Living with Asia' – amounted to a kind of realist, hard-headed foreign policy manifesto. In discussions about Australian international affairs, he argued, invocations of the geographical term 'Asia' tended to provoke a number of predictable, panicked responses: 'megalomaniac sentimentality' and guilt about decolonisation and the past treatment of colonial peoples; 'grandiose panic' and 'defeatism' about Asian nationalism and the massive population of the continent; or just 'plain fear' – and mostly from those on the left 'who profess to be liberal-minded and tolerant'. From a foreign policy perspective, he thought, the dilemma of decolonisation in Australia's region was not a moral problem but a diplomatic one:

> We can discuss our foreign policies in a practical kind of way when … we start thinking that the situation in Asia is fundamentally not one of liberation or of coloured people but of power politics and that Australia's present predicament is simply the kind of problem in which most small countries have found themselves all the time.[25]

It was, Horne argued, in the nature of countries to have clashes of interests, just as it was equally normal and historically observable that strong states would exploit weak ones, and vice versa. To treat the newly independent states of Asia as anything other than ordinary nations to negotiate with diplomatically and self-interestedly would have itself been a new kind of racism (this argument, it must be said, was a somewhat cunning inversion of the problem of Australia's imperfect record on racial matters). Even so, in the age of nuclear weapons, Horne continued, Australia need not fear an Asian invasion. In the end, 'it is power that matters, not arithmetic'. It was thus more sensible and realist for Australia to play power politics with Asian dictators than to offer unqualified support for unknown liberationist movements – some of whom had communist sympathies. Australia had no moral responsibility to support any nationalist movements where it contradicted its own interests. Nor, given the widespread and deeply entrenched racial attitudes buttressing Australia's immigration policy, should its leaders waste too much time attempting to overthrow the basic idea of White Australia, however morally untenable it had become. 'Our concern with our ways of life is that we should preserve them, not extend them.'[26]

For all of Horne's dreams of a *New Statesman*–like intellectual sophistication, his most potent and natural critical mode remained that of dissent and opposition. He excelled in the dark arts of the put down and had a sharp polemical talent for assembling straw men. Like his intellectual lodestars Brian Penton and John Anderson, he had an instinct for controversy and provocation. As a writer, he was always at his liveliest when he was able to position himself as an outsider, a maverick sticking it to the establishment, sweeping a broom through the dusty old ways of looking at things, barging in with a new view of existence.[27] He and the *Observer* crowd, he boasted four years later, were 'all gatecrashers together'.[28]

For Horne, having an outlet for such sermonising was a deeply satisfying, even life-changing development, and 1958 proved to be an obvious turning point in his life. His recollections of the birth of *Observer* always stressed a very Horne-like sense of rupture, between an old and new Australia, and between the erratic young Donald and the mature writer that eventually emerged in the mid-1960s. It was a critical moment in the life of the man and the life of the nation he would help to redefine.[29] Or, as his old colleague Michael Baume put it in 2014: before the invention of *Observer,* Horne had been masquerading as a variety of different characters and 'finding satisfaction in none of them', but in the late 1950s and early 1960s he eventually 'found an intellectual attire that gave him comfort'.[30]

And yet, despite all the long-awaited satisfactions and thrills of intellectual influence, perhaps the most truly life-changing moment for Horne in this fateful year occurred not in the pages of *Observer*, but at an office party in Baume's Kings Cross apartment. In addition to the usual *Observer* and *Weekend* crowd, his much younger colleague had taken the liberty of inviting some of his friends from *The Sydney Morning Herald*. A brown-haired, hazel-eyed young woman named Myfanwy Gollan caught his attention, and the two of them immediately hit it off, leaving the party early to continue their conversation over coffee.[31]

It was, by all accounts, love at first sight. At twenty-four, this magnetic young woman was twelve years Horne's junior, but the couple had little trouble finding common ground. Gollan had attended

Canberra Girls Grammar School at the same time Horne had been living in the sparsely settled bush capital training to be a diplomatic cadet. She was intelligent and self-assured – and had been from an early age. At fourteen, for example, she had read *Ulysses*, then, for a lark, had tried out its stream of consciousness style in a school exam. She had gained entry to the exclusive Sydney Girls High School and, like Horne, had worked on the student magazine *Honi Soit* at Sydney University. Her father, Ross, was a reporter at *The Sydney Morning Herald*, and after graduating in 1951, she, too, had gone to work for the *Herald*. But more important than their similar histories were their shared worldviews. From the very beginning, Horne recalled, they shared a 'common line in things to laugh about'. A week later, over dinner at the Chelsea in Kings Cross, Horne proposed marriage.[32]

By early 1959, Horne's future had begun to look much brighter than the one he had envisaged for himself when he had been stuck at *Weekend* just over twelve months earlier. In that short period, he had established his own intellectual magazine; carved out a new role as a critic; rapidly expanded his social circles; met the woman who would become his wife, editor and closest intellectual ally; and become an important new voice in the national political conversation. After a long, potholed journey to the intellectual dinner table, the gate-crasher had arrived. As with most gatecrashing, however, it was not then entirely clear whether he was improving the party or ruining it.

◆ ◆ ◆

After McAuley launched *Quadrant* in December 1956, Horne had begun to attend parties thrown at its shabby office on the top floor of a building at Circular Quay. Initially, he found the men at these parties not to his taste, a group of 'pompous lawyers' with reactionary lean-ings, many of whom seemed anti-intellectual.[33] Indeed, even among the Cold War warriors at the Congress for Cultural Freedom's Paris-based headquarters, the Australian branch had developed a poor reputation. When he visited in 1954, the English poet and *Encoun-ter* editor Stephen Spender had been deeply unimpressed with the local outfit, describing them as 'all the stuffed shirts in Australia in one prodigious front of bores'. He thought the Australians were too obsessed with anti-communism and advised them to involve more poets and artists.[34]

In late 1958, a little over a year after its launch, *Quadrant* was in financial dire straits. The magazine carried no advertising, and the modest grant from Paris barely covered expenses. Then, in November, the conspiracy-mongers in their ranks got a boost when *Quadrant* was denied its promised Commonwealth Literary Fund grant, even though their ideological rivals at *Meanjin* and *Southerly* had been successful. Despite Robert Menzies' Liberal–Country Party coalition coasting to a fifth consecutive Australian federal election victory on the back of preference flows from the breakaway anti-communist Democratic Labor Party, within the AACF's ranks suspicions of a progressive hold over culture grew ever stronger.[35]

It was amid such paranoid whisperings in the *Quadrant* offices in these years that Horne made several new friends, none more important than an extremely well-connected Polish émigré, Richard Krygier. Born Jewish in Warsaw in 1917, Krygier had originally been a communist fellow traveller, before the Moscow show trials and the occupation of Poland by Nazi Germany and the Soviet Union in the late 1930s had revealed the brutal authoritarian reality of both communist and fascist regimes. He and his wife, Roma, had escaped to Lithuania, travelled by train across the Soviet Union to Vladivostok and eventually made their way to Sydney via Tokyo and Shanghai. Blessed with the zeal of the convert, he had been the central figure behind the establishment of both the AACF and *Quadrant*. Like McAuley, Krygier saw the communist question in black and white. For him, neutralism and fellow travelling would only strengthen those intent on Western civilisation's destruction.[36]

Significantly for Horne, Krygier had begun to establish a vast and varied network of local and international contacts. At AACF parties in 1959, for example, Horne met and befriended several right-wing Labor figures, including Laurie Short of the Federated Ironworkers' Association, Lloyd Ross from the Australian Railways Union and Jim McClelland, a lawyer doing well out of his association with both men. All three had been present at the infamous Hobart Conference in 1955 that split the Labor Party, and all had since drifted into *Quadrant's* orbit. Also present were two other AACF lawyers, John Kerr and Hal Wootten, who now headed up what amounted to a liberal faction within the organisation, pushing back against the ideological fervour of Krygier and McAuley.[37]

In September 1959, the more ardent members of this shaky alliance of antipodean anti-communists descended on Melbourne in an attempt to – quite literally – gatecrash the Australian and New Zealand Congress for International Co-operation and Disarmament (also known as the 'Peace Congress'). The event had stirred up a considerable amount of controversy in the preceding months. The Australian attorney-general, Garfield Barwick, had already denounced it as a communist front, and there were even rumours of a covert ASIO campaign to undermine the event. Within the AACF, meanwhile, the Peace Congress exacerbated existing tensions. Hardliners, including Krygier, enthusiastically took up the cause, but others, among them Kerr and Wootten, saw no role for the AACF in such matters and determined to stay away. After a vote, the organisation's executive officially resolved to keep its distance from the 'unseemly shouting match', and Krygier's group attended in an 'informal' capacity.[38]

Horne, for his part, sided with the hardliners – as he would for the next two years. He ran an editorial in *Observer* – based on a document given to him by Krygier – detailing the communist connections of the Congress organisers. 'Don't ask me where it came from,' his well-connected friend had reportedly told him.[39] In Melbourne, Horne attended Krygier's hastily organised 'counter-conference', held in a hotel room, where he met a motley collection of Victorian dissenters, including the poet Vincent Buckley, the ex-communists Ken Gott and Stephen Murray-Smith, and Melbourne University lecturers Jim Jupp and Frank Knopfelmacher.[40]

The shouty, personal antagonisms and deeply entrenched ideological enmities of the Congress had a radicalising effect on many members of the AACF, not least Horne. Upon his return to Sydney, he wrote a short polemic in *Observer* about the perils of disarmament and the naivety of the Peace Movement, arguing that on such issues the Soviet leader, Nikita Khrushchev, was a con man and could not be trusted. If the United States and their allies in the West voluntarily gave up their nuclear weapons, he contended, they would merely weaken their bargaining position and fall into the Soviet trap. He followed this up with the satirical 'Do-It-Yourself-Guide: How to Hold a Congress', a silly diatribe about leftist groupthink, before finally getting into a spat over communism with the left-wing historian Brian Fitzpatrick in *Observer*'s letters pages.[41]

Over summer, with the heresies of the Congress still fresh in the minds of the AACF insurgents, James McAuley penned a ten-page manifesto in *Quadrant* titled 'On Being an Intellectual'. Making reference to Marx, Sorel and Hume, he set about dismantling what he saw as the delusions and self-deceptions of modern liberal progressivism. Intellectuals, he wrote, were like priests: they were sceptics and searchers, seekers of truth in a fallen world. Like monks, they had a stated duty to be free and disinterested, impartial observers, alienated from the affairs of men. Modern liberal intellectuals, however, as 'children of the Enlightenment', had instead become 'sectaries in the Religion of Progress', and this new, secular 'priesthood of dissent' was, in his view, too obsessively concerned with social transformation. He called this 'the serpent's ideology', one that cast man in the image of God in the naive pursuit of human perfectibility. Only a 'genuine realist intellectuality' that embraced culture, religion and tradition – 'the divine *cultus*' – could ward off the apocalypse of secular humanism. What was required was a robust conservative defence of civilisation against the 'delusional grip' of the secular priests. 'A choice has been set before us,' he concluded, 'of life or death, of a blessing or a curse.'[42]

Horne had long been under McAuley's spell. In one fawning *Observer* essay in 1958, he had even admitted to the formative impact his friend's 'literary puritanism' had had on his impressionable young self at Sydney University. It was the sad, fascinating young Jim McAuley, he wrote, who had first sparked his 'distrust of all cultural activity, good or bad' and his absolute rejection of the idea that 'just because a thing is new it is good'.[43] On political questions, however, the two old friends had begun to differ.

In January 1960, Horne penned a response to McAuley's essay in *Observer*. This much shorter piece, titled 'A Plimsoll Line for

Intellectuals', was to date the most detailed published expression of his fundamental political beliefs. In it, he agreed with McAuley that the word 'intellectual' had been seized by progressives, and that such intellectuals were 'physically and emotionally dull-witted' and too concerned with social transformation. But unlike his Catholic counterpart, he could not go as far as to blame secularism for the intellectual rot. To abandon all attempts at reform, on principle, would be to side with the Bow Brickhill villagers who could not comprehend street lights. Surely a more modest reform agenda, he mused, one infused with scepticism and a sense that things may not turn out as planned, was preferable to such doctrinaire oppositionism. Horne proposed a 'conservative secularism':

> One which does not destroy institutions out of squeamishness because parts of them are offensive, but operates through them, or reforms bits and pieces of them, or tries to avoid them ... It is a messy and unexciting view of life; but it is one which allows for difference and liberty; it may be the only view of life that does.[44]

Horne's avowed moderation and articulation of his sceptical reform-mindedness could not temper his newfound anti-communist zeal, nor could it deter him from getting involved in several of Krygier's political crusades in this period. If anything, 'Plimsoll Line' probably encouraged him, serving to train his insatiable reforming instincts and polemical energies on the intolerable intellectual crimes of the 'authoritarian left'. In a typically heated argument at a party in late 1959, Horne was accused – lazily, it would seem – of being a 'fascist'. To be fair to his accuser, however, in the twelve months following the Peace Congress, Horne did very little to alter public perceptions of himself as a nasty right-winger.[45]

In March 1960, he published a vicious four-page review of the historian Manning Clark's account of a three-week trip to the Soviet Union, *Meeting Soviet Man*. Despite Clark – hitherto something of a political agnostic – receiving criticism from the left for his decidedly lukewarm endorsement of Soviet communism, Horne nevertheless went to town, castigating him for his credulousness, his romanticism and his provincial 'look-at-me-mum' approach. The book, wrote Donald, 'reek[ed] of a certain kind of intellectual's attitude to Russia', one that fell over itself to excuse Russian inadequacies while enlarging Western crimes 'to the point of invention'.

> Summed up, the differences between Soviet and Western Man are, apparently, that Soviet Man is secular, optimistic, egalitarian, freedom-loving, looking for happiness and the full life here on earth; and Western Man is religious, pessimistic, expecting nothing from life on earth, regarding it as an immense darkness to be endured as well as enjoyed, as a preparation for the life of the world to come.[46]

Horne's sustained, unsympathetic and personal mockery of Clark's book earned him considerable notoriety among the 1950s Australian liberal left as one of the worst of all right-wingers. For the last year of *Observer's* existence, he later admitted, its political comment was confined to the anti-communist intrigues of the Victorian Labor Party Executive, the Democratic Labor Party and the NSW Labor Party, 'as if nothing else in Australian politics was worth writing about'.[47]

Horne's name – even for those without a personal interest in the debates – became synonymous with a kind of mean, pessimistic and hawkish Sydney conservatism, one that relentlessly poured scorn on those who sought to express even the faintest hope in the future of humanity. In the *Observer* years, alleged Clark fifteen years later, Horne was 'one of those "everything is allowable men" who wore an ill-fitting, Norman Lindsayish, bourgeois baiters mask to conceal the "kingdom of nothingness" within'.[48] For at least twelve months, recalled Peter Coleman – Horne's closest intellectual ally – he had 'personified that short-lived if tense amalgam of social activism and anti-communist zeal that often characterised the Congress for Cultural Freedom'. Such reputations, once earned, are hard to shake off.[49]

In November 1960, after basking in this newfound notoriety for close to six months, Horne zeroed in on a different target. This time, his straw man was an old acquaintance, Murray Sayle, the London-based Australian journalist with whom he had worked on *Honi Soit* and the *Telegraph* in the 1940s and a variety of British papers in the early fifties. Sayle, Horne claimed, had 'hoaxed' and brownnosed his way to the top of Fleet Street by reciting a series of lazy clichés and myths about Australian society for his British audience. Sayle's rendering of Australia, wrote Horne, read 'like a nightmare that one might have after reading Mr Russel Ward's *The Australian Legend*': the southern continent was either an illiberal, priggish, convict-ridden backwater, or else a provincial working man's paradise with a radical tradition of protest. These, he thought, were 'outrageous' myths born of a completely outdated colonial mentality that flew in the face of recent intellectual breakthroughs and 'eight years of inflationary prosperity'.[50]

Perhaps still smarting from his own disappointing Fleet Street experience, Horne seemed happy to pour scorn on Sayle for opinions with which he had himself only just dispensed. Many Australians, Horne declared somewhat autobiographically, had 'stopped regarding what goes on in London's intellectual and cultural world as the beginning and end of sophisticated conversation'. Those 'best qualified to criticise their country', he continued, were those 'still living in it'. Having only very recently adopted the necessary postcode and attitudes of this much-needed 'new kind of intellectual', Horne's resounding condemnation of Sayle was – at the very least – a bit rich.[51]

Curiously, Horne's quarrelsome and at times ungenerous public political activities in 1959 and 1960 were at odds with the immense private happiness he had found with Myfanwy. After their first meeting in 1958, Donald had set himself up in a bachelor flat in Kings Cross, not far from where he had once lived with Ethel less than ten years earlier. Though long separated, the estranged couple had had considerable difficulties finalising their divorce (a not insignificant personal detail that may have been a motivating factor behind *Observer*'s ongoing campaign for reform of Australian divorce law in these years).[52] When the paperwork finally came through in the early months of 1960, Donald and Myfanwy wasted no time, tying the knot in a small, unostentatious ceremony. In April, they moved into a small rented flat on Manning Road in the leafy harbourside suburb of Double Bay in Sydney's east. By the end of the year, Myfanwy was pregnant.

Donald and Myfanwy Horne
on their wedding day

◆ ◆ ◆

In October 1960, in an act of entrepreneurial adventurism and bold social invigoration befitting one of Horne's 'Great Men of History', Frank Packer purchased the *Australian Woman's Mirror*, a women's magazine that had been popular in the 1920s and '30s but had since fallen on hard times. Given that Packer's company already owned Australia's current most popular women's title, the *Australian Women's Weekly*, his move appeared to have been strategic, a calculating response to rumours that his upstart rival, Rupert Murdoch, was thinking of making a play for the *Mirror* to set up as a competitor for the *Weekly*. As he had with *Weekend* back in 1954, Packer decided to get in first.

In order to take the *Mirror* out of Murdoch's reach, Consolidated Press had acquired its entire parent company, Bulletin Newspaper Company, as well as the decrepit six-storey building at 252 George Street in which it was housed. Land in that part of Sydney's CBD, just a short step from Circular Quay, was becoming increasingly valuable, and even if the magazine failed, Packer could be sure of steady revenue from the building's many tenants. With such commercial concerns in mind, it was almost by accident that Packer came to own the vanquished company's other stuttering title, *The Bulletin*, one of Australia's oldest and most storied little magazines.[53]

The Bulletin, a political and literary periodical first published in 1880, had established its legendary reputation in the decades prior to World War I as a publisher of rebellious, irreverent and stridently republican poetry and prose. All the great names of prewar Australian literature – Henry Lawson, Banjo Paterson, Joseph Furphy and Mary Gilmore, among others – had used the magazine as a platform for a rural brand of literary nationalism that later became known as the 'Bulletin school'. Though it had declined considerably since those heady days, the 'old Bully' survived almost as a tribute to the golden age of the 1890s, when it was known as the 'Bushman's bible' and was one of the most recognisable symbols of the (now somewhat calcified) radical tradition in Australian literature.[54] In December 1960, Donald Horne – perhaps the most outspoken modern critic of the allegedly insatiable Australian taste for such writing – became its new editor.

In Horne's telling, the *Bulletin* that he inherited in December 1960 was a kind of living museum of a much older Australia that had ceased to exist sometime around 1930 (at the very latest). Its managing editor, Ken Prior, was a man of Horne's father's generation, whom he could not help but treat 'like an honoured digger-uncle'. Worryingly, he learned from Prior, it was for the sake of 'tradition' that the magazine's leader page still maintained its racist nineteenth-century motto, 'Australia for the White Man'.[55] Presumably it was also in deference to these 'traditions' that *The Bulletin* continued to publish columns such as 'Aboriginalities' and 'Man on the Land' and to inveigh against the 'flapper press'. Even among people of conservative views, Donald declared privately, the modern *Bulletin* had a reputation for an 'arid kind of diehard reactionaryism'.[56]

At the beginning of 1961, Horne found himself at the head of three extraordinarily different publications. With only one of them (*Weekend*) able to make a profit, however, the arrangement was never going to last. When he was inevitably given an ultimatum by Packer – he could have either *The Bulletin* or the *Observer*, but not both – he reluctantly chose the former. By April 1961, *Observer* was dead. As Patricia Rolfe later put it, the 'healthy fledgling' had been killed off in order to revive 'the albatross, the dodo'.[57]

Once again in full revolutionary mode, Horne quickly set about tearing down all the magazine's old verities and starting again with what he thought of as newer, more relevant standards. He intended to bring *The Bulletin* into the modern world. It was 'humbug,' he wrote, 'to talk of the old Australia as if it still existed'.

> The old patterns are fading. New social designs are being woven of which we do not yet know the shape. We hope to present week by week some of the raw material of the new Australia – not the picture of what Australia used to be, but what it is becoming now.[58]

The current affairs–minded Horne quickly set fire to most of what the more literary-oriented *Bulletin* held dear, including the staff, most of whom departed within three months of the takeover. Of the magazine's 'tolerated veterans' – Malcolm Ellis, Douglas Stewart and Ronald McCuaig – only Ellis survived the first six months. He also dropped the famous pink cover and the 'Australia for the White Man' slogan, changed the format, shelved the racist cartoons and phased out the poetry and short stories – most of which he thought to be a 'stale leftover from the old bohemian and underdog preoccupations'.[59]

Outraged letters poured in from the magazine's ageing, rural, racist readership – or so the story goes.[60] At the time, it seems – at least on the (somewhat questionable) evidence of *The Bulletin*'s letters page – even some of the harshest critics did not appear to see the changes as signifying the apocalypse. Most were happy with the magazine's face lift: 'It was only when I saw her new looks after the operation that I realised how deepset and fixed her wrinkles had become,' wrote one seventy-eight-year-old subscriber. 'It was inevitable that changes would have to be made in this changing world,' wrote another.[61] The most notorious response to the face lift, however – and one that has since taken a central place in the large and colourful canon of Horne bashing – came in August, when the poet Gwen Harwood managed to get two poems published in the magazine under a pseudonym which, taken together, formed two mischievous acrostics: 'so long bulletin', 'fuck all editors'.[62]

Horne thought, somewhat predictably by now, that *The Bulletin*'s stubborn commitment to a completely obsolete worldview was emblematic of the bankruptcy of the entire Australian intellectual culture. He saw his revival of the legendary magazine as a great symbolic act, his small way of helping force Australia into the modern world, knocking down a national edifice and stripping it of its racism, jingoism and chauvinism. The 'revolutionary impact' that the original *Bulletin* had had on prewar Australia, he argued, could never have come about without a firm grounding in reality. It had once been an 'an Australian paper, written by Australians and concerned with Australian problems and attitudes'.

The modern *Bulletin*'s romantic fascination with down-and-out characters, the bush and the radical tradition was, he believed, utterly irrelevant. It failed to describe present realities, and it ignored life as it was then lived in the unprecedently prosperous, middle-class, suburban Australian society of the 1960s. In early 1961, Horne announced that he was attempting to revive the original animating spirit of *The Bulletin* and to turn it once more into a 'rebellious, rambunctious thunderer living on opposition'. Under his revitalising stewardship, it would 'face unpleasant facts', maintain a cautious optimism about the future and dispense with the 'illusion that there is one "Australia".[63]

What is particularly noteworthy about this developing critique of 1950s Australian society (of which the old *Bulletin* and its sympathisers were supposedly characteristic) was that it was coming not from the left but largely from what was then thought of as the political *right*.[64] It was liberal conservative critics, such as Horne and Coleman – with their anti-nationalism, pluralism, cosmopolitanism, bourgeois hatred of radicalism in art and their critical interest in middle-class pursuits, the suburbs and consumer society – who were providing the most robust (and in some ways the most forward-looking) critique of modern Australian society. They were not, it should be said, the only group of critics finding fault with the state of the nation in the age of Menzies, but they were certainly among the loudest and most destructive. 'There is no point in flogging a dead tradition,' wrote Horne. 'It is better to have no values than false ones.'[65]

For all his revolutionary heroics, however, Horne remained a deeply unpopular figure during his editorship of *The Bulletin* – at least among liberal progressives – mostly owing to his continuing concern with what he saw as two interrelated topics: foreign affairs and communism. On such issues, Horne still saw an 'endless possibility of immediate and final external disaster', and maintained his hardline and perhaps unnecessarily pessimistic position – even as the Cold War began to assume a more complex and unfamiliar shape.[66] The dynamic of the conflict had been slowly shifting ever since Nikita Khrushchev had denounced the crimes of Stalin, initiated a 'thaw' of some of the more outrageous Stalinist repressions and begun pursuing, at a series of international summits, a policy of 'peaceful coexistence' with the West (in deliberate contrast with the more overt hostility of the Stalinist period). To further complicate matters, disagreements between the Russian and Chinese communist leadership, both of whom possessed nuclear weapons, had added a new, multipolar element to international diplomacy.

In a series of articles on 'Australia and the World', Horne acquainted *The Bulletin*'s readers – whether they liked it or not – with all the diplomatic nuances of communist polycentrism and the Sino–Soviet split. In his eyes, Khrushchev remained an untrustworthy huckster intent on 'demoralising' the West with his cynical, two-faced peacemongering and 'summit diplomacy propaganda'. Offering concessions to the Soviets, he thought, would only result in the demand for more. In international relations, there were no rules, only power. On most issues throughout 1961, Horne continued to argue – perhaps more vociferously than ever – for a hard-headed, hold-the-line approach to Cold War diplomacy: anywhere that communists sought to expand their influence, the West should be ready to resist it.[67]

Such a philosophy made sense in the ongoing struggle for control of Berlin, or even – at a stretch – in the former French colonies of Indochina. It was decidedly more complicated, however, when applied to the former Dutch colony of West Papua, situated directly to Australia's north. Australia's leaders, with their own defence interests in mind, cautiously maintained that it should become an independent state, while Indonesia, under the leadership of Sukarno, coveted the territory. The Americans, not wanting to unnecessarily antagonise their Indonesian anti-communist allies, refused to guarantee the colony's independence. Wading into this diplomatic impasse, Horne argued Australia should risk upsetting their Indonesian neighbours and support an 'International Control Commission' of South-East Asian powers that would guarantee West Papua's independence. As Horne had repeatedly argued since 1959, timidity in the face of Indonesian claims, and a willingness to give them what they wanted, betrayed a condescension towards Asian nations that was a leftover from the colonial era. It was, he thought, perfectly normal for nations to disagree: 'Just because [Australia's Asian neighbours] were once colonies does not mean that they are now children who must be spoilt, to whom the ordinary standards of foreign policy do not apply.'[68]

Even on the popular question of immigration, Horne remained on the right wing of the liberal spectrum. On this contentious issue, the man who had just taken 'Australia for the White Man' off *The Bulletin*'s masthead did not exactly foresee a utopia of the races Down Under. Horne had finally been convinced of the need for immigration reform after reading a pamphlet –'Control or Colour Bar?' – published by a group of Melbourne academics in April 1960.[69] For all the moral force of their argument, however, he still saw the problem through his Cold War glasses: Australia's safety in a region teeming with potential communist satellites, he wrote, depended on keeping 'most of the people with non-European skins on our side'.

One way for Australia to achieve such a goal, he thought, would be to demonstrate that it was at least doing something about its own racial problems – particularly its treatment of Indigenous peoples. However, Horne did not believe that this necessitated an opening of the national floodgates, so to speak. As he had written two years earlier, what mattered most in international diplomacy was 'the kind of face you pull'. One could still support a restrictionist immigration program 'on economic and social grounds', but 'if you are going to shut the door in people's faces,' he quipped, 'you have to be polite about it'.[70]

It was on the issue of domestic communism, though, that Horne really ruffled the feathers of Australian progressives throughout 1961. *The Bulletin* carried countless articles and editorials on communist influence and 'thuggery' in the Seamen's Union of Australia, which it saw as nothing less than evidence of the 'totalitarianism of the Left'. More controversially, in early 1961, Krygier and McAuley alerted Horne to a staffing dispute at the University of Melbourne that they thought amounted to a communist conspiracy. The director of the social studies department, Ruth Hoban, had become convinced that her authority was being undermined by her colleague Geoff Sharp, who was affiliated with the Communist Party of Australia. In April, Horne received a long letter from Hoban's husband, Max Crawford, the longstanding Chair of History at the University of Melbourne, alleging – in the most polite of terms – communist influence in departmental politics. In the next issue of *The Bulletin*, Horne chose to publish Crawford's letter alongside a summary of the dispute, with names anonymised. 'One cannot safely assume,' wrote Crawford, 'that in the Communist academic, the academic will always overcome the Communist'.[71]

Horne took the letter as a prompt for a full-scale campaign against communist skulduggery in Australian universities. With the aid of another secret, mysteriously sourced dossier provided to him by Krygier and McAuley, and complemented by a running telephone commentary on the matter with the hyper-conspiratorial Melbourne University anti-communist Frank Knopfelmacher, *The Bulletin* published several detailed accounts of what became known as the Social Studies Affair (written, unsigned, by Horne), multiple editorials on the subsequent 'smearing' of Crawford and numerous letters to the editor (of rapidly increasing tedium).[72] Several other journals, including *Nation*, *Prospect* and *Dissent*, also ran commentaries and letters on the controversy. In the end, no communist plot was revealed, and a number of the academics involved suffered lasting damage to their reputations – Crawford included. Many years later it emerged that the Australian spy agency ASIO had had a hidden role in the affair as part of its 'spoiling operations' and had even spoken directly with Crawford several months before the publication of the letter.[73]

Since the creation of the AACF in the mid-1950s, concern for intellectual, cultural and academic freedom had become a predictable refrain among liberal and conservative sections of the Australian commentariat.[74] In a number of high-profile cases – most prominently those involving Russel Ward and Sydney Sparkes Orr (whom Horne had long depicted as a kind of Australian Dreyfus) – much intellectual blood had been shed over the question of whether the professional prospects of an academic should be in any way impeded by their political views or affiliations. However, as Fay Anderson has argued, Ward's case – which provoked relatively little protest – occurred in the mid-1950s, at the zenith of Cold War paranoia. The Social Studies Affair, meanwhile, occurred at a comparatively less frantic phase of the Cold War, when the communist threat was less pressing and claims for intellectual autonomy 'far more resonant'. The controversy failed to set off the anti-communist alarm bells with quite the same urgency. In the future, it seemed, such threats would be treated less hysterically. On this point, Horne was probably – by his own metric – slightly out of tune with the times.[75]

Out of the public gaze, meanwhile, Horne's anti-communist gusto was greater still. After a meeting with Jack Kane, the General Secretary of the NSW branch of the DLP, Horne had agreed to write several stump speeches for each of the NSW DLP candidates at the 1961 federal election.[76] Even his intellectual allies were surprised at his commitment to the cause. In response to a letter from his old friend Doug McCallum about McCarthyism in the United States, Horne shot back with apocalyptic warnings about the possible victory of world communism, while at AACF dinners he became one of the chief partisans in the campaign to root 'naive liberals' out of the organisation.[77] In his memoirs, he even admitted to having had an ASIO contact in these years, with whom he would have lunch in an Italian restaurant on George Street to discuss the various splits within the Communist Party of Australia, before heading back to the office to fill the pages of his new, 'modern' *Bulletin* with the latest internecine communist esoterica.[78]

Like the communists themselves, the anti-ideological ideologues in the AACF could not stave off the problems of factionalism. When the association's president, Sir John Latham, announced in late 1961 that he would not be seeking re-election, the fault lines within this hazily defined cultural freedom movement became impossible to smooth over. Latham's preferred successor, John Kerr, was thought by Krygier and McAuley to be insufficiently committed to the anti-communist cause – or any cause, according to some – and Krygier's more conspiratorial and activist group quickly put up its own candidate, Lloyd Ross, an intellectually inclined union figure with DLP connections.[79] Horne, ever enthusiastic, was enlisted to get the numbers, and after some energetic work on the telephone, secured the presidency for the anti-Kerr insurgency.[80] A spate of resignations inevitably followed – including Kerr, Hal Wootten, Dick Spann, Henry Mayer and others – and Horne was elevated to the association's executive committee, which, thanks to his efforts, was now sufficiently purged of any naive, uncommitted liberals.[81]

Despite these excitements, Horne still nursed his long-held ambitions of intellectual detachment and omniscience, periodically retreating down the corridor to sit behind his three-cornered desk and think about what it all meant. If he failed to sufficiently detach from events in these years it was not for want of trying, and indeed the 'taking stock' article had become a familiar and enjoyable subgenre of his writing since the beginning of *Observer*. The '50s, as he had memorably observed in 1959, were 'the ten years that did not shake the world', while 'Living with Asia', Horne's most impressive *Observer* essay, was framed as a survey of existing attitudes to Australia's northern neighbours, rather than a polemic.[82]

At the end of 1961, Horne once again looked back on the year that was. Domestically, he quipped, it was 'not the best of years for wine, women and Mr Menzies, but it was a good one for uplift'.[83] On the international front, the Soviets had held the diplomatic initiative, he thought, testing the strength of the free world and the stability of Africa, South America and Asia. As for the future, he warned for the umpteenth time, the coming battle over communist aggression in South Vietnam held 'grave' portents for Australia, yet there were 'few Australians who could find South Vietnam on a map or know what part of a history book to look up'.[84] As the Cold War spread into Australia's region, Australians could no longer pretend they were 'not yet really part of the world'. In 1962, he predicted, they were in for some 'nasty shocks'.[85]

It was not without irony, then, that it was the unpopularity of Horne's relentless prophesying and campaigning that ultimately delivered him a nasty shock of his own. When he had begun his reforms to *The Bulletin* in December 1960, the magazine's circulation had been just over 29,000. After twelve months of Horne at the helm, it was at a still-unprofitable 34,000 – clearly not a sizeable enough increase to satisfy his ruthless boss.[86] In early 1962, while in the midst of further revolutionary planning, he was summoned to Clyde Packer's office to learn that he had been replaced as editor by his friend and rival Peter Hastings.[87] Horne was ordered, abruptly and humiliatingly, to concentrate his efforts on reviving *Weekend*, which had only recently and rather unsuccessfully been amalgamated with the *Australian Woman's Mirror* and renamed *Everybody's*. The chief gatecrasher had done his job. The dull, old-fashioned intellectual dinner party had been at least partially revived. But now he had been asked to leave.

6.

OVERTHROWALS

If you had randomly selected someone from the ranks of the organised Australian left at the beginning of the Cold War's second decade and asked them to name their least favourite conservative intellectual, there is a good chance they might have singled out Donald Horne, the mean-spirited editor of the *Observer* and *The Bulletin*, unapologetic red-baiter, Packer stooge and all-round intellectual gadfly of the political right. For those on both the socialist and the liberal left in those years, there was certainly no shortage of evidence with which to build such an argument. Horne's close working relationship with Richard Krygier, James McAuley and the Cold War warriors in the AACF, his hawkish views on foreign affairs, his immense enthusiasm for the anti-communist cause at home and abroad and his unsparing polemical assaults on prominent liberal intellectuals had all given plenty of ammunition to those who thought him 'about the most outspoken incarnation of the forces of reaction' in Australia.[1]

Yet to characterise Horne as purely oppositionist and reactionary in the late 1950s and early 1960s – regardless of how sincerely some of his enemies then believed it – would be a somewhat misleading simplification of the shifting and unstable currents of progressive and conservative thought in that transitional period. Horne might have deserved his reputation as an intellectual tyrant, a stirrer and a profoundly unsympathetic reviewer, but at heart he was no reactionary. And even at the height of his right-wing notoriety, he sustained an essentially revolutionary posture. He was, he believed, still storming Australia's intellectual Bastille, gatecrashing its ageing establishment and cautiously hoping for (if not believing in) a better future. As he had declared during *The Bulletin* takeover, he was determined to be *'for* things, as well as against them'.[2]

The paradox of Horne's idiosyncratic brand of conservatism at this time was that it was always conceived as a kind of progressivism. He believed in progress and in reform just as sincerely as his rivals on the left; he merely refused to have any illusions about the meanness and unpredictability of life. 'The harsh fact of human existence,' he wrote in March 1961, 'is that there are always clouds on the horizon.'[3] Behind the jibes, the sneers and the personal enmities was always a firm determination to make out the new and indistinct shapes of Australia's future in a radically changed (and radically changing) world. If this often resulted in muddle, contradiction and the pursuit of strange, eccentric political causes, it is partly because so little was then known of what was to come in the 1960s. The gatecrashers had cut the lights, and now everyone was reaching around in the dark.

Part of the confusion was that in these intellectually turbulent times, Horne's arguments – especially if taken in good faith – could not be easily distilled into existing stereotypes of left and right, progressive and conservative. As elements of his brief but productive editorship of *The Bulletin* had made clear, he was fully engaged with what were widely thought to be the principal issues of the age, pursuing liberal reforms to immigration and censorship and interrogating the middle class, suburban and consumerist aspects of postwar Australia – all within the context of the global Cold War. If his ultimate political position seemed ambiguous it was partly because he was always determined to acknowledge that the radically new political circumstances, particularly in Australia's region, precluded any kind of certainty about the future.[4]

In the (very retrospective) view of some of his late 1950s intellectual allies, Horne's embarrassing dismissal from the editorship of *The Bulletin* in February 1962 was one of the most critical and transformative moments of his intellectual life, a personal trauma that marked the beginning of his slow abandonment of conservative principles and his vain and self-serving drift into the waiting arms of the left.[5] Certainly, the event had a profound effect on the shape of his future, eventually releasing him from the very real (if mostly unspoken) constraints of loyalty to Frank Packer and, with the subsequent free-dom this afforded, broadening his intellectual horizons and personal acquaintance. But to infer that solely for reasons of professional envy, spite and personal vengeance Horne went out and got himself some new and more fashionable intellectual clothes is to take a rather sim-plistic view of the unsettled state of Australian political debate in the early 1960s.[6]

Horne's critics are correct to recall a subtle shift in his attitudes in this period. But his revision of some of his old arguments was prompted less by the distress of his humiliating sacking than by his genuine disappointment with the two major parties' response to Brit-ish prime minister Harold Macmillan's July 1961 announcement that Britain would be seeking entry into the European Economic Commu-nity (EEC). In Australia, this sudden and shocking declaration caused a considerable stir among the political classes. As Horne quipped in *The Bulletin*, the news 'burst upon us like a mother's sudden death'.[7] If successful, it threatened to seriously undermine many of Austral-ia's long-held and preciously guarded arrangements with the imperial metropole: economic, strategic and sentimental.

Writing in the immediate wake of this destabilising event, Horne called for the creation of a new Australian political party, one that would be 'in touch with the times' and therefore break through the 'present political stalemate'.[8] In their current guises, he declared, both major parties were unable to confront the geopolitical demands of the age; neither had any concern for the 'broad issues of Australia's sur-vival and prosperity':

> What shocks are ahead when we move out of our pleasant dream that we can go on forever as we are, with no sacrifice, no discomfort, not even an abandonment of fantasies … We cannot afford the luxury of acting as if things were still the same. We are lonely, and if we had bad luck we could become isolated and deserted – unless we help ourselves.[9]

Horne's frantic concern with Australia's survival and its need for protection from its unstable and potentially hostile neighbours was consistent with the pessimistic tenor of all his foreign affairs writing since the war. By his reckoning, the British turn to Europe had merely made official what geopolitical reality had long rendered inevitable. In the wake of the British pullout, he thought, the new Australian strategic threats that had emerged throughout 1961 – communist aggression in South-East Asia (particularly in the former French colonies in Indochina) and Indonesian expansionism and claims on the Dutch territory of West Papua – now presaged 'ghastly turmoil'. Australia was at a crossroads – a friendless, 'pipsqueak' nation in a tumultuous part of the world, confronting problems of which it was 'as yet only dimly aware'.[10]

Foreign policy was not the only topic in line for a reassessment in early 1962. What had also changed – for Horne at least – and what the perilous geopolitical circumstances demanded, was a more positive attitude to the question of government planning and intervention, particularly on domestic economic matters. Such an argument radically reversed the confident Hayek-by-way-of-John Anderson small government economic line that Horne had been very publicly prosecuting since at least the mid-1940s. On such matters, he now conceded, *Observer* had been 'a bit old hat'.[11] Australia's leaders instead needed to plan the economy in a 'comprehensive and long-term way'. In the end, the only way forward was 'planned capitalism'. If the British EEC application were indeed successful, Australia would be left without its major trading partner; it should thus concentrate its energies on strategic national development, increased migration and, in matters of trade, engage with 'countries in our own part of the world' – particularly Japan. These necessary realignments in Australia's international outlook, he believed, would soon have transformative effects on the country's domestic politics. But such an idea, he lamented, was a 'policy without a party'.[12]

By the end of 1961, more than twenty-five years after the publication of John Maynard Keynes' *General Theory of Employment, Interest and Money*, the idea that nations could and should efficiently plan and direct their economies was not exactly cutting edge. It was, rather, almost a paradigmatic political precept of the anglophone world in the postwar period. Throughout the 1950s the enthusiasm for economic planning had transcended political divides, and even ostensibly conservative governments had had little problem presiding over the creation and consolidation of massive public infrastructure projects and welfare programs – Australia included.[13] But as a Cold War liberal – and a committed contrarian – Horne had always belonged to that camp of sceptics who saw it as their duty to keep a lid on the excesses and enthusiasms of the postwar social democratic ascendancy. They saw themselves as the vigilant guards of the citadel of liberty, repelling the relentless encroachments of big government progressives. And amid such progressivist fervour, as he had written in December 1960, 'nothing better could have happened to Australia than to enjoy a long period of conservative rule'.[14]

In the eighteen months between the Peace Congress and the Melbourne University Social Studies Affair, however, Horne's shifts between activism and detachment – between a reforming optimism and an unhealthy pessimism – had mirrored, to some extent, the largely unspoken divide at the heart of global anti-communist politics. As a new decade began, it was becoming increasingly obvious to some influential Congress intellectuals that the more destructive, oppositionist aspects of anti-communism would have to be tempered if such Cold War liberals were to play any part in the politics of the future. In 1961, the American sociologist and *Encounter* regular Edward Shils became the spokesperson for such a view, officially calling for a new liberalism of 'civility' and a break from the polemical, Manichean 'free world rhetoric' of the 'uncivil Right' in the McCarthy era. Shils' 'end of ideology' politics would instead be 'something akin to the humane liberalism of the Enlightenment', where disinterested intellectuals would go beyond the 'worn out clichés' of the 1950s and lay the foundations for a new, civilised and pluralist modern society:

> The new generation has no experience of the communists of the old days, and 'fellow travelling' has become a more complicated and obscure affair. The new generation does not want to fight the old battles, partly because these battles appear to them to be irrelevant and partly because the older generation is engaged in these battles.[15]

It was this call for moderation, delivered in a paper titled 'Further Thoughts on the Congress in the '60s' and discussed at length by the organisation's executive committee in Zurich in March 1962, that provided some of the intellectual framework for Horne's subtle change of direction following his sacking from *The Bulletin*. After several years publicly (and unproductively) kicking the anti-communist can, Horne was now particularly attracted to Shils' argument that the best way to fight communism was simply to ignore it – this was, after all, an argument he himself had floated at the creation of *Observer*. In the coming decade, he intuited, what would matter most was the articulation of a new language of liberalism. Doing so, however, would require new, more constructive ideas, and perhaps even the crossing of previously uncrossable political divides.[16] In the February 1961 issue of *Encounter*, for example, the British Labour Party intellectual Anthony Crosland had wondered what politics would soon be about in this increasingly 'post-political society'. His answer sounded a lot like Horne's in 1957: it would be 'about the same things as before, but at a lower level of political temperature'. Politics was converging on the centre, Crosland wrote, and ideology was in retreat. A new politics would soon emerge.[17]

Without his weekly *Bulletin* soapbox, however, it had now become unclear if Horne would play any part in the changes he had predicted. The unwelcome clouds of misfortune had once again cast shadows on his professional future. Thrown into yet another of his recurrent career crises, he found himself back where he had started four years earlier, an exile in the intellectual desert of *Weekend* magazine (now merged with the *Australian Woman's Mirror* and renamed *Everybody's*). Certain that he could not spend the rest of his career subject to Packer's whims, he was nevertheless trapped, as he was not in a financial position to resign; his growing family had no obvious alternative source of income. Unsure of what to do, he took a week off to contemplate his future.

The mood at home was no less sombre. Myfanwy was grieving the recent death of her father, a man who had been 'a central pillar of her life'.[18] Horne was still processing the death of his own father, David, a year earlier. He spent most of the week wandering around the serpentine streets of Double Bay and Woollahra in the state of mordant self-reflection that such accumulations of personal tragedy are given to provoke. As was so often the case, what he had written about Australia in *The Bulletin* had had uncomfortable personal resonances: for Horne, things could certainly not go on forever as they were. He and Myfanwy decided he would give Packer twelve months' notice. He had a year to find an escape route.[19]

Donald and Myfanwy Horne at dinner

In such a predicament, nothing proved more useful than Donald and Myfanwy's own inexhaustible sociability. Their near-permanent presence at the innumerable office parties and dinners of the previous four years had rapidly expanded their network of personal connections among (politically sympathetic) parts of Sydney's cultural and intellectual elite. Of particular importance was the *Quadrant* circle, which met regularly for dinner parties at the home of Richard and Roma Krygier. Regulars included Peter and Verna Coleman; Doug and Ann McCallum; the political scientist Owen Harries and his wife, Dorothy; the lawyer and recently anointed AACF president Lloyd Ross; the philosopher David Armstrong; and the academic and critic Leonie Kramer. On occasion, even James McAuley would fly in from his new home in Tasmania, as would Melbourne émigré academics Frank Knopfelmacher and Sibnarayan Ray.[20]

Overlapping with this *Quadrant* group was, from Horne's perspective at least, a newer social set: an assortment of lawyers, trade union officials and anti-communist intellectuals loosely associated with the right wing of the NSW Labor Party. Parts of this crowd, including John Kerr, Hal Wootten and Laurie Short, had been drifting in and out of Horne's orbit for several years. But it was another intellectually inclined lawyer, Jim McClelland, who had the most useful impact on Horne's thinking about the Labor Party in the years following his departure from *The Bulletin*. Horne and McClelland had met through the AACF several years earlier, and, along with their wives, had started having regular dinners – ones that satisfied Horne's requirements for successful conversation: 'novels, paintings, travel, food and ... the whole range of human aspirations and follies that goes by the name of "politics"'. On New Year's Eve 1961, McClelland and his wife, Nora, had thrown an enormous party at their home in Mosman, where Horne got an insider look at the complex and conspiratorial world of Sydney union officials and Labor lawyers, one of whom – the future premier of New South Wales, Neville Wran – for a while became a part of their dinner circle.[21]

Though united in their opposition to communism, these two loose social groups were uneasy bedfellows. Some in the *Quadrant* circle saw the Labor Party as irredeemable, terminally corrupted by communist influence. Others in the Labor movement, while critical of the party, could not countenance the intellectual bankruptcy of the conservatives. Most, like Horne, were increasingly unable to comprehend either option. Similar to Horne, McClelland later attempted to portray his own involvement with the AACF as the result of a deep disenchantment with existing political parties. The *Quadrant* crowd, McClelland recalled, were a 'gaggle of disaffected ex-Marxists and political floaters' looking for a 'raft of enlightenment in a sea of confusion'.[22] Horne, alone in the intellectual abyss of *Everybody's*, no doubt felt the same, and it was to this raft that he desperately clung in his moment of professional need.

◆ ◆ ◆

Throughout the demoralising year of 1962, Horne attempted to convince himself that his exit from *The Bulletin* was not going to bring his brief career as an opinion-leading intellectual to an end. As always, he kept himself busy. Following the quarrel over the AACF presidency in November 1961, he had worked his way onto the organisation's executive committee. Then, when Richard Krygier left for Paris and Geneva in early 1962, Horne took over as acting secretary – a stroke of fortune that put him in direct contact with the Congress's European headquarters at the very moment the organisation was debating Edward Shils' calls for revitalisation. Not long after, Krygier also appointed him editor of the association's quarterly newsletter, *Free Spirit*, a rather shabby publication filled mostly with syndicated content and news from the Congress's global network of writers and intellectuals.[23] On top of this, he maintained a steady stream of freelanced opinion throughout the year, writing mostly after work or on weekends.

All of Horne's published writing in this period involved an interrogation of his own Cold War liberalism. Having already gestured at two key problems of Australian modernity – how to shore up the nation's security and image in a hostile Asia, and how to maintain Australia's present level of economic prosperity – he began to ask himself: what did it mean to be a liberal in a world that had produced both affluent welfare states and nuclear bombs? In a paper titled 'Freedom in Australia', presented to the Sydney Fabian Society in July 1962, Horne railed against the 'conformist' liberals who could only think of questions of liberty in 'traditional terms'. Instead, he proposed a more pragmatic, somewhat arbitrary definition of political freedom, one that defended civil liberties in particular cases and endorsed state action in others. Such liberalism, for example, would oppose censorship, police brutality and the bureaucratisation of life, and support Aboriginal citizenship and the liberalisation of Australia's immigration policy. At the same time, these same liberals would support illiberal restrictions – to a point – on the freedom of political parties that sought to act as 'agents of foreign totalitarian powers intent on our conquest.'[24]

This brand of liberalism – with its muscular anti-communism, its non-ideological position on economic questions and its much purer liberalism on social ones – had quite obviously begun to scramble existing political fault lines. The fact that Donald Horne, the scourge of the Australian left, was invited to address a Fabian Society event was only one example of the many tentative crossings of old political divides that were taking place in these years. Without an obvious political party or ideology to attach themselves to, socialists and conservatives of a more liberal bent found themselves fighting over the same patch of political turf. With his still nebulous ideas of a 'radical' third party in mind, Horne suggested a new political distinction:

> Anti-communist socialists, liberals and conservatives on the one hand and communists, fascists, pro-communists and proto-fascists (that is to say supporters of totalitarian tyrannies) on the other.[25]

Horne developed these themes still further in an essay for the special Winter issue of *Quadrant*, compiled under the (ironic) theme, 'What Is to Be Done?'. In 'The Metaphor of Leftness', his most substantial essay since leaving *The Bulletin*, he now explicitly sought to paint his own distinctive brand of enlightened anti-communist liberalism as the new progressive force in Australian politics. Throughout the modern era, he argued, the left had always declared itself as the 'exclusive party of reform'. However, since World War II, the economic problems upon which the left had once constructed its legitimacy and 'aura of holiness' had been 'solved', and the prevailing mixed economic model – with its role for both public and private actors – was 'not capitalism'. By Horne's reckoning, unprecedented levels of postwar prosperity had rendered economic questions less urgent. The political problems of the future – 'freedom, humanity and progress' – had 'changed in a way the left will not acknowledge'. A new, 'post-political' age was approaching, and Horne – supported by the growing band of 'end-of-ideology' progressives – once again repeated his call for a new politics. 'Let us make a bonfire of the metaphors of left and right,' he wrote.

> The friends of totalitarianism could go up in flames, and the dreary ashes of the demoralised conservatives of left and right could be mingled together in one party on the mantle shelf. Here would be a chance to form a Radical Party, its policy determined not by the problems of the nineteenth century but by the problems of today.[26]

Put simply, Horne now thought – more assuredly than ever – that the politics of the next decade would be about culture, lifestyle and questions of freedom and personal liberty, not a war over competing economic systems. Less than a decade later, of course, amid the numerous global banking and energy crises of the early 1970s, this proto–End of History argument would look impossibly naive. But Horne's polemical instincts here obscured some of the underlying optimism of his argument. The early 1960s were, after all, the twilight of the Age of Menzies, a time of full employment and unprecedented material affluence. John F. Kennedy was in the White House, promising to put a man on the moon, and Harold Macmillan's 'winds of change' were blowing through Africa. In this context, the idea that a centralised, protectionist, mass-industrialist and state-controlled version of capitalism or socialism were the only paths to human betterment seemed impossibly old-fashioned. And in such a climate it is understandable that a provocative writer such as Horne could suggest that capitalism – at least in its virulent, nineteenth-century shape – might have been reformed into something different.

This kind of writing helped Horne stay in touch, but with the majority of his time still spent at *Everybody's*, intellectual life was mostly fugitive. What was really required for a critics' culture to flourish, he thought, was talk. It was thus fortunate – for the intellectually unemployed Donald Horne, at least – that one of the central planks of Edward Shils' 1961 vision for a new international liberal community was the development of a global program of small intellectual seminars and 'conversaziones'. In the early 1960s, the Congress underwrote countless gatherings of liberal writers, poets and critics in places as diverse as Egypt, Spain and Uganda, where – in the spirit of Socratic dialogue – they would attempt to debate 'circumscribed subjects' with the appropriate level of Shilsian civility. Some of these seminars proved to be as constructive as Shils had envisioned: the French intellectual Raymond Aron, for example, organised one on 'the conditions of world order', while the legendary New York magazine *Partisan Review* – publisher of some of the biggest names in American and European writing – hosted another on 'The Idea of the Future'.[27]

For Horne, then, one of the most encouraging developments of his *annus horribillis* came not within the pages of a magazine, but between the walls of a ramshackle building in Sydney's eastern suburbs. In late August 1962, the AACF put Horne in charge of organising a one-off seminar on the subject of 'Literary Journals and Journals of Opinion'. He threw himself into the preparations, drawing up potential discussion topics and contacting the editors of fifteen Australian small magazines, along with a handful of foreign ones. The seminar was being arranged, he told them, because 'in modern industrial societies like Australia there is a great possibility that the expression of minority opinions might be crushed out of existence'.[28]

Though AACF sponsorship gave the event an international flavour, its illiberal reputation created headaches for Horne. Some potential attendees expressed reservations about the seriousness of his commitment to open discussion. Will Phillips, the co-founder and long-time editor of *Partisan Review*, had to be convinced that the seminar would encourage 'a genuine exchange of opinion between people of both diverse views and common interests'.[29] Similarly, Stephen Murray-Smith – editor of the left-leaning Melbourne magazine *Overland* – wondered, not unjustifiably, if the event would be nothing but a PR stunt for the Congress. In response, Horne assured him of its bona fides. If it were not concerned with the expression of independent opinion, he wrote, 'I could not be bothered having anything to do with it ... [Such an] occasion is all too rare in Australia when we can all actually meet and see what we have to say'.[30]

In the end, a quite eclectic collection of journalists and magazine editors did meet – for four days at The Belvedere, a sprawling old house-cum-hotel on Bayswater Road in Kings Cross. Horne was thrilled by a sense of intellectual community he rarely experienced. Alongside Phillips and Murray-Smith were Robie Macauley of the American literary magazine *Kenyon Review*, the editors of *Southerly*, *Dissent* and *The Bulletin*, the poets Kenneth Slessor and A.D. Hope and an assortment of critics, including Robert Hughes and Leonie Kramer (the sole female participant). Granted, there were no card-carrying communists present, but by AACF standards it was a diverse guest list.[31]

On day three of the seminar, Horne gave his own paper, a detailed analysis of his editorship of *Observer*. Amid this breakdown of *Observer*'s pet topics and attitudes, Horne traced the outline of his own intellectual journey and approach to politics. His only previous attempt at journalism in Australia, he wryly admitted, was in the late 1940s, an era characterised by rather simplistic and polarised political debates that 'seemed pretty far away stuff by 1958'. His new magazine, he had determined, was instead intended to espouse what he called 'radical conservatism':

Conservative in the sense that there was a realisation that hotheads, sentimentalists or crooks can put up alluring policies, but just because the policies sound good does not mean that they will necessarily happen … Radical in the sense that it wanted to see the shape of new problems, not simply recite recipes for the solution of old problems … it wanted to pull to bits both reforming and conservative conventional wisdoms; it wanted to reach towards attitudes that were not acknowledged in the prevailing conventional wisdoms.[32]

Horne's deliberately contradictory philosophy neatly captured the uncertain ways in which the prevailing atmosphere of political possibility had begun to fray old allegiances. But though he acknowledged his 'growing friendship with some trade unionists', by his own analysis Horne still remained firmly on the right wing of the liberal spectrum. Just a year had passed since the Social Studies Affair, and he was a still a fair way from feeling comfortable with the political left. Even so, there was now increasing doubt about where such boundaries lay.

As luck would have it, Geoffrey Dutton and Max Harris – both well-connected Australian publishing figures who were in attendance at the Little Magazines seminar – were inclined to agree. The two men were the founding editors of *Australian Book Review* and had both been infrequent contributors to *Observer* and *The Bulletin*. Significantly, however, Dutton had also taken a job at Penguin Books' new Australian offshoot, Penguin Australia, and – with Harris's assistance – was scouting for talent. At the event, Harris reminded both Horne and Dutton of an earlier offhand suggestion that Horne should write a book about Australia in the mould of his 'Living with Asia' articles. Presumably, Horne agreed. After four years of fortnightly opinion journalism, here was a chance to pull back, to take stock of his arguments and to make some sense of this confusing, transitional political moment.[33]

Of course, Horne, Harris and Dutton were not alone in their conviction that a nation at the crossroads was in need of a thorough dissection. That same year, a new edited collection of essays compiled by Horne's friend and colleague Peter Coleman provided a stimulating example of the very incipient Australian intellectual foment that Penguin was hoping to exploit. Coleman's list of authors for *Australian Civilization: A Symposium* was impressive: *Quadrant* and *Bulletin* liberals McAuley and McCallum; *Nation* regulars Ken Inglis and Robert Hughes; the Catholic poet Vincent Buckley; unattached critics, such as Max Harris and Robin Boyd; the celebrant of the radical literary tradition A.A. Phillips; and even Horne's old punching bag Manning Clark.

Horne himself contributed a chapter on 'Businessmen', arguing, in his typically heterodox fashion, against the prevailing stereotype of Australian business elites as conservative or reactionary. Rather, he wrote, many had 'a tolerance of socialism that would have amazed them, or their fathers, in 1939'. He fashioned this into a now-familiar argument against Australia's 'puritan obsessions about ostentation' and its discomfort with symbols of grandeur and success. To their own discredit, he quipped, Australians derived their image of themselves from English commentators who 'look down on our red-tiled roofs from their airoplanes [sic] and decide that – like Chinamen – we are all the same: a kind of vast Watford'.[34]

In the scheme of things, Horne's chapter was insignificant and has been largely overlooked in later appraisals of *Australian Civilization*'s considerable influence on the politics of the 1960s. In a broader sense, however, Horne is all over Coleman's book. Its various contributors, while not entirely of a piece, were uniformly critical of Australia's simplistic monocultural myths and traditions, its complacent suburbanites and philistinism, its wowsers and puritans, its provincialism and irrelevant radical-historical literary obsessions. In Coleman's introduction, it is almost as if he were quoting directly from Horne's *Bulletin* editorials: The 'Australianist legend', he wrote, was populist, nationalist, racist, nihilist, naively humanist and too obsessed with 'Australianity and bushwackery'. It was, in other words, 'anti-civilized'. As Frank Bongiorno noted on the book's fifty-year anniversary, *Australian Civilization* was an exercise in 'cultural pessimism'.[35]

Horne captured some of this feeling in his review of the Little Magazines seminar in *Free Spirit*. Little magazines, everyone had agreed, were 'upholders of standards and fostering grounds of an elite of serious writers and readers'. But, irrespective of one's political stripe, one issue had come up in nearly every presentation: the 'search for a national identity and national self-examination'. Over the next few years, wrote Horne with his then characteristic gloom, 'this could – if our country survives at all – become *the* problem in Australia.'[36]

Teasing out the links between national self-examination and national survival – easily his two favourite topics in *Observer* and *The Bulletin* – soon became Horne's argument du jour. By late 1962, Richard Krygier had 'sold' him to the editor of the English *Spectator*, Anthony Hartley, as someone who could write about Australia and its region for a British audience. In Horne's first piece, a blistering polemic titled 'Australia Obsolescent', he took aim at the 'senselessness, banality and parochialism of Australian opinion forming'. Nowhere was this more evident, he thought, than in foreign policy. The certainties on which Australia had built its strategic defence for nearly a century had collapsed, seemingly overnight. Since World War II, Australia's traditional protector in the region, Britain, had been gradually winding down its military presence 'East of Suez', and, to the north, the Dutch had finally ceded the territory of West Papua to the Indonesians.[37]

Horne once again argued that what was needed in this new and uncertain regional environment was an entirely fresh approach. The policies of the past had become, in a word, 'obsolescent'. Yet most Australians, he wrote, continued to maintain a blissful ignorance of such alarming developments: 'A society that for a while burst with innovation is now complacently suburban, shunning anything that is at all out of the ordinary.' On the conservative side, the long-serving prime minister Robert Menzies had lulled his party into irrelevance, 'the last great Empire statesman'. Desperation increased, however, 'when one [entered] the museum in which the Labor Party stores its totems'. Horne repeated – for a British audience this time – his Shilsian call for a 'drastic change of political generations': 'Events are rapidly making nonsense of Australia's conventional wisdoms. They will soon become insupportable.'[38]

◆ ◆ ◆

With Horne's exit from *Everybody's* fast approaching, his professional future had started to look marginally less bleak. In early 1963, his and Myfanwy's financial uncertainty was assuaged when he accepted a lucrative job as an advertising copywriter. It was another unusual addition to what was becoming a unique résumé. His morning commute now took him over the Sydney Harbour Bridge to the North Sydney offices of the advertising firm Jackson Wain. The agency, controlled by the old-school ad men John Jackson and Middleton 'Mid' Wain, was the first to advertise on Australian television in 1956 (a twenty-second plug for Rothmans cigarettes) and had been in a process of almost continuous expansion ever since. By 1963, Jackson Wain was the only large local agency to remain Australian-owned, due for the most part to its continued control of the prestigious Qantas advertising account. When the director of that account, Jack Mack, heard that the long-serving editor of *Weekend* magazine (another of the agency's clients) was looking for work, he offered Horne a job.[39]

In 1963, advertising paid his bills, but as usual it was the AACF that provided his intellectual sustenance. Towards the end of the previous year, the organisation – with its access to obscurely sourced international funding – offered Horne a possible path back to the editorship of an intellectual magazine. Ever since he discovered *The Economist* as an adolescent, he had seen small magazines as his direct line to the world of ideas. As he had told his fellow editors at the seminar at The Belvedere in August, the surprise success of *Observer* had offset his sense of intellectual loneliness, 'of dropping stones into a bottomless pit'. The furious agreement of the magazine men at the seminar itself had only strengthened this conviction.[40]

With this in mind, at the December 1962 meeting of the AACF executive committee, Horne proposed yet another new journal of opinion, once again styled in the mould of *Encounter*: 'intelligent, realistic and liberal-minded (in the best sense).' He reiterated his prophecy of the coming revolution in Australian politics and society: events, he predicted, 'are going to cause a great number of overthrowals of traditional ways of looking at things in Australia in the next decade.' In Horne's view, the best way for the association to play its part in these impending political transformations was, unsurprisingly, a 'monthly journal of opinion' – particularly one that critically examined his favourite topics: Asia, economic planning, the Australian character, 'freedom issues' and cosmopolitanism.[41]

Though the committee was enthusiastic about Horne's new venture, the Congress's Paris-based decision-makers were not, and flatly refused to fund both Horne's proposed magazine and the existing literary journal, *Quadrant*, at the same time. By Christmas 1962, Krygier had solved the problem, earning approval from Paris to switch the funds from Horne's new journal to a 'new and improved' *Quadrant*. Beginning in 1963, the magazine would have two editors: McAuley would continue to handle the literary pages, while Horne would oversee the political commentary and intellectual content. The arrangement was not without its difficulties – the job was part-time, the pay was insulting and McAuley was unenthusiastic – but less than twelve months after his exit from *The Bulletin*, Horne was back at the (part-time) helm of an intellectual magazine.[42]

Summer also brought another important new addition to the Hornes' social circle. While on holiday with their new daughter, Julia, at Kims Camp on the NSW Central Coast, Myfanwy took Donald to lunch with her old university friend Ed Campion, who was living in The Entrance and working as a priest. Campion – Jesuit-educated, intellectually inclined and, to Horne's immense pleasure, a former reader of *Observer* – gave the couple a driving tour of the area. Horne was thrilled by Campion's 'erudition' and his subtle and humorous dissection of the social makeup of the area. By the afternoon, recalled Horne, 'I became as familiar with The Entrance as with Graham Greene's Brighton.' It was the beginning of a deep and lasting friendship, begun, somewhat fortuitously, at the exact time that Donald had finally broken with Packer and started, however tentatively, to take a second look at some of his most cherished assumptions about politics and life. It was likely with Campion in mind that Horne later wrote of the Catholic influence on his own thinking, particularly 'its sense of compassion towards human complexity'.[43]

In early 1963, Krygier organised for Horne to travel to Taiwan, Indonesia, Singapore and the Philippines on behalf of the AACF to meet with politicians and diplomats – including the leader of the exiled Chinese Nationalists, Chiang Kai-shek. The trip proved to be a significant one. Horne's somewhat grandiose ideas about the centrality of the communist threat in the region, produced second-hand from newspapers and magazines and expounded in *Observer* and *The Bulletin*, were now forced into a confrontation with the reality of South-East Asia.

In Taiwan, Horne visited Quemoy, a group of islands situated less than 2 kilometres from the Chinese mainland. Hoping to catch a glimpse of one of the frontlines of the Cold War – 'the guns of Red China pointed at me' – he instead found the islands to have 'the colour and climate of a holiday resort'. From this vantage point, he wrote, communist China was nothing but 'brown earth and green grass'. Writing about the trip in *The Bulletin* in April 1963, Horne argued that there were now two types of Taiwanese: those who dreamed of a triumphant 'return to the mainland', and those who were content to hang around and 'eat the newly baked cake'. Horne favoured the latter: in his eyes, the best way to ward off the 'big mess' of Chinese expansionism in the region was to encourage the 'small mess' of European-style industrialism. Such an outcome was not ideal, he admitted, but then there were 'no tidy solutions' to political problems.[44]

As always, Horne continued to do most of his thinking on the page. By June 1963, he had published no less than eight articles on South-East Asia in *The Bulletin* and the *Spectator* on South-East Asia. Since the publication of 'Control or Colour Bar?' in 1960, he had slightly amended his attitude to the speed of decolonisation (he now no longer thought it was proceeding too quickly), but he was nevertheless still determined not to be naive about its realities. He maintained a hard-headed, sceptical outlook on foreign affairs. For Horne, the Cuban Missile Crisis of October 1962 had only confirmed the dominance of great-power politics in the nuclear age. In *The Bulletin*, he pointed out that the world was not a 'civic centre controlled by some impartial body that sorts out rights, settles quarrels, protects the weak, orders the affairs of the strong and lends a gentle predictability to everything', but rather that the reality of international relations was power politics and 'gross conflict'. No region exemplified this better, he proposed, than South-East Asia, the most 'melodramatic' part of the world. Not only did communism remain a legitimate threat in this region, even the anti-communist states mistrusted each other. 'Nothing in Africa is as bad as the mess the scuttled conquerors left floating behind them in South-East Asia', with its 'muddle of races, religions, languages and cultural traditions.'[45]

By this point, the book about Australia that Max Harris and Geoff Dutton proposed at the Little Magazines conference twelve months prior had become a distinct possibility. Horne's strident arguments about South-East Asian communism, however – coupled with his position at the AACF, the notoriety he had earned as the editor of *Observer* and *The Bulletin* and the general black mark of his close association with Frank Packer – initially gave the decision-makers at Penguin cause for concern. 'We should think carefully about Donald Horne doing the book you suggest,' Brian Stonier, Penguin Australia's managing director, wrote to Dutton in February 1963. 'I think you should ask him to give you a provisional list of contents and some sort of synopsis.' Dutton, though less sceptical, complied, and was enthused by Horne's response. 'I very much like your idea of chapters on the suburbs and on changing Australian attitudes,' he wrote to Horne in April 1963. The book was all but confirmed.[46]

In addition to all these new activities – editing *Quadrant*, writing a book, contributing pieces to various magazines, wandering around South-East Asia, not to mention fatherhood and family life – Horne also assumed responsibility for the latest AACF brainchild: a bimonthly 'Sunday seminar' series. Given the reservations about his Little Magazines conference, Horne was determined his new series would include a much more diverse range of voices than those that had traditionally dominated the *Quadrant* circle, many of whom were fast becoming anti-communists of the more illiberal variety. When they were eventually launched in mid-1963, some of these Sunday seminars did prove to be quite ecumenical gatherings. One event, called 'New Interpretations of Australian History', was essentially a debate over the first volume of Manning Clark's *History of Australia* (published a year earlier), and was attended by figures as far removed from the AACF as Russel Ward, Miriam Dixson, Robin Gollan and Clark himself.[47]

By 1963, it was becoming increasingly obvious to all but the most paranoid of conservatives that the intellectual upheavals of the post-1956 period had produced a sizeable group of anti-communist social-democratic progressives, whose general political outlook was not too far removed from the anti-communist liberal conservatism of much of the AACF set. Along with a shared distaste for communism, these previously sworn enemies found common ground in their opposition to censorship and White Australia, in their general preference for the postwar 'mixed economy' over the traditional Labor platform of full nationalisation of industry, and in their confrontation with the immense geopolitical and psychic shock of the British turn to Europe. Across Britain and America, this developing policy consensus was being feted as the 'new progressivism'.[48]

One of the chief proponents of this middle way, the British intellectual and Labour member in the House of Commons Anthony Crosland, visited Sydney and Melbourne for six days in June 1963. Despite (or perhaps because of) AACF sponsorship of his Australian trip, Crosland met with a broad cross-section of the Australian left, including Gough Whitlam, the Victorian Fabian Society and anti-communist operators, such as Knopfelmacher and Bob Santamaria. In Sydney, Crosland and Horne crossed paths several times: first at the Horne-organised AACF seminar on 'Press, Radio and Television', then at a party at Richard Krygier's house, where almost everyone took exception to Crosland's suggestion that they all join the Labor Party and reform it from within. Finally, a more intimate encounter was arranged between Horne, Crosland and McClelland in Kings Cross, where Horne experienced the bewilderment of having his political views endorsed by the author of a book called *The Future of Socialism*. Crosland's subsequent assessment of Horne – 'v. nice, bright, now Lib but? moving left' – was shrewd.[49]

All the while, Horne was putting in long hours in his new career in advertising. Alongside Trevor Wilson, Jackson Wain's art director, he had been put to work on the new Qantas ad campaign. Though he spent the majority of his time confined to a desk in an unassuming corner of the agency's drab Miller Street offices, the new job also required a considerable amount of overseas travel. In July 1963, in a whirlwind 'writing and photography mission', Horne and Wilson were ordered to visit each of Qantas's most important international stopovers to conduct research for the campaign. On three separate trips between August and October, the two men visited Singapore, Bangkok, Hong Kong, Tokyo, Manila, Delhi, Cairo, Athens, Rome, Frankfurt, London, Fiji, Honolulu, San Francisco and New York. Horne found it exhausting, unenjoyable work, spent mostly in airports and second-rate hotels. In a letter to Jim Plimsoll, he complained that he and Wilson felt like 'characters in a summer conference crisis'.[50] The mission was even more trying for Myfanwy, left alone in the Manning Road flat for weeks at a time to look after two-year-old Julia. 'I am exhausted,' she wrote.[51]

Despite the punishing schedule, Horne managed to find time for several significant meet and greets. In Delhi, he arrived just as Bill Pritchett was handing over the post of high commissioner of India to Plimsoll. In Taiwan he met Chiang Kai-shek. In New York he had lunches with *Encounter* editor Irving Kristol, the journalist Arnold Beichman and his former *Weekend* favourite Lillian Roxon. In London he met with Crosland, *Spectator* editor Iain Hamilton, 'several *Encounter* people' and Ethel, whom he hadn't seen in nearly seven years. His proposed meeting with the American intellectual Daniel Bell, author of the 1960 bestseller *The End of Ideology*, was cancelled at the last minute. Before leaving England, he even went back out to Bow Brickhill. As he wrote in *The Bulletin* soon after, it was a 'weird journey backwards to a place where I once saw what would then have been described as my future.'[52]

Donald Horne in front of the Taj Mahal, 1963

It was certainly an auspicious time to be an intellectual in London. After a tortured decade of imperial decline and seemingly irreversible damage to Britain's international standing, the British publishing industry had become increasingly enamoured with probing and acerbic works of national self-criticism – titles so ubiquitous that one writer later dubbed them the 'What's Wrong with Britain' books. With great commercial success, a number of British intellectuals – including Horne's acquaintances Hartley and Crosland – had tried their hand at diagnosing the national malaise. *Encounter*, meanwhile, had published an entire special issue in 1963 under the title 'Suicide of a Nation?'[53]

When he arrived back in Australia in late 1963, Horne went to considerable lengths to distance himself from what he saw as the distasteful opportunism of the What's Wrong phenomenon: 'There are so many intellectual careers to maintain or make in the State-of-the-Nation debate in London that after even only a week the thing begins to seem a bit of an act.' This was a strange and somewhat hypocritical response, given that Geoffrey Dutton had only recently contracted him to write, quite literally, 'something like Anthony Sampson's *Anatomy of Britain*'. Horne's first diatribe in Hartley's *Spectator*, too – with its excoriation of Australian political elites stuck between the 1920s and 1930s – was itself a kind of antipodean variation on the central refrain of the entire What's Wrong genre: that the political classes had grown alarmingly complacent in the face of British imperial decline. In this sense, Horne was merely developing an Australian perspective on what was really a crisis of the entire British world. As a consummate outsider, however, he was temperamentally unable to be a part of any club that would have someone like him for a member.[54]

This brief episode was nevertheless characteristic of the confusion and – often – the contradictions that Horne worked through in the two years after his departure from *The Bulletin*. In the early 1960s, with Australia at a geopolitical crossroads and its domestic politics seemingly on the verge of several serious 'overthrowals', it is hardly surprising that the intellectually agile (and now professionally independent) Horne began to experiment with new and somewhat conflicting ideas. Inevitably, these weathervane tendencies attracted plenty of criticism. But to focus solely on Horne's inconsistencies in this crucial period risks overlooking the intellectual energy and curiosity that lay beneath them them. From a young age, Horne had always attempted to understand and describe the world around him, but like the fox of Isaiah Berlin's famous maxim, he was never fully wedded to one way of thinking. As he himself might have put it, things had changed so fast since the British pullout that it would probably have been more of an intellectual sin *not* to call one's most cherished political beliefs into question. The proposed book in which he intended to conduct this self-interrogation would be but the next step in his never-ending intellectual odyssey, a chance to very publicly find out what it was that he now believed.

7.

THE LUCKY COUNTRY

It had been a long apprenticeship. Over the course of Horne's stop-start, two-decade-long journalistic career, his cumulative word count ran into the hundreds of thousands. He had written poetry, pamphlets and prose sketches; daily journalism, op-eds and essays; advertising copy, speeches and a lifetime's worth of fanciful *Weekend*-style dross – not to mention two unpublished novels. On top of this, he had lived abroad, travelled extensively, married twice, become a father and edited three different intellectual magazines. Given his relentless output, literary inclinations and obvious ambition, it is notable that by 1963 Horne had somehow *not* found a way to publish a book. But at forty-two, the production of intelligent, popular books remained his dream.

What ultimately provided Horne with his subject was the confluence of major geopolitical events that had occurred during his *Observer* and *Bulletin* editorships. His proposed book with Penguin had, after all, had its origins in his expanding corpus of essays about Australia's relationship with Asia. It was just before Horne's trip to Taiwan in early 1963, too, that Geoffrey Dutton had first flagged Penguin's serious interest in a book on the topic, written by Horne. And it was during these overseas trips in 1963 that it became clear to Horne that the upheavals of the Asia-Pacific region were deeply intertwined with the coming 'overthrowals' of Australian politics. His early drafts of what would become the final chapter were even written under the title 'The Demands of Asia'.[1]

Around this time, Horne also began to sketch out another big theme: the political effects of technology and the spread of affluence in Australia. This, he thought, was not something to be bemoaned, yet

151

both right and left seemed to be bewildered that people were adopting middle-class lifestyles: the right were nostalgic for old hierarchies, the left were disappointed in the new materialism. In his view, it was instead the rapidly improving technologies that were going to provoke the most consequential political dilemmas for affluent Western societies:

> We are entering a quite mysterious period of social history that is going to be unlike anything history has ever known before. Most of the drudgery that was once removed only by slaves or servants is now going to be removed … by machines and gadgets; unparalleled leisure is already available; there are huge ranges of choice in how we can use it. Can't we be happy with this wonderful change – and be patient if some of it does not come out (for the moment) as we had hoped?[2]

It was in the discussion of the implications of this change, though, that Horne landed on the germ of his most famous argument. In 'Nation Without Ideas', a longer and more substantial piece written for the Congress's West German publication *Der Monat*, Horne contended that Australia had 'not been a country of great enterprise in production'. Rather, it had 'lived on the innovations of others' and was, therefore, not culturally predisposed to deal with the coming technological revolution. Australia, he believed, would not be able to maintain its present level of affluence unless it became more open to new ideas.

To this expanding argument he added his enduring concern: Asia. Australians, he thought, remained fatally naive about the problems of their own region: to the real threat of communism in many of the politically unstable new South-East Asian states, and to the level of anti-colonial and anti-racist sentiment in these same states. On this front, Australia's racist immigration policies were 'an affront to an important world trend'. This was not substantially different from what Horne had argued in the past: that it was in Australia's self-interest to destroy the image of itself as a racist or neo-colonial country:

> Some great effort of will and imagination is needed to solve this problem so that immigration policies continue to favour the maintenance of a

predominantly Western society within Australia but allow sufficient non-European migration to enliven the Australian community and destroy the accusation of racialism.[3]

As a denunciation of White Australia, this was still relatively lukewarm. Horne continued to see immigration reform as a pragmatic foreign policy concern, rather than an explicitly moral one. Either way, he argued, the collapse of the British Empire had accentuated this national image problem. Australia was without a powerful Western protector in an unstable Asia, and it lacked the ability to develop new independent relationships with Asian countries. This threat, he declared, was now being exacerbated by an out-of-touch political class – symbolised by his new arch-villain, Robert Menzies – for whom 'mindlessness was a virtue'. They were a provincial and an 'essentially conservative' political generation, who had formed their ideas of the world 'in the intellectual desert between the two world wars'. Instead, he thought, Australia needed an intellectual class that could 'see the new shapes of the future':[4]

> Australians are not great sentimentalists. It seems that when Sir Robert Menzies goes, the true temper of what – beneath the surface – is at last beginning to look like an independent nation is likely to become apparent with almost revolutionary speed.[5]

Here in these pieces was the embryo of the central idea of Horne's book: that the twin challenges of Asia and technological change had created an existential crisis for Australia. And given the disappearance of the British Empire, the inevitable logic of Australia's geography was – by his calculation – nothing less than full political independence. In an early draft of his book, Horne called the monarchy an 'important issue', and suggested that Australia's 'retention of it is taken seriously by other countries, particularly in Asia'. When the Menzies generation was replaced, he suggested, Australia would soon need to 'start looking for a president'. A republic might thus be the best way to dramatise the twin dilemmas of Asia and technological change to 'fill Australia's traditional need for feeling that he is going somewhere into the future'.[6]

In October 1963, Stonier wrote to Horne to confirm that the book was now a definite proposition. He expected it would be an impulse buy for people, but that 'it should not be written as such'.[7] Horne was full of confidence. 'I have a lot of things already worked out,' he wrote to Dutton.[8] He sketched out a more detailed synopsis. After receiving it, Dutton wrote another encouraging letter, stating that it promised to be a 'tremendous book'. Horne's stress on the cities and suburbs was 'much needed', although on this he advised caution. 'There is a danger of swinging too far the other way, and creating a sort of inverted Australian legend.'[9]

There is a simple tale of the book's conception and writing that has been repeated over the years. On a beautiful summer's day in early December 1963, it goes, while two-year-old Julia slept in her cot, Donald and Myfanwy reclined on some deckchairs in the back garden of their Manning Road flat, and, pen in hand, Donald began writing the book, page by page on a foolscap notepad. The story became a part of the family folklore, recounted over the dinner table like an old war story. It functioned as one of Donald's regular acknowledgements of the role that family life played in his belated success. By the time the book was published twelve months later, Donald and Myfanwy would have a second child, Nicholas. *The Lucky Country* was, in this sense, a group exercise: the whole family were present at the dramatic moment when the pen hit the page.[10]

In reality, Horne wrote a lot of the book at his desk at Jackson Wain, 'when all the executives were off playing golf'. By 8 December he had already written the first two chapters. 'I find I like writing books,' he wrote to Dutton. 'Perhaps I might take it up.' Around this time he even aborted – fortuitously, it would seem – a proposed *Quadrant* essay on Manning Clark, so keen was he not to 'break off from the themes I'm taking up and write a kind of peripheral article.' Whether his book would have been received with quite the same level of enthusiasm had he launched another attack on Clark is an intriguing and not completely implausible counterfactual. Luck, however, was on his side, and less than two months later, by February 1964, he had finished the first full draft of the manuscript.[11]

He found he was surprised at some of the things he had written.

In a letter to Stonier, Horne gave yet another hint that some of his political views had begun to evolve: 'It is interesting to discover what one thinks when one gets down to detail.'[12]

> I have come out with a more favourable picture of ordinary Australians than I thought I would and an even more scathing picture of their leaders than I expected … For what it's worth – I'm quite pleased with what I've done. I think it's probably more comprehensive and also more provocative than the usual book on Australia.[13]

Though Horne's manuscript was completed by February, debate over its title continued throughout 1964. 'Australia in the Sixties', everyone agreed, was too dry. As the book was originally conceived as an Australian version of Sampson's *Anatomy of Britain*, Stonier wanted a medical term, preferably a 'synonym for anatomy'. The various draft titles of the book's final section offered some alternative possibilities, including 'A New Australia?', 'More by Good Luck', 'The Demands of Asia' and 'What Happens?' Dutton wrote back to suggest using the name Horne had eventually chosen for the final section, 'The Lucky Country'. Horne agreed: 'I think it sums the whole thing up, and makes a pleasant, intriguing title. So far as I'm concerned, use it.'[14]

Along with discussion over the book's title, Horne and Penguin spent much of 1964 in a pitched battle over the book's style. Aside from hundreds of work-related memos and costings reports, almost all the writing Horne had done since his return from England in 1954 had been for immediate publication. He had never been a great writer of letters, and almost never kept diaries. During his travels in 1963, however, as if to stave off loneliness and boredom, Horne – for one of the first and only times in his life – had begun to keep journals of the things he saw and the people he met, along with several long drafts of his proposed book, and this private literary experimentation proved fruitful. In these 'thousands of as yet secret travel words,' Horne wrote to Dutton, he had inadvertently 'discovered a descriptive narrative style' that he hoped to use in his proposed book.[15]

This, he wrote, was just one of four styles he had planned to deploy, alongside 'neat and logical' intellectualised argument, a 'reminiscent' style to provide personal feeling and a 'philosophising-about-life' style that would bring 'coherence of approach'. Most important, he believed, was readability. 'The thought of writing a book that people wouldn't read is unbearable to me,' he wrote.

> Both to make the thing physically readable, and also to present my kind of view of Australia and indeed life (if I might use that expression), I should also like to introduce certain shifts of tone, and a certain amount of discursiveness and, among the abstractions, to attempt to give something of the colour and texture of the things the abstractions are supposed to be about.[16]

Dutton agreed, and Horne went ahead and wrote his manuscript in line with this stylistic rubric. But Dutton and Stonier, as the representatives of Penguin's fledgling Australian operations, needed the tick of approval from the English bosses, and in June 1964 the English publishers took issue with Horne's approach. When the manuscript came back from Tony Godwin in London, it was accompanied by a demand for more 'facts and figures' and a suggestion that as it stood it was not suitable for publication in England. Godwin wanted 'a larger book' in the style of *Inside Russia Today*, one of a series of popular sociological books written by the American journalist John Gunther. Dutton thought it was a 'crap' idea. He wrote to Stonier: For the book not to appear in the United Kingdom would be an 'absolute crime'. '[If] I were Donald Horne, I would think of suing the company.'[17]

Nothing could have been further from Horne's conception of his book than the inclusion of a stupefying cloud of facts and figures, and understandably he flatly refused to let excessive amounts of statistics and evidence dampen the effect of his stylistic approach. He had, after all, clearly and deliberately made the case for his methodology in his proposal in October 1963. In July 1964, Horne took up his own cause in a brutal review of (his friend) Henry Mayer's book *The Press in Australia*. There was 'little flesh and blood' among Mayer's statistical tables and analysis, he wrote. 'His whole approach is static. Nothing moves, nothing changes; it's all happened before; it will go on happening.'[18] A month later he made the same argument to Dutton. 'There is nothing like facts and figures to take the meaning out of something and to detract from its readability.'

> People sometimes say they want figures but I think that all the readership surveys suggest that even quite sophisticated minds turn off when faced with even a small amount of them. What keeps people reading is a kind of this paragraph leading to that paragraph thing, a pseudo narrative effect. When you were kind enough to say that this book had a 'hypnotic effect', I took it that you meant something like that.[19]

To their credit, Dutton and Stonier backed their author, and in August 1963 decided to publish locally without the approval of Godwin – an act of colonial rebellion that chimed nicely with the book's own robust criticism of Australia's continued deference to Britain. They would instead print 10,000 insubordinate copies of *The Lucky Country* for the Australian market. It was Dutton's belief that he would eventually be able to convince the English publishers to 'come to the party'.[20]

The two men had every reason to be confident. Everyone involved could see the book's potential. Dutton's wife, Nin, sent Horne a glowing letter of encouragement. 'It puts into words a number of half-formed ideas and perhaps formed, but not generally expressed ideas,' she wrote. 'A nation isn't a nation until it's discussed how many toes it's got.' Max Harris, who had still not seen the manuscript, had nevertheless heard the good news. 'Fame is yours,' he declared.[21]

Everyone at Penguin Australia knew they were onto a winner, and the book was given top priority. Both Dutton and Stonier were clearly of the opinion that the nebulous reforming sentiments that had been bouncing around the pages of *Observer* and *Nation* since 1958 (along with the countless seminars, dinner parties and academic symposia of those years) had the potential to reach a broad and receptive audience. For all their freshness and originality, the many significant book titles of the period – including John Douglas Pringle's *Australian Accent* (1958), Robin Boyd's *The Australian Ugliness* (1960) and Coleman's *Australian Civilization* (1962) – had all produced more of a ripple than a splash. As both Horne and his publishers foresaw, the myriad new ideas of what had amounted to an Australian intellectual renaissance, bubbling away for half a decade, were clearly in need of distillation. 'I think this is a particular book for a particular time,' wrote Dutton. 'We mustn't miss this bus.'[22] 'The sooner this book is published the better,' replied Horne a month later. He added:

> I think it may have caught the mood of a number of people and, although
> this mood is not going to disappear, if we can get in first by expressing in
> a book what may otherwise dribble out in other ways, this should help
> the reception of the book.[23]

In August 1964 the Penguin promotional machine clicked into gear. Dutton promised they would do a 'crash job' marketing the book, as it would provide 'happy hours' for television, radio and newspaper critics, as well as 'reaching the schools in large numbers'. Stonier thought it would make a 'perfect Christmas book'. In September, Max Harris organised for some of the book's more controversial sections to be serialised in the newly launched national broadsheet *The Australian,* prior to its publication.[24] Harris, as editor of the newly launched *Australian Book Review,* set up a public review competition, with the best submission to be published in the magazine. Horne also called upon his own contacts and marketing experience to help drum up publicity.[25] Peter Coleman, now the editor of *The Bulletin,* promised a headline review, and Horne had Penguin send a review copy to Irving Kristol to encourage a possible US release. Elsewhere, the book was to be reviewed on ABC's *The Critics* program, and even before its release there was talk of a special *Lucky Country* episode of *Four Corners.* 'This book is going to be a wow!' wrote Dutton in November. 'I feel we have a bestseller,' wrote Stonier.[26] The stage was set: the Australian intellectual renaissance would soon have its scribe.

◆　◆　◆

As time passes, certain cultural events come to act as placeholders for entire historical eras, signposting the national narrative and in the process assuming a significance of their own. The publication of Donald Horne's *The Lucky Country* in December 1964 and the debate it stimulated in subsequent years was, in a way, one such cultural event, having long since become so closely associated with the transformative changes of 1960s Australia that it almost seems to have produced them. With over fifty years of hindsight, it now appears as a kind of singular literary manifestation of a nation (and a man) in transition, a symbolic stake in the ground at the point between the old Australia and the new; one of those books that, by exaggerating a sense of rupture, provides a simple framework for political change, an artificial periodisation between the past and the future, the *then* and the *now*.

This is not entirely a fantasy of retrospection. When it was first published, *The Lucky Country* caught on in a way that cannot simply be attributed to Albert Tucker's striking cover art, its cheap paperback pricepoint or Penguin's pre-publication marketing blitz. The initial print run – already revised upwards to 18,000 – sold out in nine days, and subsequent editions continued to sell at a steady rate for years to come: by 1966, the figure had reached 80,000. For a work of Australian non-fiction – and social criticism, no less – this was barely believable. At the height of the book's popularity, Horne – hitherto a largely obscure political commentator and magazine editor – managed to achieve something close to household-name recognition.[27]

Anyone living in Australia in 1965 could have been forgiven for coming down with *Lucky Country* fatigue. In the course of that whirlwind year, Horne shot to fame, making countless appearances on Australian television and radio. Headline reviews and articles about his controversial book ran in nearly every major magazine, periodical and newspaper (both metropolitan and regional). Before May he had received two different inquiries about a *Lucky Country* documentary series. Copies were distributed to the Australian Department of External Affairs and the Department of Immigration, and seminars were organised to discuss the book's main arguments. Qantas supplied it on their aircraft and it featured as a prize on the Channel 7 television gameshow *Terry's Hour*. At one point Horne – still employed as an advertising executive – even suggested that the book be put on sale on cruise ships to 'reach the tourist and migrant market'. By

October 1965, less than a year after it was published, the book was set for the Grade III English course for Fifth Grade in New South Wales schools. A whole generation of Australian schoolchildren would grow up reading *The Lucky Country* – whether they liked it or not.[28]

Something about Donald Horne's argumentative book clearly resonated with the reading public. In its basic concerns, it differed little from the arguments and themes that he had already outlined (to a much smaller audience) in essays, reviews and editorials in the previous two years. To these disconnected arguments he had added a potted survey of the nation, describing, for the readers of the future, 'what this huge continent was like in those early days in the 1960s before it was peopled from all over Asia'.[29] With his irreverent 'philosophising-about-life' narrative style, Horne cast his eye over early-1960s society, politics and culture, with chapters on topics such as 'The Bush', 'Migrants', 'Unions', 'Schools', 'Intellectuals' and 'The Churches'.

Despite these (deliberately) superficial claims to comprehensiveness, however, Horne insisted that the December 1964 edition of the book had no obvious overarching thesis. As he wrote less than twelve months later, if the book had a central theme it was probably in the subtitle: *Australia in the Sixties*.

> The *Lucky Country* theme is really a subplot. It comes and goes. *Overall* the book is not polemical: no single point is being driven home all the time. Nor is there any singleness of approach. A country can be looked at from a number of different points of observation. I have tried six of them, one after the other.[30]

Alongside this scattershot sociological survey, what was both appealing and confusing about *The Lucky Country* – then and now – was the application of Horne's 'tough, stylish wit' to his (heavily qualified) celebration of suburban, middle-class, 'ordinary' Australia. In Horne's newly revised view, all of Australia's unique qualities, both good and bad, emanated from the people. As he had mentioned to Stonier while writing the book, he had been surprised by his own optimism on the subject of ordinary Australians.[31]

Horne began *The Lucky Country* with a typically hyperbolic accusation of this nature. Australia had been one of the world's first suburban societies, he wrote, yet almost all Australian writers and intellectuals, whatever their politics, were 'reactionaries', whose main attitude to Australian life was either to 'ignore it or condemn it'.[32] Such thinkers, he thought, with their particular contempt for the suburbs and the kinds of people who lived there, 'hate almost the whole community'. Horne instead proposed to approach Australian life and suburban values sympathetically, to describe Australia 'as it is'. There was, he argued, 'no Australian Orwell … searching for the temper of the people, accepting it and moving on from there'.[33] It was in this spirit that Horne described what he thought were the dominant positive characteristics of ordinary Australians:

> their non-doctrinaire tolerance, their sense of pleasure, their sense of fair play, their interest in material things, their sense of family, their identity with nature and their sense of reserve, their adaptability when a way is shown, their fraternalism, their scepticism, their talent for improvisation, their courage and stoicism.[34]

Horne thought these values were, in and of themselves, 'great qualities that could constitute the beginnings of a great nation'. But viewed in a different light, he continued, these same characteristics had decidedly negative implications. That same Australian pragmatism and scepticism also manifested as philistinism, anti-intellectualism and a mistrust of expertise. In this sense Australia was a 'nation without a mind'. He also pointed out that the much-feted Australian values of egalitarianism and mateship were rarely extended to women, migrants or the Indigenous population. As Peter Coleman had written in *Australian Civilization* two years earlier, there was a rarely acknowledged dark side to the cult of mateship: 'the open smile' was so often accompanied by 'the broken bottle'.[35] Thus Horne's celebration of 'ordinary' suburban Australia was a decidedly ambivalent one:

> Australians are a largely non-contemplative people … [This] seems to come from a narrowness of imagination, the product of scepticism …

> Scepticism can combine with the egalitarian dislike of cleverness to oversimplify even the simplest issues. Like all optimists, Australians are stupendous simplifiers.[36]

What gave the book its populist appeal, however, was Horne's allegation that it was Australia's *leaders* who deserved the blame for the nation's faults. Ordinary Australians, he thought, were about as adaptable, sceptical and decent as could be expected, but these same attributes seemed to produce mediocre, narrow-minded and unimaginative leaders. 'On top,' he wrote, there remained a 'stiff-necked carrying on of old ways based on enervated wisdoms'. This argument was more or less endlessly repeated throughout the book, and was the essence of its most famous line: 'Australia is a lucky country run mainly by second-rate people who share its luck.' Australia, Horne proposed, had achieved its security and material prosperity by chance alone; it was short on visionary statesmen but long on raw materials and other people's ideas. And in his view, no politician embodied this mediocrity of leadership better than Australia's long-serving conservative prime minister Sir Robert Menzies.[37]

Among the strangest and most revealing aspects of the fraught Australian cultural politics of the past few decades has been the elevation of the 'Menzies era' – beginning not long after the end of World War II and extending to the mid-1960s – into something approaching the loose interpretability of myth. At its peak, for a brief season in the middle of the 1990s, this somewhat arbitrary bracket of historical time between the prime ministerships of Chifley and Holt became ground zero in Australia's culture wars, a political shorthand from which you could explicate a person's entire worldview. The mythic Menzies years were, from one vantage point, a time of threat, of communist conspiracy and international upheaval, of nefarious Cold War espionage and nuclear proliferation.[38] From another they were 'comfortable and relaxed', a time of peace, prosperity and affluence, of simple certainties and homespun virtues.[39] Most fashionably, however, they became a time of national drift, stagnation and obsolescence, of fogeyism and conformity, a dull period when Australians became less concerned with politics and more interested in their own private kingdoms and possessions: houses, cars and gardens, refrigerators and televisions.[40]

Of this latter interpretation, Donald Horne has a decent claim to authorship.[41] As a part-time political speechwriter and full-time ad man, he knew better than anyone that stereotypes and historical generalisations were one of the necessarily evils of political communication, distilling the impossibly broad, incoherent sentiments of vast constituencies into something concrete and actionable. And in *The Lucky Country*, he reserved some of his best and most contemptuous lines for Menzies, his Labor rival Arthur Calwell and the rest of their 'decrepit', 'antediluvian' political generation, all of whom desperately clung to power by keeping the nation 'spellbound in boredom'. In their rhetoric, Horne claimed, none of them was able to dramatise the problems facing Australia in the second half of the 1960s. Menzies' talk of empire and Calwell's talk of class instead had 'something of the flavour of progressive discussion in 1908'.[42] At times, Horne jibed, they 'seemed to be conducting a political debate that they had read about in an old book'.

One can say that since 1949 Menzies has seen few of the potentialities of the age; that his reactions have usually been those of an old-fashioned man guided by the vanishing standards of an earlier, more rural community. In some ways at times he has seemed to reflect not even the standards of his own generation, but the one before him ... If this interpretation is true, it means that throughout a period in which Australia was in need of orientation towards Asia and towards technology, it has been governed by a man who has deeply absorbed the provincial standards of Melbourne at the beginning of the century.[43]

Horne instead placed his hopes in the changing of the political guard. The current political generation, he predicted, would 'soon be writing its memoirs'.[44] He saw this as an opportunity for 'the radical overthrow and destruction of the prevailing attitudes of Australia's masters'. Only a new generation attuned to the problems of the modern world would be able to interest voters in the twin dilemmas of Asia and technological change, to encourage Australians to 'develop some new sense of identity, some public feeling of being a people who can be described – even if incorrectly – as such and such a kind of nation, and act at times as if it were so'. And only a new generation would be able to swallow his most controversial remedy: a symbolic breaking of sentimental ties to Britain and the declaration of an Australian republic. As he had argued relentlessly since the late 1950s, one thing was now clear: things could not go on as they were.[45]

Horne's excoriation of Menzies, long stereotyped as a leading figure of the political right, and his call for a break with the British monarchy may have come as something of a surprise to many of his political enemies. But it was his *bipartisan* condemnation of Australian elites that caused the most confusion. Some of *The Lucky Country*'s earliest critics could not make heads or tails of it. The book's slippery, politically unsettled, end-of-ideology arguments made it something of a blank canvas on which to project whatever political ideology one saw fit.

Who was this new Donald Horne, some critics wondered, who with equal vigour attacked both Menzies and Calwell, Labor and Liberal, businessmen and trade unions? The best that Judah Waten could come up with in the Melbourne-based communist newspaper *Guardian* was to call him 'one of Australia's extreme right-wing journalists', a 'man of monopoly' and a 'reactionary'. On the other side of politics, in the conservative Melbourne *Age*, Gerald Mayhead read Horne's arguments as 'the bitter-sweet observations of a republican, pro-American, working class, left-of-centre journalist'. A concerned Sir Allen Brown, the Australian deputy high commissioner in London, even saw fit to mention the book to Menzies himself: 'I suspect [Horne] of being some sort of Don at some university somewhere.'[46]

For other, more perceptive readers, however, Horne's lively style more than made up for his political indeterminacy.[47] This 'vigorous, not unduly scrupulous, brutally tactless, robustly quarrelsome' polemic deserved to be read, wrote H.G. Kippax in *The Sydney Morning Herald*. It summarised 'many of the views and theories which have appeared in the past few years either expensively in hard covers or obscurely in literary journals'. In *The Canberra Times*, Maurice Dunlevy was slightly more circumspect. 'Well said – but it's been said before,' was his sceptical appraisal. With regret, he predicted that 'Horne's little outburst will have been forgotten by the end of the summer and that we'll all be ready for the football season without any worries of Asia, or imperialistic hangovers or of second-rate minds.'[48]

Given the considerable longevity of Horne's 'little outburst', Dunlevy's unfortunate prediction quickly became a part of the book's mythology, and Horne was always sure to quote it at the beginning of later editions. At the time, however, Dunlevy was actually not too wide of the mark. The 1960s were certainly a decade of radical cultural change, for both Horne and the nation he dissected and described, but until the more obvious earthquakes of the post-Menzies years, for many people these changes remained either imperceptible or largely fugitive.[49]

In Australia, it is sometimes said, the remembered '60s didn't arrive until the early 1970s. At the time of *The Lucky Country*'s publication, Menzies was still in office and showed no signs of leaving. A year earlier, Queen Elizabeth II had been greeted with great enthusiasm all over Australia, just as she had on her previous visit in 1954. One could just as easily have asked: Had anything really changed? As Horne had pointed out in his book, even by the midpoint of that decade, Australia's post-imperial political crisis remained largely 'concealed'. But when it did inevitably come out into the open, he predicted, this concealed crisis would be 'quite unpredictable in effect'.[50]

Similarly, for all its success and transformational influence on his public profile, and despite its anticipation of the cultural revolutions to come, *The Lucky Country* was not necessarily the simple pivot on which Horne's decade turned. He had, after all, begun to cautiously revise some of his most sacred political precepts as early as 1961. It was, rather, the near two-year process of writing the book – informed as it was by his global travels, relentless reading, diversified social and intellectual networks, and domestic contentment – that forced him once again to confront the question of all questions, the problems that had plagued him since adolescence: Who was he, and what did he believe? In the early months of 1965, this dilemma sent him into what he later described as a 'sombre, dreamlike state of freefall' and a 'recurring state of mental depression'. Despite his long-awaited anointment as a writer of intelligent books, Horne experienced *The Lucky Country* summer as a 'period of sadness'.[51]

As had become alarmingly apparent, it was not only the book's reviewers who were confused about its politics, but also the author. In February 1965, still smarting from some of the more misguided responses and personal attacks, Horne penned a 'review of the reviewers' in *The Bulletin*, sarcastically titled 'Who Am I?': 'I find myself facing a crisis of personal identity,' he quipped, perhaps more revealingly than he had intended.[52] Three months later, when a new university appointment controversy provoked another round of public debate over academic freedom, Horne saw it as an opportunity to take up the case against his detractors. In April, Frank Knopfelmacher, the former Melbourne University academic and outspoken anti-communist, had had his appointment to the Department of Philosophy at the University of Sydney overturned on political grounds. For Horne, this was nothing less than the martyrdom of a maverick – and yet another example of the 'meanness of institutional mateship' in the face of brave and outspoken criticism. Knopfelmacher had been singled out, wrote Horne, because he was 'unclubbable':

> Any original-minded Australian who has been savaged by his own pack because he hunted outside it and who challenged its collective wisdoms and tried to go his own way will recognise in Dr Knopfelmacher's defeat a bitter repetition of his own loneliness and the frustrations imposed by mediocrity of spirit.[53]

Knopfelmacher aside, Horne's despondency in these heady months probably had more to do with the paralysing doubts and self-interrogation that are often the by-products of literary composition. In early 1965, encouraged by *The Lucky Country*'s success, or in spite of it, or both, he began a number of inchoate writing projects. One he hoped would become a second book, a fragmented memoir of his country childhood. Another he envisaged as a kind of philosophical play, set in the afterlife, about the timeless mysteries, paradoxes and absurdities of politics. Both, however, seemed to lead him down an existential rabbit hole, leaving him face to face with those same eternal, insoluble tensions of existence that had always confounded him at moments of personal crisis: of faith and doubt, optimism and pessimism, activism and detachment, scepticism and belief. Unsurprisingly, neither of these tortured, self-searching writing experiments came to anything in 1965. Donald Horne – like the nation he described – was still in a state of transition.[54]

The one new literary project that did get off the ground in the difficult post–*Lucky Country* period was a novel he had mostly written nearly fifteen years earlier. In early 1965, fed up with Penguin's ambivalence towards its Australian operations, Dutton, Harris and Stonier decided to launch their own publishing company, to be called Sun Books. Horne, feeling somewhat indebted to these three men for the role they played in his belated literary success, offered one of his old English manuscripts to them as a 'kind of housewarming present'. The agreement was mutually beneficial: Horne would finally get a novel published, while the fledgling Sun Books would trade off the name of one of Australia's hottest and most controversial authors. Horne, relieved to find a distraction from his latest personal crisis, turned the manuscript around quickly, just as he had with *The Lucky Country*, and it was in Dutton's hands by June.[55]

This farcical, anti-bureaucratic political comedy – originally titled 'The Richmond Affair' – had had its genesis in the late 1940s, when Horne had been engaged in a long epistolary battle with the Department of Education to avoid punishment for breaking the terms of his university scholarship. In the revised 1965 version – now given the Kafkaesque title *The Permit* – a young man's honest attempt to get a permit from a government department becomes tangled in an absurd web of bureaucracy, journalistic manipulation and cynical party politics. Significantly, however, to his updated manuscript Horne added some of the themes he had raised just a few months earlier in *The Lucky Country*. The delusional politicians in *The Permit* thus live in a bygone world, detached from reality and concerned only with the pursuit of power. The book's political characters are indifferent to the problems of modernity, preferring instead to reflexively spout irrelevant and hollow rhetorical slogans. Parliament is, variously, a 'circus', an 'aquarium' and a 'zoo'. One character, named 'Shennanagen', furnishes his parliamentary office like a 'wealthy, cultivated, nineteenth-century man of letters'.

Like Menzies, his social and political imagination is backward-looking, constructed around an idealised image of the past:

> 'Ah, why don't you let a man alone?' Shennanagen stared at a large globe of the world that stood beneath his window. He walked over to it and spun it around. He flicked a fingernail against the part that said 'Austro-Hungarian Empire'.[56]

It was this kind of political dinosaur, native to both sides of politics, that Horne had sought to describe and tear down in his bestselling first book. In this regard, both *The Lucky Country* and *The Permit* were natural extensions of what he had always done well, whether at an old magazine like *The Bulletin* or a new one like *Weekend*: to sweep the broom, to cut against the grain, explode old wisdoms, spark conversation and – most importantly – avoid simple categorisation. The responses to *The Lucky Country* seemed to justify Horne's repeated argument that the problems of Australian politics in the 1960s were obscured by outdated rhetoric and old ways of thinking. The political culture was shifting, and the boundaries of left and right were in flux. As the journalist Geoffrey Hutton surmised six months after the book's release, *The Lucky Country* read like 'a manifesto for what sounds like a political party, as yet unborn'.[57]

8.

AUSTRALIA LOOKS AROUND

For a book intended to be of its time, *The Lucky Country* has had a long shelf life. Unlike the rest of the handful of forgotten state-of-the-nation books of the era, Horne's snapshot of Australian life and ways in the late-Menzies years has so far managed to avoid the literary graveyard that is the fate of almost all published books: it has – miraculously – never been out of print. And whatever its shortcomings, its endurance is merited. Many of the political dilemmas it articulated and popularised in 1964 – the complicated politics of prosperity, affluence and diversity, the open question of Australia's identity and nationhood in the wake of British imperial decline, and the never-ending predicament of Australia's relationships with Britain, Asia and America – remain some of our key political dilemmas. The book's ambiguous title has a similarly timeless appeal, and is dredged up every few years for each new round of national self-critique. 'Is Australia still the lucky country?' is a question that seemingly never goes out of date.

One less obvious reason for *The Lucky Country*'s durability was Horne's ability to revise and reshape the book in response to events, and to refine and rearticulate his arguments in response to criticism. The version that is in print today is not a carbon copy of the book published in December 1964. As Horne told an interviewer many years later, he did not believe books were 'sacred', nor that there was anything about Australia that was 'eternal and unchanging'. *The Lucky Country* was instead treated by Horne as something of an open question throughout the middle and latter parts of the 1960s. And though the book's essential arguments and structure remained largely unchanged, on questions of emphasis and omission he was always happy to 'spring clean' it and move with the times. These subtle but significant revisions, he told Penguin in 1966, would give *The Lucky Country* a broader perspective and, he hoped, 'a longer life'.[1]

Penguin were understandably keen to maintain the book's saturation, and in July 1965, six months after its initial release, it was Stonier's replacement, John Stephens, who first suggested that Horne rewrite parts of his bestseller. With Penguin's eyes once again on the Christmas publishing market, Stephens asked for a 'reissue and not merely a reprint', and suggested an extension of the section on Menzies and additional chapters on the subjects of defence, investment and 'Australia in the future'. Horne told Stephens that he did not want to appear to be 'too much on the make', but he nonetheless agreed that the book would benefit from a few changes. To write about a society 'as it moves', as he would argue in his new introduction, was 'more demanding than to write as if a society were all of a piece, standing still and unchanging'. In the latter months of 1965 – close to two years after he had written his first draft – he thus set about making several adjustments.[2]

Many of Horne's initial revisions were subtle. The title of his foreign affairs section, 'Looking to Britain', became the more modern 'Between Britain and America', while the allusively named chapter 'The Bead Curtain' became the more straightforward 'The First Suburban Nation'. Women, conspicuously absent from the 1964 edition, now appeared in a chapter of their own, as did 'Catholics', while 'The Churches' became 'Wowsers', 'A Mateship of Directors' became 'Men of Business', 'Ambitions' became the brilliantly titled 'Racketeers of the Mediocre' and most of the original chapter on 'Good Taste' was folded into the new discussion of women. These changes, while superficial, Horne believed to be significant, admitting that the first edition's avowed commitment to 'topicality' may have given it 'some of the wrong emphases'.[3]

Other changes were more substantive. The reworked section on 'The Age of Menzies' (which now stood alone, separate from the section on 'Men in Power'), for example, made Horne's condemnation of Australian political leadership much more forceful and unambiguous. His populism was clearly undiminished: 'It is not the people who are stupid but their masters', he wrote, as bluntly as ever. His revision of the book, he assured readers, had mostly 'added to this criticism, not modified it'. And in another newly titled and expanded section, 'A Republic' (once again excerpted in *The Australian*, alongside 'The Age of Menzies', to coincide with the reissue), Horne restated his most controversial prophecy: that the end result of Australia's postwar geopolitical dilemmas must be full political independence. 'To people who are under thirty-five, who were still at school when Singapore fell or not even born, there is no basis of power or performance or reason in the monarchy.'[4]

Horne's most significant adjustment of emphasis, and what signalled the evolution of his thinking over the previous eighteen months, was his forceful recapitulation and extension of his original 'nation without a mind' argument – now outlined in an entirely new chapter, 'Provincial Australia'. Historically speaking, he argued, the estrangement of Australian elites from the realities of Australian life, their provincialism, their second-rateness and their 'contempt for the ordinary people of their own country' were all a product of Australia's essential 'derivativeness'. Australia was a second-hand society, thrown up in imitation of its foreign forebears, and ever since Europeans had first arrived on its shores, they had always found it easier and safer to borrow ideas from abroad than to think them up on their own:

> What other word than 'provincial' does one use to describe a nation in which most activities are derivative and most new ideas are taken from abroad? In which the main decisions in manufacturing and strategy are dominated by overseas centres and in which vogues are usually out of date? Which not only lacks a feeling of importance for the present, but which has no feeling of importance in the past? That sometimes watches the policies and trends of its twin metropolises (Britain and the USA) with more interest and knowledge than it watches its own?[5]

What Horne's new chapter prefigured were the needs to connect the dots between *The Lucky Country*'s disparate sociological observations, and to synthesise its various cultural, historical, intellectual, political and diplomatic criticisms into a comprehensive argument – a 'derivative society thesis'.[6] For Horne, then, the immediate post–*Lucky Country* years were a time of taking stock, of connection-making and consolidation. The two books he had out at Christmas 1965 were, in their own ways, both based on personal experiences and impressions, and were both coming at the same essential problems from different stylistic angles. Throughout 1966, Horne started fleshing out these fundamental problems – both personal and societal – joining the various fragments and approaches of *The Lucky Country, The Permit* and his other unfinished writing projects into one convoluted but increasingly coherent argument. 'May the Horne of plenty continue to overflow,' wrote Dutton.[7]

Donald Horne having dinner with friends, c. 1965

Perhaps more than ever before, in the mid-1960s Horne was willing and able to adjust his thinking in response to events – particularly those taking place to Australia's north. In this sense it was not the writing and publication of *The Lucky Country* itself, but rather this revision and repositioning of the book that were key to the transformation of Horne's outlook in the second half of the decade. For him, these years seemed to mark a new beginning in Australian politics, not least because Menzies finally retired in January 1966, unbeaten, after nearly seventeen unbroken years as prime minister. Even more significantly, his replacement, Harold Holt – though himself a veteran of the

Liberal Cabinet – attempted to project a more modern image than that of his predecessor, and – to Horne's heavily qualified approval – tried to promote what Menzies had always sought to downplay: Australia's role in Asia.[8]

In February 1966, for the third time in as many years, Horne set off on his own small diplomatic tour of South-East Asia. This time, the impetus was the Congress-sponsored conference on 'Democracy and Development in South-East Asia', to be held in both Singapore and Kuala Lumpur, and to which the AACF sent a large delegation, including Richard Krygier, James McAuley, Peter Coleman, Bruce Grant, Owen Harries, Doug McCallum and Brian Beddie.[9]

The international events of the previous twelve months gave a particular urgency to proceedings. In Indonesia, an attempted communist coup had been met with brutal reprisals, purges, mass killings and transition to military government. Further north, Australia's key ally in the region, the United States, had significantly increased its military presence in Vietnam, transforming the engagement into a full-scale war. Seeing the conflict as a perfect illustration of Eisenhower's domino theory of Chinese communist expansionism and as a means of keeping the Americans involved in Australia's unstable region – as many did in the early 1960s – Menzies (and later Holt) had guaranteed Australian support for the intervention, and even introduced legislation for conscription. Unsurprisingly, Horne's travelling band of professional anti-communists generally saw things the same way. For them, Vietnam was the latest and most worrying outbreak of the Cold War in South-East Asia, and on this account none of them could possibly have been brought to oppose either Australian or American involvement.

Given this basic pro-Vietnam consensus, disagreements among Horne's group were more a matter of degree – a question of how you defined your liberalism. For the hardliners, any criticism of American Cold War foreign policy, no matter how well intentioned, was viewed as a sign of weakness and a lack of commitment to the cause. As Horne himself might have said just a few years earlier, the threat of communist aggression needed to be met with equal force – there was no value in 'giving in'.[10] Since the publication of *The Lucky Country*, however, he had begun to take a marginally less hawkish view. Writing in Sibnarayan Ray's edited collection *Vietnam: Seen from East and West*, he called for greater independence and pragmatism in Australian foreign policymaking in the region (as opposed to an unquestioning obedience to whatever Washington deemed necessary), and insisted that pro-war zealots 'sacrifice the use of the word "Communism"' and 'get themselves some more exact terminology'.[11] Nevertheless, Horne's was not an argument against Australian involvement in the conflict – on the contrary, he thought doing something was probably better than doing nothing:

> In the Australian idiom, one may as well 'give it a go'. By this view we support the killing and misery in Vietnam because without it, worse killing and misery might follow … [We should] proceed in the faith that our own standards of decency, imperfect as they might be, are nevertheless of a different order from those of the regime we fight – and that our own standards, if we are firm enough, might well prevail.[12]

In Horne's view, preventing the spread of communism from North Vietnam was a tremendously important Australian foreign policy goal, but only if considered in light of what he thought of as more practical and independent calculations. Writing just a few months later in the American foreign policy journal *Foreign Affairs*, he suggested that Australia's traditional subservience to its foreign protectors, and its willingness to fight in their wars, was just another manifestation of the nation's essential derivativeness and inability to 'think up new things'. In the mid-1960s, he noted, even the principal form of public opposition to Vietnam – the 'teach-in' – came 'ready-mixed from America'. Despite this, Horne thought that Australians possessed a long-unrealised 'yearning' to go their own way, and to 'do away with the inhibitions of alliance'. What it would take to bring this into the open, he suggested, was not any specific policy on Vietnam, but rather a political generation who were able to 'dramatise' the nation's place in the region: to provide 'shocks of recognition' that would 'shake Australia into a new way of looking at things' and rid it of its derivativeness. His essay was titled, appropriately enough, 'Australia Looks Around'.[13]

Such notions of foreign policy independence, however modestly expressed, were not necessarily shared within the AACF. By the time of the conference trip to Singapore and Kuala Lumpur, Krygier, McAuley and even Peter Coleman had all noticed that Horne's recent flirtation with newer and (marginally) more radical political ideas seemed to have tempered (if not completely stifled) his previous enthusiasm for the anti-communist cause. Krygier could not countenance Horne's new friendship with the novelist Frank Hardy, one of Australia's most well-known postwar communists, while McAuley and Horne had had a longstanding disagreement over the value of liberal social reforms. Coleman, meanwhile, took particular issue with *The Lucky Country*'s republicanism and its attack on Menzies. In the Cold War minds of some of his friends, the new Horne was in danger of becoming what they all despised: a left fellow traveller. Given his otherwise impeccable anti-communist credentials, however, such a claim would only have confirmed his feeling that the AACF was drifting into reaction.[14]

None of these simmering disagreements was helped by a suggestion in *The New York Times* in April 1966 that the Congress for Cultural Freedom (and, by extension, the AACF) had long been receiving secret CIA funding through a dummy foundation first established in the early 1950s. Despite relatively little public interest in the story, at least initially, several of the organisation's biggest names – among them John Kenneth Galbraith, George Kennan, Arthur Schlesinger Jr, Stephen Spender, Irving Kristol and Melvin Lasky – immediately penned impassioned defences of its intellectual independence.[15] Reputations were on the line, and the CCF clearly intended to get out ahead of the allegations. Horne, as the editor of the Congress-sponsored *Quadrant* (and thus a personal beneficiary of the funding), was particularly attuned to questions of its public perception. That same month, he received a letter from Nicolas Nabokov at CCF headquarters with uniform instructions on how to respond to Australian media enquiries on the issue.[16] Then, in October, after the organisation had hurriedly procured new and less problematic funding from the Ford Foundation, he received another, rather disingenuous letter from Michael Josselson, one of the founders of the CCF, assuring him that 'our lawyers who have been investigating the matter for us have thus far found no basis for *The New York Times*' charges.' Nevertheless, the organisation would 'no longer need to solicit support from smaller and less well-known foundations'.[17]

In his memoirs, Horne suggested that he had been aware of the CIA funding rumours for some time prior to the first public allegations, but had disbelieved them until he was finally convinced of their truth by Lee Kuan Yew at the Singapore conference in February 1966 (two months before *The New York Times*' story). Given Horne's centrality to the Australian organisation, however, this story rings a little hollow. He was close personal friends with almost everyone on the AACF executive committee, on which he had sat since 1962. He had also edited *Quadrant* since 1963, overseen the AACF's various seminar series for several years, operated as secretary during Richard Krygier's periodic absences and had infrequent correspondence with many of the organisation's key international figures, including Nabokov, Josselson and John Hunt. As Jason Epstein, founding editor of *The New York Review of Books*, recalled: 'Nobody, of course, was supposed to know who was financing the Congress for Cultural Freedom ... But by the middle of the '60s anybody who didn't know it was a fool. *Everybody* knew.'[18]

It was not until April 1967, however, when the American magazine *Ramparts* published the damning results of its year-long investigation into the CIA funding issue, that it finally morphed into an existential crisis for the Congress and its subsidiaries. The allegations appeared during a period when previously marginal critiques of 1950s Cold War thinking were coalescing into what Frances Stonor Saunders has described as a 'backdrop of critical dissent'.[19] Critically, though, the *Ramparts*' story transformed the CCF into what looked like a CIA front at the very moment when the tide of public opinion in the West was beginning to turn on the United States' interventions in Vietnam.[20]

Countless well-known writers (including many from the formerly Congress-subsidised *Partisan Review*) lined up to take a swing. CCF intellectuals were accused of being nothing less than cheerleaders for American imperialism, 'cockroaches in a slum sink' and 'spies who came in for the gold'. Fearing for their own reputations, Congress leaders called an emergency meeting in New York in early May 1967, where many were shocked to hear both Michael Josselson and John Hunt admit that they were – and always had been – CIA operatives. A wave of resignations followed, including *Encounter*'s original editor, Stephen Spender, and his recently appointed replacement, Frank Kermode.[21]

Horne did not resign from the AACF in the wake of the CIA revelations, but he did continue to stir the possum. For several years he had been expressing his frustration with the increasingly inflexible political line taken by many of his oldest comrades. Chief among his criticisms of the AACF in the mid-1960s was what he suspected was its inability, and maybe even its unwillingness, to keep pace with the times. He had conveyed this very Horne-like concern to Krygier – in writing – as early as June 1964: 'We are now seeing the beginning of an intellectuals' breakthrough. Over the next few years, there is going to be a shift in habits and attitudes that is unimaginable to most people now. If the AACF does not associate itself with this trend it should go out of business.' To add insult to this intellectual injury, Jim McAuley – who lived in Tasmania on a professor's salary – had continued to draw his *Quadrant* coeditor's fee despite Horne doing almost all the editorial work. Something had to change – though Horne was unwilling to break with an organisation to which he had contributed for half a decade, he was now increasingly reluctant to promote it.[22]

It was convenient, then, that in November 1966, Frank Packer once again presented him with a way out of an awkward career impasse, offering Horne his old job back as editor of *The Bulletin*. Packer's latest offer – which was full-time, well paid and included permission to 'write books which you claim as a hobby' – was too good to pass up.[23] With his enthusiasm for both advertising and hysterical anticommunism all but exhausted, he quickly resigned at both Jackson Wain and *Quadrant*. The latter, in fact, had become a particular burden, part-time, poorly paid and barely read. In his resignation letter he did not mince words: the *Quadrant* job, he told Krygier, had turned out to be nothing but a 'nagging public duty, skimped and unsatisfactory. One of the most disappointing ventures I have ever been connected with.' Horne had grown so bored with *Quadrant*, recalled Krygier, that by 1966 he had passed on most of his editorial duties to Myfanwy. In December that year, it was agreed that after half a decade of intellectual independence, Horne would return to *The Bulletin*.[24]

The years 1966 and 1967 were the beginning of the end for the AACF. The CIA funding issue had turned it into a political lightning rod: you were either with it or against it. For some, then, Horne's resignation from *Quadrant* in late 1966 and his relatively cautious critique of Australian foreign policy subservience suggested a weakening of his anti-communist commitments and an even more suspicious dose of anti-Americanism. James McAuley, for example, thought the whole saga was 'bogus hysteria', and that CIA palm-greasing had done nothing to influence their already fervent anti-communism.[25] This may have been true, but in the AACF's moment of crisis, its formerly reliable journalistic megaphone Donald Horne was not exactly screaming it from the mountaintop. He was one of the few dissenters on the executive committee who thought that the AACF needed to publicly apologise for the scandal.[26] When this was rebuffed, he took care to distance himself from the whole debacle, privately repeating his previous assertion that the association had 'image problems'.[27]

Given the existing suspicions that Horne had gone soft, it would have been tempting for the hardheads to assume that he was merely protecting his *Lucky Country* reputation in the wake of the CIA revelations and, worse still, that he had become one of the naive liberals that he had himself enthusiastically ousted from the organisation's leadership five years earlier. The old Horne, they might have thought, would have stayed to defend the citadel; the new one was playing both sides, compromised by his *Lucky Country* fame. It was not a decisive break with the organisation, nor with the cause of anti-communism, but the seeds of serious disagreement had been planted.

The slow deterioration of Horne's relationship with the AACF intellectuals highlighted the subtle changes in political sensibility that he had been working through since the early 1960s. Staunch ally to the anti-communist hardliners in the AACF presidential election of 1961, he had now become one of their critics, if not their enemy. As he recalled many years later, when the time had come to revise *The Lucky*

Country in 1965, he had decided to 'soften' its original discussion of communism, a topic on which he admitted he had 'simply overdone it in regard to the local people'.[28] The threat of a communist fifth column, which had seemed so real to Horne in 1961, had by the mid-1960s become almost an irrelevance. Similarly, Vietnam – initially sold as a Cold War defence of Western liberalism against communist tyranny – had turned out to be a much more complicated affair.

Discussing a second revision of *The Lucky Country* with Penguin's new management team not long after Menzies' retirement, Horne declared his intention to put the old man and the whole political era he represented 'into the past tense'.[29] Communism and anti-communism, he sensed, would not play a significant role in the politics of the coming decade: they had almost ceased to matter *now*. Horne's revisions to his book in 1965 and 1966 certainly gave it a 'longer life'.[30] That this was so, however, owed everything to his deliberate and self-conscious contemporaneity, his desire to dispense with out-of-date issues and attitudes – even if they were once his own – and, it must be said, his weathervane critical instincts. Horne would not hang around to fight yesterday's battles. As he wrote to Penguin in 1967, he hoped to rewrite a lot of his book, but not to alter its structure in any way: more than anything, he simply wanted to make it 'true, not false'.[31]

◆ ◆ ◆

In February 1965, just over two months after the publication of *The Lucky Country,* Donald Horne had received a letter from his publisher, Geoffrey Dutton, asking him what he planned to do next. As the most famous author in the country, Dutton implied, he could write whatever he pleased. At the time, however, Horne was despondent. The reviews of his book had seemed to revive the most difficult questions of his adolescence. What lay behind all his different personas: the republican radical and the anti-communist conservative, the irrepressible optimist and the fearful pessimist, the outraged activist and the level-headed observer? Was there a 'true' Horne, an essential set of principles and ideas that directed all of his thinking? Or was he simply a writer who changed direction with the breeze?[32]

In search of a satisfactory answer to these questions, Horne responded in the only way he could: he sat down and wrote. What spilled from his pen, though, was not social criticism, nor was it an apology for his political beliefs. Rather, it was an attempt to go right back to the beginning, to a much younger version of himself, to the person he thought he had once been. In those confusing summer months, he had penned a series of autobiographical 'scraps', short literary re-creations of the most cherished scenes of his boyhood: playing bridge and mahjong with his parents, singing songs around the pianola, sleeping out on the front verandah. It was writing as therapy, he recalled, the confrontation with his former hopes and fears akin to 'confession and absolution'.[33] Thinking it worth pursuing, he quickly informed Penguin that he had indeed begun work on a second book. Its working title, he said, was 'Half My Luck'.[34]

Throughout 1965, Horne returned obsessively to these scraps of memories, chiselling away at the shape of his early life. He paid careful attention to the historical accuracy of his account – checking dates, interviewing his grandmother, reading the *Muswellbrook Chronicle* and consulting his boyhood diaries.[35] It was an autobiography, he thought, honest and true. But the more he wrote, the more he suspected that it was not the mere recounting of facts that most interested him: it was the ways that such facts could be made to represent different social categories and historical ideas. 'I wasn't quite sure what I was doing,' he remembered a few years later, 'but since I had come up with a lot of generalisations in *The Lucky Country* [I thought] it might be interesting to test them by comparing them with my own personal experience.'[36]

As with *The Lucky Country*, his thematic canvas was broad: the joyfulness and innocence of boyhood and family life, Muswellbrook's strictly enforced social and sectarian prejudices, generational differences, public rituals of war commemoration and imperial allegiance, the stifling moral conformity of the interwar years, the discovery – through books, friends and *The Daily Telegraph* – of a world beyond provincial Sydney, and the various political and intellectual fashions that had constituted an undergraduate education at the University of Sydney in the early 1940s. In keeping with this critical approach to both his young self and the society that formed him, he eventually settled – via Henry Adams – on the book's title: *The Education of Young Donald*.[37]

It was not until early 1966, however, with both *The Permit* and the revised edition of *The Lucky Country* behind him, that this autobiographical experiment began in earnest. It was a fitting coincidence, then, that at the precise moment Horne was attempting to pick apart the intellectual lodestars of his youth, one of the most important of them all, the novelist Evelyn Waugh, passed away at his country home at the age of sixty-two. In April, Horne took this famous literary death as an opportunity to publicly reflect on the English writer's influence on his impressionable young self in an uncharacteristically personal piece in *The Bulletin*. He had first read Waugh as a 'perplexed, unhappy and sceptical high school boy' and found in him a sense of 'relevance': he and this rebellious son of the English aristocracy seemed to see the world in exactly the same way, that life was 'absurd compared with the aspirations we have about it'. But now, nearly thirty years hence, he wondered what effect this adolescent literary discovery had had on the trajectory of his life, and the 'reality' of his perception:

> Did my life subsequently turn out something like an Evelyn Waugh novel, because that's the way life goes? Or because, having read Evelyn Waugh, I was determined that this was how life should be?[38]

In Waugh's novels, hollow words and ideals were presented in deliberate contrast with harsh, fickle reality, thus exposing their meaninglessness and, in this way, 'solving' what Horne now took to be one of the modern writer's central problems: 'how to cast off old rhetoric, without adopting a neo-primitivism.'[39] What were *The Lucky Country* and *The Permit* but attempts to throw out a similarly moribund political language, to scrutinise old worldviews in light of modern realities and to reveal their redundancy in a much changed and a much changing world?[40] From an early age, Horne realised, Waugh had instilled in him a conviction that there was really no stifling the human capacity to ignore reality, to project prefabricated ideas onto events and to turn to old explanations that no longer made sense.

In his and Waugh's cruel, complicated world, this kind of self-delusion knew no bounds.[41]

In *The Education of Young Donald*, Horne sought to poke fun at such self-deception, and in the process uncover the key to both himself and the society that had made him. In order to marry these twin aspirations, he conceived of a hybrid literary form, 'sociography', which he described as an 'attempt to show what social history can look like when told through *people*'.[42] Though he mimicked many of the conventions of both autobiography and fiction, Horne's intentions were explicitly sociological, and in this sense *Education* can be thought of as a prequel to *The Lucky Country*.[43] As he explained in a letter to Frank Knopfelmacher, 'the creation of a society through a person can have a significance that is different from a "scientific" account.'[44] The personal history of Donald Horne would thus double as a narrative account of Australia in the 1920s and '30s, and a continuation of the de-provincialising project he had begun in his first book.

As he had with *The Lucky Country*, Horne placed supreme importance not merely on the marshalling of historical and sociological facts, but also on the manner of their presentation. In all writing, he believed, style *was* substance, and indeed his search for an ideal narrative tone while writing the book became something of an obsession. Between early 1965 and late 1966, for example, he wrote more than ten full drafts of the opening chapter, in each new version tweaking a word here and there, subtly adjusting the emphasis or rhythm, then throwing it out and starting again.[45] What he was looking for, he later recalled, was a tone of 'non-intrusive detachment' and an ironic interplay between two voices – with the voice of his impressionable young central character being filtered through that of an older, wiser narrator.[46] Ideally, the self-evident truths that would spill out of the mouth of his young protagonist – imperial patriotism, mistrust of Catholics and, later, adolescent political posturing – would appear either absurd or meaningless.

In the section on his country childhood, to take one example, Horne remembers a speech he had given as a schoolboy at an Empire Day ceremony, for which he had received much acclaim. 'Now, think of the heart of this mighty Empire,' proclaimed the patriotic young Donald.

'There lives our King, and from there come the men who have made our Empire what it is … In a few years we will be men and women, and we will have to keep up the fame of our Empire. Upon us rests the task of keeping the flag flying high.' Not long after, however, the narrator delivers his (suspiciously republican) judgement on such fantasies:

> Our allegiance to this monarch did not have much positive effect on most of us. Its effect was mainly destructive: our formal allegiance to this bearded gentleman seemed so improbable that in reality we bore formal allegiance to nothing.[47]

Horne clearly did not intend for his literary ambition to replace the book's historical or sociological objectives, but rather to enhance them. He wanted to 'patch facts together in what was really a literary way' to show 'how literary techniques can still be used for serious intellectual purposes'.[48] His intention was to present his childhood as a kind of 'microcosmic world', a doll's house in which the national story could be played out in miniature.[49]

In Horne's telling, Muswellbrook was presented as a scale model of interwar Australia – its characters, institutions and class structures all carrying symbolic weight. Despite outward pretensions to equality, he wrote, those socially situated below the landed rich and above the homeless and jobless poor found themselves subject to a complex system of prejudices and snobberies. Owing to David Horne's job as a schoolteacher, the family were welcome at the golf club. For the same reason, however, they were not welcome at the more exclusive Picnic Races Ball. Religious differences, too, were complicated. From the three sides of his verandah, Horne could survey Muswellbrook's four churches: Anglican, Presbyterian, Methodist and Catholic. As Anglicans, they could think of themselves as lower-ranking members of the dominant social group. Catholics, he had been told, sat at the bottom. He was taught to despise them, yet found that this general rule had not seemed to apply to his Catholic neighbours, with whom his family had enjoyed good relations.

When *The Education of Young Donald* was eventually published to great critical (if not commercial) acclaim in late 1967, readers immediately recognised the book's literary qualities. Manning Clark praised his 'marriage of the gifts of the novelist and those of the historian'.[50] Horne, wrote the poet Vincent Buckley, 'was less interested in recalling than composing: the textures of the world are less important to him than the shape his own past can be induced to take in the process of recasting his society.' *The Education of Young Donald* was, in Buckley's view, a 'sociological document'.[51] Horne was so pleased with this analysis that he wrote Buckley a long letter of gratitude. He was, he confirmed, especially concerned with the book's structure and, in a broad sense, its style.

> The style I wanted to achieve was that of the narrator, so that his approach to recovering the past and his general approach to things ('style') not only shaped the book but indirectly provided some of its themes, without being directly stated.[52]

An important model for such a style was the nineteenth-century French novelist Stendhal, whom Horne had first discovered as a gunner in the army in the early 1940s. Stendhal's two great novels, *The Charterhouse of Parma* and *The Red and the Black*, were early works of literary realism, placing fictional characters and stories at the heart of real historical events, such as the Bourbon Restoration and the Battle of Waterloo. *The Red and the Black*, Horne now told several friends, was a much better fictionalised account of a life and a society than James Joyce's celebrated *A Portrait of the Artist as a Young Man*.[53] Set amid the tumults and conspiracies of revolutionary France, Stendhal's novel told the story of Julien Sorel, a bookish, self-conscious and ambitious young man from a provincial town, who rises far beyond his modest station through a combination of luck, talent and deception. With great psychological subtlety, Stendhal placed his duplicitous hero at the centre of French politics and society, nobility, clergy and peasantry, royalist and revolutionary, the better to reveal the cant and hypocrisy of all.[54] Stendhal's work was subtitled *A Chronicle of the Nineteenth Century*, but in modern times, Horne lamented, few novelists still fostered such nineteenth-century ambitions to show 'a whole society in operation'.[55] Fiction, he thought, had instead retreated inward, to the psychological and the sentimental. For Horne, one key exception to this tendency was Anthony Powell, whose still-unfinished multi-volume autobiographical novel *A Dance to the Music of Time* he had discovered while living in England and had been following ever since. Powell's books painted a highly detailed portrait of upper-class and bohemian English society between the wars – like a kind of anglophone Proust. They were, wrote Horne, 'an epic of English society in the period when England was being done for before anyone knew how very much it was going to be done for.' His books brought to life not just a single voice but an entire social world. In this regard, and despite their immense differences, both Powell and Stendhal were proof that in certain circumstances the 'novelist's eye' could be a lot sharper than the 'sociologist's or historian's'.[56] As Horne told Geoff Dutton in 1967, in *The Education of Young Donald* there were two things he had tried to avoid:

One was self-importance. And the other was the writing up of emotion and sensitivity. Considering the author and the central character, the avoidance of self-importance was quite a task. But since I believe that we are primarily social animals and that the 'private' bits of us are both elusive and very largely non-communicable I had to set to and treat myself as just one of the other animals.[57]

Instead, Horne sought to re-create Young Donald as an agent of history, to present his younger self as a 'social animal', 'shaped and coloured by social circumstance.'[58] In this way, wrote Frank Knopfelmacher, the book was not merely a prequel to *The Lucky Country*, but a psychological accompaniment.[59] It was memoir as social history, a fable of a man and a nation on the bumpy road to maturity. *Education* evoked an older, more innocent but still deeply provincial Australia, and it was precisely the political nostalgia for such a world that Horne had critiqued in his 1964 bestseller. It was for this reason Max Harris thought that Horne had 'explained the intellectual post-war revolution in Australia'. Horne's prewar generation, Harris wrote in his review of *Education*, had been the first to sense the fraudulence of the dominant Australian national myths – the bush, masculinity, whiteness, Britishness and philistinism – and they sought to replace them with a 'new, bitter, bleak, but sociologically constructive image of Australia'. This book, he surmised, was no mere memoir: it should be read to 'understand the Australian mind'.[60]

Other critics compared *Education* favourably with two other acclaimed Australian autobiographical works of the period: Hal Porter's *The Watcher on the Cast-Iron Balcony* (1963) and George Johnston's *My Brother Jack* (1964).[61] All three books drew upon personal histories to highlight the contrast between interwar Australia and the Australia of the 1960s. But what was most interesting about Horne's book, thought H.G. Kippax in *The Sydney Morning Herald*, was the way his adolescent identity crisis echoed the national crisis of identity he had just recognised in *The Lucky Country*[62] For Horne, it seemed, the personal was the national.[63] He had admitted as much in his discussion of his 'sociographical' approach in the book's foreword:

> In some of the ideas that beset the central character – reform, revolution, experimentalism, freedom, nihilism, fraudulence, 'reality', alienation – is to be found some of the intellectual history of our times, in a particular context.[64]

It should be said that this was not a simple case of Horne projecting his own personal crises onto the nation itself. The two issues were not necessarily linked – one did not obviously lead to the other – and many Australian intellectuals had made and were still making similar observations in this period.[65] But it was also not some kind of cosmic coincidence that Donald Horne was looking for new political opinions at the very moment that Australia seemed to be looking for new ways of representing itself to its neighbours in the Asia-Pacific. As Horne had noticed, Australia's new foreign policy dilemmas were part of much broader changes to the shape of politics in Western democracies. Decolonisation and the global civil rights struggle had brought racial questions to the forefront of domestic and international policymaking, while conflict in Vietnam had begun to provoke disagreement over the nature of the communist threat – even among committed Cold War warriors. If anything, it is once again to his enduring credit that in this transitional period, and unlike many of his old anti-communist friends, he was willing and able to adjust his attitudes and dispense with old opinions as circumstances changed.

It is also precisely this somewhat egotistical ambition – to reconstruct both a personal and social past in a deliberately literary way – that makes reading *The Education of Young Donald* such a challenge for the historian. Autobiography is a difficult source at the best of times, but it is tempting to treat *Education* as a particularly trustworthy personal account of the past, to quote it as if it were a primary source rather than a carefully constructed memoir written more than two decades after the fact for personal, literary and even political purposes. This is perhaps due to the book's detached, almost documentary style, which gives Horne's recount of past events the impression of authority and of verifiability, and of the success with which he had (like a novelist) so engagingly reconstructed the social world of Sydney in the 1930s and 1940s.[66] But as the critic John Colmer argued in 1989, historians would be mistaken to read Horne's 'sociographical' book as a record of documentary facts. Like *The Red and the Black*, *Education* was a fictive re-creation of the past.[67]

Nothing exemplifies this problem better than the book's presentation of the central character's boyhood diaries. These sections ('Extracts from the Diary of D.R. Horne', 'Extracts from the Diary of a High-School Boy', 'Extracts from a Student's Notebook') are presented (but not described) as primary sources, reproductions of real diaries that authenticate the narrative unfolding around them. These diaries, if they existed, are not included in Horne's manuscript papers at the State Library of New South Wales. But in the several drafts of the book that survived, it is apparent that many of the diary entries are highly constructed, drafted and redrafted in order to achieve the written voice of a high-school boy, complete with spelling errors, strange syntax, odd banalities and carefully placed historical references. 'Bradman scored a double century,' goes one. 'The Commonwealth Parliament meets on Wednesday to pass the Statute of Westminster,' says another, quite implausibly.[68]

The diaries, as they appear, were just another part of Horne's literary re-creation of a personal and social past. The book was a useful historical source in the way *David Copperfield* or *The Red and the Black* are useful historical sources (of such a comparison Horne would have been immensely satisfied). As he wrote decades later:

> [I am very proud of] my autobiographical trilogy, which I think is better than most people's. It belongs I think to the great tradition of autobiographies – as distinct from memoirs – set by Saint Augustine and Jean Jacques Rousseau. [In] so many of these autobiographies – people are just trying to square-off and make themselves look good. I think that if you're going to write a critical autobiography, you must first of all be critical of yourself.[69]

Horne had indeed been quite critical of himself. After reading the manuscript, Nin Dutton worried that it sounded as though Horne didn't like himself much.[70] Horne explained to Geoff Dutton that he was 'trying to get under my own skin and have a pick at those bits of Young Donald that survived, so that there was a kind of confessional effect which has changed "me" a bit.'[71] The book dramatised the Stendhalian interplay between what Horne thought of as his two dominant 'selves': the curious, optimistic 'Young Donald' and his bitter, obnoxious and outspoken public alter ego 'D.R. Horne'. Like Stendhal's Julien Sorel, Young Donald's natural innocence and good-heartedness are slowly corrupted by the pessimism of his education. The gentle ambivalence of his boyhood is subsumed by ego and Napoleonic ambition. The Young Donald side of his personality 'accepted muddle, stupidity and deceit as amusing and necessary characteristics of the conduct of human affairs', but the now-dominant D.R. Horne side 'remained morally outraged and still dreamed, vehemently, that all this evil might be blown up'.[72] For Horne, it was this 'confession' – the exposure of D.R. Horne, narcissist, bully and fraud – that ultimately made the writing of the book feel like an act of 'absolution'.[73]

Horne's confession did not go unnoticed by his old enemies. Manning Clark thought it a long-overdue repudiation of his old Andersonian pessimism.[74] Judah Waten – the critic who had once called

Horne a 'reactionary' – was a lot closer to the mark this time around, now seeing him as a 'respectable conforming man who has never been able to fully conform' and a 'rebel who dislikes the left'.[75] Murray Sayle, who had not spoken to Horne since he was subjected to the long attack in *Observer*, now wrote him a fan letter. 'I don't know where you and I stand personally after all these years … [but] anyone who can write a book as good as this one is entitled to have his case reviewed.' The old Horne, he thought, was a 'posturing prick', but *Education* 'makes me see you with new eyes'.[76] Horne responded with grace and contrition: 'I have wondered several times why I wrote at such length and so bitterly'.[77]

Horne's autobiography was itself an attempt to understand why he had written and acted so bitterly in the past. Its publication, just over two years after *The Lucky Country* had launched him into the national consciousness, helped reshape his public persona. But it was the long saga of its writing – which coincided with both the geopolitical confusion around the escalation of the Vietnam War and the AACF civil war over the CIA funding scandal – that encouraged Horne to finally work through much of the pessimism of his worldview. It was a key period of his political and intellectual evolution, a revelatory few years in which he tried to find a way to embrace his innate enthusiasm for change without abandoning his scepticism or his penchant for critical heterodoxy. The achievement of the book, argued Horne a few months after its publication, was the way in which it tried to see through the 'posturing' of adolescent proponents of both left and right, 'not only to the political reality beneath, but to the people beneath who found this posturing necessary to their own self-esteem'.[78]

9.

TIME OF HOPE

In late January 1967, two months before he began his second tenure as the *Bulletin* editor, Horne embarked on yet another whistle-stop tour of South-East Asia. It was his fourth trip in as many years. Organised at the behest of the Congress for Cultural Freedom, it was also his most comprehensive. In less than a month he visited Indonesia, Singapore, Vietnam, Korea, Japan, Hong Kong and the Philippines. His brief, though, beyond the maintenance of Congress networks, was vague.[1] He was not necessarily in search of critical facts, nor did he have any particular diplomatic purpose. The whole exercise, he told his old friend Jim Plimsoll, was more of a 'reshaping and background affair'.[2] In each place, he sought out politicians, dignitaries, journalists and intellectuals, so that he might better understand what he saw as most crucial: their attitudes to the vast continent to the south.[3]

By Horne's account, two key experiences stood out. The first was a brief and somewhat disillusioning stopover in Vietnam. Over the previous two years, the Americans had significantly escalated their role in the conflict, and by January 1967 had over 300,000 troops stationed on the ground. During his brief visit, Horne was confined mostly to the area just north of American-controlled Saigon. His observations, though, were largely superficial, reminiscent of his tales of boredom in an outback army camp during World War II: drinking, standing around and 'jumping in and out of trucks'. Taken on a patrol with an Australian Task Force, he witnessed a futile village search and a large army gun firing at nothing. His overall judgement, as he put it to CCF secretary John Hunt, was that Vietnam had become a 'controlled crisis'. The 'sense of emergency' that had initially characterised the conflict was exaggerated. And the 'sense of catastrophe' that had marked South-East Asia itself for twenty-five years, he thought, might soon begin to 'blow away'.[4]

Donald Horne addressing a dinner in Tokyo, 1967

This stability, he conceded, was largely contingent on what happened in Indonesia. For several years, the country had been mired in immense violence and civil unrest. Since 1965, a brutal and ongoing mass purge of the Indonesian Communist Party had undermined the Sukarno government's hold on power. When Horne visited Indonesia in January 1967, he was not ignorant of these atrocities. The massacres, he wrote a few months later, were yet another addition to the horrors of the twentieth century. Even so, in the midst of this revolutionary fervour, he detected a yearning for a different kind of future, particularly among younger Indonesians. In his brief dealings with a group of anti-Sukarno student activists and in his conversations with the dissident journalist Mochtar Lubis, he thought he saw a 'boredom with the old nationalist or Afro-Asian rhetoric' and a desire for pragmatism and modernisation.[5]

To most Indonesians, Horne wrote, Australia didn't exist. It was a relic of the imperial age, an 'anomaly that history might correct when it got around to it'. But he believed that in the interests of regional stability, the two countries would likely need to forge much closer relations in the future: economically, strategically and even in 'matters of the spirit'. Indeed, by coming into increased contact, Indonesians and Australians might 'cross-fertilise' their worldviews in ways that could 'extend human consciousness'. He did not mean to sound utopian. South-East Asia, he thought, was not a 'sanitorium to which Australians go for a cure'. It was nevertheless through interactions with such places that Australia was beginning to lose its provincialism and develop a new sense of self-confidence and independence. South-East Asia remained unstable, he wrote, but Australians had already thought about what to do if things went wrong. 'We should now start thinking about what we should do if things go right.'[6]

As always, Horne placed great emphasis on political leadership. In his social schema, political leaders – and particularly prime ministers – were the chief national image-makers, tasked with drawing a people's attention to the broad outlines of the nation's collective consciousness. Through their activities, behaviour and public performances, they 'set an example' for the nation to follow, adjusting or changing the terms of the debate, laying stress on particular issues and ultimately forming 'an image of reality that can justify old habits or prompt new actions'.[7] The greatest feature in a politician, Horne wrote, was not necessarily a set of policies, but a *style*: the possession of the 'intellectual capacity to conceptualise policy and dramatise it, the open-heartedness to speak to their countrymen, and that sense of a future that can make new sense of the present and the past'.[8] In the age of television, he believed, 'good speeches [could] have more profound (if immeasurable) effects than legislation'.[9]

The thing that Horne most wanted Australian leaders to make speeches about was Asia. In August 1967, the foreign ministers of Indonesia, Malaysia, the Philippines, Singapore and Thailand founded a new organisation, ASEAN, to promote economic and strategic cooperation in the region. If Australia was to play a part in such arrangements in the future, he thought, it would need to do a lot more to adjust its image in these countries. In his view, the best way to do that was to overhaul Australia's racially restrictive immigration policies. Immigration reform was 'probably the single most effective piece of image changing we could engage in,' thought Horne. As it stood, the image of Australia was still that of a 'vulgar American toady, pushing its snout into Asia'.[10] Even the positive steps towards addressing Australia's mistreatment of its Indigenous people via a historic referendum in 1967 were offset by the continued problem of Australia's colonial claims on New Guinea.[11]

For Horne, the problem of Australia's international reputation was rendered even more acute when American leaders began making noises about winding back their direct presence in the region. In an October 1967 issue of *The Bulletin*, he published an article on the subject by Richard Nixon, then the frontrunner to be the Republican candidate in the 1968 American election. Titled 'Asia after Vietnam', it predicted that America's role as 'world policeman' would soon be rapidly scaled back. It was in their own interest, wrote Nixon, that the nations 'in the path of China's ambitions' should move quickly to establish 'an indigenous Asian framework' for their own collective security'.[12] The Americans were not going to do it all themselves. A few months later, as if to drive this point home, the British, too, indicated their intention to remove what remained of their own military presence in Asia. Australia, it seemed, would soon have to pay its own way in the region.

In the late '60s, barely a week would go by without another missive from Horne on these approaching foreign policy headwinds or the need to renovate the nation's image at this critical moment.[13] In intellectual circles, at least, this relentless hobbyhorsing did not go unnoticed. In *The Sydney Morning Herald*, Phillip Adams used a review of one of Horne's books to grumble about his 'interminable' articles on Asia.[14] In *The Australian*, Geoffrey Jukes took similar issue with the 'low moan of the prophets of doom'.[15] Max Harris declared himself fed up with 'knocking' books about Australia: 'If my old mate Donald doesn't let-up I'm going to thump him one with my silver-topped cane.'[16]

Horne did not let up. The geopolitical ructions to the north, he thought, had finally begun to provide Australians and their political leaders with the 'shock of recognition' that he had long prophesied, the kind of dramatic political theatre that could 'shake Australia into a new way of looking at things'.[17] And of Menzies' two immediate successors, he felt it was John Gorton who experimented most with what that new vision of the country might be. During the first six months of his prime ministership, Gorton increased spending on education, green-lit the establishment of the Australia Council for the Arts and questioned the efficacy of foreign investment in Australian resources. When asked by a reporter to choose between Britain and America, Gorton even insisted that he was 'Australian to the boot-heels'.[18]

For Horne, though, the main problem with Gorton's brand of nationalism was that it was too limited in scope. He saw it as mere chest-thumping about Australian growth, development and investment, painting Australia as a land of vast mineral resources and little else. In October 1968, in a headline feature in *The Bulletin* called 'The New Nationalism?', Horne speculated instead that behind such crude economic patriotism lay the potential for a much broader revival of national sentiment, and a rediscovery of a long-lost spirit of Australian uniqueness and excellence. The time was ripe for political ambition, he thought, for a politician who could 'make us see ourselves as being perhaps a bit more idealistic than we usually admit'. In their rhetoric, styles and policies, he argued, Australia's political leaders would do well to tap into much older Australian ideals of the 'fair go', of egalitarianism and fraternalism, comradeship and brotherhood, and the 'American-style belief that here we were establishing a new society of a quality that would be better than any other in the world'. This was nationalism not in its exclusivist, xenophobic guise, but as a unifying, 'noble and liberating ... ideal of the good'.[19]

The unabashed political idealism of this essay was the clearest manifestation yet of the changes Horne had undergone over the previous few years. Gone was the doomsday prophet of 'Has Australia Got A Chance?' (1958) and the anti-communist campaigner of the early 1960s, worrying whether Australia would 'survive' the threats posed by a newly decolonised South-East Asia. Gone, too, was the overpowering cynicism that had pervaded *The Permit* as recently as 1965. In its place was something approaching a declaration of faith in the potential of both humans and governments to change things for the better, an 'idealisation of some good new interesting thing that Australians might become'.[20]

It was not that Horne had become naive about Australia's external pressures and geopolitical challenges. As a foreign policy-watcher, he remained as hard-headed as ever. What had changed was that he now chose to view threats to national survival as opportunities for civic renewal. In 'The New Nationalism?' he even offered up four particular issues – the treatment of Indigenous Australians, immigration policy, foreign aid and Vietnam – as areas in which Australia might begin to form 'generous, imaginative, subtle and intelligent policies', expressions of political optimism that would give the Australian people a 'proud sense of contribution to the future'.[21] And if, as one critic pointed out, he was slowly coming to see Australia's essential qualities as something like 'easy-going optimism' and a sense of human brotherhood, this probably said less about Australia and a great deal more about Horne, 'the Donald Horne they used to know in the Hunter Valley, before he went to Sydney and got himself sophisticated'.[22]

◆ ◆ ◆

In the 1960s, Sydney experienced a dining-out boom. By 1970, there were over 500 licensed restaurants in the city (up from ninety-nine in 1950). Within the surrounds of inner Sydney, you could now eat mussels at an Italian restaurant, eggplant and cabbage rolls at a Greek eatery and 'nouvelle cuisine' at a French brasserie. Dutch, Chinese, German, Swiss and Hungarian fare was all on offer. At a constellation of cafes and bistros you could drink espresso coffee and cappuccino, and at a new suite of registered licensed clubs you could combine your meal with a dip in a swimming pool or a spin on a poker machine. Between 1966 and 1976, per capita consumption of wine more than doubled. In these years, a combination of demographic changes, increased leisure time and a gradual loosening of immigration restrictions occasioned something of a revolution in food and restaurant culture. Australia, as the writer Frank Moorhouse put it, underwent a 'gastronomic awakening'.[23]

This awakening, of course, went well beyond restaurant culture. In the late 1960s, there were times when it seemed as if the entire society was changing. Galvanised by a growing opposition to the Vietnam War, a new generation of protestors engaged in highly visible forms of mass organisation and street theatre. In doing so, they forced new issues onto the political agenda, from gay and Aboriginal rights to environmentalism and women's liberation. Australia's censorship regime was dismantled and permissiveness became the watchword of the era. Depending on where you stood, wrote Horne several years later, it was either a time of hope or a time of threat.[24] For the first time in living memory, Australia's prevailing national myths were up for debate. The idea of Australia as fundamentally white, male and British was – for those in the new social movements – no longer tenable; even the Australian cult of economic development was being called into question. Change, argued the political historian Paul Strangio, was nothing less than the 'leitmotif of the times'.[25]

Under Horne, *The Bulletin* positioned itself as an interested – if somewhat sceptical – chronicler of these changes. The young journalist Sandra Hall wrote a column called *Out and About*, covering topics such as 'light entertainment' television, cigarettes and new ways of packaging consumer products. Moorhouse, too, wrote expansively about different aspects of consumerism, youth culture and modern life, scrutinising things like coffee, cars, milkshakes, marijuana and drinking in hotel bars. A dose of scepticism, meanwhile, came in the form of Peter Coleman's weekly column. Horne, for his part, was broadly optimistic about the liberalising impulses of the time, though he remained quite dismissive of some of the rhetorical excesses. In an essay titled 'Anarchism – What do the Students Want?', written in the wake of the May 1968 student protests, he described the goals of anarchism as 'one of the greatest humbugs of all'. The desire for freedom, he wrote, perhaps with an eye on his own youthful enthusiasms, often betrayed a 'fear of responsibility'.[26]

The dining-out boom, though, was enthusiastically welcomed by Horne. *The Bulletin* of the late 1960s and early 1970s, recalled Hall and two of her colleagues, Marion Macdonald and Sandra Forbes, was a place where lunch was 'indivisible from work'. Horne, they wrote, liked everyone to be finished whatever they were doing by midday, so that they might go out and discuss ideas over a meal.[27] Not everyone could sustain this level of sociability. During the week, they recalled, some *Bulletin* staff were known to hide under their desks while Horne stalked the corridors looking for someone willing to go to lunch with him. With deadlines to meet and families to feed, they could not afford another long, alcohol-fuelled ideas session with the editor.[28]

Indeed, along with being a chain-smoker, Horne was also a prodigious drinker. Lunch with him would often begin with a brandy, followed by at least two bottles of wine (usually Cawarra Claret), and then, if things were going well, something else to finish. *Bulletin* staff writer Peter Manning remembered some hardy souls going on to a hotel afterwards to get 'properly sloshed', before heading back to the office to file their copy. In the world of mid-century newspapers and magazines, heavy drinking was simply part of the culture.

Horne, recalled his friend Meaghan Morris, was one of the 'great old-school Sydney lunchers'.[29] The talk was always wideranging and intellectual, sprinkled throughout with quips and bon mots. According to Peter Coleman, Horne was a sensational mimic, delighting in impressions spoofing 'Pecksniffs, parasites and *pomposi* of church and state, big business and universities'. No one was off limits: journalists, politicians, intellectuals and academics all got the treatment.[30] In conversation, he had a tendency to declaim, offering ideas to see what people thought of them. He would, in effect, hold court, taking charge of discussion and keeping it on topic. To keep up, you needed to have read every one of the daily newspapers for the past month.[31]

The Bulletin crowd had a standing booking at the New Hellas, a Greek restaurant not far from the office on Elizabeth Street. At lunchtime each Friday, they would congregate at a corner table at 'The Greeks'. The mainstay of the group was Patricia Rolfe, the deputy editor and beating heart of the magazine, who had been there since Horne's first resuscitation of it in 1961. Other regulars included staff writers Ross Campbell, Denis O'Brien, Brian Hoad, Elisabeth Wynhausen and Peter Manning, as well as Hall, Forbes and Macdonald. These editorial lunches were not exclusive to *Bulletin* staff. Contributors and like-minded people were also regularly drafted in to offer their thoughts on the issues of the day: Peter Coleman, Jim McClelland, *Nation Review* editor Richard Walsh, the journalist Richard Hall, and the writers Don Anderson, Frank Moorhouse and Ed Campion.[32] Taken together, quipped Rolfe, they made up the 'New Hellas school of journalism'.[33]

As Walsh recalled, lunches with Horne in these years sometimes had the atmosphere of a 'last supper', as if everyone were showing up to sit at the feet of the master.[34] For younger journalists, meeting Donald Horne in the flesh could be an intimidating experience. Nearing fifty, he had become a living legend of the Australian journalistic scene, the author of a famous book and a veteran of the Brian Penton–inspired postwar generation of rebellious Sydney newspapermen. Manning, for example, felt the full force of his no-bullshit management style and exacting editorial standards. He had initially been hired by Horne's predecessor, Peter Coleman, but after Horne arrived, his copy was deemed 'boorish' and 'academic' – 'You don't have dot points in journalism, Peter' – and he was sent to *The Sydney Morning Herald* to learn how to write.[35] Two years later, however, when Manning's cadetship was complete, Horne pinched him back. From that point forward he was taken seriously, and Horne later credited him with bringing environmentalism, anti-Vietnam sentiments and 'other manifestations of a secular bleeding heart' to the magazine.[36]

For all his grumpiness (and sometimes rage) with bad copy and general incompetence, Horne could be a great mentor and fosterer of talent, and many young Sydney journalists credited him with teaching them how to write. Michael Baume, who had first come under Horne's tutelage during his comparatively crankier *Observer* days, recalled being taught by his angry boss to structure his articles in the shape of an hourglass, rather than following the journalistic tradition of the inverted pyramid.[37] Others recall the novelty of Horne allowing them to write longer, more discursive introductions or to use words with more than two syllables.[38] Just as he had once done with *Weekend* magazine, Horne also regularly dispatched instructional staff memos – 'The Bulletin on *The Bulletin*' – chockfull of usage rules and editorial tidbits: 'Never say "America" when you mean the United States'; 'People are not flocks of birds. They are immigrants (or emigrants) not migrants'; 'Woman, not lady'.[39] One memorable command read like a defence of Horne's own journalistic style:

Colloquial expressions should never be put in quotes. If they are worth using, they are worth using with belief and dignity. A juxtaposition of colloquial and literary English makes the language sound as if it is alive and shared, and not ashamed of itself. But if you are not sure if you are alive and shared and if you think there is something funny about mixing up colloquial and written English – don't. Colloquialisms must come from the heart.[40]

Horne's literary imagination – first nurtured on the stylistic experimentation of modernist poetry and fiction – rendered him particularly hostile to constraints of form, whether journalistic or academic. He would always insist that he was first a writer, not a journalist. 'You're writing essays, not stories,' he told Manning.[41] On one occasion, tired of the idea that each *Bulletin* journalist should confine themselves to any one particular field, Horne experimented with swapping everyone around, so that the finance writer wrote the politics story, the sports writer wrote the finance story and so on. The results, according to some of those involved, were 'entertaining'.[42] Moorhouse's experience, too, shows how enthusiastic Horne was about good writing, regardless of the medium. In 1970, when Horne heard that the upstart author of *Futility and Other Animals* had missed out on a Commonwealth Literary Fund grant, he promptly rang Moorhouse and invented a secret $50-a-week 'Frank Packer Fellowship' in order to keep him going, on the proviso that he write one article a week for *The Bulletin*.[43]

Though he had not lost his maverick temperament, Horne was no longer the same intellectual outsider that he had once fashioned himself as at the *Observer*. One reason was that he knew too many important people. In the years since he started out as a press gallery reporter in the mid-1940s, he had crossed paths with quite a few members of the political and journalistic generation who were now coming to power. Many of his closest friends and associates now occupied positions of serious influence: Adrian Deamer was editor of *The Australian*, Bill Pritchett was high commissioner to Singapore, and – partly at Horne's urging – Jim McClelland had become a federal Labor senator.[44] Further afield, Jim Plimsoll was secretary of the Department

Donald Horne [left] speaking with
Peter Manning and Gough Whitlam

of External Affairs (then, from 1970, ambassador to the United States), while Gough Whitlam – though only a very distant acquaintance from university days – was no less than the leader of the federal Opposition.

By his time of his second *Bulletin* stint, Horne had instead become something of a political *insider*. It was not uncommon for him to have audiences with senior political figures, often in his own office. His published recollections of the period are full of sentences such as 'When [South Australian premier] Steele Hall came to see me' and 'When [his successor] Don Dunstan ... sat expansively in the leather chair beside my desk.'[45] After Harold Holt died in 1967, the Horne family decamped to Canberra so that Donald could speak personally with individual Liberal politicians, including Billy McMahon, Billy Snedden and John Gorton.[46] At one party thrown by Frank Packer during this time, Horne even found himself standing between McMahon and one of his main political rivals, Malcolm Fraser.[47] Horne and his postwar milieu, it seemed, had muscled their way to the decision-making table. As Richard Hall – *The Bulletin* writer turned private secretary to Gough Whitlam – joked sarcastically to Frank Moorhouse in the early 1970s: 'We are the masters now.'[48]

◆ ◆ ◆

The Lucky Country was that rarest of books: a bestseller that went on selling. By late 1966, when Horne was weighing up his return to *The Bulletin*, its Australian sales had gone past 90,000. Including hardbacks and international editions, the real number was in six figures. For Donald and Myfanwy, the financial windfall from such success was significant: enough for them to trade in their small Double Bay flat for an elegant four-bedroom house in nearby Woollahra.[49] Beginning in 1966, this high-ceilinged, timber-floored terrace, just a stone's throw from Bondi Junction, formed the new centre of their universe. For the next four decades, it was the site of their family life, much of their social life and, increasingly, the majority of Donald's writing life.

Horne's penchant for the long lunch in these years did little to dampen his writerly productivity. Between March 1967 and December 1969 alone, he penned 110 columns in *The Bulletin* – often written under the pseudonym 'Observer' – as well as eleven feature-length pieces and several book reviews.[50] Between 1964 and 1972, he wrote and published no less than eight books, plus three revisions of *The Lucky Country* and several essays on the book's main themes for international magazines. On top of this he put his name to other miscellaneous work, often undertaken in the service of friends, such as his introduction to Frank Hardy's 1968 study of Aboriginal Australia, *The Unlucky Australians*, or, slightly later, his foreword to Bob Ellis and Michael Boddy's political drama *The Legend of King O'Malley*.[51]

The books that Horne wrote during this period were, per his agreement with Frank Packer, an entirely 'after-hours performance'.[52] In practice, this meant that on weekends, after a long family breakfast on their square cedar dining table overlooking the courtyard, he would retreat upstairs to his book-lined study, away from the noise and chaos of their domestic existence.[53] As Myfanwy recalled many years later, Donald was rarely burdened with household chores.[54] Instead, they had decided early in their relationship that he would be in charge of the paid work and she would be in charge of the rest. Donald's incredible literary output in this time was a direct result of this domestic arrangement. As Horne acknowledged many years later, his books 'wouldn't have happened' had it not been for his wife's efforts in this regard.[55]

Myfanwy, though, was not simply her husband's domestic help-meet. After setting aside her own journalistic career, her literary talents were largely used to assist Donald with his writing. From the beginning, she became his first reader and most assiduous editor. Theirs was an intellectual partnership. In *The Bulletin* years, Donald wrote his first drafts longhand in a fountain pen, after which the manuscript would be typed by a secretary, before being submitted to Myfanwy for impressions and editorial suggestions. During this process, he remembered, the two of them would sometimes have terrible arguments, as Myfanwy went through his copy 'nitpicking and correcting words'.[56] When they disagreed, Myfanwy recalled, Donald could be a 'pain in the neck', boiling into anger as he argued his point of view. She knew, though, that this was mostly a function of his 'shoot-from-the-hip argumentativeness'. If proven incorrect, he would always retreat.[57] 'I have learned patience through Donald,' she reflected, 'but not always from him'.[58]

Myfanwy Horne in the Hornes' study in 1973

Commercially, Horne's books continued to do well, though none came close to the stratospheric success of *The Lucky Country*.[59] If his writing suffered from anything in these years, it was a kind of stubborn repetitiveness. His 1969 effort, for example, *God Is an Englishman* – conceived over a dinner with James McAuley in 1967 – was essentially an inversion of *The Lucky Country* thesis. After the collapse of the European colonial empires, he argued, myths of English pre-eminence and moral leadership had been exposed as fantasies. In his view, the English now faced their own crisis of identity, born of this deep-seated myth of global superiority. Though they were wont to admit it, the British – and particularly British elites – now had to think of themselves as a nation among equals.[60]

Horne's latest effort was one of the last of the so-called 'What's Wrong with Britain' books, the genre of popular sociology that had emerged at the beginning of 1960s and provided an early model for *The Lucky Country*. By the time *God Is an Englishman* came out in October 1969, the trend was just about exhausted – a fact brought home by the publication in the same year of Christopher Booker's *The Neophiliacs*, a retrospective study of the British self-searching of the 1950s and '60s.[61] Horne was even told as much by an apologetic British publisher in August 1968, who initially rejected his manuscript on the grounds that 'Britain has been so much anatomised recently that we wouldn't be able to do well enough with it to satisfy either you or ourselves.'[62]

This wariness about the continued impact of state-of-the-nation writing was not exclusive to British publishers. In January 1970, not long after the Australian release of *God Is an Englishman*, Horne sent a letter to Penguin proposing yet another update of *The Lucky Country*. This time, he wrote, he wanted to take the book 'out of the 1960s', to give it 'broader perspectives' and add many of the 'good points I've thought of since I wrote it.'[63] By April, however, when Horne presented his new manuscript to Penguin, their initial enthusiasm had evaporated. His new ideas, it seemed, had so overwhelmed the text that it had become not a mere update of *The Lucky Country* but an entirely new book. Penguin – who had a considerable and ongoing financial interest in the original title – were understandably reluctant to dilute its sales, and turned him down.[64] Instead, Angus & Robertson – or more specifically, John Abernethy, who had briefly worked under Horne at *The Bulletin* in the early 1960s – picked up the book and scheduled it for a Christmas release under the title *The Next Australia*.[65]

Though these two new books dealt with ostensibly different topics, they both remained wedded to some of Horne's key 1960s themes. In *God Is an Englishman*, for example, Horne recycled much of *The Lucky Country*'s populism, putting forward a trademark populist excoriation of British elites – the 'Upper English' – whom he depicted as delusional 'dealers in fake antiques', hopelessly addicted to a comforting, false version of the past.[66] And despite their many differences of culture, region and religion, he saw the mass of ordinary British people – 'average Britons' – as foreign cousins of his much-feted ordinary Australians: fraternal, democratic and possessed of 'little social snobbery'.[67] British intellectuals, meanwhile, came in for special censure, no doubt due to Horne's association of the term with the more utopian elements of the socialist left. So detached were these thinkers from the actual lives of ordinary British people, he argued, that they were in an almost constant state of disenchantment: 'It is one of the hazards of a radicalism that professes to be populist that the people might let down the ideals of the radical: they might want something different from what he wants them to want.'[68]

The Next Australia (1970), meanwhile, owed more to Horne's late '60s thinking and writing about Australia, and in particular his escalating concern with the need for a new and relevant articulation of an 'Australian character'. In this sense it was less a rewrite of *The Lucky Country* than it was a book-length explication of his essay 'The New Nationalism?' (1968), especially in its repeated confrontation with some of the conceptual dilemmas of nationalism itself. In its more xenophobic early-twentieth-century guise, went this story, the idea of nationalism had been unashamedly premised on notions of cultural and ethnic exclusivity. As George Orwell once quipped in his famous essay on the subject, 'Notes on Nationalism', this kind of nationalism assumed that human beings could be 'classified like insects' and that tens of millions of people could be 'confidently labelled "good" and "bad"'.[69] Horne's desire for a 'new nationalism', then, had first to contend with this thoroughly discredited definition of the term. The problem, though, was that a pluralist, benign and inclusive conception of the nation risked becoming so broadly defined that it was stripped of meaning. To characterise a people by their heterogeneity, diversity and tolerance was to describe not a nation but humanity itself.[70]

In *The Next Australia,* Horne had become conscious of this dilemma. Given the 'imperfections of reality', he wrote, a modern nation could never be accurately 'described'.[71] Australians, therefore, were 'inscrutable':

> They are both larrikins and conformists. They oscillate between terrified conservatism and wild adventurism. They see themselves as a rural people when they are the world's most urbanised nation. They dislike great men, yet they hate their leaders for not being great. They possess both optimism and a highly developed sense of catastrophe.[72]

For some years now, Horne had been arguing that without an understanding of its own identity, Australia was at risk of becoming 'the country without qualities', the 'world's one non-nation'.[73] 'Without self-definition', he wrote in July 1968, '[it is doubtful that] the human species, whether individually or collectively, can release its creative forces, or even survive'.[74] By the end of the '60s, Horne believed that such a problem could only be overcome by the kind of logical sleight of hand he had been experimenting with since *The Lucky Country*: that if nationalism was nothing but a 'hollow vessel', why not make it an expression of a nation's best and most noble qualities, a 'creative force' and 'an ideal for future'?[75] 'National identity', so defined, would be less a description of a people than an *aspiration* towards which they might strive.

In *The Next Australia,* Horne even offered up three distinctly Australian ideals that might form the basis of such a self-characterisation: an informality and relaxation in social relationships; a belief in human progress and social improvement; and a commitment to tolerance. Such ideals, he argued, could be used to justify all kinds of policy reforms, including the rational planning of cities, the development of an independent foreign policy, better policies towards Indigenous peoples and even the development of a national system of super-annuation. 'In a secular, democratic society,' he wrote, 'some of the strongest and most enduring ideals can come from the attempt to ennoble a nation with a sense of mission, even if turning the ideals into flesh is marred by human weakness.'[76]

Ultimately, however, both Penguin and the British publishers of *God Is an Englishman* were vindicated. Published twelve months apart, the two books sold modestly and were given some rough treatment by critics. Phillip Adams – who might have had an axe to grind after Horne fired him as *The Bulletin*'s theatre reviewer – called *God Is an Englishman* 'the verbal counterpart of Yorkshire pud': 'Those of us who have been *Bulletin* contributors were under the impression that God is Donald Horne,' he jibed.[77] Two different readers called *The Next Australia* a 'yawn'.[78] 'I cannot believe that any French or English intellectual would display the same concern with his country's soul,' wrote John Douglas Pringle.[79] In *Nation Review*, Trevor Kennedy summed up this general feeling with the blunt assertion that Horne had simply 'run out of ideas'. After five books in as many years, he thought, 'one tends to come up with the exhausted feeling that it has all been said before.'[80]

◆ ◆ ◆

In late 1971, Horne began to experience serious problems with his right eye. Merely glancing at something as benign as a streetlight would cause the light's rays to bend and 'shatter into fragments'. The problem, he soon found out, was cataracts: the lens in his eye had hardened and clouded over. He would need major surgery to repair it. At the time, Horne recalled, cataract extraction operations were considered to be 'ceremonies of fear and care'. There was a very real chance of failure. Potential complications were myriad. He would not, for example, be able to cough during the surgery – a difficult ask for someone who had smoked up to sixty cigarettes a day for over thirty years. On doctor's advice, he was told he would need to quit smoking altogether.

Horne went cold turkey. On the Thursday before the operation, he smoked his full allotment. Over the weekend, spent on a
family driving trip to the country, he got himself down to ten. On
the Monday, the day before the surgery, he smoked two. On the
Tuesday – due at the hospital at three o'clock – he enjoyed his last
cigarette. This heroic five-day effort, though, took its toll. Horne's
operation was a terrifying failure: first, his eye haemorrhaged while
the doctors were making anaesthetic injections into his head, and
the procedure was abandoned. Then, while awake in recovery, the
strain on his distressed lungs had triggered a coughing fit – later
diagnosed as a laryngeal spasm – that closed his windpipe and
began to suffocate him. Had he had this spasm during the surgery,
doctors told him, he would have been permanently blinded. Giving
up smoking – his well-intended attempt at physical reform – had
nearly resulted in disaster. John Anderson's law of unintended consequences remained as relevant as ever. Once again, he was left to
reflect on its meaning.[81]

Horne's life, to date, had been full of obvious turning points: the
horrific army injury in 1943; the decision to choose journalism over
the public service in 1945; the expatriation to England in 1949 and the
sudden repatriation five years later; Frank Packer's gift of *Observer*;
meeting Myfanwy a few months later; the sudden fame brought about
by *The Lucky Country*; the slower and more inward transformation
brought about by the writing of his memoir in the mid-to-late 1960s.
But by his own admission, and as far as such a thing is possible, he was
altered by his experience in early 1972. If he had a road to Damascus
moment – a clear and obvious point at which his outlook shifted –
it was here, in the two months he spent listening to classical music
while he recovered from surgery. 'I had a kind of feeling it was time
I changed myself,' he told an interviewer four years later.[82] Both the
brush with death and the physical strain of quitting smoking seemed
to signal that it was time for a clean break.[83]

This desire for change, of course, was tied up with Horne's gradual
realisation that the political and cultural upheavals of the 1960s had
not only changed the terms of the debate but also his whole worldview. In the latter part of that decade, the liberalisation of censorship

and immigration laws, the emergence of radical social movements and a vibrant youth culture, the increasingly vocal demands for racial and sexual equality, and the rise of a more sophisticated Australian artistic and cultural scene had all seemed to indicate a break with the cultural pessimism and political inertia of the late Menzies years. Real social change was possible.

By 1972, even seemingly unshakable Australian commitments to racial homogeneity and Cold War ideology appeared to be not long for this world. Between July and August 1971, President Richard Nixon had presided over twin global shocks: first, announcing the United States' intention to establish diplomatic ties with communist China, ending over two decades of diplomatic isolation and permanently altering the dynamic of the Cold War; then, a month later, taking the United States off the gold standard, bringing a similarly abrupt end to the Bretton Woods system of fixed exchange rates that had been in place since the end of World War II. The scramble to get out of Vietnam, the Sino–Soviet split, the meteoric rise of Japan as an economic force, the further economic integration of Europe and the continued commitment of 'Third World' nations to non-alignment – all portended a more complex, multipolar world.

Given that nearly every review of Horne's work in the late 1960s had commented on his nascent political idealism in the face of these events, it is surprising that it was not until late 1971, after reading a long review of *The Next Australia*, that he came to accept more confidently the party-political implications of his own intellectual metamorphosis. In the December 1971 edition of *Meanjin*, Jim Davidson had argued that Horne possessed all the characteristics of a nineteenth-century romantic nationalist. In Davidson's view, Horne showed a 'faith in the Australian people that verges on the mystic'. His problem, thought Davidson, was that he still carried too much intellectual baggage: he was a 'soured conservative', convinced of the 'intellectual bankruptcy' of the Liberal Party but unable to offer anything more than 'tepid support' for its opponents. But on the evidence of *The Next Australia*, he thought, this need no longer remain the case: Horne and Labor were now offering similar programs, and theirs were the 'healthier, more progressive visions'.[84]

The title of Davidson's piece, 'Notes on a Nationalist', was an explicit reference to the famous essay by another plain-spoken, romantic progressive, George Orwell – and he was not the only critic to make such a connection. The English reviewers of *God Is an Englishman*, in particular, had pegged this famous dissident of the English left as one of Horne's key critical predecessors. Like Orwell, noted Barry Carman on the BBC, Horne wanted the upper English to 'come and join the human race'.[85] Also like Orwell, thought Iain Sainsbury in *The Daily Telegraph*, was Horne's taxonomy of the virtues of average Britons, which he listed as 'decency, sincerity, tolerance and reasonableness'. 'Decent,' he added, 'is a word that recurs in Orwell's writing without ever being identified.'[86] Horne's unwavering belief in the basic goodness of the people, too, proposed the English critic John Mander, was 'essentially Orwellian'.[87]

The comparison with the famous English socialist, though flattering, was not necessarily one that Horne would have always welcomed. On the surface, their political journeys were quite different. Orwell was an Eton-educated British radical, and though he came to see the folly of Stalinist communism earlier than most, he had been a committed reformer and democratic socialist for the majority of his adult life. Horne, on the other hand, was born a generation later in the far antipodes, and cut his political teeth on liberal conservatism and Cold War anti-communism. In fact, Horne's totalising Cold War suspicion of liberal progressives might have been the only reason for his relative lack of interest in Orwell throughout the 1950s, considering the undeniable similarities of some of their arguments and stylistic approaches. After all, as Horne had himself argued in *The Lucky Country*, Australia needed its own Orwell, someone who could use their own experience to come up with sociological concepts that were both organically Australian and more usefully descriptive of how Australian society actually operated.

The widespread critical comparison of Horne and Orwell in the late 1960s was one of the most telling indications of the intellectual transformation that Horne had undergone since the beginning of that decade. By 1972, he had become tired of being called a right-winger by virtue of his connection with Frank Packer. If it truly was going to be a turning point in his life, then the time would soon be right for a change of employment. For several months following his operation, he and Myfanwy thought long and hard about this impending career change. At one point they even systematically compiled a list of their options in order to get a clearer picture of their situation. What they wanted, they wrote, was security, 'reasonable affluence' and for Donald to be creative in a way of his own choosing. His preferences were either a university or a government department: ideally, somewhere that needed Donald 'as the head of an Aust studies org, journalism course or whatever'. They might need to invite some people round for dinner, they speculated. 'N.B. THINK BIG.'[88]

In November, Horne sent Packer his letter of resignation. He was exhausted, he wrote, having returned to work too soon after his eye operation. He had also not had a raise in six years, which meant, after inflation, 'a big proportionate drop in purchasing power'. But most importantly, he had a suspicion that there was nothing more he could offer *The Bulletin*, 'other than changes of a kind you wouldn't want.' Their political differences, long suppressed and avoided by Horne, had now become an insurmountable obstacle. Packer accepted this letter with uncharacteristic grace, describing their long working relationship as a 'happy association'. Horne responded in kind. By January 1973, he would be looking for a job.

Around this time, he was asked by Max Harris at *Australian Book Review* to name the most influential books of the 1960s. Horne wrote reflectively:

> I've used books this decade as a kind of demolition job against all those certainties that I got from other books in the two decades that preceded it and out of the resulting rubbish I suppose I have been trying to construct some beliefs that, however inadequate, are at least something that could begin to seem real.[89]

Much of this reading had been historical. In 1963, Horne helped organise an AACF seminar on 'New Interpretations of Australian History', attended by a range of professional historians, including Manning Clark, Allan Martin, Robin Gollan, Russel Ward and

Miriam Dixson.[90] In *The Lucky Country*, too, he had praised the 'diffuse re-examination' of received Australian wisdom that had been going on in historical writing since the beginning of the '60s.[91] But it was not until the mid-to-late 1960s that Horne had developed a serious interest in writing history itself, first with *The Education of Young Donald* and then in the reading and research for a one-volume social history of Australia that he called *The Australian People: Biography of a Nation*.

For Horne, what made the writing and publication of this book so significant was not merely its role in his intellectual evolution, but rather its decisive impact on his professional life. *The Australian People* was well received by professional historians, many of whom had long been far to his left. Clark wrote approvingly of it in *The Australian*, while Russel Ward, of all people, called it 'the best social history of Australia we have'.[92] Ian Turner thought its combination of hope and cynicism to be both fascinating and perceptive. Horne, wrote Turner, had 'graduated with honours'.[93] Several academic historians, too, including Frank Crowley, who was the dean of the Faculty of Arts at the University of New South Wales, and Geoffrey Blainey, then a Professor of History at the University of Melbourne, had attended the book's launch at an old house in The Rocks.[94] Horne certainly had the contacts, if not the necessary credentials, for a career in academia.

It was appropriate, then, that in his latest hour of professional need, it was Doug McCallum and Owen Harries – both members of the School of Political Science at the University of New South Wales – who eventually came to his rescue. On the day his departure from *The Bulletin* was announced in the press, Harries rang to say that Crowley had put together some money for a research fellowship. At a time of increasing budgets, the dean was looking to expand the School of Political Science and he wanted people who could teach politics from an Australian perspective. If Horne was interested, the job was his. Soon after, the deal was done (at a French restaurant on Elizabeth Street). In January 1973, Horne – a career journalist who did not have an undergraduate degree – would become an academic.[95]

IO.

SHOCK THERAPY

The Blacktown Civic Centre is not a particularly memorable building. At its entrance, a wide concrete staircase opens out onto a featureless square of grass, as if it were a suburban school. From one angle, it looks like an oversized demountable classroom, dropped unceremoniously on top of an older, smaller structure. Its auditorium, too, has the feel of an assembly hall, all bricks, floorboards and open space, with a curtained stage at one end. Its style is one of outer suburban modesty. Yet it was here in November 1972, on what was then the fringes of western Sydney, that the federal Labor leader Gough Whitlam produced one of the most memorable election campaign launches in Australian history.

At the lectern, like a headmaster addressing his pupils, Whitlam reeled off the items of an ambitious reform agenda: universal pre-school education, universal health insurance, the abolition of university fees, a 25 per cent increase to the pension, big investments in cities and urban renewal. He went on for over half an hour, working his way through 'The Program' one item at a time, as if reading out a grocery list: Aboriginal land rights, self-government for Papua New Guinea, a ban on 'racially selected' sporting teams, the end of conscription.[1]

On the face of it, there was nothing unusual about a politician expounding his policy priorities in front of a crowd of enthusiastic supporters. It had been the basic template for political campaigning for as long as anyone could remember. But for Donald Horne – who witnessed at least one Whitlam rally himself, on election eve in the Sydney CBD – the mood surrounding the Labor leader was different. The excitement seemed genuine. And Horne's impression, at least, was that it was not any particular policy that was generating the euphoria around Whitlam: it was the sense of expectation. People were packing out the town halls for Labor because they believed that new things were about to happen. Change was in the air, and they wanted to be a part of it.[2]

Before then, Horne had only ever welcomed one Labor election victory: that of John Curtin's in 1943, when the 'dismembered' wartime conservative parties had appeared to Horne to be a bunch of 'incompetent fools'.[3] Now, nearly thirty years later, he sensed that Whitlam had managed to produce a similar feeling in the Australian electorate. Labor's campaign slogan, 'It's Time', perfectly captured what he thought was a growing contempt for the political status quo. Similarly, Labor's television commercial, which featured a slew of Australian artists, actors and musicians organised into a beaming gospel choir, gave the impression that the cork was about to come out of the bottle. In his stump speeches, Whitlam painted the 1972 election as a choice between the past and the future, between a party that was permanently handicapped by old ways of thinking and another that looked optimistically towards a new kind of society and a 'new vision of what we can achieve'.[4] The Australian people's decision on this matter, he declared, would decide no less than the fate and future of the nation.

Horne agreed. By 2 December, when he reclined in front of his television to watch the election of the first federal Labor government in twenty-three years, he found himself almost completely in sympathy with the man on the screen. In the next issue of *The Bulletin*, prepared before election night in expectation of a Labor victory, he had already declared the 'end of the age of Menzies'. At long last, he thought, Australia had reached one of those moments when the people expected the nation to 'become different'. Despite the stop-start reform-mindedness of the previous half decade, he declared, the post-Menzies Liberals had remained hamstrung by the 'troglodyte elements' of their party. They had repeatedly fallen back on the hopes and fears of a bygone age, 'the great truths with which Sir Robert battled against Chif and the Doc.' And the longer they had gone on doing this, he believed, the easier it had been to see Labor as 'the party of the future'.[5]

What appealed to Horne about Whitlam was his self-conscious sense of contemporaneity, his ability to draw attention to newer and more relevant political issues. The Labor leader had high hopes for what Australia could be, and he was willing, if necessary, to impose this vision upon the nation.[6] He was, in Horne's view, a 'shock therapist', waking up a sleepy nation and reorienting it towards the future.[7] There was a deliberate urgency about his government, designed to suggest that after two long decades of conservative stasis, there was simply no more time to waste. Just three days after his election victory, for example, Whitlam formed a two-man Cabinet with his deputy leader, Lance Barnard, to begin enacting parts of Labor's Program before the official swearing in of the full ministry. Over the next two weeks, the two men established diplomatic relations with China, announced the full withdrawal of any remaining Australians in Vietnam, abolished the imperial honours system and ratified international conventions on human rights and nuclear arms. 'I think God has sent him to us,' wrote Horne, to create 'a disbelief and a confusion so great that only good can come of it.'[8]

Horne had not previously been one to tie his mast to a political party, but by early 1973, mere months after Labor's victory, he became – by his own admission – an 'unqualified supporter' of the Whitlam government.[9] According to Frank Moorhouse, it was a dramatic change that surprised everyone, especially those who knew Horne before *The Lucky Country*.[10] Back then, he had been one of the Labor Party's true nonbelievers. He and most of the other writers who had contributed to Peter Coleman's *Australian Civilization* symposium in 1962, for example, had expected to find their great modernising leader somewhere within the ranks of the Liberal Party.[11] To have suggested at that moment that their political opponents could produce a leader in touch with the problems of Australian modernity would have been, for Horne at least, laughable. When Anthony Crosland suggested as much to Horne and his friends at a dinner party in 1963, he had been roundly ridiculed.[12] Labor's 1972 policy agenda, too, would have been anathema to the libertarian Horne of the 1940s and '50s, the acid-tongued enemy of the postwar 'planners'. It was apt, then, that Whitlam's choice of personal adviser on economic policy and the arts was none other than H.C. 'Nugget' Coombs, the former director-general of the Department of Post-War Reconstruction and one of the chief objects of Horne's disdain as young journalist.[13]

Horne's embrace of Whitlam might have been surprising to some, but this was no sudden epiphany. In fact, in 1967, the year Whitlam was elected to the Labor leadership, Horne had reached out to him, sending several copies of his new *Bulletin*. 'Well done,' wrote Whitlam in a courteous response. 'Never again must so many years elapse before we meet again.'[14] In the magazine that year, Horne speculated hopefully that the only way that Harold Holt's incumbent Liberals might effectively counter the new Labor leader would be to 'become a better government'.[15] In 1968, he praised Whitlam again for bringing Labor 'closer to the aspirations of the Australian people' and commended his ability to talk intelligently about foreign policy.[16] And at the 1969 election, he thought Whitlam had made Gorton seem like 'an old-fashioned Labor man'.[17]

What was truly surprising was that it had taken Horne so long to rally in support of Whitlam's Labor Party. The two men were contemporaries, having both been students at Sydney University in the late 1930s, soldiers during World War II, Cold War opponents of communist influence in the Labor Party and unapologetic advocates of a new Australian cultural sophistication.[18] And unlike some other members of the *Quadrant* circle, Horne had never conceived of Whitlam as a kind of liberal antichrist, a destroyer of moral standards and a meddling socialist. He was, rather, almost a model of the kind of politician Horne had called for in 'A Plimsoll Line for Intellectuals' in 1959: sophisticated, reform-minded, anti-communist and Asia-focused.

To his own surprise, Horne displayed unusual levels of defensiveness when it came to Whitlam. By his new calculus, it seemed, it was more useful to praise the government than it was to criticise it. Frank Moorhouse recalled a lunch with Horne in the early '70s during which they both agreed they felt oddly 'protective' of Whitlam and his political project. This, they decided, was 'uncharacteristic' for both of them: their default attitude to politics and political activity had traditionally been a rigorous scepticism. Politicians were clowns and not to be trusted. Not long after, then, they were relieved to hear reports of government interference with the ABC. Finally, they thought, they would have an opportunity to express their disapproval of Whitlam. They would be free of their uncharacteristic roles as protectors. Normality would be restored. Unfortunately, however, the reports proved false. The government had acted appropriately. The opportunity to criticise was gone.[19]

Of course, Horne was not the only Australian intellectual to see the coming of Whitlam as a fundamental point of departure for the nation. Writing in *Meanjin* in September 1973, Manning Clark described the long period of postwar conservative government as 'the years of unleavened bread'. In his view, the Menzies era had been an age of 'hollow men', whose anglophilia and philistinism had stunted the growth of a more intellectually stimulating and spiritually enriching national culture. But Whitlam, declared Clark, was 'a teacher who had a chance to lead us out of darkness and into light'. Similarly, after an initial period of scepticism, the press gallery journalist Mungo MacCallum confessed to being won over to 'lifelong Whitlamolatry'. Russel Ward, too, welcomed Whitlam's victory as 'the end of the ice age' and a long-awaited rejection of 'the most fossilised and discreditable aspects of Australian society'. And in service of his claim that Whitlam was tapping into the innate national feeling of ordinary Australians, Ward – a left-wing intellectual whose work had been pilloried in the *Observer* a decade earlier – even drew on examples from Donald Horne's most recent book, *The Australian People*. It was the surest sign yet that Horne's worldview had undergone some radical revisions.[20]

◆ ◆ ◆

When Horne joined the School of Political Science at the University of New South Wales (UNSW) in January 1973, more than a few eyebrows were raised among his future colleagues. It is not hard to see why. The former editor of Frank Packer's *Bulletin* had arrived in his new office in the Morven Brown Building with no degree, no teaching experience and no record of academic publication. He had written several popular books (a source of eternal suspicion) and was a minor celebrity among journalists and literary types. His résumé was uneven, and included stints at a lowbrow magazine and an advertising agency. He had no formal training in the field of political science and no real command of existing scholarly debates. He had never even used a footnote.

Horne had his own reservations. He was baffled by the seeming lack of sociability in the department. For a writer accustomed to the vibrancy and confrontations of the newsroom, academic common areas seemed eerily quiet. There appeared to be few opportunities for casual conversation and almost none for discussion. Conscious of his non-existent academic credentials, too, he suspected many of his new colleagues viewed him with serious scepticism. Prior to his arrival, Vietnam had been a source of deep division in the department, and many of Horne's friends in the department – such as Doug McCallum, Owen Harries and George Shipp – were supporters of Australian involvement. Few department members were fond of Gough Whitlam, either, while others simply chafed at what they saw as Horne's special treatment. For the most part, many of his colleagues were no more than names on a door. 'There was never any comparing of notes on teaching,' he recalled.[21]

His timing, though, was impeccable. The 1970s were an excellent decade to be in the market for an academic job. Since the end of World War II, the university sector had been in a process of almost continuous expansion, spurred on by favourable government policies and an influx of upwardly mobile baby boomers. When the Whitlam government abolished university fees in 1974, hundreds of thousands of new undergraduates poured into tertiary institutions without incurring a single cent of student debt. As a result, participation in higher education increased by 25 per cent during the Whitlam years alone. In these boom years for the sector, the demand for academic teachers and researchers briefly exceeded the supply. If ever there was a time for a degreeless former magazine editor to find a job at a university, this was it.[22]

Horne was an obvious beneficiary of these changes. A sudden increase in enrolments meant a sudden increase in the amount of first-year classes to be taught, and the school's new research fellow was on hand to provide relief. He gave his first university lecture – on the 'new nationalism' – to an Australian history class in 1973. Over the next two years, he contributed fourteen more lectures to a first-year Australian politics course run by another new recruit, John Paul (a deeply conservative man who delivered his lectures in full academic gown). Horne structured these sermons around topics that had animated him at *The Bulletin*: foreign affairs, the national image, new social movements, the 'It's Time' campaign. In these fits and starts, he proved himself to be a useful lecturer.[23]

Academia was a significant change of pace. Barring his stint as an advertising executive in the mid-1960s – during which he had edited *Quadrant* in his spare time – it was Horne's first job outside journalism in more than twenty years. There was no weekly deadline, no staff to manage and no mistrustful boss looming overhead threatening to put an immediate end to it all. Within his vaguely defined field of 'the development of Australian political thought', too, he was free to read and write whatever he wanted. Such freedom had been unimaginable even a few months prior.[24]

Initially, the price of this intellectual freedom was a substantial pay cut: Horne's research position at UNSW was worth less than half his *Bulletin* salary.[25] Ever practical, he contrived to supplement his radically reduced income with freelance work. Through a friend of Myfanwy's, he found a job fact-checking subbed copy for the new revised edition of the *Australian Encyclopedia*. Via his contacts in Sydney media and journalism, he published irregular commentary in *Nation Review* and *The Bulletin*. And after a chance meeting with the editor of *Newsweek International*, Bob Christopher, in mid-1972, he was contracted to write a monthly column.[26] It was not until late 1974 – two years into his academic job – that Donald received a promotion – and a raise. When the dean of the Faculty of Arts, Frank Crowley, decided that the School of Political Science needed a new upper-level course on 'Politics and the Media', he created a senior lecturer position at twice Horne's research associate salary and hired him for it.[27]

Horne's *Newsweek* and *Nation Review* columns traversed familiar territory: foreign policy independence, political leadership, the 'new nationalism' and the effects of cultural change and 'suburban radicalism'. But all of this public commentary was now coloured by a sense of enthusiasm for the future direction of the country. In an article titled 'A Return to Idealism', he wondered whether he was living though a 'fundamental shift in what Australian politics appears to be about'. Suddenly, new issues, including regional development, the environment, prison reform, country arts centres and pre-school education, were being publicly discussed. Almost overnight, he thought, Australia found itself 'back in the game of political progress'. In the arts, Patrick White's Nobel Prize, the opening of the Sydney Opera House and the government's purchase of Jackson Pollock's *Blue Poles* all pointed towards an increasing cultural sophistication. Even the intellectuals no longer felt like 'outcasts in their own nation'. Perhaps Whitlam's greatest contribution to Australian political debate, he speculated, would be this fostering of an 'intelligent expression of an Australian sense of hope'.[28]

This is a decidedly rosy view of the Whitlam government, which – despite its considerable legislative achievements – was also beset with crisis and scandal for much of its three years in office. From the moment of its election, the Opposition parties had used their control of the Senate to block aspects of the government's agenda. In February 1973, Labor's attorney-general, Lionel Murphy, had led a controversial police raid on the offices of the Australian intelligence services, which he suspected might be hiding information from the government. From December 1974, a media circus surrounded the deputy prime minister and treasurer, Jim Cairns, who had appointed a personal acquaintance as his principal private secretary, a matter made more salacious by her being female. Perhaps most controversially, in 1975 the government was embroiled in a scandal over its pursuit of a $4-billion private loan from a Pakistani businessman, an affair that saw Cairns removed from the Cabinet.

Certainly, there were circumstances beyond Labor's control. In October 1973, an OPEC oil embargo initiated a threefold increase in the price of oil and triggered a global economic recession. By December 1973, Australian inflation was running at 13.2 per cent, to which belligerent trade unions responded with increasing wage demands, further compounding the problem. In this 'stagflationary' economic environment – high inflation and high unemployment – the Keynesian economic faith of the postwar years was increasingly called into question. When Bill Hayden replaced Cairns as treasurer in 1975, for example, he quietly shelved the government's long-held commitment to full employment. Around the same time, Horne predicted that 'economic nationalism won't survive the new year.'[29]

Horne was not ignorant of the government's shortcomings. After the 1974 election, he wrote that Labor would certainly need to be seen to be doing something about inflation or risk political annihilation. But in his mind, these issues were ephemeral, mere turbulence. Whitlam had instituted a more profound shock, one that would outlast the crisis of stagflation: he had moved the boundaries of Australian political debate so far that there would be no turning back. He had changed Australian politics 'decisively'. His vision was one of 'national independence, contemporaneity and self-confidence'. If the Liberals were to regain office, it would be in Whitlam's Australia.[30]

◆ ◆ ◆

On 11 November 1975, just under three years after he had attended Whitlam's final election rally in the Sydney CBD, Horne sat down to a sociable lunch with a few colleagues at the UNSW staff club. Not long into the meal, a distressed waitress approached their table. She said she had just heard on the radio that the prime minister had been sacked. 'Nonsense,' replied Horne. That was impossible – she must have misheard. It was against the principles of responsible government. The prime minister had the confidence of the House. He sent her away, seemingly reassured. Five minutes later, though, she was back. They were still saying it, she said. The governor-general had sacked the prime minister.[31]

In no other domestic political crisis have Australians been as convulsed with so sudden a sense of shock and disbelief as they were in the few hours following the Whitlam government's dismissal on Remembrance Day 1975. It was, by most accounts, the most dramatic event in the history of Australian politics. For a moment on that

Tuesday afternoon, ordinary life ground to a halt. People sat huddled around radios and televisions, waiting for updates from Canberra. A spontaneous rally formed on the front steps of Parliament House. As word spread, the crowd swelled as locals rushed down in a fever of excitement and horror. Across the country, rumour and misinformation swirled. Phones rang, jaws dropped.[32]

In his now famous impromptu speech to the crowd on the steps of Parliament House, Gough Whitlam predicted that Malcolm Fraser, the leader of the Opposition, would 'go down in Australian history' as a villain, as 'Kerr's cur'.[33] Most of the prime minister's supporters shared this feeling of momentousness. Less than two weeks after the event, *The Bulletin* magazine ran a 'where were you when you heard the news' article. Manning Clark, informed by a secretary in the ANU history department, reported a 'sinking feeling in the stomach'. The former Liberal prime minister John Gorton – an outspoken critic of Fraser's political tactics – described feeling 'angry and shattered'. Others testified to a long moment of disbelief and confusion as the news sank in, the traditional two minutes' silence of Armistice Day that year coming after rather than before lunch.[34]

For Horne, listening to the radio in the UNSW staff club, the news had the 'shock of an assassination'.[35] Of all the possible outcomes to the crisis, he thought, none could have been more outrageous. Repulsed by Kerr's actions, and overcome by a strong desire to contribute to the Labor response, he dove headlong into political activism. Before 1975, he recalled, the only protests he had ever signed were open letters complaining about the treatment of Soviet intellectuals. Now, in the eye of Australia's constitutional firestorm, he put his name to 'anything and everything'.[36] He sent Kerr an angry telegram. He did interviews on the BBC, on ABC's *PM* and the youth radio broadcaster 2JJ. He wrote impassioned articles in *The Bulletin* and *The Catholic Weekly*. He taunted the crowd at a meeting of the Killara branch of the Liberal Party. He contributed to a letter of protest from a group of political scientists. He even appeared on a television commercial alongside Patrick White.[37]

Amid the heightened emotions of those initial weeks, Horne was animated by an intense partisanship. He sent additional telegrams to

Whitlam and the federal president of the Labor Party, Bob Hawke, offering his support. He joined the (ostensibly non-party-aligned) action group, Citizens for Democracy (CFD), which had been set up in the wake of the dismissal to circulate anti-Kerr petitions and raise money for newspaper advertisements. On 17 November, he even spoke at a rally organised by the Labor Party in Sydney's Hyde Park. Of the seven speakers to address the crowd, Horne was the only one who was not a sitting Labor MP. Opposition complaints about the government's economic mismanagement were bogus, he told the 8,000 people assembled there. Despite every country in the Western world going through some kind of economic crisis, the Liberals had used Labor's economic record as a justification for bringing down the government.[38]

Donald Horne speaking at an anti-Kerr rally in November 1975

The intensity of Horne's outrage was amplified by another sudden and distressing problem with his vision. Sitting in a restaurant with a colleague in late November 1975, he began to experience 'fireworks' in his right eye. At an emergency appointment with an ophthalmologist, he was diagnosed with a retinal detachment and booked in for surgery the following day. It was his second major optical issue in three years. Unlike in 1972, however, the operation went off without a hitch. The only side effect – some small damage to the macula – meant that for the rest of his life his right eye became 'like a television set that jumps out of control'.[39]

As part of his recovery, he was required to be completely blind-folded for two weeks – just as the post-dismissal election campaign was heating up. From his hospital bed, sitting in a 'tunnel of darkness', he relied upon the radio and visits from friends for the latest updates.[40] The news was not promising: opinion polls pointed to a decisive Labor defeat. He had Myfanwy read out newspaper articles, letters and protest advertisements. He received a personal letter from Whitlam, wishing him a speedy recovery.[41] He dictated a message to be read out at a rally at Paddington Town Hall, he considered urgent changes to the manuscript of a book he had been working on all year and made plans to write a new book about the event, should Labor lose the election.[42] Not that that was to be expected – opinion polls were not the gospel truth, and the energy at Labor rallies was elec-trifying. In the end, however, this energy did not translate into votes. On 13 December, the day after Horne was discharged from hospital, Whitlam led Labor to a historic election defeat.

In *Death of the Lucky Country*, the short polemic Horne pro-duced in the three weeks between mid-December 1975 and early January 1976, he made his case against the usurpers. On one level, he argued, the events were an assault on democratic norms. A legiti-mately elected government had been prematurely ousted, deliberately and deceptively, via constitutional arcanum. In their cynical grab for power, the conservatives, the governor-general and their enablers in the media had undermined faith in the democratic system, perhaps fatally. By getting involved in Fraser and Whitlam's stand-off in the Senate, Kerr had gone well beyond his largely ceremonial remit. As Horne argued repeatedly, Kerr's carefully planned actions were no less than a 'constitutional coup d'état': an illegal seizure of power by a minority force acting in the name of law and order.[43] In this sense, it mattered little which party was on the receiving end of Kerr's inter-vention; the intervention was wrong. Only the people should have the power to remove a government. Kerr's actions were undemo-cratic and unjust, and Australians should be able to recognise them as such.[44]

On another level, though, it did matter which party had been wronged. For years, Horne had waited for a political leader with a confident and optimistic vision of Australia's future, someone willing and able to raise the standards by which Australians judged themselves. Even more eagerly had he awaited someone willing to shake off the habits of deference to Britain, to launch a full-scale assault on Australian derivativeness, colonial-mindedness and cultural cringe. And then along came Whitlam, infuriating conservatives with his abolition of royal styles and titles, his pursuit of a new national anthem and his overall spirit of national independence and self-respect, an attitude that informed everything from his foreign affairs posture to his arts policy. A revolt against Whitlam, thought Horne, was a revolt against the same modernising impulses he had himself been promoting since he wrote *The Lucky Country* in 1964. That book, he now claimed, may even have provided 'a kind of John the Baptist role for "Whitlamism".'[45]

It was this second, symbolic interpretation of events, more so than complicated disagreements over constitutional interpretation, that produced such a visceral response in Horne. This was not any old government Kerr had thrown out of office: it was one that had directly challenged the Menzies-era idea that Australia was small, loyal and 'didn't do too much thinking for itself'. It was a government that encouraged innovation, a 'new national consciousness' and 'an Australian sense of excellence'.[46] In this respect, it mattered immensely that it was Whitlam who was on the receiving end of the dismissal. Horne's long-awaited political visionary had been cut down by a man who 'dressed like somebody from the members stand'.[47] As he had argued in his message to the Paddington Town Hall rally: 'To endorse [Kerr's] action on December 13 will return us not only to the days of the colonial past, but also to the days of the cultural cringe.'[48]

Like many Australians who had spent time in Britain, Horne remained deeply sensitive to expectations of colonial obsequiousness. In his English village in the early 1950s, it had been a truth universally acknowledged that Australians were second-rate. The social hierarchy was widely believed to be immutable, and to question it was considered ratbaggery, a crude affront to good taste. Likewise, Australian governments were expected to keep their heads down, to narrow their vision of what was possible and pay tribute to their great and powerful friends. This was the worldview, shared by many Australians, that had so demoralised Horne throughout the Menzies years. In his view, Whitlam – with his insistence upon Australian independence, assertiveness and excellence – had offended these colonial sensibilities. That was what had made his government so refreshing; it was also what had made the manner of its removal so galling.[49]

This personal history may go some way towards explaining Horne's conferral of outright martyrdom upon the ousted Labor leader. In *Death of the Lucky Country*'s titular final chapter, intended to sum up his argument, he rather brazenly suggested that Whitlam was a prime minister 'born to be king'. He was bold like a king, he was boastful like a king, he sacked ministers like a king. He had visions like a king and he indulged his pleasures like a king. There was a 'gallantry' and a 'heroic aspect' in the three-year struggle of his government, pushing the Labor program forward, despite the cynicism and obstruction of his opponents. *Blue Poles* – the Jackson Pollock painting Whitlam had controversially approved for acquisition by the National Gallery in September 1973 – was a 'princely purchase'. And then, like a king, he was assassinated, twice: first by Kerr, and again by an 'illegitimately called election'. He was 'a double martyr, but still living among us'.[50]

Death of the Lucky Country sold handsomely and was reviewed more widely than anything Horne had written since *The Lucky Country*.[51] The 'Whitlam as king' passage, in particular, drew comment from nearly every reviewer. Here was the most overwhelming evidence yet of Horne's new role as a mouthpiece for the Labor Party, thought his critics. Anointing Whitlam as a king was an 'odd compliment for a republican to pay', wrote one. 'It suggests to the reader that Donald Horne … may be at heart a monarchist or at least a royalist.'[52] Another called Horne and Manning Clark the 'prophets of hysteria' and the 'professors of shame'.[53] Others feigned alarm at the intensity of Horne's partisanship, noting the metaphorical implications of the very literal blindness that had handicapped him for most of the election campaign. Overwhelmed by rage, they said, he had surrendered his judgement.[54]

For all Horne's previous enthusiasm for Whitlam, it was this intense period of political activism – beginning in late 1975 and extending to the end of the '70s – that earned him a reputation as a Labor apologist which he would find difficult to shake in later years. As he lamented to an interviewer two decades later, the whole episode 'wrecked' his public persona.[55] By defending Whitlam, went the criticism, Horne and the other intellectuals and cultural elites were looking after their own. In April 1976, for example, Donald and Myfanwy Horne and Gough and Margaret Whitlam were among the many prominent guests at an exclusive 'People for Whitlam' event at the North Shore home of the architect Harry Seidler.[56] Poking fun at this phenomenon in a public lecture in 1976, James McAuley – a fierce Whitlam sceptic – conjured an image of the Labor leader returning from the clouds on a chariot 'pulled by four diversely formed heraldic beasts'. The names of the four horsemen, he joked, were 'hidden in eternity', but here on earth they were known as Donald Horne, Germaine Greer, Manning Clark and Patrick White.[57]

McAuley's lecture, titled 'Culture and Counter-Culture', was a quasi-autobiographical essay on the eternal virtues of history and tradition in politics. It was, in effect, an argument against the new middle-class radicalism of which Horne had become a figurehead. The majority of the political mainstream, McAuley contended, accepted piecemeal change, hoped for something better and possessed no expectation of heaven on earth. They knew instinctively that the world was 'exceedingly complex and opaque' and largely resistant to attempts to 'predict and control its future developments'. By contrast, he thought, the new radicals – like the communists of old – had 'apocalyptic' worldviews, so impatient for change that they yearned for catastrophe, fantasising about nuclear war, the destruction of the ozone layer and liberation through 'extra-parliamentary mob action'. It was, he admitted, 'absurd and paranoid' to ascribe any major influence to the Communist Party of Australia (CPA) at this point in history. But he nevertheless warned that Australians needed to be vigilant about the 'organisers and manipulators' that moved among the new counterculture. In his view, the probable infiltration of these social movements by the remnants of the CPA was one of the key risks of an increasingly permissive society.[58]

Even if McAuley had not invoked the image of Whitlam on the chariot, it would still have been possible to read his lecture as an

In this 1976 George Molnar cartoon,
Gough Whitlam rides a chariot pulled by Donald Horne,
Germaine Greer, Manning Clark and Patrick White

oblique critique of the former prime minister's intellectual boosters. Horne, who was in the audience the day of the lecture, could have harboured no doubt about what was being implied: that fellow travelling liberal intellectuals who saw the new social movements as a force for progress – Horne, Clark, White, Greer – were the unwitting dupes of the 'organisers and manipulators' intent on the destruction of the system. For McAuley, what was required in the face of such a threat was a radical defence of the status quo. In the circumstances, it is hard to interpret his lecture as anything other than a clear endorsement of Kerr and Fraser. In McAuley's view, their actions were entirely justified.[59]

Horne, understandably, disagreed. A few months later, in the same issue of *Quadrant* that reproduced the text of McAuley's lecture, Horne penned his own oblique quasi-autobiographical essay, an account of the many different ways that the fall of the Roman Empire had been interpreted over the course of his life. It was a curious piece of writing, and he waited until the final paragraph to make his point. In the '60s and '70s, he argued, Rome was once again being used by opponents of change as a sloppy metaphor for the way that a society can crumble under the weight of its own decadence. But those who sought to use the example of Rome to condemn the 'permissiveness' and 'degeneracy' of recent years, he observed, were always conspicuously silent on the 'brutishness' and 'despotism' of those same Romans. 'It is as if R movies are more degenerate than throwing Christians to the lions,' he quipped. Horne's implication was as obvious as McAuley's: the threat to Western civilisation in the 1970s was not a generation of hippies and student radicals; it was a yearning for political strongmen who sought to roll back hard-won democratic freedoms in the name of law and order. Those who were now predicting a retributive fall, he concluded, might be 'nostalgic for despotism's strength'.[60]

◆ ◆ ◆

Horne spent the next two years in a whirlwind of political activism. He spoke anywhere and everywhere: at political rallies; meetings of the NSW and Victorian Fabians; ANU, Monash, La Trobe and Newcastle universities; Adult Education Tasmania, the UNSW History Society, the Institute of Chemical Engineers Symposium, the United Theological College. He churned out articles for *Newsweek*, *The Age*, *The National Times* and *Reader's Digest*. Between August and November 1976, he wrote a series in *Nation Review* that included 'The Case Against the Senate', 'The Case For a Republic' and 'The Cult of November 11'. He wrote a satirical novel, *His Excellency's Pleasure*, in which Australians lived under a 'governor-generalate'. He coedited a book called *Change The Rules! Towards a Democratic Constitution*. He wrote another pamphlet, *Power From the People*, and he contributed a chapter to Geoffrey Dutton's 1977 edited collection, *Republican Australia?*[61]

Most of these endeavours fell under the banner of Citizens for Democracy.[62] After its initial burst of activity in those frantic early weeks, the organisation had withered on the vine until Horne and the novelist Frank Hardy contrived at a lunch at the New Hellas restaurant in mid-1976 to revive it. Their intention was to project a veneer of respectability onto the increasingly dispersed and disorganised anti-Kerr forces, which they complained were being depicted in the media as an unrepresentative fringe movement of professional stirrers and suspect types. Horne and Hardy believed that dissatisfaction with the events of 11 November was instead a mainstream political issue, something a large swathe of ordinary Australians would surely rally behind if given a suitable forum in which to do so. During the lunch, they decided they would stage a public meeting and put this idea to the test.[63]

On 20 September 1976, over 3,000 people crammed into the Sydney Town Hall for Horne and Hardy's protest meeting. According to some reports, another 1,500 waited outside. At the suggestion of Myfanwy, they had called the event 'Kerr and the Consequences'. Attendees were handed badges, car stickers and copies of a leaflet titled 'Where Do We Go From Here?' At the entrance, they were encouraged to sign a petition to the House of Representatives calling on John Kerr to resign. Throughout the proceedings, they listened to works by Albinoni, Bach and Vivaldi and joined in renditions of 'Waltzing Matilda' and 'Advance Australia Fair' (the latter sung with particular gusto as the words had been printed in the leaflet).

On the stage, beneath a huge banner of the Southern Cross – designed by the artist John Coburn and adorned with the words 'It's Time For A New Constitution' – were a diverse collection of Australian public figures: Horne, chair of proceedings, was joined by trade unionists Jack Mundey, Joan Evatt and Sarah Sheehan; Manning Clark; Indigenous lawyer and activist Pat O'Shane; filmmaker and cartoonist Bruce Petty; folk singer Alex Hood; actor John Gaden; federal Labor senator Jim McClelland; and emerging NSW Labor figures Bob Carr and Franca Arena. Patrick White, then holidaying in Greece, sent a short statement that was read aloud.[64]

In his own remarks, Horne argued that the Australian constitution was a 'weapon' that was being used against democracy. The 'reactionary lawyers,' he said, kept pointing out that Kerr's actions were expressly sanctioned by the constitution, as if it was a sacred and unchallengeable document designed to be interpreted literally. If that were so, he continued, all kinds of outrageous actions were authorised by the law: parliament could restrict the franchise, for example, or disqualify people from voting on racial grounds. The governor-general, as commander-in-chief of the Australian defence forces, could summon the army. None of these actions would likely attract majority support in Australia, he believed, yet all were within current constitutional constraints. Australia's founding document was 'monarchical'; it contained 'no democratic clauses'. It was, in short, thoroughly out of date.[65]

Horne was in line with most of the other speakers in all but one significant respect: the new constitution, he thought, should be a *republican* one. For Horne, the problem of Australia's antiquated, monarchically inclined political institutions was inseparable from the issue of its independence and thus with the prospect of a republic. The time had come, he argued, for Australians to rid themselves of the notion that they were so 'second-rate' that they could not provide their own head of state. Rectifying this, he believed, would provide Australians with a powerful and long-overdue symbol of their 'national maturity and national unity'. A truly democratic constitution, in other words, could only be a republican one.[66]

Even as late as 1976, after all that had occurred in the previous twelve months, this was still considered a somewhat eccentric view. Of all the speakers to address the Kerr and the Consequences meeting on 20 September, only two – Horne and John Gaden – explicitly called for a republic. In his statement, Patrick White even declared the question of a republic to be of 'secondary importance'. According to opinion polls, support for a completely independent Australia hovered somewhere between 25 and 39 per cent. Gough Whitlam, too, remarked a few weeks later that though a republic was sure to come, it would not be in his lifetime. Not for the first time, Horne was largely out on his own on the republican issue.[67]

In the wake of the Town Hall meeting, Citizens for Democracy set up branches in Sydney, Newcastle, Perth, Adelaide, Melbourne and Brisbane. Myfanwy, the most active behind-the-scenes member, started a CFD newsletter, *The Democrat*, to provide the organisation with a sense of concreteness and shared purpose (it was packaged and put into envelopes on the Hornes' dining table by a group of CFD helpers).[68] Over the next few months, Donald went on an impromptu media tour, appearing on radio, in newspapers and at public events all over the country. And on 11 November 1976 – the first anniversary of the dismissal – meetings were staged by all the newly launched CFD branches, including another large event at the Sydney Town Hall.[69]

For Horne, though, still intent on keeping republicanism alive, it was the Queen's visit to Australia in March 1977 that provided the most obvious opportunity for provoking debate on the question of Australia's head of state. And this time, Citizens for Democracy got behind the cause. They started by putting together yet another Town Hall meeting, their third in six months, titled 'Towards an Australian Republic'. They planned peaceful demonstrations at which protestors followed the royal motorcade with pro-republican placards. And on the day of the Queen's arrival, Horne spoke at the National Press Club, arguing that after the events of 11 November 1975, it was no less than his 'democratic duty' to provide a republican 'counterstatement' to the whole royal charade. The cult of Britishness, he said, underpinned Australia's 'delusional' political structure, and only a clean break with Britain would force Australians to confront the reality of their circumstances. In Horne's mind, there was a kind of post-imperial logic to republicanism, as if it were the inevitable outcome of British imperial decline and Australia's proximity to Asia. The republic was predestined; it was not a matter of 'if' but 'when'. He predicted that by 1980, debate over Australian independence would be a 'political reality'.[70]

Aside from the call for new constitutional arrangements, this argument was basically identical to the one Horne had presented in *The Lucky Country* over ten years earlier. The only major difference in 1977 was that he was now making his republican noises in the presence of the royal person (he later claimed that the Queen and the Duke of Edinburgh had listened to his Press Club address on the car radio between Canberra Airport and John Kerr's residence at Government House).[71] In return for this supposedly egregious display of disrespect and disloyalty to the Crown, however, Horne was subject to a tidal wave of hostility and abuse. He was called a 'little old man', 'undistinguished', 'pathetic', 'a self-appointed prophet' and the 'leader of the republican stormtroopers'. *Newsweek* discontinued his column. Old friends stopped talking to him. He even attracted the attention of ASIO, whose officers reported on him during the Queen's tour and tracked him for several years afterwards.[72]

The protests held in March 1977 were the first substantial show of opposition to a royal tour since British settlement. Unfortunately, they also marked the high point of republican sentiment in the immediate post-dismissal years. Despite their continued program of meetings and demonstrations throughout the late '70s, both Horne and the rest of the Citizens for Democracy found themselves speaking to an increasingly uninterested electorate. By 1979, when CFD held their last 'Republic Day' rally, barely anyone noticed.[73]

In early 1978, both Donald and Myfanwy stepped back from most of their Citizens for Democracy activities (though Donald continued to speak publicly at their events). For Donald, travel, writing and university commitments began to take precedence.[74] As the rage of 1975 slowly subsided, too, both he and Myfanwy had found themselves increasingly at odds with the organisation's inner circle over questions of strategy. Donald wanted a small, directive leadership that would make the majority of public appearances, decide on key talking points and lay out a new constitutional framework. Others, taking their cue from the New Left, wanted a more horizontal, participatory structure. For these activists, Horne's preferred approach was elitist, concentrating idea generation and decision-making power among a select few.[75] But for Horne, this was how politics – or, rather, political criticism – worked: enlightened minds came up with ideas (or repackaged existing ones) and threw them into the mixer. If the ideas were good enough, people would start talking about them. A debate would begin. The goalposts would move. Things would happen. If his opponents within CFD could not appreciate this, he would take his ideas elsewhere.

For those, like Horne, who had been sold on the vision of the country that Whitlam had offered in 1972, the 1970s ended in disappointment. The energy of that famous election had evaporated, weighed down by political controversy, economic insecurity and a doom-and-gloom atmosphere. In April 1979, over 400,000 Australians were out of work. During 1980, the figure went past one million. Full employment, the bipartisan policy goal of the postwar years, seemed a distant memory. In his 1979 Boyer Lectures, the Australian Council of Trade Unions (ACTU) president Bob Hawke argued that it was an 'exercise in futility' to imagine a simple, cosmetic fix to the problem. The system that had produced the prosperity of the post-war years now appeared to have broken down. The luck might finally have run out.[76]

II.

——

THE GREAT MUSEUM

In 1949, when Horne first set sail for England, international leisure travel was practically non-existent. Between 1925 and 1955, fewer than 50,000 Australians ventured abroad in any one year. Generally, only the wealthy, certain types of businesspeople, the odd scholar and a handful of adventurous young escapees could afford to spend an entire month on a boat just to get to their destination. Even within Australia's borders, getting around was no easy task. During World War II, it had taken twelve days for Horne's artillery unit to get to Darwin. Before the late 1960s, too, travellers heading north by car from Sydney to Brisbane were forced to take a roundabout route via Tenterfield, lest they become trapped on the unsealed, flood-prone Princes Highway. Outside of wartime, most people stayed put.

In the postwar years, that changed. More Australians saw more of the world, more of the time. Partly this was the result of the commercialisation of air travel, which drastically reduced both international and domestic travel times. Between 1955 and 1965, traffic through Australian airports increased tenfold. By the mid-1970s, Sydney airport alone was servicing nearly two million travellers per annum. And it was not only aircraft that were changing the nature of space. An explosion in car ownership, the improvement of roads and an expansion in the number of motels all provided new types of travel experiences to an increasingly affluent population. The revolution in national consciousness that occurred in the postwar decades – perhaps even the unravelling of Australia's imperial imagination – had much to do with this increase in mobility. Distance became less tyrannical.[1]

Donald Horne's career was shaped by these changes. It was air travel that had got him to Kenya in 1954, where his brief experience of anti-colonial conflict directed some of his future views on decolonisation and its implications for Australia. In the early 1960s, planes had taken him all around Asia, and his world tour in 1963 – organised to collect images of foreign destinations for a Qantas advertising campaign – had a direct influence on his subsequent concern with Australia's own image and identity. Even the AACF seminar series – with its regular smattering of international guests – was only made possible by the invention of commercial air travel. In Australia, at least, there would be no cosmopolitanism without this improvement in mobility.

Before the 1970s, most of Horne's travel experiences had been serendipitous, informed by whatever he was doing at the time: a journalistic assignment to Finland to report on an espionage scandal, a stopover in New York to collect images for *Weekend*, a six-week trip to London to salvage his first marriage.[2] From the 1970s onwards, however, he began to take a more deliberate and systematic approach to travel. One reason for this was that with two school-aged children, sightseeing had now become a family affair. In 1971, the Hornes embarked on their first overseas family holiday, to Bali, Jakarta and Singapore. Then, in 1974 and 1975, they went on a series of long road trips: an overland journey to South Australia for a holiday on Kangaroo Island, a drive through outback New South Wales to Broken Hill, another to the South Coast and Snowy Mountains.[3]

Travelling with Donald Horne was not a passive experience. Nor was it a time for relaxation and leisure – at least, not entirely. It was, rather, an opportunity for observation, a prompt for ideas and discussion, and an endless source of new material. Like any good journalist, he never travelled without a notepad and he scrawled down much of what he saw and thought. When he got older and his handwriting deteriorated, he travelled with a portable typewriter. Only on a few occasions did this endless notetaking have any clear and immediate purpose. More often than not it was simply a compulsion, part of his eternal need to translate experience into words. It was usually only much later that he would digest, process and manipulate the hieroglyphics in his yellowing notepads into more usable forms.[4]

The Horne family road trips around Australia in 1974 and 1975 are a case in point. Detailed planning would begin months in advance. The family would convene around the dinner table to study guidebooks and map out routes. Eleven-year-old Julia was charged with typing up detailed itineraries for each family member. Eight-year-old Nick was responsible for marking out their route with a blue Pentel pen on an 'NRMA Motorist's Map of South East Australia'. When they were on the road, the seminar would begin, with Myfanwy behind the wheel and Donald lecturing at the windshield from the passenger seat. As they approached each town, he would give a rundown of its history and significance, and when they arrived they would set about inspecting every major landmark and building on offer. Each day the four of them would discuss which images, ideas and stray thoughts might go in the holiday journal. Then, in the motel each night, Donald would sit in front of his typewriter and write them down.[5]

This unstructured process of image collection, description and explication was Horne's critical trademark – it is the reason his books were so often described as 'impressionistic'. It was the images in his writing that often left the strongest impression, that lingered longest in the memory. In *The Lucky Country*, there was the man in the open-necked shirt, solemnly eating his ice cream; in *The Education of Young Donald*, the young boy standing in front of the mirror wearing his father's war medals and slouch hat; in *The Next Australia*, the man choosing, against type, to sit in the back seat of the taxi; in *The Permit*, the bumbling Menzies-era politician pointing to a map of the Austro-Hungarian Empire. Seen in this light, the Horne family's systematic hoarding of images and impressions of the places they visited in 1974 and 1975 was merely the adaptation of a process Horne had been unofficially practising for several decades.

In his first few years as an academic, Horne experimented with new theories and ideas in much the same way. At the Mitchell Library in Sydney, he began two different research projects: one was an essay on Fijian politics, based upon observations he had made when he had visited the country in the 1960s; the other was an exhaustive study of Australian prime ministerial rhetoric in the first half of the twentieth century. Back on campus, he devised an idiosyncratic system of notetaking using index cards and familiarised himself with the latest trends in academic political science. Picking up where he had left off in his diplomatic cadet studies in the 1940s, he read (and, in many cases, re-read) several canonical works of political philosophy and sociology. As he put it many years later, he was attempting to make sense of things that he already knew, but 'didn't know the names of'.[6] At a distance from the urgency and immediacy of weekly journalism, however, it was not obvious how he would translate all of this new material into something worth saying.

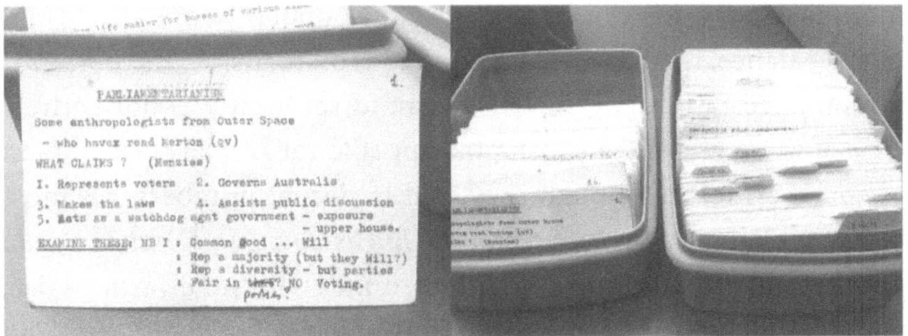

One of the index cards Donald Horne used for recording his research notes

The road trips provided one possible answer. In late 1974, he decided he would try a study of what he called 'the Australian imagination'. It would be an examination of dominant Australian myths and beliefs. In a series of essays, he would show how these myths – economic, impe-rial, racial – were represented in (and reinforced by) 'cultural forms': like the statues, buildings and memorials that he and his family had observed on their travels around the country. He started with what he called the economic prism, the idea of 'Australians as Economic Man'.[7] With hundreds of pages of notes, however, it quickly became a book of its own. He called it *Money Made Us*.

The research for and writing of Horne's first academic book was a classic example of his process. It was the product of huge amounts of travel and real-world observation. It was informed by reading that went back decades: nearly three years as an academic, four years working on *The Australian People* and nearly twenty years of public debate over the state of the nation. As he began to do more teaching, it was workshopped, with immediate feedback, in the lecture theatre and the seminar room.[8] And it was shaped by discussion: with family, friends and colleagues. It was an unsystematic system for writing books – an intuitive process of observing, reading, talking, teaching and writing – and the model for nearly everything he would produce in the next decade.

◆ ◆ ◆

When Horne first sat down to write *Money Made Us* in the early months of 1975, his career as a writer of popular books was, if not in the balance, then at least at a kind of crossroads. As the new economic uncertainties of the '70s began to set in, it was not entirely clear if there was still a substantial appetite for his particular brand of social criticism. Though they sold in decent numbers, his most recent sociological books – *God Is an Englishman*, *The Next Australia* and *The Australian People* – had been met with lukewarm praise, and a fair degree of fatigue with his arguments. In *The Bulletin* and *Newsweek*, too, he had produced more editorials on Asia and Australia's post-imperial identity dilemma than any other comparable Australian writer.

By the time *Money Made Us* was published in December 1976, however, two months after the 'Kerr and the Consequences' rally, Horne's public persona had changed dramatically.[9] His criticism of conservatives had become much more pointed, and his new book's underlying concerns reflected this change in outlook. What, he wondered, were the cultural and institutional forces that supported the interests of conservatism over those of progress? What determined the boundaries of the Australian imagination?

These questions about the nature of Australia's political culture were the foundations on which Horne built his belated academic career. Politics, he believed, was not simply something that was done by officials in distant cities, with a few elections here and there to give the impression of participation. In all of his writing, teaching and public roles in these years, he was impatient to show the connections between politics and everyday life. In his view, the realm of the political went far beyond the chambers of parliament: at a fundamental level, it was shaped by the unexamined attitudes and beliefs of ordinary people, by what they valued and what they did not, by what a society defined as its 'common sense'.[10]

The many books and articles Horne produced in this period were all informed – at least implicitly – by these ideas. At a 'Man and the Biosphere' symposium in 1974, for example, he presented a hypothetical 'social history' of Barry Humphries' satirical alter ego, Edna Everage.[11] In 1978's *Right Way, Don't Go Back* – his unexpurgated account of the Horne family road trips around Australia – he gave a behind-the-scenes look at his family life, the very mundanity of his observations serving as an argument about the political meanings that can be found in an examination of the quotidian. In 1979's *In Search of Billy Hughes*, he dissected the myths and legends that had been built up around the life of one of the country's most influential early prime ministers. And in 1980's *Time of Hope*, he produced a full cultural history of the fertile half decade between Menzies' retirement and Whitlam's election.

By any measure, the pace and quality of Horne's output was outstanding. Though he had more time to work on his writing since becoming an academic, books still remained a predominantly after-hours affair. He had a journalist's ability to write at speed and to deadline, which he combined with strategic catnaps and what he saw as his unique 'powers of concentration'. Since his handwriting had deteriorated, he wrote all his manuscripts on an electric typewriter. A typical Sunday, he told a journalist in 1985, involved 'breakfast, writing, lunch, sleep, more writing, dinner, more writing'. Every book since *The Education of Young Donald* was at least partially written in the Hornes' upstairs study, though, as his daughter, Julia, recalled in 2014, there were times when Donald would close the door to keep out the noise, 'and only my mother would dare enter'. As Horne told an interviewer in 1994, 'When I am writing ... I write'.[12]

In the late 1970s, Horne's publishers marketed each new book as a major literary event. They sent him off on nationwide author tours, talking not only to newspaper journalists but also to radio and television programs.[13] They solicited lists of famous and influential names to invite to his book launches. *Billy Hughes*, for example, was launched by Gough Whitlam at the Nimrod Theatre and was written up in the social pages of *The Sunday Telegraph*.[14] Every book elicited at least one new biographical newspaper profile, usually conducted from the front room of the Grosvenor Street terrace, in which Horne would be asked to give yet another abridged account of his personal history.[15] Almost as a rule, these profiles would recount his expanding list of personal accolades, and none was complete without a mention of the one book that towered over the rest (by 1975, Penguin had sold over a quarter of a million copies of *The Lucky Country*).[16]

As a writer, this personal celebrity had him at a distinct advantage. Horne had little trouble interesting publishers in his books. Almost anything with his name on it would sell. *Death of the Lucky Country*, for example, moved over 50,000 copies in its first two months.[17] Ostensibly minor Horne releases did well, too: *Money Made Us* sold 21,000 copies; *Southern Exposure*, a coffee table book largely recapitulating his *Lucky Country* arguments, sold 10,000. Nearly every book he wrote was excerpted in at least one major newspaper, often several days in a row. On at least one occasion this led to a bidding war. In 1977, a representative of Curtis Brown publishers even contacted him about a reissue of his long-forgotten 1965 novel *The Permit*. They planned to market it as an under-read classic by 'Australia's greatest living writer'.[18]

Horne was a very public kind of academic. He positioned himself somewhere between journalism and the academy, comfortable in both the lecture theatre and the opinion pages.[19] Alongside his writing and teaching, he took on numerous public roles. He continued to sit on the advisory board of the *Australian Encyclopedia*, meeting monthly in its Rose Bay office until well into the 1980s.[20] At the request of the NSW premier Neville Wran, he also sat on the NSW Cultural Grants Advisory Committee. In the early 1980s, he was chairman of the Copyright Agency and president of the Australian Society of Authors. Throughout, he made regular public appearances: in newspaper and magazine commentary; on television and radio; in lectures and speeches. Between 1977 and 1989 he gave four separate addresses to the National Press Club.[21]

Horne collected people almost as enthusiastically as he collected images and ideas. When the academic Meaghan Morris presented a paper on the cultural meanings of a new Sydney skyscraper at a conference in Hobart in the early 1980s, he approached her afterwards with great excitement. 'That's what I do!' Morris recalled him saying, after which she was invited to lunch about once a month for the next fifteen years.[22] Another academic, Helen Irving, had an almost identical experience. After Horne heard her speak at a conference in 1992, he called her up a few days later and joked that he was 'doing a little talent scouting'. They, too, began to meet for regular lunches at the Bayswater Brasserie, which went on for many years.[23] Countless others considered themselves regulars on Horne's lunch roster.

Horne's closest colleague in the department of political science, though, was Elaine Thompson. A generation younger than him, she had arrived at UNSW in 1974 with a freshly minted PhD from the University of Sydney and an instruction to teach an American politics course. Their first serious encounter had come in early 1975, when Thompson arrived at a department meeting with a competing idea for a first-year course in Australian politics. After glaring at each other across the desk for the duration of the meeting, they reconvened in her office afterwards to resolve the dispute, only to discover that their ideas were quite similar. Following an amicable discussion, they agreed to teach the course together. It was the beginning of a long and successful professional relationship.[24]

As his friend and colleague Owen Harries observed many years later, Horne possessed all the qualities of a good teacher: enthusiasm, imagination, a sense of the dramatic and, above all, the ability to convey 'a sense of the cosmic importance of whatever happened to be occupying his attention at the time'.[25] He was, after all, an inveterate explainer, the kind of writer who tried to make complicated things comprehensible. In a tutorial setting he was talkative and animated – to the point where one former student recalled it being 'more like a lecture on the thoughts of Donald'.[26] Though less cantankerous than he had once been, he still had hard edges: he was apt to yell 'shut up' at anyone who interrupted his thought process (as he sometimes did to Myfanwy at dinner parties) and he could be remote and reserved if you caught him one on one in his office.[27] But he treated his seminars as a long lunch without the alcohol, an opportunity for discussion, argument and wide-ranging debate.

In front of an audience, Horne could also be tremendously entertaining, with his talent for humorous anecdotes and bon mots.[28] His humour was often self-referential: sometimes he began lectures by warning the students that he would be making a joke every twenty minutes.[29] Mark McKenna, who tutored for him in the late 1980s, recalled his sparkling wit – infectious, ironic and caustic – and an educated accent that was 'reminiscent of a prewar Australia'.[30] At a National Press Club address in 1989, for example, Horne began by recounting the time he had welcomed Queen Elizabeth to Australia in her capacity as the representative of one of Australia's 'most highly respected ethnic groups'.[31]

He grew no less unconventional with age. In the course outline for one of his upper-level seminars, his instructions for tutorial preparation included 'Know thyself' and 'Look around you ... trust your own experiences'.[32] Conal Condren, a colleague in the Department of Political Science, remembered talking to Horne at a staff meeting after a particularly uptight honours seminar. In order to loosen things up, Horne told him, he had asked everyone – on the count of three – to yell out the word 'fuck'.[33] During a debate over the Hawke government's proposed Australia Card in the 1980s, one of his students was brazen enough to liken it to the illiberalism of Nazi Germany. In response, Horne mounted his chair, placed his finger over his upper lip and shouted 'Heil Hitler!' After a long pause, he then delivered his verdict: 'No, it is not like Nazi Germany'.[34]

As much as possible, Horne did things his own way. In 1977, not long after the publication of *Money Made Us*, he embarked on the most ambitious project of his writing life. In all likelihood, he thought, it would occupy him for at least three years.[35] His 'eccentric' idea, as he described it to UNSW pro-vice-chancellor Rex Vowels, was to examine museums, monuments and historical sites in every European capital city and major provincial centre.[36] It would require two huge trips, each around four to five months long, and thus a considerable amount of study leave. But the outcome, he assured his university overseers, would be a book on 'European cults of the heroic' – likely with an international readership – and a new political science course on a similar topic.[37] It was, in essence, tourism as an intellectual exercise, an attempt to apply the *Money Made Us* formula to the entirety of the European continent. And it was yet another example of Horne's talent for dovetailing these intellectual pursuits with family travel, always with a keen eye on commercial opportunities in the publishing market.

The trips, once again, were meticulously researched and planned. With the help of Myfanwy and the children, he drew up several draft itineraries, packed with detail, not only about which museums to visit but about which specific items they wanted to view and, sometimes, even floor and room numbers.[38] He contacted the embassy of each country he planned to visit, soliciting lists of key cultural sites and where to find them.[39] The first trip, from December 1977 through to March 1978, was focused mostly on Western and northern Europe, and included detours to his old English haunts of Bow Brickhill and Polperro; the second, from December 1978 to April 1979, covered central and eastern Europe, every capital except Tirana in Albania. In all, he would visit eighty European cities. The children, now teenagers,

Donald and Myfanwy Horne in Europe in the late 1970s

would accompany them for the first two months. And aside from the final portion of the second trip, Myfanwy would travel with him all the way.

These European journeys were more comprehensive and focused than his Australian road trips. He received funding grants from the university and the Australia Council (topped up with the proceeds of *Right Way, Don't Go Back*).[40] He wrote several research proposals and, on his return, filed reports on his research 'findings'.[41] And while *Money Made Us* had confined its focus to the economic realm, his European project, from its very conception, was much more ambitious: nationalism, war, fascism, communism, religion, imperialism, science, industrialism and revolution were all among his proposed themes.[42] His field of interest – and the literary stage on which he sought to perform – was fast expanding beyond Australia to include more global concerns.

In their different ways, all of Horne's intellectual activities in the late 1970s – his writing, his teaching, his travelling and public performances – were examinations of what would eventually be called 'political culture'. They took as a precondition the idea that politics was not the plaything of politicians and statesmen, but rather was embedded in the broader culture in complex and often revealing ways.[43] This was an idea he had arrived at intuitively, the product of two decades of reading, observation and discussion. In an unending stream of published books and articles, written in various styles and from different angles, he had chronicled, prodded, dissected and described the world as he saw it. He had trusted his own eyes. But it was only in his research and his teaching that he had begun to explicitly connect his own political and cultural observation with sociological models and theories of power. The time had come to put it all together.

◆ ◆ ◆

On a windy, overcast day in September 1980, a television crew escorted Horne onto a yacht in Sydney Harbour to film material for an episode of the ABC current affairs program *Four Corners*. Bobbing up and down in a matching brown suit and tie, with a halo of wispy white hair flailing in the breeze, he was asked for his thoughts on the upcoming federal election. Like a tour guide in a large open-air museum, he explained to interviewer Peter Ross that most of the key themes of the campaign could be found on the harbour itself: in the growth of the city skyline, 'sound economic management'; in Fort Denison, 'safe government'; in Luna Park, the 'razzamatazz' and 'nonsense' of electioneering; and in the governor-general's residence, Britishness and 'the shades of 1975'. But all of these issues, he declared, were illusions. They were older, more familiar definitions of reality that would be used to reassure the public that nothing much had changed. The things that really had changed – global capitalism in the wake of the oil shocks, inflation and mass unemployment, Australia's self-definition in a post-imperial world – would not be talked about. They were not yet part of reality.[44]

A month earlier, in a much less public setting, Horne had proposed his own intellectual framework for this kind of analysis. In a paper titled 'Hegemony: An Australian Model', delivered at the Australasian Political Studies Association Conference in Canberra, he suggested that in order to understand power in Australia, it was necessary to identify the common habits, behaviours and beliefs shared by Australian elites ('the deciding classes'). He listed several preliminary examples of these kinds of shared assumptions, among them a respect for the rules, a belief in progress, an emphasis on individualism and a 'priority for the economic'. He called this collection of dominant attitudes 'the directive culture'.[45]

As he acknowledged right from the start, this idea was explicitly adapted from the work of the Italian Marxist Antonio Gramsci, whose hitherto obscure writings had been rediscovered by the New Left in the 1970s. In his *Prison Notebooks*, written from a fascist jail in the 1930s, Gramsci had described how ruling elites warded off working-class revolution not simply through violence and coercion, but through culture. Hegemonic ruling-class power, in the Gramscian sense, was produced and maintained by ideology, by the monopolisation of a society's generally accepted beliefs, its values and norms. As long as this conventional wisdom favoured ruling-class interests, he argued, revolution was impossible.[46]

Horne had first begun to take a serious interest in Gramscian ideas in the mid-to-late 1970s, not long after he finished *Money Made Us*.[47] In the theory of hegemony, Horne saw a version of his own thinking about political culture. It was, in the words of one former student, his 'dialectic touchstone'.[48] In Horne's adaptation, however, he detached hegemony from its theory of working-class revolution and deployed it instead as a general framework for understanding power in modern societies. A directive culture, he thought, was not coercive or exhorted from on high. It was, rather, a *demonstration* – through style and ritual and public rhetoric – of what to do, what to think and what to value. Nor was it static or inflexible. Large parts of it were actually 'pseudo-dominant' and contested, and it was always subject to challenge and critique. Taken as a whole, though, it operated as a society's conventional wisdom. You could not change a society unless you changed its directive culture. Overturning its most pervasive elements, he quipped, would 'require the imagination of a Pol Pot'.[49]

Horne had never been a theorist or a philosopher. Before the 1980s, none of his books was – in a narrow sense – theoretically rigorous or systematically argued. To the annoyance of some of his reviewers, they rarely betrayed any single overarching idea about how politics and society worked.[50] Theories, for Horne, were new ways of clarifying his own observations. After learning of the existence of the French critic Roland Barthes in a review of *Money Made Us*, for example, he had gone out and read everything of Barthes that he could find, then added him to his undergraduate reading list.[51] Many other forerunners of the 'cultural turn' in the humanities – writers including John Berger, Susan Sontag, Stuart Hall, Erving Goffman and Michel Foucault – received similar treatment.[52] As Robert Dessaix pointed out several years later, Horne's engagement with 'postmodern' thinkers was actually somewhat uncharacteristic of intellectuals of his generation.[53] But he was never afraid to read his way into different fields and disciplines if he found them useful. He might have rarely used footnotes, recalled Elaine Thompson, but of one thing you could always be sure: he had read it all.[54]

Horne's concern with questions of power, though, was at least partially related to the Labor Party's continuing lack of success at the federal level – or rather, that in its pursuit of electoral legitimacy since 1975, it had drifted closer to the values and rhetoric of the conservatives. After Labor's narrow loss at the 1980 election – its third in a row – he put some of these thoughts into a slim post-election pamphlet titled *Winner Take All*.[55] He was clearly disappointed. Both parties, as he had predicted in his *Four Corners* interview, had been almost uniquely uninterested in the major issues of the day. The media, he added, had made things worse by presenting a myopic and often trivial account of national affairs. Worse still, he thought, the vagaries of the constitution had made the results of the election somewhat ambiguous: a party with a 1 per cent advantage in voter preferences had won 20 per cent more seats in the parliament. The generally accepted rule in Australia, it seemed, was 'woe to the conquered'.[56]

As Horne lamented in his titular chapter, however, his very public activism on constitutional matters had narrowed his public persona to some degree. He was now seen by many people as someone who talked primarily about constitutions and republics. As recently as February 1980, for example, he had helped organise a public conference on constitutional reform called 'Change the Rules'. Designed to come up with common ground on the matter among Australian elites, it was attended by high-profile political figures, such as Gareth Evans, Don Chipp, Billy McMahon and Gough Whitlam.[57] Eight months later, then, when Horne delivered a wide-ranging National Press Club address on an entirely different topic, it came as no surprise that he was asked by a journalist to outline his current level of rage at the actions of John Kerr. He was, after all, Australia's chief republican. Horne, though, dismissed the question as 'irrelevant'. His real line as a critic, he insisted, was not constitutions, but power and culture.[58]

In the early 1980s he did his best to correct this mistake. At UNSW, he was the driving force behind the establishment of a new interdisciplinary MA program in Australian Studies, designed to offer students a much broader view of politics, society and culture. In *Winner Take All*, he included a chapter titled 'Power and Democracy in Australia', in which he reiterated his idea of a hegemonic directive culture. He also began renaming his junior- and senior-level courses to accommodate this change in emphasis: 'Australian Political Culture' was changed to

'Australian Dominant Culture'; 'Politics and the Media' became 'Power and Mass Culture'; the first-year course he taught with Thompson, too – initially 'Australian Politics: Issues, Parties, Policies' – became 'Power and Democracy in Australia'.[59] And across myriad articles, book chapters, seminars, lectures and conference papers, he repeated his core analysis: power in Australia rested with those whose interests aligned most neatly with the country's dominant myths and beliefs.[60]

His biggest project on this theme was the Europe book. Conceived in 1977, it had been repeatedly delayed: first by the writing of other books, and then by the more practical problem of putting it all together. It total, he had around 140,000 words of polished notes and short essays. As he told an interviewer several years later, he felt like a 1920s film producer who had shot enough footage to last a week but did not know what to do with it.[61] It was not until 1980 that he found the time to transform this raw material into a viable manuscript. He wrote several drafts, but was not pleased with the results. Soon after, Ed Campion went through the entire manuscript and made several suggestions.[62] Then, in 1981, after taking a break to write *Winner Take All*, he implemented some of Campion's advice, paring it back, giving it more coherence and structure, and sending it off to his agent. He thought he would call it 'The European Imagination'.[63]

In his attempt to pitch the book to an international audience, however, he came up against an unfamiliar problem: he could not find a publisher. Curtis Brown passed on the manuscript in early 1982, then, after several months at Anthony Cheetham & Co., it was deemed to be 'excessively long'. In 1983, both Penguin and Oxford University Press passed too, while Faber & Faber suggested that only an internationally recognisable writer such as Arthur Koestler could get away with such an ambitious book.[64] In the midst of it all, Horne sacked his agent.[65] Eventually, at a picnic in Sydney, he met a representative of the small left-wing publisher Pluto Press, who finally agreed to publish the book. Even then, it would not appear until October 1984, four years after he started writing it and seven years after his first European trip. It was called *The Great Museum: The Re-Presentation of History*.

The long saga of *The Great Museum*'s production had at least one positive effect: it gave Horne time to work through his ideas about power. In April 1984, not long after he finished the book, he travelled to Melbourne to discuss a series of essays written for an upcoming edited collection called *Australia: The Daedalus Symposium*. His contribution, 'Who Rules Australia?', was a synthesis of his last ten years of thinking, writing and teaching. In a highly bureaucratised modern society like Australia, he argued, power was diffuse. It did not derive from some obvious source like the Crown or the constitution, nor could it reliably be said to come from 'the people' (especially while nearly every parliament in the country persisted with unrepresentative upper houses). Instead, he wrote, it was the collective worldview of the 'governing classes' in the increasingly professionalised bureaucracies – government, business and trade union – that determined whose interests would naturally triumph at a time of conflict. There was, therefore, no 'ruling class' in Australia. There were simply groups who 'prevailed' by default, the natural beneficiaries of decisions and policies shaped by the 'common sense' of bureaucratic decision-makers.[66]

Throughout the early 1980s, Horne had experimented with different labels for what he described as his 'liberal-democratic modification' of Gramsci.[67] In 'Who Rules Australia?', what was previously 'the directive culture' and 'the dominant culture' became 'the prevailing culture'. Later, he would settle on an even broader idea of 'the public culture'. All, though, were attempts to theorise what he had already observed in *Money Made Us*: that in Australia, prevailing attitudes and beliefs almost always favoured business interests. As he had quipped in that book, Australia was a 'white man's resource-ripping country'.[68] The election of the Hawke Labor government had only confirmed it. Hawke's flagship National Economic Summit in 1983 brought together the decision-makers in government, business and the unions, or as Horne dubbed them, 'the finalists in answering the question: "Who governs Australia?"' The participants at the summit, he added, were predominantly male, university-educated and of British origin, and what they demonstrated (for a televised audience) were the 'bargaining realities of managed capitalism'.[69] Capitalist imperatives directed all significant decision-making in Australia. To challenge this common sense, Horne suggested, was to challenge capitalism itself.[70]

Horne threw these ideas – either explicitly or implicitly – into everything he wrote in the mid-1980s. As always, his output was prodigious. Between 1983 and the middle of 1984, for example, he taught several university courses, presented a small handful of conference papers, completed his *Great Museum* manuscript, wrote a second volume of his autobiography, and rewrote his 1972 social history (published in 1985 by *Reader's Digest* in coffee-table format as *The Australian People: Biography of a Nation*, with new colour images and biographical sketches written by Myfanwy). In early May 1984, he left for a month-long lecture tour of California, visiting eight universities as part of an Australian Studies exchange program.[71] Returning for a few days, he and Myfanwy then departed on another six-month tour of the United States and Europe. While overseas, he researched and wrote an updated version of *The Great Museum*, describing power in industrial societies more generally.[72] Adding examples from the United States to his existing observations of Europe, he completed most of the manuscript on his portable typewriter while camped out in various hotel rooms and, occasionally, the homes of friends living abroad.[73] He called it *The Public Culture: The Triumph of Industrialism*.

As one reviewer proposed after reading *Winner Take All*, Horne had now repositioned himself somewhere to the left of the Labor Party.[74] Given his personal history, this could seem a somewhat radical position to have reached. But Horne was not calling for an end to capitalism. His critique, as he put it, was simply of capitalism as the only possible view of existence, and of capitalist imperatives and economic indicators as the only constituent parts of 'reality'. For Horne, reality as expressed in the public culture was always hypothetical; it was a mirage. It operated, as it were, like a museum, directing you where to look and, in the process, providing a judgement about what was valuable and what was not. Abstractions that had always appeared natural and given – the nation, the middle class, the economy – were first and foremost creations of the mind. If they could be created, then they could just as easily be taken apart and put back together again in different forms. For Horne, the examined life always revolved around two great questions: 'How can we describe existence?' and, ultimately, 'What can we believe?'[75]

◆ ◆ ◆

In March 1984, a few months before Horne left for the United States, the Minister for Home Affairs in the newly elected Hawke government, Barry Cohen, contacted him with an intriguing proposal. The Australia Council, the government organisation charged with slicing up the pie of federal arts funding, was looking for a new chairperson. It was no honorary position. At a time of high unemployment, the Council was under increasing pressure to justify its claims on public finances. In the view of the outgoing chair, Timothy Pascoe, it was in need of an advocate, a high-profile figure who could make the case for its relevance and, most importantly, for its funding in difficult economic times. By making the role part-time, Pascoe thought, they could attract a 'busy person of distinction', someone who could lend their credibility to the organisation.[76]

By the mid-1980s, Donald Horne was – by any definition – a busy person of distinction. According to reports, he had emerged from a field of potential candidates that included the former South Australian premier Don Dunstan, the novelist Morris West and Gough Whitlam.[77] Like these figures, Horne had become something of a cultural icon. *The Lucky Country*, of course, had much to do with it: in recent years, the recording artists Richard Clapton and Midnight Oil had both written songs about the phrase and columnists continued to trot it out whenever it suited their purposes. A pub in Newcastle had even renamed itself 'The Lucky Country Hotel'.[78] For Horne, it was an age of accolades. He was given an Order of Australia and a Personal Chair at UNSW.[79] The State Library of New South Wales purchased forty-eight boxes of his personal papers.[80] He had a street named after him in Canberra and two different students had made him the subject of their undergraduate theses.[81]

In April 1984, after mulling over Cohen's offer, Horne accepted: he would be glad to lend some of this credibility to the task of arts advocacy. In many ways, it was a role he was born to play. The Council itself was a product of the cultural reforms of the late 1960s and early 1970s, when successive Australian governments had been moved by moral, national and geopolitical concerns to pursue a less tight-fisted approach to arts subsidy. As Australia's British connection became increasingly untenable, prime ministers from Holt to Whitlam were persuaded that the cultivation of the arts was a means by which Australia might begin to shore up the flimsy foundations of its nationhood. A nation without its own culture, they surmised, was no nation at all. Almost overnight, artists and intellectuals counted. As Horne had written in his own book-length account of the period, honour had suddenly been conferred on the arts in a language that people could understand: government money.[82]

Horne's own career was deeply intertwined with the intellectual and cultural breakthroughs to which these governments attached themselves in the post-Menzies years. For nearly two decades, he had been both an advocate and a beneficiary of this new cultural sophistication. *The Lucky Country* owed much of its success to the rapid growth of Australian publishing in the 1960s, especially books and magazines. At the same time, its diagnosis of a moribund, intellectually impoverished political culture had appealed strongly to a growing cohort of white-collar, university-educated professionals, many of whom hoped that Australia could become something more than a white man's country, hostile towards new ideas and committed principally to economic development. In the decade following the retirement of Robert Menzies, Horne's was one of many voices – in the press, in the parliament and on the streets – who welcomed an alternative, civic-minded vision of the country, founded instead on principles of diversity, tolerance and cultural sophistication.

Of all the administrative roles that Horne had taken on during his long public career, the Australia Council job was by far the most prominent – and controversial.[83] The organisation was under almost constant pressure: from governments threatening funding cuts; from arts organisations lobbying for a bigger slice of the pie; from prominent critics sceptical of its very existence. Though it was a statutory body, with allocation decisions made by a collection of independent boards operating at 'arm's length' from Canberra, the spectre of ministerial interference loomed large. Indeed, the appointments of both Horne and the incoming managing director, Di Yerbury, were in part driven by their assumed sympathy with

Labor's (vaguely defined) policy goals in the area of arts support: increased funding and fairer distribution.[84]

Horne's first two years at the Council were among the most turbulent in the organisation's short history.[85] Within the arts community itself, a series of funding allocations by the theatre and music boards led to several ugly public spats, as did the governing Council's attempts to streamline the organisation by amalgamating many of its boards (which, for a while, involved secret Council meetings at Horne's house).[86] Relations with government were no better, especially after a letter leaked in August 1985 that seemed to show arts minister Barry Cohen trying to influence funding priorities.[87] In response, the arts community, most of whom saw this as a clear violation of the arm's length principle, galvanised around a new political action group, the Arts Industry Alliance. The arts, though, were never high on the Hawke government's list of priorities: in the 1985 budget, the Council's overall funding was cut by 1.3 per cent. The restoration of these funds a year later came at the expense of a $1 million cut to the Council's administrative budget.[88] In the midst of it all, Horne and Yerbury's working relationship deteriorated beyond repair, and in August 1986 the latter departed for a job at Macquarie University.[89]

Horne took a philosophical view of these power struggles: politics was an imperfect business, and to his mind, principles of Council independence, democratic oversight and the federal government's duty to the 'national' interest in the arts were always bound to come into conflict.[90] On the whole, he was an efficient and capable chair, managing meetings and keeping them on task. He had considerable experience in boardrooms, having sat on the NSW Cultural Grants Committee, the Arts Faculty Board at UNSW and, further back, in the court of Sir Frank Packer. Don Aitkin, who worked with Horne in the 1990s, remembered him as the 'second best' chair he had ever seen in action (after Bob Hawke).[91]

His style was often more declarative than consultative. Yerbury's replacement, Max Bourke, recalled Horne's propensity to dominate meetings, lecturing and sermonising from the head of the table. Another colleague at the Council, Andrea Hull, described Horne as someone with strong views who was usually 'unambiguous about what he felt'.[92] Among those with whom he disagreed, he developed a reputation as someone who did not like to hear too much feedback.[93] But Horne's tendency to declaim, thought Bourke, was not aggressive or overtly masculine: he was simply a talker, an enthusiast. He was also quite adaptable, if necessary. In meetings, for example, the two men developed a system whereby Bourke would tap Horne on the knee when it was time for someone else to speak.[94]

Horne saw his move to the Australia Council as being continuous with his ongoing concern with power and culture. He admitted as much to a journalist in November 1984, suggesting that his academic work had provided him with a 'full theoretical base' for his new role.[95] In his inaugural address as chair, delivered at the Art Gallery of New South Wales in January 1985, he had explained that he wanted to get Australians to think about the creative imagination as an indispensable feature of modern life, as an activity that was central to existence in a post-industrial world.[96] There was more to life than jobs and economic growth, he thought: 'the arts' and 'the economy' were, in fact, completely interdependent. The creative industries were one of the dream factories of modern industrial societies, articulators of its common sense, one of the most important means by which humans simplified, criticised and thus made sense of existence. They helped define what was meant by the word 'reality'.

The problem, of course, was that not every group in Australian society was fairly represented in this public 'reality'. Some, he thought, were 'culturally deprived'. Without access to the means of cultural production, they had few avenues by which to make their criticisms of existence; they were, in all respects, invisible. If stability in modern societies rested upon the pervasiveness of dominant values in the public culture, then change would come through the injection of new voices and ideas into the public realm, from challenges to the common sense. Horne's hope for the Australia Council, therefore, was that by giving artistic platforms to previously under-represented groups, they would pose new challenges to the prevailing culture, throw up new issues for public debate and make new criticisms of existence. Reality, in essence, would be redefined.

Horne's great passion at the Council, then – and the one that aligned most neatly with his theorising in *The Public Culture* – was community arts. Horne loved the idea of art being practised by ordinary people. In his inaugural address, he had spoken of his desire to 'normalise' artistic activity in Australia, to make it an essential part of the lives of Australians. After the amalgamation of the Council's boards in 1987 (from eight to five), Horne became the head of the newly created Community Cultural Development Unit.[97] During his six years as chair, he recalled, he likely spent the equivalent of at least twelve months visiting museums, galleries and community arts centres in all corners of the country. Museums, he thought, had a storytelling function. They were, in a way, another kind of book, another way of reaching and engaging a general audience, provoking them, challenging them, getting them to have a think. Indeed, two of the books he published in these years – 1985's illustrated reissue of *The Australian People* and 1987's *The Lucky Country Revisited* – were essentially museum-like in their presentation.[98]

For Horne, grassroots support for the arts was fundamentally progressive. By broadening access to creative activity, organisations such as the Australia Council acted as 'enliveners of social change', expanding the horizons of the Australian imagination. In his view, just as Indigenous Australians had certain land rights, different groups in a society could have 'cultural rights'.[99] Such a notion might even provide a model for navigating life in the post-industrial age – a white-collar world of ideas and intellect, where traditional notions of work were in flux. His role, as he saw it, was to convince Australians that this was something to welcome – a richer, more diverse and fulfilling world than the one they were leaving behind. He wanted to convince them that in the future, the examined life really would be the only one worth living.

12.

PUBLIC INTELLECTUAL

Donald Horne made more public appearances in his first few years as Australia Council chair than most of his predecessors combined. In fact, outside of teaching and socialising, to which he remained enthusiastically committed, almost all of his spare time in the late 1980s was devoted to something that could plausibly be described as public work. He toured arts facilities, attended gallery openings and wrote newspaper columns. He was a member of the Constitutional Commission's Advisory Committee on Executive Government, sitting in on public hearings in every major capital city. He travelled regularly to conferences and events, and made speeches all over the country: at the Gippsland Institute of Adult Education, at the opening of the Australian Theatre Studies Centre; at a meeting of the Double Bay branch of the Liberal Party; at the opening of a Brunelleschi exhibition. By his own estimation, he spent close to seventy days a year on such activities. And between 1984 and 1989, as he approached seventy years of age, he wrote, promoted and publicly discussed no less than seven books.[1]

Intelligent public discussion was central to Horne's vision of a healthy democratic culture. A nation that did not discuss its problems, he thought, could never resolve them. In an address to graduating students at the University of New South Wales in 1985 – one of many he delivered in these years – he spoke of his firm belief in the possibility of a shared intellectual discourse, one that sought to transcend the 'great and debilitating intellectual divisions' of modern society. Contemporary intellectuals, he lamented, too often lost themselves in the 'legitimating rituals' of scholarship. They operated in increasingly specialised fields and disciplines. They spoke in 'secret languages' and 'moribund Talmudisms', addressing ever smaller and more disconnected audiences. The effect of this was not to enhance intellectual life, he said, but to stifle it. It betrayed a 'thin and deprived' view of the world. For Horne, a shared culture of ideas was more like an all-you-can-eat restaurant, one in which anyone with a brain could pick and choose their intellectual dish: poetry, novels, history and philosophy; economic, social and political analysis; music, paintings and architecture; texts and performances of plays; scientific theory and research. If a person wanted to say something true – about art, about society, about life – how could any of these fields be ignored?[2]

In his lament for a disappearing culture of general discussion, Horne was merely adding his voice to a more widespread anxiety about the retreat of intellectual life into the universities in the 1970s and '80s. As the story went, in the relatively recent past, a tough species of iconoclastic freelance intellectual had dominated public life, a kind of morally courageous writer who could combine a disdain for fashionable groupthink with a talent for speaking to a (vaguely defined) general reader. It was said that this type of independent-minded maverick had once proliferated in the bohemian urban enclaves of major American and European cities, where he or she had made a living writing for a broad range of little magazines (themselves aimed at a non-academic audience of educated generalists). In the years since the war, however, rents had risen, the enclaves had disappeared and the little magazines had become less viable. If an intellectual wanted to pay the bills, the only place left was university. And in this increasingly professional and bureaucratic habitat, the public trade in ideas was withering on the vine.[3]

American scholar Russell Jacoby coined the term 'public intellectual', in his much-discussed 1987 book on this topic, to describe a contemporary thinker who attempted to buck this trend.[4] Over the next decade, the label became ubiquitous, fuelled by the same concern about academic obscurantism and intellectual decline that Horne had identified in his UNSW graduation address. In Australia, straw polls of prominent public thinkers became standard newspaper fodder. In 1991, the literary magazine *Meanjin* devoted an entire issue to the discussion of public intellectuals. A few years later, *Australian Book*

Review held a symposium on the same topic.[5] By 2001, the American legal scholar Richard Posner had even devised a complex ranking system for prominent public thinkers (to which one sceptical reviewer replied that you might as well try to build an economic model to explain prayer).[6]

Despite the sudden popularity of Jacoby's neologism, its meaning was always ambiguous. What, some asked, did 'public intellectual' denote that the existing labels 'critic', 'commentator' – or even simply 'intellectual' – did not? In a series of influential lectures in 1993, the critic Edward Said made a case for what might be called the 'maverick' definition: of a fiercely independent, passionately engaged freethinker speaking truth to power on matters of social, moral and political significance.[7] Others, though, scorned the label altogether, insisting that it referred chiefly to shallow, brand-name intellectuals with a taste for the spotlight; media darlings who placed too much emphasis on the publicity and not enough on the ideas. A public intellectual, wrote David Carter in 2004, might even be defined as someone who calls for more public intellectuals.[8]

Either way, Donald Horne was almost immediately considered to be a prototypical Australian exponent of public intellectualism. In the 1990s, his name was a permanent fixture on newspaper lists (and a small handful of book-length studies).[9] Even as late as 2005, when *The Sydney Morning Herald* conducted a poll of Australia's top 100 public thinkers, Horne – aged eighty-three – came in at number nine.[10] It is not hard to see why. His credentials were impeccable. He had made his name commenting on general matters of public concern and attacking what he saw as the unexamined orthodoxies of Australian life. He had a sharp and wide-ranging intellect, a natural simplicity of expression, an innate scepticism and nonconformism, an inclination to prod and provoke, a supreme talent for aphorism, an ability to *perform*. He was always looking for some new tyre to puncture, for some conventional wisdom to up-end, some illusion to unveil. Topical, provocative, well-informed public thinking was in his bones.[11]

Given his widespread reputation as a stirrer, however, Horne's own idea of public intellectualism was surprisingly non-adversarial. As he argued repeatedly throughout the 1990s, the most influential public thinkers were those who could say what people already knew – or perhaps might want to know – but had not yet fully articulated. This, he told Robert Dessaix in 1998, was 'a truism of the advertising business'.[12] The immense influence of Horne's early writings in the 1950s and 1960s, for example, was at least partly derived from his clear and self-conscious sense of his *audience*. These were *Observer*'s 'New Men': the concerned, 'educated but classless' white-collar professionals who had emerged out of universities and business and government bureaucracies. It was to this reform-minded, 'rising class' that Horne had deliberately attached himself in the late 1950s. This cohort, he wrote in 1957, 'do not know what they think, who they are, or where they are going. We should tell them'.[13]

In the 1960s, Horne had been one of the chief articulators of the worldview of this new and politically indeterminate group. In that transitional period, it was as if he had been given a glimpse into the future. Almost all of the issues Horne took up between the launching of *Observer* in 1958 and the publication of *The Lucky Country* in 1964 had made their way to the mainstream of public debate by the end of the Whitlam years: the need to forge more productive relationships with Australia's Asian neighbours, the need to reconsider Australia's British connection, the need to encourage the development of the arts and intellectual life, the need to reform Australia's racist immigration policy, the need to relax censorship, abortion and divorce laws, the need to take the suburbs seriously, and to embrace the full diversity of Australia life. By the late 1970s, reasonable people were even talking about republicanism. As Hugh Stretton observed in 1976, few Australian intellectuals had ever had the satisfaction of seeing such concrete results of 'a generation of persuasion'.[14]

Horne had not been – nor did he ever claim to be – the sole author of these ideas. As several of *The Lucky Country*'s reviewers had pointed out, his famous book was in some respects simply a summary of issues that had been widely discussed in various little magazines and learned journals in the half decade before its publication. For Horne, though, this was precisely the point. Trafficking between the highbrow and the general was the modus operandi of the public intellectual. They were translators and explainers, addressers of different and diverse publics. They were performers, willing and able to capture the attention of non-specialist audiences, stimulating new discussions and interesting people in important issues and ideas. And this, he insisted, did not necessitate simplification. It was, rather, a matter of style and presentation (Horne's 1984 book *The Great Museum*, for example, was favourably reviewed in both *The Sydney Morning Herald* and the *International Journal of Museum Management and Curatorship*). The best description of the task of the public intellectual, argued Horne, was the French term *haute vulgarisation*. Its literal translation is 'high popularisation'.[15]

◆ ◆ ◆

In late 1990, not long before the end of his six-year tenure at the Australia Council, Horne was treated to an elaborate farewell dinner at the Australian Museum in Sydney, where writers, journalists, politicians and arts industry heavies listened to a steady stream of tributes to the 'wizard of the Oz Council' himself. Max Bourke spoke of the profound impact *The Lucky Country* had had on him as a young man. The minister for the arts, David Simmons, called him 'one of the choice and master spirits of this age'. In a newspaper column a few months earlier, Humphrey McQueen even declared that Horne had helped remove 'intellectual' from the list of Australian swear words.[16]

Horne, though, was not quite ready for canonisation. Talk of retirement, he said, was premature. At sixty-eight, in good health and in full command of his faculties, he was at work on a new book, one that examined the absurdities and self-deceptions of the modern tourist experience. As he told journalist Lenore Nicklin, only death and senility could turn a writer off, 'and often *that* doesn't silence them'.[17] Nor did he have any intention of disappearing from public view. In early 1991, he was slated to begin a new role as chairman of the Ideas for Australia program – a government-endorsed thinktank operated from Monash University's Centre for Australian Studies. Less than twelve months later, he was invited to become chancellor of the University of Canberra. Far from signalling the end of his public career, recalled

David Marr, Horne's departure from the Australia Council was merely the beginning of a 'long non-retirement as the sage of Woollahra'.[18]

During the last year of his Australia Council chairmanship, Horne had become increasingly fixated on finding new ways to support the promotion of intelligent public discussion. For him, there was no reason this could not be done with government money. A productive and creative Australia, he argued, needed robust and complex 'intellectual infrastructure' – clear and formal pathways by which new ideas could be put onto the public agenda. In recent years, the Australian of the Year award had been won by Paul Hogan, Dick Smith and Allan Border. Horne's vision was to give intellectuals as prominent a place in the Australian imagination as cricketers, actors and business entrepreneurs, to give thinkers a seat at the decision-making table. He wanted, in short, more public intellectuals.[19]

The Ideas for Australia program was consistent with Horne's ideas about good public discussion. It had grown out of a series of heavily publicised conferences and seminars initiated by Horne and the Australia Council throughout 1990: big, media-friendly ideas jamborees attended by academics, politicians and artists. The first, February's National Ideas Summit, had been a two-day event at Old Parliament House in Canberra, with speakers including Hugh Stretton and Henry Reynolds (both academics), Diana Gribble (a publisher), David Throsby (an economist) and Noni Hazelhurst (an actor). In subsequent months, Horne had then presided over a series of Clever Country Seminars on topics such as media diversity, science and 'Unlocking the Academies', all of which were eventually brought under the Ideas for Australia umbrella.[20]

These public ideas symposia were only the latest manifestation of Horne's near four decade-long campaign to raise the standard of Australian public debate. To his mind, they served a similar function to the magazines he had edited in the 1960s and '70s: they were open forums in which a variety of leading Australians – journalists, academics, businesspeople and politicians – could imagine themselves to be part of a single, ongoing conversation about politics, culture and society. Horne's *Observer*, after all, had given space to figures as politically and intellectually diverse as Robert Hughes, Lillian Roxon,

Bruce Beresford, Judith Wright, Henry Mayer, Barry Humphries, Peter Coleman, Manning Clark, James McAuley, Brian Fitzpatrick, Christopher Koch, Jack Lang and Bob Santamaria. At *The Bulletin* in the late 1960s, writers Frank Moorhouse, Don Anderson, Ed Campion and Sandra Hall had been added to the conversation. He had even run an article by Richard Nixon.

At a National Press Club event in 1989, when asked by a journalist what he would like on his tombstone, Horne responded: he was a 'writer and talker'. After a short pause, however, he made an important addendum: 'and luncher'.[21] With Horne, what mattered most was discussion, and his ideal model for good public discussion remained the long lunch. Intelligent conversation over a meal and several bottles of wine, he thought, could be the most productive form of intellectual work, a chance to figure out what you might think. Like his contemporaries in the UNSW Political Science Department, Doug McCallum and Owen Harries, he was a kind of mid-century liberal, someone who believed in rational argument and putting the contrary case. Dialogue was important. Contestation was essential. If you weren't disagreeing, you weren't really talking.[22]

As such, Horne made a point of cultivating a relatively diverse collection of friends and acquaintances. As Peter Manning recalled, the frequent dinner parties hosted by Donald and Myfanwy at Grosvenor Street were always attended by a 'catholic' mixture of intellectual types: artists, writers and 'soft lefties' on one side of the table; Sydney powerbrokers and 'rabid neocons' on the other.[23] For Horne, too, fierce disagreement was no impediment to friendship. If anything, it was a precondition. Some of his dinner party rows with Adrian Deamer were 'legendary', remembered Gillian Appleton, but they never led to lasting rifts. Elaine Thompson called him a 'bully – but a very nice bully'. When they fought, she said, they were both aware that it was mostly a charade. Their absolute statements had 'no necessary depth'.[24] Max Bourke, as well, remembered that although they had several 'major blues' at the Australia Council, it never seemed to affect their working relationship. If he knew he was wrong, said Bourke, Horne would accept it and move on. Arguing was simply a way to arrive at the truth.[25]

Horne had different rules for public criticism. If you attacked him publicly, he would never forget. Beginning in the late '60s, he had a habit of responding directly to some of his reviewers, 'one critic each book'.[26] The most irritating mistake a book reviewer could make, he grumbled in 1970, was the 'failure to decide what kind of a book it is that is being reviewed, and what kind of standards apply to that kind of book'.[27] In 1980, when Frank Devine wrote a negative review of *Time of Hope*, Horne cut him off completely. 'I never want to see him again,' he wrote in a letter to a friend.[28] Richard Walsh, at one point an infrequent guest at Donald and Myfanwy's Grosvenor Street 'salons', alleged that he was dropped from the invite list after he accepted a job as the managing director of Australian Consolidated Press. Any association with the Packers, he speculated, was viewed by Horne as a betrayal.[29] For someone in such an 'unassailable position', recalled Appleton, Horne was 'strangely sensitive'.[30]

Criticism is the price of a lifetime of public intellectual combat, and Horne had no shortage of detractors. During the Australia Council years, in particular, he had found himself the subject of a number of serious critical essays. One of the most penetrating appeared in *Island* magazine in 1988. Its author, Tim Rowse, took aim at what he saw as Horne's 'Cold War complacency' on economic matters. In his view, Horne was a middle-class radical, a whimsical iconoclast whose ideas were rarely harnessed to any concrete political goals. He used irony without purpose; he practised polemic without values; he wrote 'criticism as urbane cultural consumption'. For Rowse, Horne's obsessive focus on culture was based on a naive postwar assumption that capitalism had been reformed out of existence. Amid the social wreckage of 'economic rationalist' policymaking in the 1980s, he thought, this ignorance of material politics was a recipe for critical impotence.[31]

Rowse's characterisation of Horne as a social critic either ignorant of or uninterested in the hard stuff of politics and economics was not new. As far back as 1970, the South Australian politician Don Dunstan had made an almost identical critique of Horne's book *The Next Australia*.[32] What was fundamentally at issue was the question of power: who had it and where did it reside? For Horne, no issue could not be further illuminated by examination through a cultural lens – including economics. In *Money Made Us*, for example, he had attempted to explain Australia's seemingly innate materialism and developmentalism though various cultural forms, such as habits, behaviours, monuments and buildings. In Horne's view, ideas always preceded politics: you first had to imagine something before you could act on it. For those like Rowse, however – watching on glumly as Horne's cultural studies approach worked its way through the academy in the 1980s – cultural power was always downstream of more concrete things: capital, institutions and the coercive capacity of the state. Without serious consideration of the harder forms of power, he thought, Horne's sophisticated brand of cultural criticism was simply a middle-class entertainment product.

Twelve months later, in a lively group study of several prominent Australian public thinkers, the critic Mark Thomas produced a more sympathetic portrait. Horne, he agreed, was certainly preoccupied with the cultural forms of power and 'myths' that societies entertained about themselves. But in Thomas's view, aside from an ongoing concern with Australia's colonial mentality and cultural cringe, he was a largely uncategorisable thinker: there was no particular set of ideas that could be reliably associated with him, no intellectual framework or tradition to which he could be tied. Instead, Thomas suggested, what was unique about Horne was less the ideas themselves than his approach to their contestation. He was a 'crystallising agent', a 'stirrer' and a 'signposter', constantly hoovering up a dizzying variety of competing cultural and intellectual currents and putting them back together in new forms. Viewed in its entirety, Horne's career was one unending Ideas Summit, his thoughts and opinions constantly evolving, overlapping, shifting, blending and grating in a more or less relentless stream of published work. If it was difficult to paint a coherent picture of Horne, he concluded, it was likely because there was too much evidence to draw from.[33]

Horne was nothing if not productive. In the few years before Rowse's and Thomas's essays, he had not only produced several wide-ranging works of social and political theory – culminating in 1986's *The Public Culture* – but also two successor volumes to his 1967 autobiography, *The Education of Young Donald*. And unlike the somewhat varied critical reactions to Horne's more explicitly sociological work, the tone of the responses to his autobiographical books was largely admiring. In *The Australian*, Denis O'Brien called him a 'master of the autobiography-as-an-art-form' and his books a shining example of 'social history made vividly evocative'. Vincent Buckley agreed, repeating his earlier judgement of *Education* as a 'masterpiece', and Horne as someone who was largely 'interested in himself as a reflector of the age'.[34] What was increasingly obvious to those who kept up with Horne's books was that his multi-decade interrogation of his own past was basically inseparable from his concurrent interrogation of the nation itself. As Mark Thomas observed in his 1989 profile (borrowing an idea from D.H. Lawrence), Horne had 'wrestled with the problem of himself and called it Australia'.[35] For Horne, both then and now, there was only one way out of this predicament: the declaration of an Australian republic.

◆ ◆ ◆

The 1980s were not a good decade for republicanism in Australia. Under Bob Hawke, the Labor Party had sought to distance itself from the controversies of the Whitlam years, and instead project an image of cautious and sound economic management. In this environment, there was little enthusiasm for republican ideas at government level. In 1985, Hawke attempted to usher in several modest constitutional reforms – including four-year terms and an acknowledgement of basic rights and freedoms – but even these had been firmly defeated at a referendum in 1988. Hawke's *Australia Act* of 1986, too, closed off a number of the remaining constitutional impediments to Australian independence (such as the ability for British parliament to legislate for state governments) which, in effect, neutered some of the more practical republican arguments for the removal of the Crown. The moment for serious constitutional change seemed to have passed. In 1990, while working on a PhD thesis on the history of republicanism in Australia, the historian Mark McKenna found himself facing an ocean of ambivalence. The republican issue, he was told, was a 'dead duck'.[36]

In May 1990, at this apparent nadir of republican sentiment, the Hornes received an encouraging letter. Its author, the NSW Labor MP

Franca Arena, was a long-term acquaintance, having been one of the speakers at the original Citizens for Democracy rally at the Sydney Town Hall in 1976. Like Donald and Myfanwy, she was a republican true believer, and had remained so throughout the demoralising decade that followed the collapse of CFD. In 1988, with the encouragement of the former NSW premier Neville Wran, she had begun recruiting prominent personages to a fledgling organisation that she hoped would put republicanism back on the political agenda in Australia. Twelve months later, when Arena's letter arrived at Grosvenor Street, she thought she had enough names to make it work. Would the Hornes lend their support? Myfanwy responded enthusiastically. Donald, she wrote, already had some strategic ideas. When his Australia Council tenure ended in December, she added, he would be a willing participant.[37]

Six months later, Horne was one of thirteen public figures who met in the Sydney office of a well-connected thirty-six-year-old merchant banker, Malcolm Turnbull, for the first meeting of the newly formed Australian Republican Movement (ARM). They were a tiny vanguard, organised around a dormant political issue, but there was some cause for optimism. To begin with, the end of the Cold War had reconfigured the republican debate in Australia to some extent, potentially taking some of the sting out of the accusations of disloyalty and subversion that would inevitably come their way. The next decade, too, would see centenaries of the famous constitutional conventions of the 1890s: modern-day Australians might even be inspired by their spirit of democratic experimentation. There was a growing media interest in the approaching new millennium and Sydney was making a bid to host the 2000 Olympics. Beyond that, there was the centenary of federation. Meanwhile, the passing of some of the most divisive figures in the post-dismissal era – Patrick White in September 1990, John Kerr in March 1991 and Manning Clark in May 1991 – gave a sense of new beginnings for the movement, free from the deep personal enmities of the past.[38]

In July 1991, the ARM officially launched at a media event at the Regent Hotel in Sydney's Circular Quay. In an inaugural press conference, eleven of the founding members of the organisation sat

Donald Horne and his fellow members of
the Australian Republican Movement in 1991

side-by-side on a long table: among them the writer (and founding ARM president) Thomas Keneally, the fashion designer Jenny Kee, the architect Harry Seidler, the civil rights activist Faith Bandler and the journalists Mark Day and Geraldine Doogue. And at the centre, directing proceedings as the MC, was Horne, the honoured veteran of struggles past.[39] In the temporary absence of Geoffrey Dutton (not to mention White and Clark), he was one of the presiding godfathers of modern Australian republicanism, an ageing symbol of historical continuity at the centre of a movement that sought to present itself as youthful, contemporary and future-focused.

Horne, though, had no intention of playing the museum piece. From the beginning, he positioned himself as one of the chief media faces of the organisation, spruiking the republican cause at every available opportunity. In the three years following the launch of the ARM, he penned a small avalanche of feature articles on the subject in major mastheads.[40] As chairman of the Ideas for Australia program, he oversaw a series of seminars on citizenship, media, cultural diversity and the Centenary of Federation.[41] In 1992, he also edited and contributed to a book, *The Coming Republic*, intended as a kind of primer on the key republican arguments. Its various authors were agreed not only on the practical need for change but also on its symbolic power. An Australian republic, argued Keneally, would 'let us know at last what an Australian is'.[42]

Like Keneally, Horne saw the republican issue as one that was, at least in part, a question about citizenship and national identity, about deciding who Australians were and what ideas they shared. Before the 1960s, Australia's official public sense of itself had been largely based around an ethnic Britishness. Since the social, cultural and geopolitical stirrings of that decade, however, no new consensual idea of the nation had moved in to take its place. After several decades of debate, there was still no obvious answer to the question of what would hold Australians together once they could no longer describe themselves as a British people. The basic question of Australia's national self-definition remained unresolved.

In the 1990s, with the republican issue back on the agenda, Horne became fixated on the articulation of a civic definition of the Australian nation. Nations, he argued, following Benedict Anderson's famous formulation, were 'imaginative constructs', existing mostly in the mind, in a people's shared idea of themselves. All modern industrial societies, he thought, required some imaginative or mythic set of ideas, some commonly held values and beliefs that allowed them to sustain and organise themselves. That such myths were not always declared by the state did not mean that they were not there: they were a feature of modernity. For Horne, the republic was an opportunity for Australia – itself an increasingly complex, multiracial society – to put its identity confusion in the past, and to enshrine a new, civic definition of the nation into its founding document. It was a chance to declare new, more relevant myths around which the nation might organise itself in the twenty-first century.[43]

In Horne's view, such navel-gazing over the national character was not simply a parlour game for newspaper opinion columnists and 'patio intellectuals'.[44] As he wrote in *The Coming Republic* (and, explicitly or implicitly, in nearly everything he wrote in the 1990s), it was constitutive of Australian politics itself. The way that people imagined the world ultimately determined the way that they would act. As an example, he offered the long dominance of 'the bush' in the Australian imagination, a pervasive national myth that for many decades had worked to conceal the fact that Australians were actually a largely urban people. This misunderstanding of reality, he thought, had had all sorts of adverse consequences for government policymaking, not least the long political neglect of the suburbs. The question of Australia's identity, history and nationhood, therefore, was not simply a hollow intellectual debate over symbols, images and signs: it was a program for action.[45]

It was for this reason that the republican question became so central to the intense debates over culture, history and national identity that dominated Australian public life in the 1990s. These culture wars, as they came to be known, were a contest over the two broad and largely incompatible visions of the nation and its essential character that had emerged out of the 1960s – one older, more homogenous and socially conservative; the other more diverse, cosmopolitan and sympathetic to 'post-material' issues, including feminism, environmentalism and multiculturalism. One took a somewhat Whiggish view of the Australian past, keeping the focus on economic progress and Anglo-Saxon achievement; the other was motivated by impulses of self-criticism and social justice, tending to complicate and sometimes undercut standard national narratives, particularly where it concerned Australia's treatment of its Indigenous population.

These claims for control of the national narrative were turbocharged by the ascension of Paul Keating to the prime ministership in December 1991, six months after the ARM launch. Keating assumed office during an economic slump that was at least partially initiated by some of the drastic economic reforms he had himself unleashed on the country during his seven years as treasurer. But just months into his leadership, in a barbed speech delivered on the floor of parliament, Keating redirected the national agenda towards matters cultural, presenting a sweeping interpretation of Australian political history that positioned the Labor Party as the one true 'aggressively Australian' party of progress, and the Liberals as a rabble of nostalgic conservatives with an obsolete attachment to Britain (a country, he said, that had abandoned Australia during World War II). In subsequent months, Keating laid out the elements of a 'big picture' for the country, tying Labor's recent economic reforms to a much broader social and cultural program that included Indigenous reconciliation and land rights, engagement with Asia, multiculturalism and, ultimately, a republic.[46]

Before the 1990s, this contestation over the character of the nation had periodically attached itself to particular political events and intellectual controversies – such as the South African Springboks' rugby tour of Australia in 1971, Geoffrey Blainey's criticism of the pace of Asian migration in 1984 and disagreement over the nature of the Bicentennial celebrations in 1988 – without it ever becoming fundamental to party politics. In the 1990s, that changed. Between 1992 and 1994, Keating campaigned openly for a republic, while the Opposition remained staunchly against it (or rather against 'Keating's republic'). At the same time, Keating's big picture became a target for a new cohort of economic and cultural conservatives. Fashioning themselves as a 'New Right', they pushed back against this newer, more civic-minded vision of the country, depicting it instead as the hobbyhorse of a new left elite, a cohort of Whitlamite intellectuals who had come to dominate the arts, the media and the universities in Australia.[47]

In this new political environment, Donald Horne came to be seen by conservatives (and even some on the left) not as a political maverick or a gadfly but as one of the leaders of a left-liberal cultural establishment. In their view, Horne's persistent inquiring into the national ethos appeared, somewhat perversely, to have earned him an exalted social standing. In *The Bulletin*, Patrick Cook called his February 1990 Ideas Summit a 'Festival of Lovely Little Thinkers' (with Horne as 'Professor Trumpet'). In *Quadrant*, Robert Manne argued that Horne's symposia were a reflection of the consensus ideology and corporate politics of the Hawke era.[48] The sociologist Boris Frankel, too, thought the contributors to the first Ideas for Australia conference were representative of a 'loose cultural mafia' that had dominated Australian public culture since the 1970s. This group, he suggested, shared a vision of Australian identity that was basically simpatico with Keating's big picture. If this was oppositional public intellectual life in Australia, he concluded, 'then God help us'.[49]

These were not baseless accusations. Horne was a well-paid author and public commentator, the chair of multiple government arts bodies and the chancellor of a university. He had an Order of

Australia and several honorary degrees. In 1991, the Ideas For Australia program had even initiated an annual Donald Horne Lecture. He moved freely in Sydney literary, academic and media circles. His books were often launched by Labor or Labor-sympathetic figures: Manning Clark and *Money Made Us*, Gough Whitlam and *The Great Museum*, Jim McClelland and *The Public Culture*, Barry Jones and *The Lucky Country Revisited*. And since the late 1960s, he had been one of the most prominent campaigners for constitutional reform and an Australian republic.[50]

Horne's passionate advocacy of a more civic-minded vision of the country had certainly turned him into a partisan in the new war over culture, but this image of him as a deified darling of the left-liberal cultural establishment is nevertheless too simple. First there was a matter of generational difference. As David Carter wrote in 2004, by comparison with the majority of the new cohort of public intellectuals that emerged in the 1990s, Horne was an 'old stager', someone who had come to prominence at an earlier moment: socially, culturally, politically.[51] Despite his activism on behalf of Whitlam's agenda in the late 1970s, his party-political attachments were never especially clear-cut. While Horne saw the Labor Party as more sympathetic to his vision for the country, his writing spoke less for a party than it did for a particular social type: professional, white collar, liberal, educated, urban. Before the 1990s, neither party had a monopoly on this particular demographic. In 1989, for example, Horne's book *Ideas for a Nation* was launched by the Liberal premier of New South Wales, Nick Greiner.[52]

On the issue of Indigenous reconciliation, meanwhile – one of the defining political concerns of the '90s – Horne's was not a particularly prominent voice. The issue burst onto the national agenda in 1992, following a High Court decision to partially recognise Indigenous land rights and, six months later, a moving admission of past government misdeeds by Paul Keating in a speech at Redfern Park. Horne, of course, was not opposed to such developments: he had been publicly supportive of attempts to redress Indigenous disadvantage since at least the late 1960s, when he had written a foreword to Frank Hardy's book on the subject, *The Unlucky Australians*. At the time, too, he had argued that reconciliation was not simply a matter of improving Australia's international reputation: it was something to be done for its own sake. To treat Indigenous Australians like dogs, he had written, was 'to treat ourselves as a nation of dogs'.[53] It is safe to say, though, that over the course of his public career the issue had never fully fired Horne's imagination. His idea of an Australian republic, for example, was almost entirely premised on the need to expunge Australia's public culture of any traces of Britishness and to replace it with pluralist ideals of tolerance and diversity. The need to reckon with Australia's origins was, for Horne, always subordinate to this grander civic project.

Nor was Horne's relationship with Paul Keating particularly straightforward. The two men had crossed paths several times throughout the 1980s, and Keating and his wife, Anita, had even dined at Grosvenor Street.[54] Though Horne had an obvious sympathy with Keating's cultural agenda, he was not enthusiastic about other key aspects of the prime minister's program. As treasurer, Keating had been an advocate of 'economic rationalism', the byword for a suite of policies designed to deregulate an ostensibly stagnant Australian economy and expose it to the invigorating influence of global markets and financial flows. Horne, by contrast, was generationally inclined towards a more social democratic idea of national economic management, and was highly critical of this new policymaking consensus. Through the Ideas for Australia program, he had even tried – unsuccessfully – to rebrand it as 'economic fundamentalism'.[55]

In the 1990s, Horne used his newspaper columns to dole out advice to the prime minister. In 1995, their hitherto cordial relationship collapsed in a catty newspaper exchange over the details of a lunch that had occurred during his Australia Council term. In Horne's account, he had used this meeting to present Keating with the idea for what eventually became a lucrative series of Creative Fellowships. In response, Keating penned a dismissive editorial in *The Sydney Morning Herald*, describing Horne's Australia Council as 'stale' ('you could smell the thing') and claiming that he had come up with the fellowships himself. He had only agreed to the meeting, he wrote, after he was told that he would need to drop the knee to Horne, lest the 'cranky old joker' tried to find a way to wreck the whole idea. 'To prick the conscience of a toff is a big undertaking,' he concluded.[56]

Perhaps the biggest wrinkle in the image of Horne as a powerful cultural elite was his lack of influence within the republican movement. After Keating's adoption of the issue in 1992, and his government's subsequent establishment of a Republic Advisory Committee in 1993, the ARM had become only one voice in a much wider conversation about the republic. On the face of it, this was not really a cause for concern: if anything, the mainstreaming of republican debate was a sign of the organisation's success. But it did render the ARM meetings less important and, increasingly, less well attended. In 1993, Tom Keneally stepped down as president. His replacement, Malcolm Turnbull, was less consultative and more inclined towards private meetings and dealmaking. Horne's suggestions – written and verbal – increasingly fell on deaf ears. During one committee debate over who should speak at a public event, Neville Wran had suggested that Horne should appear on the stage not as the main performer, but simply in a show of solidarity with the 'other icons'. The most important conversations, it seemed, were happening elsewhere.[57]

Horne continued to go to ARM meetings, but he had less and less access to the powerbrokers behind the movement. When John Howard defeated Paul Keating at the 1996 election and announced a Constitutional Convention, Horne was not among the delegates chosen to represent the ARM, nor was he chosen by Howard as one of the non-elected delegates, despite prompting from NSW premier Bob Carr. When the convention ran in February 1998, Horne, the grandfather of the modern Australian republican movement, watched from home, on the couch, shouting at the television set. Not long after, he quietly resigned from the ARM.[58]

◆ ◆ ◆

As an old man, Horne lost none of his zest for new things. The rise of Pauline Hanson, the calamity of the Iraq War, the normalisation of profanity on the television show *Sex and the City*, watching strangers on public transport: all were sources of interest and inquiry.

Lunches, too, remained an important window onto the world, although they had evolved from large group affairs to more intimate encounters. Perhaps uncharacteristically for a man of his age, Horne was an enthusiastic adopter of the home desktop computer. 'I could talk about nothing else at lunch for weeks,' he recalled.[59]

Horne took to computers partly because he was – as he put it – a 'dirty writer', someone who wrote many drafts, fiddling around with his sentences, cutting and pasting, experimenting with different words and phrasings and tones.[60] Since his retirement from teaching, he had kept up a rigorous writing schedule. Each day, after eating breakfast and scanning the papers, he would dive straight into a long morning of work, punctuated here and there by short breaks in the garden or to talk to the cat. After lunch, he would take a nap, and if he had nothing on that day would do some more writing in the afternoon. For most of his career, he would go again after dinner, sometimes working late into the night. Elaine Thompson remembered getting phone calls from Horne at 10 p.m. to boast about how many papers he had marked or words he had written. In his seventies, though, he was forced to put an end to after-dinner writing. He simply did not have the energy for it.[61]

By the mid-to-late 1990s, Horne had reached the lifetime achievement phase of his career. He was a receiver of honorary degrees and a deliverer of graduation addresses. At the University of Canberra, he joked, one of his main jobs had been to shake hands at ceremonies, as if he were a 'department store Santa Claus'. Between 1992 and 1995, he had participated in three separate longform biographical oral history interviews about his life and work. In 1997, he was included on a list of National Living Treasures, chosen by public vote and described as 'exceptional Australians with substantial and enduring accomplishment in their field'.[62] At a book launch in 1998, Noel Pearson called him an 'elder'.[63]

Indeed, ageing had taken a toll on Horne's public profile. To younger Australian intellectuals, he was a grandfatherly figure, wise and experienced, but also increasingly at a remove from the cut and thrust of contemporary political debates. In *Gangland*, Mark Davis's much-discussed 1997 book about the dominance of an older generation over

Australian public culture, he barely rated a mention. In 1998, in a review of a re-released compendium of Horne's three volumes of autobiography, the journalist Matt Condon mentioned that it was 'still possible, on occasion' to witness Horne engaging in Australian cultural life.[64]

This declining relevance was also partly a by-product of Horne's somewhat old-fashioned self-presentation and writerly tastes. Large parts of *The Coming Republic*, one of his early contributions to the Australian Republican Movement, were presented as an imaginary lunch conversation, a stylistic choice that came across to some readers as slightly patronising, as if he and his contributors were talking down to their audience. Amid a cacophony of new media voices, Horne had the accent and the appearance of an educated postwar Australian, not one but two generations removed from the new wave of public intellectuals. In his 1992 book *The Intelligent Tourist*, he included a picture of himself visiting a slum in the South African city of Soweto – in a full suit and tie.[65]

He was also a partisan of the written word in an age of television. He was a perfectly capable and articulate media performer, but his true metier was the book-length critical essay and the newspaper column, not the panel-show discussion or lecture. Provocative books and columns could still cause a stir, but they were no longer the only game in town. The fate of *The Avenue of the Fair Go* – Horne's most ambitious book from this late period – was illustrative of this dilemma. He had begun working on it in 1993, in the midst of his fervour about civic identity and republicanism, envisioning it as a comprehensive account of the history of political ideas in Australia, wise and erudite, but made accessible through a straightforward, common-sense style. His idea had been to invent an imaginary theme park of political philosophy and to have a small group of Australians – each representative of a different demographic and social type – discuss various abstract concepts in a kind of Aristotelian dialogue, not dissimilar to the conversational format of *The Coming Republic*. So the 'Aboriginal Postgraduate Student' and the 'Sceptical Older Woman', among others, would debate different notions of liberty at the Manning Clark Memorial Verandah, or the 'Guy with the Ponytail' and the 'Singapore-born Australian' would discuss the

Australian cult of national development in front of the Memorial to the Ruins of Optimism.[66]

Horne spent several years on *The Avenue of the Fair Go*, showing different sections to close friends and family, as was his habit, and rewriting it based on their suggestions. When he finished, the manuscript was shopped around by his agent. Multiple publishers declined, unsure of how it would be received.[67] When the book finally appeared in 1997, this proved a shrewd judgement. Horne had hoped that his common-sense discussion of general political precepts might make the book a standard text for schools and universities, a kind of civics handbook for ordinary Australians. *Avenue's* reception, though, was muted. While most reviewers found its basic premise admirable and its arguments wise and erudite, they found Horne's stylistic and formal choices strange, almost quaint. Murray Sayle called it 'original', 'quirky' and 'weird.' In *Australian Book Review*, John Button wondered why Horne had indulged himself with a 'bunch of weirdos' in a theme park when he could have 'told it straight'. The book's weakness, wrote Ross Fitzgerald, was that it dealt with political ideas far too earnestly. Horne's imaginary discussions between ordinary people were necessarily fantasies, but in his attempts to remain contemporary, he had resorted to gimmickry. The book sold fewer copies than anything else he had published.[68]

Peter Coleman's response to the book in *The Australian*, meanwhile, occasioned one of Horne's most vigorous ripostes. His former *Observer* colleague devoted the majority of his review to a predictable critique of Horne's unorthodox political evolution – from 'crusted Tory' to 'born again Whitlamite' – and fixated on the fact that the book had been launched by Cheryl Kernot, leader of the Australian Democrats. In response, Horne expressed outrage at what he saw as a gross misrepresentation of himself and his work. In a letter to the editor, he took issue with Coleman's unwillingness to say anything about the actual book itself. Coleman, he wrote, had 'forgotten the difference between reviewing a book and making cheap shots at parliamentary question time'. Horne then sent two separate three-page letters to his 'former friend', detailing Coleman's indiscretions, and another to the paper's literary editor, Barry Oakley, demanding an explanation for why the review was allowed to run. The episode ended Horne's near forty-year relationship with Coleman.[69]

The disappointment of *The Avenue of the Fair Go* was accompanied by an alarming physical decline. While packing the car on a driving trip around New Zealand in 1997, he noticed he was becoming increasingly breathless. Back home, doctors suggested it might be emphysema, or possibly lung damage from the intense smoking habit he had kept up until the 1970s. The ailment was eventually diagnosed as pulmonary fibrosis – a hardening or thickening of the lung tissue – which was liable to progress over time. Short trips to the shops at Bondi Junction soon began to leave him exhausted and prone on the couch. For perhaps the first time in his life, too, he found himself unable to write with any clarity or vigour. His remarkable powers of concentration, it seemed, were slowly succumbing to the realities of ageing.[70]

Indeed, as his ninth decade approached, Horne had finally begun to show some signs of slowing down. After 1996, when he finished his term as chancellor at the University of Canberra, he kept up a much less intense calendar of public commitments. In the late 1990s, life for Donald and Myfanwy became increasingly dominated by health concerns. Myfanwy was diagnosed with osteoarthritis and in 1998 had a hip replacement (her second), from which she then developed a serious medical complication. Not long after she arrived home from hospital, Donald came down with a severe bout of pneumonia that left him hospitalised and prone to heart failure. Soon after, he had an operation to remove a cancerous growth from his bowel.[71] As Horne's body faltered, he and Myfanwy began to spend an increasing amount of time in their second home at Wentworth Falls in the Blue Mountains, which they had purchased in 1989 with the windfall from the sale of an investment property.[72]

None of this stifled Horne's creative energies. He was never happy unless he had a writing project, and despite his increasing frailty, he continued to work – albeit at a much slower pace. In the late 1990s, he amalgamated his three autobiographies into a single volume, *An Interrupted Life*, making over a thousand changes. Two years later, he published a memoir of his public life, *Into the Open*. The New Zealand trip in 1997 proved to be his last overseas adventure, but,

where possible, he still travelled within Australia, attending conferences, delivering lectures and speaking at writers' festivals.[73] He got
involved in preparations for the Centenary of Federation in 2001, sitting on the Australian Citizenship Council and organising a series of
public lectures on the topic 'What holds Australians together despite
their diversity?'[74]

Even in the early 2000s, in his eighties, Horne managed to mus-
ter the energy to produce two final book-length works of social
criticism, *Looking for Leadership* and *10 Steps to a More Tolerant
Australia*. Both were attempts to defend a liberal, social-democratic
vision of the country from the ghosts of anti-intellectualism and
xenophobia that the Howard government and its sympathisers had
recently reawakened, particularly in the aftermath of the contentious
2001 'Tampa' election. With its weaponisation of culture and its gestures towards an older, more homogenous idea of Australia, this new
social conservatism was in part a backlash against several decades of
national self-criticism – the three-decade period, beginning in the
1960s, in which many of the great certainties that had long underpinned Australian life were abruptly and sometimes reluctantly
called into question: among them White Australia and Britishness,
the nation's relationship with Asia and the difficult realities of Australia's colonial past.

In *10 Steps*, Horne called this a 'thirty-year truce', the agreement on
both sides of politics to maintain a basic level of tolerance and pluralism in both rhetoric and policy.[75] In the 1990s, he thought, this truce
had come undone. Populist appeals to a vanishing homogeneity were
exploited politically. If nothing else, John Howard's political success in
these years showed that the disagreement over the civic definition of
Australia that Horne had pursued in the wake of empire's end was still
far from settled. As Guy Rundle argued in his review of *Looking for
Leadership* in 2001, the 'vision of life' promoted by Horne – criticising,
taking things apart, putting them back together again – probably only
occurred naturally to the 'intellectually trained'. It had less appeal, he
thought, for those who looked for 'a more concrete story of their identity'.[76] Australians, as Howard famously proclaimed, were 'over all that
sort of identity stuff'.[77]

Horne, though, did not see this populist backlash as a reason to disavow the three decades of social progress that had been enabled, at least in part, by his perpetual seminar on the nation's identity and basic values. Indeed, in his final years, he even took to calling himself a liberal humanist. On matters of basic principle, he had aligned himself with what he saw as the forces of reason, tolerance, basic equality and the good life for all. As his son Nick put it several years later, Horne was a 'child of the Enlightenment'.[78] This did not mean that he was naive to the complexities and contradictions inherent in the pursuit of progress – he remained a sceptic to the end – but nor did he succumb to cynicism either. If there was a basic difference between the young Horne and the old – one that went to the heart of his political evolution – it was that where he once saw futility in action, he now saw opportunity. That actions sometimes produced unintended consequences was no argument against them: if anything, he believed, doing nothing was itself a form of action – and one that often produced worse results. Hope, he thought, might be our only guide.[79] As he had written in the final line of *The Lucky Country*, many problems threaten the future of Australia, but it was always worth 'giving it a go'.[80]

Horne said as much in one of his last significant public appearances, at a graduation ceremony in the Great Hall at the University of Sydney in late April 2005. He was receiving an honorary degree, sixty-four years after World War II had cut short his undergraduate studies at that same institution. He was physically frail and in serious ill health, aware that his time would soon be up. In his address, delivered from a wheelchair with the aid of a breathing apparatus, he warned this last group of graduates that as good, critical-minded citizens, they should always beware of 'phoney vocationalism' and 'hyper-naive utilitarianism'. The point of a good humanistic education, he insisted, was to pursue ideas 'for their own sake'. Thinking imaginatively, experimentally, creatively, curiously, without recourse to practical outcomes, without instrumental intent, could, he thought, be one of the most practical things a person could do. The life he encouraged them to live – the one he had himself lived – was one of relentless observation and examination, of perpetual thought, discussion and argument. 'Go,' he said, 'in the name of imagination,

of wonder and curiosity, of the spirit of enquiry, of critical engagement, of the ethic of the producer and of enterprise, and see what
you can make of them.'[81]

13.

REQUIEM

Donald Horne died as he lived: by interrogating his own experiences and impressions, then writing them down for public consumption. In the last few months of his life, confined almost entirely to his home and its immediate surrounds, he kept a diary of his terminal illness and his final thoughts on matters political and philosophical. With the aid of Myfanwy, Julia, Nick and several medical professionals, he attempted to dissect the predicament of his physical decline with the same curiosity and insight that he applied to everything else he had come across over the course of his long life: to the design and functions of his oxygen tank, the difficulties of doing basic household tasks, the installation of a stair lift in his house, his creeping sense of isolation and confinement, the joy of watching movies with his young granddaughter, the pleasures of reading *The New York Review of Books* and the annoyances and amusements of his increasingly frequent hospital stays. If you looked at things with the same attentiveness that people give to paintings, he wrote, then 'the whole world becomes a great museum'.[1]

This last, seemingly futile writing project captured so much of what made Horne a great public thinker and writer. His curiosity was boundless, his penchant for extrapolating grander meanings out of everyday things insatiable. His criticism combined an incredibly sharp eye for detail with a kind of worldliness and wisdom. He was always focused on the bigger picture. Nothing was irrelevant. In 1989, reviewing Horne's book *Ideas for a Nation*, Maurice Dunlevy speculated that Horne might have got close to his great boyhood desire to 'know everything'.[2] Horne, he wrote, 'seems to have been everywhere, seen everything'.[3] He was a consummate generalist, an inveterate autodidact, one of Australia's most prominent, stimulating and entertaining know-alls. As Mungo MacCallum reflected in 2006, Horne could mount a fair claim to being Australia's last genuine public intellectual.[4]

Horne's erstwhile friend Peter Coleman once remarked on the many Donald Hornes – the multiplicity of public characters and roles that he seemed to have played over the course of his life.[5] In the small avalanche of remembrances, reminisces and tributes that followed the news of his death on 5 September 2005, many obituarists did the same. There were, of course, the familiar figures: Horne the author of *The Lucky Country*; Horne the famous writer and public intellectual; Horne the pugnacious magazine editor; Horne the activist and republican; Horne the Professor of Political Science; and Horne the chairman of the Australia Council. There were, too, odd mentions of more obscure, earlier characters: Horne the young libertarian and *enfant terrible*; Horne the trainee diplomat; Horne the anglophile conservative expat; Horne the editor of a lowbrow tabloid magazine; Horne the advertising executive; Horne the crusading anti-communist.

However, these were the public faces. At a small private funeral, followed by a memorial service at the State Library of New South Wales, many of Horne's friends and intimates spoke of the man behind the many roles and personas – Horne the 'dishwasher unstacker', recounted his friend Ed Campion, and the father and husband who, when he wasn't making breakfast for Myfanwy or folding laundry, would be lecturing to the windshield on family holidays.[6] As his son-in-law Stephen Garton remarked, the boundaries between the public and private Hornes were never clear-cut: the ideas that made it into his books were always tried out first over lunch or dinner. The 'riotous, argumentative but convivial' company of family and friends, said Garton, was Horne's basic model for a healthy public culture.[7]

Speaking to an interviewer in 1968, Horne speculated that he was 'a bit Italian', in the sense that his first loyalty was always to his family.[8] If there was an essential Horne, a basic biographical fact that held together all the different personas, it was this one: the man at the head of the table, arguing, declaiming, conceding or simply just trying to get a hearing in the 'noisy republic of ideas' that he built for himself at Grosvenor Street.[9] For half a century, said Campion, Horne's family and friends were 'enrolled in the ongoing Donald Horne seminar whose foundation member was Myfanwy'.[10] In the debate among this highly collaborative family were the origins of nearly everything he ever wrote. Indeed, once the commotion of the tributes and memorials had passed, the Donald Horne seminar promptly restarted, as they all went back to work editing, reshaping and discussing what eventually became Horne's last and most intimate book, *Dying: A Memoir*. Published posthumously in 2007, it was the first of his works for which he and Myfanwy publicly shared authorship; a fitting tribute to a long, productive literary partnership.

Almost every obituarist remarked on the eccentricity of Horne's intellectual odyssey, from youthful libertarianism through liberal conservatism and Cold War anti-communism, to his eventual arrival as a social democrat, republican and self-described 'secular liberal humanist'. But while Horne did change his mind on certain fundamental political questions, it is somewhat superficial to suggest that he simply switched his allegiance from the right to the left, from conservative to progressive, as if these labels signified a set of unchanging policies and positions rather than a constantly evolving dynamic of politics. Horne's long march from right to left was not a straightforward rejection of an earlier conservatism, but rather the evolution of a reforming liberalism that he had always espoused. As MacCallum suggested, Horne was at all times an advocate of 'a decent and fair society in which the right to dissent was jealously protected'. He was the constant, MacCallum argued, 'it was the society around him that moved'.[11]

In Horne's view, his most consistent theme, the issue that held his work together, was a concern with the construction of 'reality'. He had an intuitive sense that out of the meaninglessness of existence, people created their own realities, sets of attitudes and beliefs that were always 'hypothetical' and thus always open to critique. Either consciously or not, this idea ran through the entirety of his vast and eclectic catalogue of books, from his commentary on Australian politics and culture to his works on tourism, museums and public culture, from his autobiographies and histories to his novels and satires. *The Lucky Country*, he told Ann Turner in 1994, was 'concerned with the fact that how we act depends on how we see things'.[12] His shift to the left was, in this sense, the result of his own recalibration of reality, his belated discovery – to borrow a phrase from the book – of some 'new ideas of the possible'.

Mark McKenna recalled once asking Horne how to effect social and political change. Horne's response was typically straightforward: 'Just get out there and talk ... take part in the conversation.'[13] One of the things that distinguished Horne from many of his contemporaries was not any particular political position or idea, but rather his approach to their discussion. You could not know the value of an idea, he thought, unless you had discussed it, poked it, seen whether it interested people.[14] As he often wrote in the 1960s, the Australian people had long been castigated for their lack of interest in big ideas, but perhaps the problem was simply the quality of the ideas that had been presented to them. Horne's talent was to constantly refresh the public discourse, to relentlessly re-tune his cultural antennae to whatever was on people's minds, and then to articulate it with extraordinary clarity, verve and sagacity.[15]

In *The Lucky Country*, Horne famously described the stereotypical image of Australia as 'a man in an open-necked shirt, solemnly eating an ice cream. His kiddie is beside him'.[16] That this portrait of the national essence now seems impossibly out of date is partly the result of one of the many endless public seminars initiated and perpetuated by Donald Horne. As he well knew, the sheer complexity of modern Australia – the basic fact of its pluralism – meant that a simple image of the nation that was in any way representative of its diversity would always be elusive. These days, in an age of air travel, dual citizenship and smartphones, the concept itself seems almost quaint.

It is worth reminding ourselves that *The Lucky Country*, Horne's first and most successful act of political criticism, was not a straightforward attempt to capture the national image, but rather a lively, eclectic and impressionistic survey of how Australia looked in the early 1960s, in all its diversity – at least in the view of one keen-eyed and sharp-tongued observer. The book's novelty was to think about the present on its own terms, and to refuse to rely uncritically on received wisdoms, on what Horne saw as the old ways of looking at things. If, in his public life, Horne had a tendency to abruptly shift gears, to suddenly take on new interests and abandon old ones, it was in large part a product of this committed contemporaneity, this relentless desire to keep the conversation going.

It is tempting to think of Horne's achievements as a public intellectual as a thing of the past, a time when critics had the platform and the ability to shift the public agenda. We are reminded time and again of the disappearance of such figures, of the decline of public discourse, of the fragmentation of our media environment. But it is pessimistic to assume that good ideas, well expressed, cannot be taken up and turned into a framework for action. Technology and media may have changed, but we have not. We still try to make sense of the world, to construct our hypothetical realities. As Horne might have said, we are all political critics.

We will not, though, have another Donald Horne, another *Lucky Country*. We must have something else, something new, something similar but distinctive. If we are looking for a guide to the future, as Horne always was, we should begin by trying to think carefully about the real problems of the present. As he once said of *Observer*, his first serious contribution to public debate, its aim was to see the shape of new problems, not to 'recite recipes' for the solution of old ones. *Observer* was interested, primarily, in providing a forum for debate.[17] And in this sense, at least, Horne did come up with an alternative national ideal: it involved several men and women, some of them in open-necked shirts, vigorously debating a point over lunch. Three empty bottles of wine are beside them.

ACKNOWLEDGEMENTS

I started working on this book in 2017, when I enrolled in a PhD program in the Department of History at the University of Sydney. The subsequent six years have not been without their challenges, and I am grateful to have been surrounded throughout by a wonderful network of friends, family and colleagues.

This book was a marathon, not a sprint, and it was always reassuring to know that when my form dipped all I had to do was get on the phone to Mark McKenna. As a mentor, friend and unofficial literary agent, he has been an unfailing advocate and sensitive critic of my writing for as long as I have known him. I would not have had the stamina to complete it were it not for his relentless encouragement and support.

I owe a great debt of gratitude to Chris Feik, who saw the potential of the book from the very beginning, and showed such patience and understanding during the times when life got in the way of writing it. Thanks, also, to Chris's team at Black Inc. / La Trobe University Press, and to Kate Morgan and Kate Hatch for their editorial brilliance.

Special thanks are due to Julia and Nick Horne, who were generous with their time, shared several photographs, were always willing to confirm facts for me and granted me permission to publish from the Donald and Myfanwy Horne Papers. Thanks, also, to Charles Woolley, who spent a good deal of time rummaging for photographs in a garage on the other side of the world and allowed me to reproduce much of what he found.

Thanks, as well, to the many friends, colleagues and acquaintances of Donald Horne's who made time to talk to me and answer my questions, including Phillip Adams, Don Aitkin, Michael Baume, Max Bourke, Edmund Campion, Peter Coleman, Conal Condren, Robert Darroch, Glyn Davis, Geraldine Doogue, Graeme Eggins, Lindsay Foyle, Sandra Hall, Andrea Hull, Helen Irving, Peter Manning, Michael McKernan, Meaghan Morris, Brad Norrington, Ross Poole, Elaine Thompson and Richard Walsh.

The Mitchell Library has been my second home for the last five years, and I would especially like to thank the archivists there, who were always willing to meet my requests and whose expertise I was the grateful beneficiary of. Thanks also to the cafe staff, who regularly gave me staff rates for coffee, even though I was clearly not an employee. Thanks, too, to the archivists at the National Library of Australia and the National Archives of Australia.

I am especially grateful to those who read the manuscript, in whole or in part. Mark McKenna read and commented on every chapter, usually more than once. James Curran, Chris Hilliard, Dominic Kelly, Billy Griffiths, Daniel Seaton, Robert Manne, Judith Brett and Elaine Thompson all offered invaluable feedback at different stages. Thanks in particular to Cathy Perkins, whose conversation and editorial acumen improved this book immeasurably. Peter Browne, too, not only read the entire manuscript at the last minute but also signed me up to write for *Inside Story* when I had barely written a word in public.

I am also indebted to those who have extended a helping hand in myriad other ways, big and small: Bridget Griffen-Foley, Emily Millane, Justin Macdonnell, Robert Milliken, Cassandra Pybus, Carl Reinecke, Peter Rose, Tim Rowse and Stuart Ward.

My friends and colleagues at the University of Sydney have been an endless source of support and motivation. In particular I would like to thank James Curran for first sparking my interest in Australian history, and for giving me the initial push in Horne's direction. Chris Hilliard provided invaluable guidance in the book's early stages and gave perceptive feedback on several chapters. As Head of Department, Kirsten McKenzie has also been immensely supportive.

I was lucky to be surrounded by a brilliant group of postgrads at the University of Sydney. Ben Vine, Emmet Gillespie, Dan Dixon, Orla McGovern, Daniel Seaton and Frank Yuan are among those whose friendship and intelligent conversation I have relied upon for many years. Thanks also to Anne Thoeming and the USyd Biography Reading Group for many enjoyable and stimulating discussions.

Thanks to those whose friendship has sustained me throughout the writing of the book. You know who you are. Thanks in particular to Michael Roddan and Thomas Mitchell, who both started (and finished) writing books long after I began mine, and have been invaluable sounding boards for my entire adult life – on much more than matters literary. Sorry for all the text messages.

Finally, none of this would have been possible without the love and support of my family. To my parents, thank you – especially for the child care. To Deirdre, my partner in everything, thanks for coming on the journey with me. To Patrick and Hazel, who joined us along the way, this book is for you.

NOTES

NOTE ON REFERENCING
Unless otherwise stated, citations of correspondence and documents refer to Donald Horne's manuscript papers at the State Library of New South Wales, MLMSS 3525.

INTRODUCTION

1   'Son of the Lucky Country', *Four Corners*, ABC television, aired 1 November 1968, NAA: C475, 1550790 Item ID: 13447813.

2   Mark Thomas, *Australia in Mind: Thirteen Influential Australian Thinkers* (Sydney: Hale & Iremonger, 1989), p. 121. H.G. Kippax thought *The Lucky Country* 'summarised' many of the ideas that had already appeared 'either expensively in hardbacks or obscurely in literary or learned journals', H.G. Kippax, 'Australians: Lucky or Unlucky?', *The Sydney Morning Herald*, 19 December 1964. Horne, wrote the academic Paul Reynolds, 'transcended disciplines and the boundaries of professional life': Paul Reynolds, 'Donald Horne: Public Intellectual', *Australian Parliamentary Review* 20 (Spring 2005), p. 8.

3   Donald Horne, 'The Art of Political Criticism', paper presented at the 1974 Australasian Political Studies Association Conference, MLMSS 3525 Add on 1871, Box 23 AD-1 (b).

4   Cited by Horne in 'Son of the Lucky Country'.

5   Horne described his 1989 effort *Ideas for a Nation* as an 'affectionate adieu' to the phrase, see Donald Horne, *Ideas for a Nation* (Sydney: Pan Books, 1989), p. 12.

6   Geoffrey Blainey, 'The Dashing Bee Who Tried to Wake Australia', *The Age*, 10 September 2005.

7   Donald Horne, *In Search of Billy Hughes*, 2nd ed. (Melbourne: Black Inc., 2000 [1979]).

1. WILD YOUNG SAVAGE

1   'Sex Leader Causes Big Stir', *Honi Soit*, 10 October 1941.

2   'Ulysses Banned after 20 years', *The Courier-Mail*, 19 September 1941; on *Ulysses* ban, see Patrick Mullins, *The Trials of Portnoy: How Penguin Brought Down Australia's Censorship System* (Melbourne: Scribe, 2020), pp. 14–16.

3   Donald Horne, 'Sex! – Isn't It Dreadful', *Honi Soit*, 2 October 1941.

4   Donald Horne, 'Argumentum Ad Hominem', *Honi Soit*, 10 October 1941.

5   Donald Horne, 'Sex Censorship Is Defeatist', *Honi Soit*, 10 October 1941.

6   Donald Horne, 'Let Us Rejoice', *Honi Soit*, 16 October 1941; 'Is Honi Soit Punk? – "No", They Say', *Honi Soit*, 23 October 1941.

7   K.S. Inglis and Jan Brazier, *This Is the ABC*, cited in Geoffrey Bolton, *The Oxford History of Australia Volume 5, 1942–1995: The Middle Way* (Melbourne: Oxford University Press, 1996), p. 6; Robert Menzies quoted in Stuart Macintyre, *Australia's Boldest Experiment: War and Reconstruction in the 1940s* (Sydney: NewSouth, 2015), p. 19; Frank Bongiorno, 'The Search for a Solution: 1923–1939' in Alison Bashford

and Stuart Macintyre (eds), *The Cambridge History of Australia Volume 2: The Commonwealth of Australia*, (Port Melbourne: Cambridge University Press, 2013), pp. 84–86; John F. Williams, *The Quarantined Culture: Australian Reactions to Modernism 1913–1939* (Cambridge: Cambridge University Press, 1995).

8 Horne, interview by Radio Helicon, n.d., National Archives of Australia, Series: C100, Item ID: 13333400; on extended family, see Donald Horne, *The Education of Young Donald* (Sydney: Angus & Robertson, 1967), pp. 36–56.

9 David Horne enlisted on 1 May 1915 and was discharged on 1 May 1919: NAA, Series B2455, Horne D. 4404.

10 Cited by Horne in 'Son of the Lucky Country'; Horne, *The Education of Young Donald*, p. 31.

11 On extended family, see Horne, *The Education of Young Donald*, pp. 36–56; 'Be yourself', p. 55.

12 Donald Horne, interview by Phillip Adams, Radio National, 5 May 2005; *The Education of Young Donald*, pp. 26–27.

13 Horne, *Australian Biography*; Morley to Horne, 12 February 1969; Horne, *The Education of Young Donald*, 2nd ed., (Melbourne: Sun Books, 1968), p. 12. See also Donald Horne, 'The Nineteen-Thirties', Ideas Articles, MLMSS 3525 Add on 1978, Box 11 J-10.

14 Horne, *Australian Biography*; *The Education of Young Donald*, pp. 131–34; on leaving Muswellbrook, see p. 109.

15 Horne, interview by Radio Helicon; 'systematic view' and 'tense' in *Australian Biography*. See also Horne, *The Education of Young Donald*, pp. 138–39; Journal of 1972 Eye Operation, unpublished, Horne Papers, Collection 5, Box 2.

16 Horne, *The Education of Young Donald*, pp. 118, 167–68, 170, 178.

17 Horne, *Australian Biography*; *The Education of Young Donald*, pp. 155–63.

18 Horne, Diary, MLMSS 3525 MLK 2137 G-3; *The Education of Young Donald*, pp. 200–01.

19 Curtin (criticising Robert Menzies) cited in Macintyre, *Australia's Boldest Experiment*, p. 39; Max Harris quoted in Alan Barcan, *Radical Students: The Old Left at Sydney University* (Melbourne: Melbourne University Press, 2002), p. 123, Deirdre Cable is quoted p. 121. Another student, Frank Williamson, from the Labor Club, punched Horne on the nose outside the *Honi Soit* offices and hated Horne for the rest of his life: Barcan, *Radical Students*, p. 122; Horne, *Education of Young Donald*, pp. 322–23. Alan Barcan alleged that Horne was 'not well liked': Barcan, *Radical Students*, p. 121.

20 Brian Kennedy, *A Passion to Oppose: John Anderson, Philosopher* (Melbourne: Melbourne University Press, 1995); Creagh McLean Cole, 'John Anderson's Political Thought Revisited', *Australian Journal of Political Science* 44, no. 2 (2009), pp. 232–33, 240; James Franklin, *Corrupting the Youth: A History of Philosophy in Australia* (Sydney: Macleay Press, 2003); W.M. O'Neil, 'Anderson, John (1893–1962)', *Australian Dictionary of Biography Volume 7, 1891–1939: A–Ch* (Canberra: Melbourne University Press, 1979). For physical description of Anderson, see Horne, *The Education of Young Donald*, pp. 204–05; John Passmore, *Memoirs of a Semi-Detached Australian* (Melbourne: Melbourne University Press, 1997), p. 93; Peter Coleman, *Memoirs of a Slow Learner* (Pymble: Angus & Robertson, 1994), p. 40.

21 David Armstrong, 'John Anderson Remembered', speech to the John Anderson Conference, 9 July 2005. By the standards of the day, too, Anderson was unusually approachable. It was not uncommon to see the gangly professor arguing with students in the Quadrangle, or holding court in the union cafeteria. It was rumoured that he even invited especially gifted young men to his home in Turramurra: P. Shrubb, *The Bulletin*, 30 June 1962, cited in Franklin, *Corrupting the Youth*, pp. 33–34; Passmore, *Memoirs of a Semi-Detached Australian*, p. 111 (Passmore was one such visitor). Coleman discusses Anderson's approachability in *Memoirs of a Slow Learner*, pp. 40–41. He was also a teacher of 'impressive psychic impact', recalled John Kerr, who counted himself among the professor's many acolytes: John Kerr, *Matters for Judgement: An Autobiography* (Artarmon: Macmillan, 1978), p. 43.

22   Clive James, 'Renegade at the Lectern', *The Monthly*, June 2005; Kennedy, *A Passion to Oppose*, p. 9; 'Einstein' see Passmore, *Memoirs of a Semi-Detached Australian*, p. 96 ('Socratic gadfly'); Horne, *The Education of Young Donald*, pp. 205–06 ('God Save the King'). The same story was recalled by Bill Pritchett in an oral history interview: William Pritchett, interview by Garry Woodard, 28 October 2002, transcript of audio recording, NLA, p. 14. On Anderson's long-term influence, see McKenzie Wark, 'The Libertarian Line', in *The Virtual Republic: Australia's Culture Wars of the 1990s* (Sydney: Allen & Unwin, 1997), pp. 60–83; John Docker, 'The Origins of Paddy McGuinness', *Arena* 3 (1993), pp. 21–24. The philosopher A.J. Baker called Anderson 'the most original, all-round philosopher Australia has had' in *Australian Realism: The Systematic Philosophy of John Anderson* (Cambridge: Cambridge University Press, 1986).

23   '1941 Student Handbook – Sydney University SRC', Horne Papers, MLMSS 3525 MLK 2137 G-5.

24   Pritchett, interview by Woodard, p. 13; the journalist and politician Michael Baume expressed similar sentiments: Michael Baume, interview by Gary Sturgess, 5 September 2012, digitised audio recording, NLA; Donald Horne, 'Donald Horne Reflects on John Anderson & Australian Civilisation', *Arena*, February–March 2004, pp. 39–41.

25   Political freedom, wrote Anderson, always depended on 'the existence of a plurality of movements which take their chance in the social struggle', John Anderson, 'The Servile State', *The Australasian Journal of Psychology and Philosophy* (1943), pp. 115–32; Cole, 'John Anderson's Political Thought Revisited', pp. 232–33; Franklin, *Corrupting the Youth*. On 'unceasing conflict', see Donald Horne, *Into the Open*, Sydney: HarperCollins, 2000), p. 5; Horne, *The Education of Young Donald*, pp. 239–40.

26   Donald Horne, 'A Message to Adelaide', *Honi Soit*, 11 September 1941.

27   Barcan, *Radical Students*, pp. 115–18.

28   James McAuley, *The Bulletin*, 30 June 1962, p. 29, cited in Franklin, *Corrupting the Youth*, p. 7. Horne later compared Freethinking to 'playground bullying' in 'On the Fringe', *Observer*, 29 November 1958. In *Honi Soit*, Horne deployed such arguments to attack both the outdated moral codes of the religious right and the 'authoritarian' inclinations of the campus left in 'On Student Fascism', *Honi Soit*, 17 July 1941, 'Fascisti at Bay', *Honi Soit*, 24 July 1941 And untitled thoughts on 'Educational reform', Horne Papers, MLMSS 3525 MLK 2137 G-3.

29   According to Barcan, 'the Andersonians devoted much energy in 1940 to the Literary Society': *Radical Students*, p. 111. For Horne's assessment of the group, see 'Portrait of an Un-Australian', *Observer*, 4 October 1958. On the bar scene, see Cassandra Pybus, *The Devil and James McAuley* (St. Lucia: University of Queensland Press, 1999), p. 8; Donald Horne, *Confessions of a New Boy* (Ringwood: Viking, 1985), p. 277. Joan Fraser (later known as Amy Witting) gives a radically different view of this bohemian milieu: 'there wasn't any [intellectual life]. Everybody has this feeling that we all sat about and quipped marvellously' . . . [University years were] 'a bore' . . . 'It was a background of uncertainty, want and personal unhappiness': Amy Witting, interview by Peter Coleman, 13 July 1992, audio recording, NLA.

30   Pybus, *The Devil and James McAuley*, pp. 5, 7 (on personal magnetism), 22 (on thesis).

31   Reflecting on this teenage hero worship just under twenty years later, Horne confessed to being 'too young, too impressionable, and too much under [McAuley's] spell': Donald Horne, 'A Time of Sadness', *Observer*, 20 September 1958. On befriending McAuley, see Donald Horne, Diary, 15 September 1939, Horne Papers, MLMSS 3525 MLK 2137 G-3; *The Education of Young Donald*, pp. 223–26, 229–34; 'Dysfunctional Exorcism', *The Australian's Review of Books* 4, no. 6 (July 1999). On the literary mannerisms adopted by Horne, see Pritchett, interview by Woodard. From McAuley's perspective, Horne was largely peripheral: 'Donald was very much around in that slightly junior echelon with other people like Bill Pritchett': James McAuley, interview by Catherine Santamaria, 5–7 May 1976, audio recording, NLA.

32   Horne, *The Education of Young Donald*, pp. 226–37; 'Donald Horne – Annual Election Board of Directors Nomination Form' in Horne Papers, MLMSS 3525 MLK 2137 G-4.

33   Horne, '"Angry Penguins" a Trifle Incoherent', *Honi Soit*, 2 October 1941.

34   Ibid. See also John Anderson, 'Literature and Life', cited in Passmore, *Memoirs of a Semi-Detached Australian*, p. 112. On objections to the ban on *Ulysses*, see 'English Lecturers to Speak', *Honi Soit*, 2 October 1941 and John Anderson, 'Ulysses Ban to Be Expected – Society Is Bourgeois', *Honi Soit*, 25 September 1941. In his own pretentious letter to *Honi Soit* on 14 April 1942, Horne argued that overturning the ban was more important for Australia than the construction of the Sydney Harbour Bridge: 'Bridges come and go, but great works of literature are irreplaceable. They are drops whose purification takes many years but whose evaporation is final, whose loss is irreplaceable. My life, without the right to read what I like, is rubbish, and the sooner it is disposed of the better'.

35   Horne, 'Should Art Be Moral?', quoted in *Honi Soit*, 18 April 1941, p. 1. See also Horne, 'A Time of Sadness', pp. 487–78.

36   Donald Horne, untitled poem; 'Homage to W.H.'; 'Railway Cafeteria, 1940', MLMSS 3525 MLK 2137 G-2.

37   Donald Horne, 'Tiddlywinks Old Man!'; 'The Service Done'; two untitled poems; 'Joan Austral Fraser – Life and Contacts', MLMSS 3525 MLK 2137 G-2.

38   Amy Witting, interview by Peter Coleman, July–September 1992, audio recording, NLA.

39   Peter Ryan, 'Donald Horne: A Self Made Man', *Quadrant*, 1998; Pat Donovan quoted in 'Is *Honi Soit* Punk?'; Miller quoted in Barcan, *Radical Students*, p. 122. Murray Sayle wrote to Horne in December 1967: 'I admired you greatly when I was seventeen to your twenty-one', MLMSS 3525 MLK 2135 L-22. Horne described some of his antics in his undergraduate diary (MLMSS 3525 MLK 2137 G-3): 'Bought an eye shade a Kogarah and being an exhibitionist enjoyed the pipe, eye-shade combination immensely'. See also Horne, *The Education of Young Donald*, p. 261; Barcan, *Radical Students*, p. 115

40   Bill Pritchett, 'Can They Take It?', *Honi Soit*, 3 April 1941, p. 2; 'These Were Some of the Odd Bits', *The Daily Telegraph*, 13 April 1941, p. 12; Patrick Buckridge, *The Scandalous Penton: A Biography of Brian Penton* (St Lucia: University of Queensland Press, 1994). See also Patrick Buckridge, 'Antagonism as an Art Form: Brian Penton and the Politics of Provocation', *Journal of Australian Studies* 21, no. 54–55, pp. 81–90. For Horne's first impressions of Penton, see *The Education of Young Donald*, pp. 296–97.

41   Pritchett, interview by Woodard, p. 7; Buckridge, *The Scandalous Penton*, pp. 89, 105, 118; Bridget Griffen-Foley, *The House of Packer: The Making of a Media Empire* (St Leonards: Allen & Unwin, 2000), pp. 61–62.

42   Brian Penton, *Think – Or Be Damned: A Subversive Note on National Pride, Patriotism and Other Forms of Respectable Ostrichism Practices in Australia* (Sydney: Angus & Robertson, 1941), p. 1. On intellectual influences, see Buckridge, 'Antagonism as an Art Form', pp. 83–86.

43   Donald Horne, 'Grin and Be Damned', *Honi Soit*, 14 August 1941.

44   'Program: 1941 Inter-Varsity Debate', MLMSS 3525 MLK 2137 G-4; 'Great Interest Shown in Inter-Varsity Debates', *Honi Soit*, 11 September 1941.

45   'Report of Editor, "Honi Soit", July 11 Onward, 1941', MLMSS 3525 MLK 2137 G-4. Some examples: Horne, 'Sex! – Isn't It Dreadful'; 'Sex Censorship Is Defeatist'; 'Argumentum Ad Hominem'.

46   Penton, *Think – or Be Damned*, p. 2.

47   Ibid., pp. 1–20.

48   Menzies cited in Stuart Macintyre, *The Oxford History of Australia Volume 4, 1901–1942: The Succeeding Age* (Melbourne: Oxford University Press, 1993), p. 327.

49   Horne, 'Let Us Rejoice'. At a debating competition in Canberra, Horne helped to make the successful affirmative case 'that freedom of the Press and Radio is essential for the successful prosecution of the war': 'Great Interest Shown in Inter-Varsity Debates', *Honi Soit*.

50   Horne, *The Education of Young Donald*, pp. 324–26. 'I hadn't read a Dostoyevsky novel since I was an undergraduate, and in my mind the themes of the various novels had run together in one great novel called Dostoyevsky', Horne, *Confessions of a New Boy*, pp. 55, 238.

51   Donald Horne, 'Poem Commemorating the Development of a Soul Through the Conflict of Social Forces and Other Types of Strange Disturbance', MLMSS 3525 MLK 2137 G-2.

52   Donald Horne, 'Manifesto', MLMSS 3525 MLK 2137 G-2.

53   Donald Horne, 'In Search of My Self', n.d., Horne Papers, MLMSS 3525 MLK 2137 G-3 'Undergraduate Prose'.

54   Horne, 'Homage to W.H.' See also Horne, untitled poem, possibly called 'From the French', 1940, MLMSS 3525 MLK 2137 G-2.

55   Horne, 'In Search of My Self'.

56   Ibid.

57   Horne was devastated by this blow: 'The shock and defeat I received on Dec 2 1941 set me back just as far as the other few great shocks that have shaken up my life – although at first . . . it may have seemed comparatively trivial, it was a blow whose pain numbed for months afterwards and from which recovery was very slow,' Horne to Miller, 3 November 1943, Horne Papers, MLMSS 3525 MLK 2131 L-5. Similarly, Horne to Miller, 1 January 1944: the current strain 'has yet to reach the apex of, say, late 1941'.

58   Horne enrolled on 28 November 1941: 'Certificate of Enrolment, Australian Military Forces', MLMSS 3525 MLK 2131 L-3. 'All male students' in Barcan, *Radical Students*, pp. 123, 128.

59   John Curtin, 'The Task Ahead', *The Herald* (Melbourne), 27 December 1941. See also Stuart Ward, *Australia and the British Embrace: The Demise of the Imperial Ideal* (Melbourne: Melbourne University Press, 2001), p. 15; Bolton, *The Oxford History of Australia Volume 5*, pp. 6–7.

60   'Chronology of the War' in Joan Beaumont (ed.), *Australia's War, 1939–45* (St Leonards: Allen & Unwin, 1996), pp. xiii–xix.

61   For the details in this paragraph, see Bolton, 'The People at War' in *The Oxford History of Australia Volume 5*, pp. 5–7; Kate Darian-Smith, 'World War Two and Post-War Reconstruction, 1939–1949', in Bashford and Macintyre, *The Cambridge History of Australia Volume 2*, p. 101.

62   Horne, 'Let Us Rejoice'.

63   On McAuley in Newcastle, see Pybus, *The Devil and James McAuley*, p. 26. On Miller at the ABC, see Barcan, *Radical Students*, p. 133.

64   Twelve months later, Donald recalled 'wasting months on my back with head injuries in an Aust Gen Hosp' in 1942: Horne to Miller, 6 February 1944. He thought this brush with death cured him of his despondence over his *Honi* sacking: 'A sudden impact was needed to set the patient on his feet – or on the way to getting on them. I got that blow – a small smack on the face. A good, really hard smack across the face has a certain curative value, you should try it some time,' Horne to Miller, 3 November 1943. For a full autobiographical account see Horne, *Confessions of a New Boy*, pp. 46–47. As he describes on p. 362, Horne had regular and recurrent nightmares about the incident for years to come.

65   Horne, *Confessions of a New Boy*, pp. 54–55.

66   'I am in regular correspondence with about 12 people,' Horne to Florence Horne, 5 September 1943. 'You know I think my exile is doing me good', Horne to Miller, 12 September 1943.

67   See, for example, another complaint about the *Ulysses* ban in April 1942, in Donald Horne, 'Ulysses Ban Must Go', Letters to the Editor, *Honi Soit*, 14 April 1942. The 1942 *Honi* editor was Peter Gibbons, who had worked on Horne's staff in 1941.

68   Donald Horne, 'Where Are the Judges?', Letters to the Editor, *Honi Soit*, 30 April 1942. The poet in question was a female student by the name of Shewcroft: T.F. D'Arcy-Burke, 'A Democrat', Letters to the Editor, *Honi Soit*, 7 May 1942.

69   D'Arcy Ryan, 'Irresponsible', Letters to the Editor, *Honi Soit*, 21 May 1942.

70   J.M. Collocott, 'But Unappreciative', Letters to the Editor, *Honi Soit*, 7 May 1942.

71   A.D. Hope, 'This Freedom', Letters to the Editor, *Honi Soit*, 14 May 1942.

72   Horne, *Confessions of a New Boy*, pp. 54–55.

73   There were sixty-four Japanese air raids on Darwin between February 1942 and November 1943: George Vazenry, 'Attacks on the Australian Mainland', cited in David Horner, *The Gunners: A History of Australian Artillery* (St Leonards: Allen & Unwin, 1995), p. 379.

74   Horner, *The Gunners*, pp. 379–81.

75   Ray Buttery, *Legion of the Lost*, cited in Horner, *The Gunners*, p. 381.

76   Horne to Florence Horne, 14 November 1943.

77   Horne to Miller, 12 September 1943.

78   Donald Horne, 'McNaughton', prose sketch written in the army, MLMSS 3525 MLK 2137 G-7.

79   Horne to Florence Horne, 7 August 1943.

80   Horne to Florence Horne, 15 July 1943.

81   Horne to Florence Horne, 16 August 1943.

82   Horne, *Australian Biography*.

83   Ibid.; Morley to Horne, 12 February 1969. Donald Horne, 'Reading and Thinking', in Donald Horne and Myfanwy Horne, *Dying: A Memoir* (Penguin, 2007), pp. 178–82.

84   Horne to Florence Horne, 15 July 1943 (asking for newspapers); Horne to Miller, 19 August 1943 (reading Shakespeare); Horne to Florence Horne, 12 September 1943 ('I have been doing quite a lot of reading up here'); Horne to Miller, 17 August 1943 ('Mr Norris'); Horne, *Confessions of a New Boy*, pp. 93–94 (reading *Scrutiny*).

85   Horne, 'McNaughton'; Horne to Miller, September 1943. On *Horizon*, see Horne to Miller, 3 November 1943. Horne also wrote a chronicle of his battery's long rail and bus journey to Darwin: Horne to Florence Horne, 22 June 1943; Horne to Florence Horne, 5 September 1943.

86   Horne to Miller, 29 August 1943. Horne was not the only bored soldier in Northern Australia contemplating turning his army experience into literature. The playwright Sumner Locke Elliott based his controversial 1948 play, *Rusty Bugles*, on his experience working in an army supply camp in the Northern Territory in 1944: Jill Roe, 'Elliott, Sumner Locke (1917–91)', *Australian Dictionary of Biography Volume 19: 1991–1995, A–Z* (Acton: ANU Press, 2014).

87   Horne to Miller, 23 January 1944. He was 'attempting to stay in the arena and pen the eyewitness account': Horne to Miller, 16 December 1943.

88   Horne to Miller, 1 February 1944.

89   Horne, *Confessions of a New Boy*, p. 51.

90   Ibid., pp. 51–52. 'When I read *War and Peace*, it explained me. I think that view of fiction as a form of revelation is no longer held, but it certainly applied to me': Donald Horne, quoted in Caroline Baum, 'Donald Sails Further Round the Horn', *Arts Extra*, n.d. [~1985].

91   Horne to Miller, 12 September 1943

92   Horne to Miller, 29 August 1943; 1 January 1944: 'Personally I think it would be nice to sit back and write *The Enormous Room* right now'. See also *Confessions of a New Boy*, pp. 3–4.

93   Horne to Miller, 1 January 1944; 3 November 1943 (The blow in 1941 'whose pain numbed for months afterwards and from which recovery was very slow'); 1 January 1944 (the current strain 'has yet to reach the apex of, say, late 1941').

94   Horne to Miller, 1 January 1944.

95   Donald Horne, 'Unca Donald on Hooton', *Honi Soit*, 23 September 1943.

96   Donald Horne, 'Silly Bitter Experience', *Honi Soit*, 14 October 1943; 'Pity from Horne', *Honi Soit*, 7 October 1943.

97   Horne to Miller, 16 December 1943; 1 January 1944.

98   Horne to Florence Horne, 7 December 1943; 18 February 1944; Horne to Miller, 23 January 1944; Horne to Florence Horne, 12 January 1944. On Conlon, see Graham Sligo, *The Backroom Boys: Alfred Conlon and the Army's Directorate of Research and Civil Affairs 1942-46* (Newport: Big Sky Publishing, 2012).

99   Horne to Miller, 20 November 1943; Joan Beaumont, 'Creating an Elite? The Diplomatic Cadet Scheme, 1943–56', in Joan Beaumont et al. (eds), *Ministers, Mandarins and Diplomats: Australian Foreign Policy Making 1941–1969* (Melbourne: Melbourne University Press, 2003), pp. 19–44; Horne to Florence Horne, 7 December 1943 ('a couple of thousand applications').

100   Horne to Florence Horne, 11 May 1944; 'Nine Servicemen in Diplomatic Cadets', *Newcastle Morning Herald and Miners' Advocate*, 15 May 1944; Horne to Miller, n.d. [~1944]; Horne to Florence Horne, 12 January 1944.

2. THE GOLDEN AGE

1   W.K. Hancock cited in Jim Davidson, *A Three-Cornered Life: The Historian WK Hancock* (Sydney: UNSW Press, 2010), p. 374; Nicholas Brown, *A History of Canberra* (Melbourne: Cambridge University Press, 2014), pp. 85–100. Stuart Macintyre described Canberra as 'a country town masquerading as a national capital': *Australia's Boldest Experiment*, pp. 70, 115. James McDonald, 'A Good Sheep Station Ruined', *Australian Journal of Biography and History* no. 2 (2019), p. 35. See also the testimonies of public servants quoted in Beaumont, 'Creating an Elite?', p. 23.

2   Horne, 'Canberra, City of Dreadful Nights', *The Daily Telegraph*, 10 April 1948.

3   Horne, *Confessions of a New Boy*, pp. 123–35.

4   Beaumont, 'Creating an Elite?', p. 35. For a first-hand account, see Paul Hasluck, *Diplomatic Witness: Australian Foreign Affairs 1941–1947* (Carlton: Melbourne University Press, 1980). On bicycles, see John Rowland, interview by Ken Henderson, September 1985, digitised audio recording, NLA; Horne, 'The Story of the Diplomat Who Couldn't Afford an Overcoat', *The Daily Telegraph*, 22 July 1946. Horne, *Confessions of a New Boy*, pp. 123–35; Rowland, interview by Henderson.

5   Beaumont, 'Creating an Elite?'; Macintyre, *Australia's Boldest Experiment*; Samuel Furphy (ed.), *The Seven Dwarfs and the Age of the Mandarins: Government Administration in the Post-War Reconstruction Era* (ANU Press: Canberra, 2015).

6   Donald Horne, 'Australia's Diplomatic Growing Pains: We Are Noisy, but Have We a Better Name?', *The Daily Telegraph*, 22 June 1948. When war broke out, Australia's only overseas representative had been the high commissioner in London, Stanley Bruce (who still reported directly to the prime minister): Beaumont, 'Creating an Elite?'.

7   Beaumont, 'Creating an Elite?', pp. 19–20, 25–26.

8   Cadet recruitment was reflective of broader changes in culture of the Australian public service throughout the 1940s: Beaumont, 'Creating an Elite?', pp. 20–23.

9   Between 1946 and 1949, the department grew from 210 to 642 staff, and the number of overseas missions from 9 to 26: Alan Gyngell, *Fear of Abandonment: Australia and the World Since 1942* (Carlton: La Trobe University Press, 2017), p. 21.

10   While interviewing Bill Pritchett, the Australian diplomat and academic Gary Woodard remarked that the 1944 and 1945 intakes were 'probably the best ever'. Pritchett also described Horne's 1944 group as 'brilliant': Pritchett, interview by Woodard.

11   'Nine Servicemen in Diplomatic Cadets', *Newcastle Morning Herald and Miners' Advocate*, 15 May 1944. Like Horne, both Beddie and Jockel came from artillery: Horne, *Confessions of a New Boy*, pp. 130–32.

12   In the cadetship program, women were not taken seriously, and did not get the same rate of pay as the men until a 1944 decision: 'All Diplomatic Cadets to Get Same Conditions', *The Herald* (Melbourne), 11 February 1944. John Rowland recalled there only being one woman in their cohort, Kathy Jones: Rowland interview by Henderson. A public-service ban on married women also ensured that very few were able to pursue the career for which they were being trained: Beaumont, 'Creating an Elite?', p. 28. On the female quota, see Yves Rees, 'The Pioneering Envoy Who "Waged War" on Canberra', *Inside Story*, 7 March 2019.

13   A few years later, Manning Clark also taught the cadets. Not all teachers thrived with this precocious group: 'What an array to have to deal with', remarked Pritchett in his interview by Woodard. Horne, *Confessions of a New Boy*, pp. 136–45.

14   Horne to Miller, 2 July 1944; Beaumont, 'Creating an Elite?', p. 30.

15   Rowland, interview by Henderson.

16   Officially, it included Homer, Herodotus, Thucydides, Plato, Aristotle, Machiavelli, Bacon, Montaigne, Tawney, Hobbes, Locke, Rousseau, Burke, plus contemporary political philosophers such as Laski, Oakeshott, von Mises, Hayek, Dickinson and Lange: School of Diplomatic Studies, 'Interim Statement (1944)', Horne Papers, MLMSS 3525 MLK 2138 G-10. The foreign language requirement had been dropped in order to attract soldiers to the program. See also Horne, 'The General Failing of University Education', *The Australian*, 6 December 1995.

17   Beaumont, p. 34.

18   Diplomatic Cadet Exam, 18 December 1943, MLMSS 3525 MLK 2138 G-10.

19   Beaumont, pp. 29, 35.

20   Horne to Miller, 24 May 1944.

21   'The Rise of Nationalism in Australian Literature', Essays while a Diplomatic Cadet, MLMSS 3525 MLK 2138 G-9. Horne on Fitzhardinge see *Confessions of a New Boy*, pp. 142–43.

22   Horne to Miller, n.d.

23   Beaumont, 'Creating an Elite?', p. 27.

24   Horne, 'Canberra, City of Dreadful Nights' ('adult intellectual interests'); 'The Story of the Diplomat Who Couldn't Afford an Overcoat' ('crowded buses').

25   Horne, 'The Story of the Diplomat Who Couldn't Afford an Overcoat'; Horne to Miller, n.d.; 23 March 1945

26   See Horne, untitled essay about planning, Essays while a Diplomatic Cadet, Horne Papers MLK 2138 G-9.

27   Horne to Miller, 15 July 1942. Alf Conlon and John Kerr were also present: Horne, *Confessions of a New Boy*, p. 156; Rowland, interview by Henderson.

28   Donald Horne, 'The Career of Alcibiades', Essays while a Diplomatic Cadet, MLMSS 3525 MLK 2138 G-9.

29   Horne, *Confessions of a New Boy*, pp. 118–20.

30   Ibid., pp. 175–78.

31   See the following articles by Horne in *The Daily Telegraph* for example: 'Sydney Declared Empire Show-Place', 5 January 1945; 'Extensive Damage in Freak Storms', 22 February 1945'; 'Film Star's Thighs on Poster Censored', 24 February 1945. Bridget Griffen-Foley, 'Operating on "an Intelligent Level"': Cadet Training at Consolidated Press in the 1940s', in Ann Curthoys and Julianne Schultz (eds), *Journalism: Print, Politics and Popular Culture* (St Lucia: University of Queensland Press, 1999), pp. 142–54.

32   Lambert had published a book a poetry called *The Map* (Sydney: Viking Press, 1940). She later became a famous writer of cookbooks, publishing under the name Elisabeth Lambert Ortiz. According to the *Times*, she was 'a food writer, but she might as well have been called a food historian or a cultural anthropologist', *The Times* (London), 25 November 2003.

33   Elisabeth Lambert to Donald Horne, MLMSS 3525 MLK 2132 L-8; Horne, *Confessions of a New Boy*, pp. 161–218; Horne, *Australian Biography*.

34   See Lambert letters. See also Horne to Miller, 2 July 1944; 27 September 1944; 13 October 1944; 12 November 1944; 9 December 1944.

35   Donald Horne, 'Frontier Settlement', in Plan for a Book about Australia, n.d. [~1945], Donald Horne Papers, MLMSS 3525 MLK2137 G-8. For other quotations, see Horne, 'The Story of the Diplomat Who Couldn't Afford an Overcoat'.

36   Lambert to Horne, n.d. [~1945].

37   Horne to Miller, 21 August 1945.

38   See Scrapbooks of Newspaper Articles, Donald Horne papers, MLMSS 3525 MLK 2176.

39   Cited in Macintyre, *Australia's Boldest Experiment*, pp. 34–35. For planning as an early war goal, see Jo-Anne Pemberton, '"O Brave New Social Order": The Controversy over Planning in Australia and Britain in the 1940s', *Journal of Australian Studies* 28, no. 83 (2004), p. 39. One of the questions on the 1943 diplomatic cadet exam referred explicitly to the 'Atlantic Charter', see Diplomatic Cadet Exam, 18 December 1943, MLMSS 3525 MLK 2138 G-10.

40   Macintyre, *Australia's Boldest Experiment*; James Curran, *Curtin's Empire* (Melbourne: Cambridge University Press, 2011); David Day, *John Curtin: A Life* (Sydney: HarperCollins, 1999); David Day, *Chifley* (Sydney: HarperCollins, 2001).

41   H.C. Coombs, *Trial Balance* (South Melbourne: Macmillan, 1981), p. 60. Coombs had a doctorate from the London School of Economics. Macintyre called him 'the pivotal figure in the history of postwar reconstruction': *Australia's Boldest Experiment*, p. 110. See also Tim Rowse, 'Coombs the Keynesian', in Furphy (ed.), *The Seven Dwarfs*, pp. 143–67. In his diplomatic studies classes, recalled Horne, they studied Keynes' *General Theory* closely, 'as if this were the Talmud and was all we really need know', *Confessions of a New Boy*, p. 193. Leslie Crisp, a political scientist who lectured the cadets on 'Political Organisation', was also an influential member of the Department: Horne to Miller, 24 May 1945.

42   On high expectations, see Macintyre, *Australia's Boldest Experiment*, pp. 314–15.

43   On Bakunin, see Army Diary, MLMSS 3525 MLK 2137 G-5. On Oscar Wilde, see McCallum and Hooton letters, MLMSS 3525 MLK 2132 L-9. Horne, *Confessions of a New Boy*, p. 91.

44   Anderson's 'producers ethic' – the idea that societies should organise themselves around 'productive activities' rather than the pursuit of material outcomes – was a direct adaptation of Georges Sorel's arguments, constituting a kind of ethical socialism focused on 'ways of life' rather than 'things to be secured'. Productive activities, he argued, were creative, 'enlivening' and rewarding, while consumption, by contrast, was shallow, spiritless and acquisitive, circumscribing human possibility. It was not economic security but the struggle of the productive act itself that unlocked human potential. Productive activity, properly conceived, carried moral value. See Anderson, 'The Servile State', pp. 119–21 and Cole, 'John Anderson's Political Thought Revisited', pp. 232–33, 240. Peter Coleman thought that Anderson 'proletarianised' Sorel's broader original distinction between 'the creative and the possessive, the free and the conformist, the disinterested and the egoistic, the bohemian and the philistine': 'Was Georges Sorel an Andersonian?', *Quadrant*, September 2002, p. 54.

45   Donald Horne, 'John Anderson: University's Stubborn No-Man', *The Daily Telegraph*, 14 September 1946. In *Confessions of New Boy*, Horne writes: 'Some of us discussed ['The Servile State'] as if it were the announcement in *Pravda* of a new party line' (p. 158).

46   Friedrich Hayek is quoted in Pemberton, '"O Brave New Social Order"', p. 40. *The Road to Serfdom* got an Australian release in July 1944: Macintyre, *Australia's Boldest Experiment*, p. 261. Many of the thinkers on the right of this international debate over planning were included on the reading list for the diplomatic studies course, including Hayek, von Mises, Oakeshott, Laski and (in Australia) Lange: School of Diplomatic Studies, 'Interim Statement (1944)'. Horne regurgitated Hayek's argument in a diplomatic studies essay on 'Nazism as a Social Phenomenon'. In another, he declared that 'there is still no guaranteed process by which the future can be predicted scientifically, nor even one which enables us to discuss whether one hypothesis about it is really better than another': Essays while a diplomatic cadet, MLMSS 3525 MLK 2138 G-9. See also Donald Horne, '1954: A Lot of Rubbish in the Bin', *Overland* 62 (1975).

47   Macintyre, *Australia's Boldest Experiment*, pp. 137–40, 257, 261–63.

48   For a full account of the fourteen powers referendum see Ibid., pp. 253–70.

49   Holt quoted in Ibid., p. 261.

50 Horne, untitled essay about planning.

51 Horne, Plan for a Book about Australia. The book was to be co-written by Bruce Miller: Horne to Miller, 23 January 1944; 6 February 1944.

52 Donald Horne, '"Bureaucracy" by Ludwig von Mises', *The Daily Telegraph*, 2 June 1945.

53 As a diplomatic studies student, Horne had been put through a unit called 'Economic Calculation in a Planned Economy': School of Diplomatic Studies, 'Interim Statement (1944)'. See also Donald Horne, *Money Made Us* (Ringwood: Penguin, 1976), p. 182 'In the economics course I took as a diplomatic cadet, we were run through this and that in the first year, then in the second year when we sat down to Keynes's *General Theory of Employment, Interest and Money* we knew it was the main meal.'

54 Robert Menzies quoted in Martin in Darian-Smith, 'World War Two and Post-War Reconstruction', p. 106.

55 Bolton, *The Oxford History of Australia Volume 5*, pp. 30–31.

56 Horne, *Confessions of a New Boy*, pp. 204–06. For Canberra address, see Donald Horne, Australian Journalists Association membership application, 22 August 1945, Papers of the Australian Journalists Association, Canberra Branch, Noel Butlin Archives, Z70, Box 1.

57 Donald Horne, Lecture on 'The Press', July 1947, MLMSS 3525 MLK 2138 G-11; *Confessions of a New Boy*, pp. 245–38.

58 Donald Horne, 'Quota Migration System Urged: Replacement of White Australia Policy Suggested', *The Daily Telegraph*, 29 January 1946; 'Miners Settle in Xmas Camps: Canvas Towns Spring up on Lake Macquarie', *The Daily Telegraph*, 8 December 1945.

59 For example, see Horne's profile of John Anderson: 'John Anderson: University's Stubborn No-Man'.

60 Horne, *Confessions of a New Boy*, p. 271.

61 Ibid., pp. 322–24.

62 Ibid., pp. 278–79, 283–85, 297–98, 300.

63 Ibid., p. 312.

64 Bolton, *The Oxford History of Australia Volume 5*, pp. 40–47; Macintyre, *Australia's Boldest Experiment*, pp. 428–34

65 Warwick Eather and Drew Cottle, 'The Mobilisation of Capital behind the "Battle for Freedom": The Sydney Banks, The Institute of Public Affairs (NSW) and Opposition to the Australian Labor Party 1944–49', *Labour History* 103 (2012), pp. 165–85; Robert Crawford, 'Supporting Banks, Liberals and the Australian Way: The Freelands and the 1949 Election', *History Australia* 2, no. 3 (2005), pp. 1–23.

66 Donald Horne, 'Bonapartist Chifley', *The Daily Telegraph*, 23 August 1947. Horne had mentioned the High Court issue in his July 1947 lecture on the press at Sydney University: 'The Bonapartists of the government hate all this. As the people's choice they see themselves so bestowed with the people's will that they would like to do away with legal tomfoolery like the High Court. Then, knowing what is best for the people, they could legislate any way they liked, allegedly in the people's interest.'

67 Brian Penton, *Censored! Being a True Account of a Noble Fight for Your Right to Read and Know, with Some Comment upon the Plague of Censorship in General* (Sydney: Shakespeare Head, 1947).

68 Horne, Lecture on 'The Press'; similar arguments made in: Horne, 'These Are Newspaper's Three Main Critics', *The Daily Telegraph*, 15 July 1947; 'Beware of Schemes to Stop Press "Abuses"', *The Daily Telegraph*, 16 July 1947; 'A "Breathing Space" for the Press?', *Australian Quarterly* 11, no. 3 (1949).

69 A good example of this is Horne, 'Canberra, City of Dreadful Nights', *The Daily Telegraph*, 10 April 1948. See also Horne, *Confessions of a New Boy*, p. 333.

70 Horne, Lecture on 'The Press'.

71 Horne, *Confessions of a New Boy*, p. 333; Scrapbooks of Newspaper Articles, Donald Horne papers.

72 Donald Horne (writing as 'David Mileham'), 'Our Mystery University', *The Daily Telegraph*, 3 April 1948; Horne, 'Our Newest Censorship: the "Handout"', *The Daily Telegraph*, 17 April 1948; Horne, 'An Englishman's Home Is His Castle', *The Daily Telegraph*, 10 July 1948; Horne (as 'David Mileham'), 'Public Service: Growth of a Leviathan', *The Daily Telegraph*, 17 July 1948.

73 Horne likened Bland to 'international villains like London's Professor Karl von Hayek and New York's Professor James Burnham': Horne, 'Professor Who Bought into Fights', *The Daily Telegraph*, 12 June 1948; Horne, 'He Dislikes the "Obstinate Bureaucrat"', 24 July 1948. In Horne's profile of John Anderson, he wrote that Anderson 'dislikes modern "progressives", with their talk of social security, nationalisation, and a New Order. He believes that capitalist countries are moving in the direction of regimentation, and that the ideology of servility is gaining ground': Horne ,'John Anderson: University's Stubborn No-Man'. See also Horne, 'A New Book about Australia', review of *Australia* by C. Hartley Grattan, *The Daily Telegraph*, 24 July 1948.

74 Horne, *Confessions of a New Boy*, p. 336

75 Horne, 'Copland Sees No Golden Age', *The Daily Telegraph*, 30 October 1948. Coombs is cited in Macintyre, *Australia's Boldest Experiment*, pp. 390–91.

76 Jo-Anne Pemberton, '"O Brave New Social Order": The Controversy over Planning in Australia and Britain in the 1940s', *Journal of Australian Studies* 28, no. 83 (2004), pp. 35–47.

77 Gordon Jockel was serving on the Australian mission to the United Nations in New York, John Rowland was a Third Secretary at the Australian embassy in Moscow and Bill Pritchett was part of the Australian contingent of the United Nations Commission to Indonesia (UNCI), which was engaged in the mediating the dispute there. See Rowland, interview by Henderson; Pritchett, interview by Woodard; Horne, *Confessions of a New Boy*, pp. 348–49.

78 Horne, 'Australia's Diplomatic Growing Pains'.

79 Donald Horne, 'Asia, Achilles Heel of the West: Communism Spreads in Burma, Japan, India', *The Daily Telegraph*, 26 August 1948; 'Australia's Unexploited "Empire": This Is the New Guinea Canberra Neglects', *The Daily Telegraph*, 5 August 1948; 'The Peninsula the Communists Covet: Malaya, Land Flowing with Tin and Rubber', *The Daily Telegraph*, n.d.

80 Donald Horne, 'Great Purge of the Golden Age', *The Daily Telegraph*, 21 August 1948.

81 Donald Horne, 'Your Humble Servants', *The Daily Telegraph*, 9 October 1948. Other titles include 'White Collar Slaves, Arise!', 'The Girls of the Golden Age', 'Democratised Arts' and 'Hamlet Democratised'.

82 Donald Horne, 'Greatest of All Reports', *The Daily Telegraph*, 7 August 1948.

83 Buckridge, 'Antagonism as an Art Form', pp. 81–90. See also Buckridge, *The Scandalous Penton*.

84 Horne, *Confessions of a New Boy*, pp. 340–41. Patrick Buckridge tells a similar story about a party at Frank Packer's house, at which Penton goaded Winston Churchill's son, Randolph, into storming out in a similar fashion: Buckridge, 'Antagonism as an Art Form', p. 81.

85 Buckridge, 'Antagonism as an Art Form', p. 86.

86 Horne, *Confessions of a New Boy*, p. 342.

87 Ibid., pp. 343–44.

88 See, for example, Horne, Lecture on 'The Press', p. 9: 'The history of progressive movements shows that the men of good will are soon ditched once the big boys get in the saddle … The sweetest democrats of the opposition become the sternest tyrants of the government when the pendulum swings and the whips start cracking'.

89 Horne, Lecture on 'The Press'.

90 Horne, *Confessions of a New Boy*, pp. 369–70. Horne recalled being asked to write 'five or six' articles. A long archival search returned two: 'Labor's Price Rise Election Conspiracy', *The Daily Telegraph*, 14 February 1949; 'Everyone Should Have a Home of His Own: House Builders Need Subsidies to Meet the Increased Costs', *The Daily Telegraph*, 1 March 1949.

3. THE GREY CLIFFS OF DOVER

1   There is a large literature on Australian expatriation to London, see Peter Morton, *Lusting for London: Australian Expatriate Writers at the Hub of Empire, 1870–1950* (New York: Palgrave Connect, 2011); Stephen Alomes, *When London Calls: The Expatriation of Australian Creative Artists to Britain* (Melbourne: Cambridge University Press, 1999). 'Curious and migratory, [Australian] journalists were drawn towards the next big story – somewhere else': Bridget Griffen-Foley, '"The Crumbs Are Better than a Feast Elsewhere": Australian Journalists on Fleet Street', in Carl Bridge, Robert Crawford and David Dunstan (eds), *Australians in Britain: The Twentieth Century-Experience* (Clayton: Monash University ePress, 2009). See also Bruce Bennett and Anne Pender, *From a Distant Shore: Australian Writers in Britain 1820–2012* (Clayton: Monash University Publishing, 2013). From a different angle, see Ros Pesman, *Duty Free: Australian Women Abroad* (Melbourne: Oxford University Press, 1996).

2   A.A. Phillips, 'The Cultural Cringe', *Meanjin* 9, no. 4 (Summer 1950), pp. 299–302. See also Rollo Hesketh, 'A.A. Phillips and the "Cultural Cringe": Creating an "Australian Tradition"', *Meanjin* 72, no. 3 (2013); Hesketh, 'In Search of a National Idea', pp. 13–72.

3   Horne, 'A New Book about Australia'. More than twenty people came to see Donald and Ethel off: Horne to Florence Horne, 31 October 1949, MLMSS 3525 MLK 2132.

4   On books, see Donald Horne, *Portrait of an Optimist* (Ringwood: Penguin, 1988), pp. 48, 56. On reading the literary canon, see Horne, '1954', pp. 28–29.

5   'I was never going to have the dust of Australia on my heels again. I was one of the, you know, expatriates who despised the country, its philistinism, all that stuff': Horne, *Australian Biography*. In 1946 he wrote, 'Overseas writers accuse us of elevating mediocrity and being suspicious of men with brains and vision. They point to the many great Australians who have had to go overseas to achieve their greatness. But we can't afford to break the hearts of the brilliant young men in the government service forever. Some day the supply of unemployed young intellectuals may run out': Donald Horne, '20-Year-Old Rules and Prejudices Tie the Public Service', *The Daily Telegraph*, 2 August 1946. He also recalled 'planning to stay there [England] for the rest of my life': Donald Horne, 'Whatever Happened to Europe?', *Newsweek*, 23 June 1975.

6   Phillips, 'The Cultural Cringe', pp. 299–302.

7   Moorehead cited in Geoffrey Serle, *From Deserts the Prophets Come: The Creative Spirit in Australia 1799–1972*, rev. ed. (Melbourne: Heinemann, 1987), p. 125. On the expatriation of Australian creatives, see Morton, *Lusting For London*, p. 1; Alomes, *When London Calls*; Bennett and Pender, *From a Distant Shore*.

8   This was one of the few periods of Horne's life for which there remains detailed personal correspondence. For quotes, see Horne to Florence Horne, 2 December 1949; 14 November 1949; 28 November 1949.

9   Horne to Florence Horne, 16 December 1949. Donald and Ethel arrived in London on 14 December 1949: Board of Trade: Commercial and Statistical Department and Successors: Inwards Passenger Lists; Class: BT26; Piece: 1256; Item: 56, The National Archives of the UK, Kew, Surrey, England. Donald's occupation was listed as 'journalist', Ethel's as 'almoner'.

10   Horne to Florence Horne, 11 January 1950; Donald Horne, 'Village Boss', *The Bulletin*, 16 December 1961.

11   See Donald Horne, 'Will England Revolt against Britain?', *Newsweek*, 18 June 1973 ('Anglophile stage'); Horne, '1954' ('Anglophile'); 'Political History of Donald Horne', *Death of a Lucky Country* promotional material, 13 February 1976, MLMSS 3525 MLK 2175 R-9 (in England, 'highly Anglophile; general conservative line, although still libertarian on censorship, and little regard for English aristocracy').

12   For example, see Robert Menzies' famous diary entry on a trip in 1935: 'At last we are in England. Our journey to Mecca has ended', cited in Brett, *Robert Menzies' Forgotten People* (Chippendale: Macmillan, 1992), p. 135.

13   Horne to Florence Horne, 6 March 1950; Horne to Florence Horne, 16 December 1949. Horne recalled his first impressions in a 1967 magazine article, noting 'there was a sense of familiarity in the little brick cottages, the hawthorn hedges, the elms, the chickens scratching around a cartwheel near the old farmhouse. This was the kind of calendar picture I had been brought up on': Donald Horne, 'The Australian Image', *The Bulletin*, 6 May 1967.

14   Horne, 'Britain May Try a Tenpenny Shilling', *The Daily Telegraph*, 30 June 1951, MLMSS 3525 MLK 2176 Folder 20. Horne to Florence Horne, 21 February 1950; 29 April 1950; 23 March 1950; Ethel Horne to Florence Horne, 6 January 1950. The 'colonial' story appears in Horne, 'Will England Revolt against Britain?'. See also Horne, 'The Koala Invades an Englishman's Castle', *The Daily Telegraph*, 30 November 1953.

15   Donald Horne, 'Bow Brickhill Takes the Elections Calmly', *The Daily Telegraph*, 17 February 1950; 'How the Light Came to Bow Brickhill', *The Daily Telegraph*, n.d. [~February 1950]. Horne lifted most of his quotes for these articles from the dowagers: Horne to Florence Horne, 13 February 1950 (the article 'encapsulates a few foolish things said in this household'). On farming conservatives, see George Eliot, *Middlemarch* (London: Wordsworth Classics, 1994), p. 326.

16   Horne, *Portrait of an Optimist*, pp. 70–71, 80, 101; Horne to Florence Horne, 6 March 1950. On the 1950 British election, see David Kynaston, *Austerity Britain Britain 1945–51* (London: Bloomsbury, 2007), p. 503.

17   Horne, 'How the Light Came to Bow Brickhill'.

18   Horne to Florence Horne, 13 February 1950; 29 April 1950; 16 May 1950. The couple also went on a longer trip to Sheffield to visit Ethel's cousins, where Donald was disappointed not to get a better glimpse of the 'mean terraces' and 'smoke and grey' of the industrial north. Instead, they were preoccupied by more genteel pursuits like inspecting old houses, visiting tourist sites and watching cricket matches: Horne to Florence Horne, 20 July 1950; Horne, *Portrait of an Optimist*, pp. 40, 44.

19   Horne to Florence Horne, 18 September 1950; 7 October 1950.

20   Horne to Florence Horne, 20 June 1950; 4 November 1950; 18 September 1950. On Ethel's inheritance, see Horne, *Portrait of an Optimist*, pp. 32–33 ('Ethel had borrowed enough to see us through the summer'); Horne, *Portrait of an Optimist*, pp. 48, 56. On reading the literary canon see Horne, '1954'.

21   By December, he had written '136 pages' and expected that 'most of it should be finished by Christmas': Horne to Florence Horne, 8 December 1950.

22   Donald Horne, 'One Can Always Tell a Gentleman', draft manuscript, MLMSS 3525 MLK2139 G-13b.

23   Ibid., p. 27.

24   Ibid., p. 40.

25   It is unlikely that Horne would have missed Wilson's collection when it was published. In *The Bulletin* in 1961, he wrote that Wilson's 'stories of university people broke new ground in England after the war' and that his 'attitude to his subject was not snobbish but critical': Donald Horne, 'The Short Story and The Bulletin', *The Bulletin*, 15 July 1961.

26   See Donald Horne, 'Harris Draws the Blind', *Honi Soit*, 13 July 1944.

27   J.D. Scott quoted in Harry Ritchie, *Success Stories: Literature and the Media in England 1950–59* (London 1989), pp. 1–24. See also Blake Morrison, *The Movement: English Poetry and Fiction of the 1950s* (Oxford: Oxford University Press, 1980); Humphrey Carpenter, *The Angry Young Men: A Literary Comedy of the 1950s* (London, 2002); Kynaston, *Austerity Britain 1945–51*, pp. 507, 524–25.

28   Horne, 'One Can Always Tell a Gentleman', p. 40.

29   Florence James quoted in Griffen-Foley, '"The Crumbs Are Better than a Feast Elsewhere'. See also Alomes, *When London Calls*; Ray Boston, *The Essential Fleet Street: Its History and Influence* (London: Blandford, 1990).

30 This was common practice, see Griffen-Foley, "'The Crumbs Are Better than a Feast Elsewhere'", p. 08.5.

31 Bridget Griffin-Foley, 'McNulty, Clarence Sydney (1903–1964)', *Australian Dictionary of Biography Volume 15 1940–1980: Kem–Pie* (Carlton South: Melbourne University Press, 2000); Horne, *Portrait of an Optimist*, pp. 14–15.

32 Horne, 'Bow Brickhill Takes the Elections Calmly'; 'How the Light Came to Bow Brickhill'; 'Myth of the Bath-Loving Englishman – If You're Going to England, Take Your Own Bathroom', *The Daily Telegraph*, 3 April 1950; 'English Clerics Are on the Breadline', *The Daily Telegraph*, 18 April 1950.

33 For some recollections of Horne's train journey to Germany, see Horne, 'Whatever Happened to Europe?'. See also Horne, *Portrait of an Optimist*, p. 59; David Childs, *Britain Since 1939: Progress and Decline*, 2nd ed. (Hampshire: Palgrave, 2002), pp. 95–97; Kynaston, *Austerity Britain 1945–51*.

34 Donald Horne, 'Reds Have Made West Germans Panicky', *The Daily Telegraph*, 2 April 1951; Horne, *Portrait of an Optimist*, pp. 60–62.

35 Donald Horne, '8 Million German Expellees Are Threat to World Peace', *The Daily Telegraph*, 9 April 1951; '5 Million German Women Will Never Marry', *The Daily Telegraph*, 18 April 1951'; '"Rearmament: Count Us Out", Say West Germans', *The Daily Telegraph*, 6 April 1951; 'Few West Germans Can Afford Cream Cakes', *The Daily Telegraph*, 23 April 1951; *Portrait of an Optimist*, pp. 59–62, 71.

36 Horne to Florence Horne, 12 April 1951.

37 Horne, *Portrait of an Optimist*, p. 71.

38 J.R. Stewart to Donald Horne, 28 May 1951. For examples of his unpublished freelance articles, see 'Oxford: It's Greatest Brawl', 'He Grew Up in America', 'Hearts and Flowers', 'Wellington – He Battled Alone', 'Prospective Candidate', 'Democracy Comes to Rotterdam', MLMSS 3525 MLK 2136 G-12 Unpublished English writing. On the Hornes' farming efforts, see: Ethel Horne to Florence Horne, 25 October 1951; Horne, *Portrait of an Optimist*, pp. 64–69; Horne to Florence Horne, 4 October 1951.

39 Kynaston, *Austerity Britain 1945–51*. On nationalisation, see Childs, *Britain Since 1939*, pp. 99–102; Kenneth O. Morgan, *Britain Since 1945: The People's Peace*, 3rd ed. (Oxford: Oxford University Press, 2001), pp. 29–111; L.A. Monk, *Britain 1945–1970* (London: G. Bell and Sons, 1976), pp. 43–49; C.J. Bartlett, *A History of Postwar Britain 1945–1974* (London: Longman, 1977), pp. 51–59; Ritchie, *Success Stories*, p. 4.

40 Horne to Florence,Horne, 28 December 1950; 15 December 1950.

41 Horne, 'Nobody Loves British Nationalisation', *The Daily Telegraph*, 11 August 1951. According to Kynaston, the 1951 proposals to nationalise the British steel industry were unpopular, but by then it had become Labour's 'deeply ingrained belief' that public ownership was 'integral to the party's "very soul"': Kynaston, *Austerity Britain 1945–51*, p. 537.

42 Horne, 'Nobody Loves British Nationalisation'. On Conservative Party organising, see Ethel Horne to Florence Horne, 25 October 1951; Horne, *Portrait of an Optimist*, pp. 76–77; Horne, 'Village Boss'.

43 Horne also discovered the novels of Anthony Trollope: Horne to Florence Horne, 22 June 1952; Ethel Horne to Florence Horne, 6 August 1952. See also Horne to Florence Horne, 1 January 1953; Garry Kinnane, 'Johnston, George Henry (1912–1970)', in John Ritchie (ed.), *Australian Dictionary of Biography Volume 14, 1940–1980; Di–Kel* (Carlton South: Melbourne University Press, 1996); Garry Kinnane, *George Johnston* (Ringwood: Penguin, 1986); Nadia Wheatley, 'Clift, Charmian (1923–1969)', *Australian Dictionary of Biography Volume 13 1940–1980: A–De* (Carlton: Melbourne University Press, 1993); Nadia Wheatley, *The Life and Myth of Charmian Clift* (Pymble: HarperCollins, 2001).

44 Ethel Horne to Florence Horne, n.d. [~March/April 1953]. 'Margaret' to Donald Horne, 16 October 1952, MLMSS 3525 MLK2133 L16; Eleanor Daniels (associate editor at Macmillan) to Donald Horne, 11 November 1952; 'Bets' to 'Jay and Margaret', 12 November 1952, MLK 2132.

45   Ritchie, *Success Stories*, p. 7.

46   Cyril Connolly quoted in ibid., p. 3.

47   On the Angry Young Men 'movement', see ibid.; Morrison, *The Movement*; Carpenter, *The Angry Young Men*.

48   On the National Gallery, lunches and newsreel theatres, see Horne, *Portrait of an Optimist*, pp. 95, 98, 120. On Australians in London, see Patricia Rolfe, *No Love Lost* (London: Macmillan, 1965).

49   Horne, 'We'll Get Through, You Know, We Always Do . . . Says the Average Englishman', *The Daily Telegraph*, 23 January 1952. Other *Telegraph* articles included: 'Empire Plan for New US Aid', 'UK Cuts Plan Attacked', 'Dollar Cuts Not Favoured', 'Move for Council', January 1952; 'It's Still Merrie England', *The Daily Telegraph*, 26 January 1952, MLMSS 3525 MLK 2132.

50   Ethel Horne to Florence Horne, 8 January 1952; 4 February 1952; Horne to Florence Horne, 7 April 1952. On being rejected for job at the Melbourne *Herald*'s New York bureau, see J.F. Williams to Donald Horne, 18 March 1952, MLK 2132. On being rejected for job in Cornwall, see D.H. Rawcliffe to Donald Horne, 28 April 1952, MLMSS 3525 MLK 2133 L-16. See also 'Margaret' to Donald Horne, 16 October 1952 ('I haven't told [anyone] about your new, possible, maybe, perhaps job, but I hope you get it'); Horne to Florence Horne, 20 November 1952 ('We have been eating all our own vegetables since last spring').

51   Clarence McNulty to Donald Horne, 20 December 1951, MLMSS 3525 MLK 2133 L-16.

52   Donald Horne, *The Australian People: Biography of a Nation* (Sydney: Angus and Robertson, 1972), p. 245.

53   Horne, *Portrait of an Optimist*, pp. 87–88.

54   Ethel Horne to Florence Horne, 18 October 1952. Horne had just won a minor literary competition for humour writing for his short story 'Appointment in Barnhampton', MLMSS 3525 MLK 2177 J-2. Austen Kark to Donald Horne, 9 June 1952, MLMSS 3525 MLK 2133 L16.

55   Horne to Florence Horne, 20 November 1952.

56   Horne to Florence Horne, 1 January 1953. Ian Wilson, 'Professor Brian Beddie, 1920–1994', *ANU Reporter*, 23 March 1994, p. 11. Both Bill Pritchett and Gordon Jockel also visited London during this time: Horne, *Portrait of an Optimist*, pp. 98–99.

57   Ethel Horne to Florence Horne, 7 January 1953.

58   Horne, *Portrait of an Optimist*, pp. 57, 74–75.

59   Letters from Ethel Horne to Donald Horne, March 1951, MLMSS 3525 MLK 2133 L-16.

60   Donald Horne, 'The Loved Ones', *The Sun*, 28 June 1953. On the royals, see Donald Horne, 'London's Little Man at the Coronation', *The Sun*, 31 May 1953, p. 15; 'Queen Mother Glad to See Australians', *The Sun*, 29 May 1953, p. 3; 'It's Quicker to Walk in Packed City', *The Sun*, 29 May 1953, p. 3. On crime, see Donald Horne, 'Moon-Mad Murders: Maniac Kills Women', *The Sun*, 29 March 1953; 'The Man Who Hanged Christie Faints As Star Witness', *The Sun*, 5 April 1953; 'Ghastly Strangling Details', *The Sun*, 26 April 1953; 'New Sensations in Moon Murder Case: Two Skeletons Shown in Court', *The Sun*, 3 May 1953; 'Murder Trail to a Pauper's Grave', *The Sun*, 10 May 1953.

61   Horne to Florence, 16 October 1953. On journalism as the 'drudge sister' of literature, see McNulty to Horne, 20 December 1952.

62   On British imperial decline, see John Darwin, *Britain and Decolonization: The Retreat from Empire in the Post-War World* (Basingstoke: Macmillan, 1988); P.J. Cain and A.G. Hopkins, *British Imperialism: Crisis and Deconstruction, 1914–1990* (London: Longman, 1993); R.F. Holland, *European Decolonization, 1918–1981: an Introductory Survey* (Basingstoke: Macmillan, 1985); John Hargreaves, *Decolonization in Africa*, 2nd ed., (London: Routledge, 2014). See also Bill Schwarz, 'The End of Empire', in Paul Addison and Harriet Jones (eds), *A Companion to Contemporary Britain, 1939–2000* (Oxford:Blackwell Publishing, 2005), pp. 482–98; John Darwin, 'Decolonization and the End of Empire', in Robin Winks (ed.), *The Oxford History of the British Empire, Volume V: Historiography* (Oxford: Oxford University Press, 19p9). On the 'new Elizabethan age', see Morgan, *Britain Since 1945*, pp. 126–28.

63   A small sample of the vast literature on the Kenya Emergency includes David Anderson, *Histories of the Hanged: Britain's Dirty War in Kenya and the End of Empire* (London: Weidenfeld and Nicolson, 2005); Caroline Elkins, *Britain's Gulag: The Brutal End of Empire in Kenya* (London: Jonathan Cape, 2005); Huw Bennett, *Fighting the Mau Mau: The British Army and Counter-Insurgency in the Kenya Emergency* (Cambridge: Cambridge University Press, 2012); Bruce Berman and John Lonsdale, *Unhappy Valley: Conflict in Kenya and Africa* (London: J. Currey, 1992). On the deaths resulting from the conflict, see Susan Carruthers, 'Being Beastly to the Mau Mau', *Twentieth Century British History* 16, no. 4 (2005), pp. 489–96.

64   Horne, *Portrait of an Optimist*, p. 117.

65   Donald Horne, 'No One Knows Who's a Mau Mau', *The Daily Telegraph*, 24 February 1954; 'Noise Is Worse than Mau Mau', *The Daily Telegraph*, 27 February 1954; 'Tough Aussies Are Hunting Mau Mau', *The Daily Telegraph*, 10 March 1954.

66   Horne, 'No One Knows Who's a Mau Mau'.

67   Donald Horne, 'Nairobi Becomes "City of Fear"', *The Daily Telegraph*, 23 February 1954; 'Kenya Anger: UK Urged to Say Whole Govt', *The Daily Telegraph*, 26 February 1954; 'Death Comes Horribly . . . Too Slowly', *The Daily Telegraph*, 7 March 1954.

68   Donald Horne, 'Only Angry Kenya Whites Were Awake', *The Daily Telegraph*, March 1954; 'And He Bought a Gun', *The Daily Telegraph*, 13 March 1954; 'Bullets, Spears and Blood in Kenya's Forest . . . Then Back to Nairobi for Afternoon Tea', *The Daily Telegraph*, 15 March 1954; 'Unhappy Kenya Needs a Strong Man – and Also a Policy', *The Daily Telegraph*, 16 April 1954.

69   Ethel Horne to Florence Horne, 30 March 1954.

70   On the Petrov affair, see Robert Manne, *The Petrov Affair* (Sydney: Pergamon, 1987); Nicholas Whitlam and John Stubbs, *Nest of Traitors: The Petrov Affair* (Milton: Jacaranda Press, 1974); David Horner, *The Spy Catchers: The Official History of ASIO 1949–1963* (Crows Nest: Allen & Unwin, 2014).

71   The Australian chargé d'affaires in Moscow, Brian Hill, had been a diplomatic cadet with Horne in Canberra in the early 1940s. During the crisis, he and Horne spoke several times over the phone, though they mostly 'chatted about mutual friends': Donald Horne, 'Soviet Arrested an Australian', *The Daily Telegraph*, 24 April 1954 ('We were friends as fellow trainee diplomats in 1944–45 in Canberra'). See also Donald Horne, 'Affair May Lead to Restrictions', *The Daily Telegraph*, 25 April 1954; 'Anti-Red Finns Ready to Welcome Australians', *The Daily Telegraph*, 28 April 1954; 'Embassy's Food, Liquor Sold', *The Daily Telegraph*, April 1954; 'Diplomats at Farewell Parties in Moscow', *The Daily Telegraph*, April 1954; 'In Clutches of Dread NNYK', *The Daily Telegraph*, April 1954; 'It Was a Fine Moment to Be an Australian', *The Daily Telegraph*, 2 May 1954; 'Aussies from Moscow Greeted with Song', *The Daily Telegraph*, 2 May 1954. In his memoir, a member of the Australian delegation only mentioned 'Waltzing Matilda' being sung by diplomatic friends when the train departed Moscow, not by crowds in Helsinki: Richard Woolcott, *The Hot Seat: Reflections on Diplomacy from Stalin's Death to the Bali Bombings* (Sydney: HarperCollins, 2003), p. 18.

72   Ethel Horne to Florence Horne, 19 November 1953; Donald Horne to Florence Horne, 16 November 1951; Donald Horne to Florence Horne, 5 January 1954; Ethel Horne to Florence Horne, 4 November 1953; Ethel Horne to Florence Horne, 30 March 1954; Donald Horne to Florence Horne, 23 April 1954.

73   Ethel Horne to Florence Horne, n.d. [~March/April 1953]; Donald Horne to Florence Horne, 16 October 1953; Ethel Horne to Florence Horne, 3 December 1953; Buckingham Conservative Association to Donald Horne, 23 December 1953, MLMSS 3525 MLK 2133 L16; Horne, *Portrait of an Optimist*, p. 110.

74   On being 'more Whig than Tory', see Horne, *Portrait of an Optimist*, p. 96.

75 Horne left little written evidence of his reasoning. In his surviving papers from the period, there are no letters to his mother after April 1954 – likely because the launch of the new magazine was such a closely guarded secret, timed to beat the rival magazine *Reveille* to the punch. See Donald Horne letters to Florence Horne from England, MLMSS 3525 MLK 2132. In 1973, Horne described the move as 'unexpected': Donald Horne, interview by Hazel de Berg, 24 January 1973, audio recording, Hazel de Berg collection, NLA. See also Donald Horne, 'The Court of Sir Frank Packer', *The Sydney Papers*, Winter 2000, p. 53 ('out of boredom, in a kind of privateering adventure', verbatim from Horne, *Into the Open*, p. 2); Horne, *Portrait of an Optimist*, pp. 122–23. The 'six-month' idea is mentioned in two memos from Donald Horne to Frank Packer, on 21 September 1954 and 30 December 1954, MLMSS 3525 MLK 2147.

4. BLIND MAN'S BLUFF

1 On Consolidated Press premises see Griffen-Foley, *The House of Packer*, pp. 53, 70–72. Horne called these 'cramped', 'rundown' buildings of Packer's 'duchy': Horne, *Into the Open*, pp. 2–5.

2 On Horne's likening of Packer to a king with courtiers: Horne, 'The Court of Sir Frank Packer', *The Sydney Papers* 12, no. 3 (Winter 2000). Horne claimed to have got the idea from a reading of Denis Brogan's *The American Political System* in the mid-1940s: Horne, *Portrait of an Optimist*, p. 133. When Peter Coleman took over *The Bulletin* in 1964, Horne's advice to him was to 'read Milovan Djilas's *The New Class* and note how Stalin's courtiers dealt with the Kremlin tyrant': Peter Coleman, '*The Bulletin*, the Editor and *The Cherry Orchid*: A Tale of the 1960s', *Voices* 7, no. 1 (Autumn 1997), pp. 88–95.

3 For concise summaries of Australia's early Cold War, see John Murphy, 'A War-Haunted World', in *Imagining the Fifties: Private Sentiment and Political Culture in Menzies' Australia* (Sydney: UNSW Press, 2000), pp. 91–104; Judith Brett, 'The Menzies Era, 1950–1966', in Bashford and Macintyre, *The Cambridge History of Australia Volume 2*, pp. 115–21; David Lowe, *Menzies and the 'Great World Struggle': 1949–1954* (Sydney: UNSW Press, 1999), pp. 3–4.

4 The phrase 'great world struggle' was used by Menzies himself in his second 'The Defence Call to the Nation' broadcast on 22 September 1950: cited in Lowe, *Menzies and the 'Great World Struggle'*, p. 2.

5 Australian Public Opinion Polls, *Australian Gallup Poll* no. 555 (October–November 1948), cited in Murphy, *Imagining the Fifties*, p. 92.

6 For example, John Murphy has criticised the traditional left's interpretation of Menzies 'cynically sounding the war drums for political advantage', noting instead that Menzies was 'magnifying rather than fabricating' widespread and popular anxieties about communism: Murphy, *Imagining the Fifties*, p. 91. For a similar critique, see Lowe, *Menzies and the 'Great World Struggle'*; Brett, *Robert Menzies' Forgotten People*; Brett, *Australian Liberals and the Moral Middle Class*. For select left interpretations, see Ann Curthoys and John Merritt (eds), *Better Dead than Red: Australia's First Cold War: 1945–1959* (Sydney: Allen and Unwin, 1986); Robin Gollan, *Revolutionaries and Reformists: Communism and the Australian Labor Movement, 1920–50* (Sydney: Allen & Unwin, 1985).

7 John Murphy argues that the popular understanding of the 1950s as a time of placid optimism and increasing material prosperity only applies to the second half of the decade, when the economic and political instability that marked the immediate postwar years finally began to fade. Even by the mid-1950s, he writes, 'none knew they were at the beginning of a quarter century of growth. Hindsight is deceptive; social experience was different, more tremulous and uncertain. The worst years of the cold war coincided with the worst years of economic uncertainty': Murphy, *Imagining the Fifties*, p. 106. On the timing of Horne's arrival, see the first letter in Horne's *Weekend* correspondence file, dated 22 July: Donald Horne to Howard French, 22 July 1954, MLMSS 3525 MLK 2148.

8   Donald Horne to Frank Packer, 21 September 1954; 30 December 1954, MLMSS 3525 MLK 2147. In both letters, Horne asks Packer to tell him what his future is beyond December – e.g.: 'I would really like to know what you want me to do after January 18th – which will be six months after I left London with some empty layout sheets in my pocket' (30 December 1954). On Packer's 'liaisons', see Horne, *Portrait of an Optimist*, p. 134. On myths about Horne's stay at the Australia Hotel: Lillian Roxon, Unpublished manuscript of a novel, Lillian Roxon Papers, MLMSS 3086, Box 2, p. 116; Frank Moorhouse, 'Donald Horne – Profile of a Republican', in *Days of Wine and Rage* (Ringwood: Penguin, 1980), p. 110 ('champagne and manicures'). See also Horne, *Portrait of an Optimist*, pp. 122, 134; Horne, '1954', pp. 28–29.

9   Roy Greenslade, 'Howard French: A Shrewd Editor Who Helped Create the *Daily Mail*', Obituary, *Guardian*, 5 December 2008. Horne worked directly under French in London: Howard French to Donald Horne, 1 December 1952, MLMSS 3525 MLK 2133 L16.

10   *Weekend*, 28 August 1954. On French's trip to Australia, see Horne to French, 29 July 1954; French to Horne, 23 September 1954. Horne, *Portrait of an Optimist*, pp. 134–35.

11   Robert Hughes, *Things I Didn't Know: A Memoir* (North Sydney: Vintage, 2007), p. 208; Moorhouse, *Days of Wine and Rage*, p. 110; Horne, interview by De Berg. In a 1962 interview, Horne said editing *Weekend* was 'a bit like directing a B grade movie': see Richard Walsh, 'More from the Dark Ages', *Honi Soit*, 20 March 1962, p. 12, MLMSS 3525 MLK 2175 R-12.

12   Ross Poole, interview by author, 15 August 2018.

13   Horne to French, 21 October 1954; 13 October 1954; 27 September 1954.

14   On *Junior Telegraph*, see Horne to French, 13 October 1954; 6 November 1954; 25 March 1955. See also Horne, *Portrait of an Optimist*, pp. 145–48. '*Weekend* never recovered from the consequences of its success. It took me years to do so': Horne, '1954', pp. 28–29.

15   Horne, *Into the Open*, p. 9.

16   'He [Clyde] was for me a buffer, critical and uncertain but usually helpful': Coleman, '*The Bulletin*, the Editor and *The Cherry Orchid*', pp. 88–95. Baume suggested that Clyde was Horne's patron and protector, defending him when Frank took issue with something he had done: Michael Baume, interview by author, 13 June 2019. In an interview with Peter Coleman, Clyde Packer had this to say about his relationship with Horne: 'I was working very closely with Donald in those days. And [*laughs*], I really enjoyed working with Donald': Clyde Packer interview by Peter Coleman, October 1991, audio recording, NLA.

17   'The only writing I did was to compose headings and sign dockets': Horne, '1954', pp. 28–29.

18   The McCallums returned in 1956: Horne, *Portrait of an Optimist*, p. 164.

19   French to Horne, 23 September 1954.

20   Horne, *Portrait of an Optimist*, p. 125.

21   Horne, *Australian Biography* .

22   Horne, *Portrait of an Optimist*, pp. 149–50; Donald Horne, *An Interrupted Life* (Sydney: HarperCollins, 1998), p. 747.

23   Horne to Packer, 30 December 1954.

24   Nick Horne and Michael Baume, 'Oh Lucky Man?', *The Spectator* (Australia), 8 November 2014.

25   Moorhouse, *Days of Wine and Rage*, p. 110. 'Donald was not universally loved: there are people who worked with him at some stages of his life who still bear the scars', recollected Gillian Appleton in 'Remembering Donald', *New Matilda*, 20 September 2005. Horne himself recalled 'continuing rows with everybody from the switch girl to Packer': Horne, '1954', pp. 28–29.

26   Graeme Eggins, correspondence with author, 4 August 2017.

27   Two junior staff on *Weekend* recalled Horne as a distant and intimidating figure: Lindsay Foyle, interview with author, 5 June 2019; Robert Darroch, interview with author, 27 June 2019. Neither were close to Horne at any point.

28 Eggins, correspondence with author; Packer, interview by Coleman. In Coleman's interview with Packer, he recalled the British journalist Malcolm Muggeridge's observation of Horne's complex personality at this time: 'he was bitter one minute, he was very amusing the next, and he was full of ideas'. On the 'anti-Horne' cult, see Horne, *Portrait of an Optimist*, p. 161.

29 Horne to French, 25 March 1955; Horne to Packer, n.d. [~1956]; Horne to Packer, 30 August 1957. For a list of *Weekend* staff and their roles, see Horne to French, 25 March 1955. Boys was the assistant editor and Murrant the chief subeditor. On 'life's desperate dilemmas', see Horne, *Portrait of an Optimist*, p. 162.

30 Horne, *Portrait of an Optimist*, pp. 150, 165–66, 173, 175. See also Horne, '1954', pp. 28–29. Horne thought Cary's book to be a 'finely drawn study of the irresponsibility and innocence of internal enchantment': Donald Horne, 'Another Look at Xavier Herbert', *The Bulletin*, 5 August 1961.

31 *Threepenny Novel* was one of the first books Horne reviewed in *Observer*: Horne, 'Written on a Fence', *Observer*, 28 June 1958.

32 Donald Horne, 'Blind Man's Bluff', *The Bulletin*, n.d., 'Other 1960s Writing', MLMSS 3525 MLK 2177 J-3. Horne may have borrowed the name for this article from the infamous July 1963 'Suicide of a Nation?' issue of *Encounter* magazine. Tolstoy also used the metaphor of the Russian game of 'blindman's buff' to describe the unpredictable movements of large armies in *War and Peace* (Ringwood: Penguin, 1978), pp. 1264–65.

33 He also read biographies of 'Lloyd George, Churchill, Birkenhead, Beaverbrook', and Kingsley Amis's *Lucky Jim*: Horne, *Portrait of an Optimist*, pp. 166, 175. In 1975, he claimed that he had started reading biographies because he had finished the literary canon: Horne, '1954', pp. 28–29.

34 Horne, 'McCarthyism', *Observer*, 28 May 1960. Horne left England on 19 July 1954.

35 Horne, 'In a Private Requiem', *Quadrant*, March 1977. This story is also recounted in Horne, *Portrait of an Optimist*, p. 168. See also Horne, 'Dysfunctional Exorcism', *The Australian's Review of Books* 4, no. 6 (July 1999); Horne, interview by Ann Turner, May 1994, digitalised audio recording, NLA. Horne recalled 'discussing the great evils of the Communist Party with McAuley until 4 o'clock in the morning over brandy'.

36 McAuley, interview by Santamaria. Stephen Spender toured in September 1954, Malcolm Muggeridge, Leszek Kolakowski and Zbigniew Brzezinski in 1955 and James T. Farrell in 1956. Horne remained at a distance from the ACCF in the early years, and it is doubtful that he attended any of these lectures: Coleman, *The Heart of James McAuleyLife and Work of the Australian Poet* (Sydney: Wildcat Press, 1980), p. 68; Peter Coleman, 'The Prodigal Sons: The Unlikely Story of Richard Krygier and the Australian Association for Cultural Freedom', *Quadrant*, November 1986; Richard Krygier, 'The Making of a Cold Warrior: The Prehistory of the Australian Association', *Quadrant* 30, no. 11 (November 1986), pp. 38–43; Pybus, *The Devil and James McAuley*; John Sutherland, *Stephen Spender: The Authorised Biography* (London: Viking, 2004), pp. 376–77.

37 The two most comprehensive works on the CCF are Frances Stonor Saunders, *Who Paid the Piper?: The CIA and the Cultural Cold War* (London: Granta, 1999) and Peter Coleman, *The Liberal Conspiracy: The Congress for Cultural Freedom and the Struggle for the Mind of Postwar Europe* (New York: Free Press, 1989). See also Tony Judt, *Postwar: A History of Europe Since 1945* (London: William Heinemann, 2005).

38 John McLaren, *Writing in Hope and Fear: Literature as Politics in Postwar Australia* (Cambridge: Cambridge University Press, 1996), pp. 77–78.

39 *Weekend*, 27 July 1957.

40 McAuley was confirmed as editor on 30 March 1956: Coleman, *The Heart of James McAuley*, p. 71.

41 On feeling a 'communion', see Horne, *Portrait of an Optimist*, pp. 169–70. See also Horne, *Into the Open*, p. 67. On the origins of *Encounter*, see Saunders, *Who Paid the Piper?*, pp. 165–89.

42   Judt, *Postwar*, p. 217; Stefan Collini, *Absent Minds: Intellectuals in Britain* (Oxford: Oxford University Press, 2006), p. 145; Coleman, *The Liberal Conspiracy*, pp. 12–13 (on civility), 59–80; Saunders, *The Cultural Cold War*, pp. 165–89. See also Horne, *Into the Open*, p. 67.

43   Horne, 'In a Private Requiem', *Quadrant*, March 1977; Coleman, *The Heart of James McAuley*, p. 70 (quoting McAuley on the 'colourless, odourless' mind); James McAuley to Rosemary Dobson, 26 February 1956, quoted in Pybus, *The Devil and James McAuley*, pp. 152–53 ('totalitarianism').

44   Horne, *Into the Open*, pp. 29–31. On move to Kirribilli, see Horne, *Portrait of an Optimist*, p. 164.

45   Horne, *Portrait of an Optimist*, p. 172; Horne, *Into the Open*, pp. 29–31.

46   Horne, *Portrait of an Optimist*, pp. 174–75. On the timing of the trip, see Horne to French, 12 July 1956 (from Sydney); Horne to French, 22 August 1956, MLMSS 3525 MLK 2148: 'It was very pleasant indeed seeing you again'. While in London, Horne also met up with the new editor of the *Weekend Mail*, Brian May: Donald Horne to Brian May, 22 August 1956, MLMSS 3525 MLK 2148.

47   *Weekend* sold 461,000 copies in September 1956: Donald Horne to Gordon Laing, 20 May 1957, MLMSS 3525 MLK 2148. On Horne's despondency, see Horne, *Portrait of an Optimist*, pp. 195–96. Clyde Packer remembered Horne being 'very depressed by editing *Weekend*': Packer, interview by Coleman. 'Although my name might appear in the *Daily Telegraph* two or three times a week, it was on the jackets of books, not in a newspaper, that I wanted to see "By Donald Horne"': Horne, *Confessions of a New Boy*, p. 366.

48   McAuley, Warner and Harris are quoted in Coleman, *The Heart of James McAuley*, pp. 73–75.

49   Horne, 'Review of JFC Fuller, *The Decisive Battles of the Western World: Volume 3*', *Quadrant*, December 1956, p. 100.

50   Though presumably not sharing *The New Statesman*'s political perspective: Horne, *An Interrupted Life*, p. 799.

51   On *Weekend* circulation, see Horne to Laing, 20 May 1957. Nothing about the deal is mentioned in Packer and Horne's correspondence, MLMSS 3525 MLK 2151.

52   Horne, *Into the Open*, pp. 1–3. In his time at the helm of *Weekend*, Horne had already overseen several minor crises: the *Junior Telegraph* debacle, circulation-crippling labour strikes, budget cuts and consistent rumours of the launch of a rival publication.

53   A.E. Bradd to Donald Horne, 28 May 1957, MLMSS 3525 MLK 2151; quotes for printing costs received on 27 May, 28 May, 19 September, 16 October, MLMSS 3525 MLK 2151; Donald Horne, 'Policy and Practice in the *Observer*', paper delivered to the AACF 'Little Magazines' Seminar, August 1962, MLMSS 3525 MLK 2151.

54   Horne, *Portrait of an Optimist*, pp. 196–97; *An Interrupted Life*, p. 803. Tom Fitzgerald remembered Packer indicating that the *Observer*'s first editor would be George Baker. 'I don't recall Donald Horne being mentioned but the person whom [Packer] rang may have been Donald Horne, I couldn't tell you': Tom Fitzgerald, interview by Ken Inglis, 1988, audio recording, NLA. Robert Hughes remembers Baker, not Horne, as the *Observer*'s first editor: Hughes, *Things I Didn't Know*, pp. 206–07. It is unlikely, though, that either of these men were aware of Horne's arrangement with Packer. Baker was to run the magazine, but Horne called the shots.

55   Three summaries of these lunchtime conversations survive. The first two are written by Baker but appear to be summaries of prior conversations. For example, 'That was plain from the analysis of contents you showed me and from the editorial policy you proposed': George Baker to Donald Horne, 'Notes on the Observer II', 12 July 1957, MLMSS 3525 MLK 2151. Many phrases from the earlier written correspondence are reproduced word-for-word in the third, typed document, and it is filed in Horne's papers alongside this correspondence.

56 'Magazine Proposal', MLMSS 3525 MLK 2151 ACP-1. On economic matters, they
    intended to follow the middle road and focus on the 'results of actions' rather than
    'what it says in the book of directions'; 'right wing' was likely Baker's interpretation
    of Horne's 'radical conservatism': see Baker to Horne, 'Notes on the Observer II',
    12 July 1957. 'I based its structure on the familiar European model': Horne, 'Policy
    and Practice in the *Observer*'. One proposed section, '*Observer*'s Diary', was to
    be explicitly modelled on 'Kingsley Martin's column in the *New Statesman*': see
    'Magazine Proposal'.

57 Horne, 'Policy and Practice in the *Observer*'; 'Observer: Contents', n.d., MLMSS 3525
    MLK 2151; 'Magazine Proposal'; Baker to Horne, 'Notes on the Observer Series III',
    16 July 1957.

58 'Magazine Proposal'. Versions of Horne's prescient passage about the *Observer*'s 'New
    Men' appeared in three of his memoirs, always with reference to the 'educated but
    classless group': Horne, *Portrait of an Optimist*, p. 187; *An Interrupted Life*, p. 804;
    Into the Open, p. 17. In *Into the Open*, with a journalist's flourish he reorganised the
    passage, splicing together its two key elements and dropping the more fluent reworked
    quote inside some authoritative quotation marks. The new quote read: 'a rising class
    who didn't really know what they thought, who they were, or where they were going'
    (p. 17).

59 Baker to Horne, 'Tabloid Observer', 28 October 1957.

60 Ibid.

61 Baker to Horne, 'Notes on the Observer Series III', 16 July 1957.

62 Ward, *Australia and the British Embrace*, pp. 41–68.

63 'Observer: Contents'.

64 Baker to Horne, 'Notes on the Observer Series III', 16 July 1957.

65 Horne's correspondence with Frank Packer is almost entirely devoted to *Weekend*.
    Horne, *Into the Open*, pp. 5–6; Horne to Packer, 28 November 1958 (detailing
    Coleman's personal history); . Coleman, *Memoirs of a Slow Learner*, p. 58; Horne, *Into
    the Open*, pp. 15–16; Horne, *An Interrupted Life*, p. 803.

66 Clyde Packer to Frank Packer, 13 November 1957, MLMSS 3525 MLK 2147; Horne,
    Portrait of an Optimist, p. 199; Horne to Baker, 3 October 1957.

67 Letter to Horne from the editor of *Australian Women's Weekly*, MLMSS 3525 MLK
    2150; Queensland Literature Review Board, Annual Report, June 1958, MLMSS 3525
    MLK 2150. The first attack appeared in Sydney's *Catholic Weekly* on 7 November
    1957. The quotes appear in 'Sexy Publications Corrupting Australian Youth' and
    'Objectionable Papers a Disgrace to Australia', *Advocate*, 28 November 1957.

68 *Catholic Weekly*, 12 December 1957; MLMSS 3525 MLK 2150; Horne, *Portrait of an
    Optimist*, pp. 200–04; Coleman, *Memoirs of a Slow Learner*, pp. 89–90; Donald Horne
    to *Catholic Weekly*, 26 November 1957, MLMSS 3525 MLK 2150.

69 The best contemporary evidence is a memo from Clyde Packer on 8 January 1958
    announcing Baker as an 'associate editor': Horne Papers, MLMSS 3525 MLK 2151.
    There are many anecdotal accounts of the incident: Horne, *Portrait of an Optimist*
    pp. 204–06; Horne, *An Interrupted Life*, pp. 810–12, Horne, *Into the Open*, p. 15;
    Coleman, *Memoirs of a Slow Learner*, pp. 89–94. Robert Hughes remembers Baker,
    not Horne, as the *Observer*'s first editor. Given the evidence to the contrary, it is
    possible Hughes assumed that because Baker had hired him he must be the editor:
    Hughes, *Things I Didn't Know*, pp. 206–07.

70 Coleman, *Memoirs of a Slow Learner*, pp. 90–94; Horne, *Portrait of an Optimist*, p. 197.
    See also, Robert Hughes: Baker was an 'obese dandy' and 'deep-in-the-closet gay' who
    was 'devoted to his unaware mother': Hughes, *Things I Didn't Know*, pp. 206–07.

71 Clyde Packer: 'Dad let him start the *Observer* because [laughs] Donald was very
    depressed by editing *Weekend*, or *Everybody*, whichever it was called, and this was
    a little consolation for him, a little fortnightly consolation': Packer, interview by
    Coleman; Horne, Portrait of an Optimist, p. 207.

5. GATECRASHING

1   On acquisition and the new *Weekend* office, see Griffen-Foley, *The House of Packer*, p. 254; Horne, *Into the Open*, pp. 5–6.

2   *Observer*, 22 February 1958; *Into the Open*, p. 15.

3   *Into the Open*, p. 31; Horne, 'Policy and Practice in the *Observer*' ('ad hoc'). See also Hughes, *Things I Didn't Know*, p. 209; Coleman, *The Heart of James McAuley*, p. 74; Horne, *Into the Open*, pp. 15–35. Just over a decade after the magazine started, the Australian sociologist Warren Osmond labelled this group of its writers the 'New Critics': Warren Osmond, *The Dilemma of an Australian Sociology: An Analysis of 'Equality and Authority'* (Melbourne: Arena Publications, 1972), p. 7. See also Tim Rowse, *Australian Liberalism and the National Character* (Melbourne: Kibble, 1978), particularly the chapter 'The New Critics and the End of Ideology', pp. 189–246. Peter Coleman also used the term 'New Critics' in *Memoirs of a Slow Learner*, p. 98.

4   Rowse, *Australian Liberalism and National Character*, pp. 176, 180; Horne, 'Policy and Practice in the *Observer*'.

5   In early 1959, Horne told *Observer*'s advertisers that the magazine 'wore its conservatism with a difference: If you are interested in an attempt to provide a counter attraction to the intellectual enticements of the left, or merely to help a magazine that is trying to foster intelligent discussion, the *Observer* deserves your support': Horne to Packer, 19 February 1959, MLMSS 3525 MLK 2147. Some of the small magazines Horne had in mind included *Meanjin*, *Angry Penguins*, *Overland* and *The Bulletin*. On the intellectual climate, see McLaren, *Writing in Hope and Fear*; Lynne Strahan, *Just City and the Mirrors: Meanjin Quarterly and the Intellectual Front, 1940–1965* (Melbourne, Oxford University Press, 1984).

6   Horne, 'The Great Australian Fraud', *Observer*, 31 May 1958, p. 247. Horne's distaste for nationalist literature had a long history: '[Since World War I, nationalism] has been a stultifying rather than a stimulating factor in Australian letters', he wrote in his diplomatic cadet essay 'The Rise of Nationalism in Australian Literature', n.d. [1944 or 1945], MLMSS 3525 MLK 2138 G-9. Coleman was allegedly the president of the 'Anti-Folk Song Society of Australia': *Semper Floreat*, 10 April 1958 (MLK 2175 R12).

7   'Patrick White's Nightmare', *Observer*, 22 February 1958; Horne, 'Portrait of an Un-Australian', *Observer*, 4 October 1958, p. 517; Another favourite was Xavier Herbert, see for example Horne, 'Another Look at Xavier Herbert'.

8   Horne's , *Observer* reviews include 'The Big Takeover', 31 October 1959; 'His Son's Father', 19 September 1959; 'McCarthyism', 28 May 1960; 'Beaverbrook for Beginners', 26 July 1958; 'No Bunker for Napoleon', 12 July 1958. In England, he had wiled away one slow winter [January– March 1952] reading biographies of turn-of-the-century English statesmen (Horne, *Portrait of an Optimist*, p. 80); in the early days of *Weekend*, he read A.J.P. Taylor's biography of Bismarck (, p. 157), 'Lloyd George, Churchill, Birkenhead, Beaverbrook', also some sociology (pp. 166–67) and 'Isaac Deutscher's biography of Trotsky'(p. 175). While working at *The Daily Telegraph* in the mid-to-late 1940s he had reviewed several Great Man biographies, including one of Henry Wallace: MLMSS 3525 MLK 2176.

9   Horne, 'No Bunker for Napoleon'. Horne gave two lectures to a Workers Education Australia Summer School in the late 1950s on the subjects of 'Ambition' and 'Conformity', as well as contributing an article to the WEA journal. See Donald Horne, 'The Organisation Don', *The Australian Highway*, December 1959. All were in response to W.H. Whyte's 1956 book *The Organisation Man*, which argued that there was a collectivist ethos within modern organisations that discouraged individual creativity and freedom.

10   Horne, 'Written on a Fence'.

11   See the following of Horne's *Observer* articles: 'Like Talking to Himself', 19 April 1958;
      'Anxious Footnotes', 19 April 1958; 'Love Among the Conservatives', 17 May 1958;
      'Sexifiers', 31 May 1958.

12   Donald Horne, 'How to Hoax the English (and the Australians)', *Observer*,
      12 November 1960, p. 5.

13   Coleman, *Memoirs of a Slow Learner*, pp. 89, 94.

14   Donald Horne, 'Pasternak's Novel', *Observer*, 15 November 1958, p. 631.

15   Donald Horne, 'Giving In', *Observer*, 6 September 1958. 'I could spray out derision like
      a cat marking its territory': Horne, *Into the Open*, p. 28

16   In later years, Horne was always quick to point out *Observer*'s allegedly pioneering
      interest in Asia. 'The cocky pundits of the 1980s and 1990s thought it was *they* who
      had discovered "Asia". Yet in 1958 the idea of "Asia" at once become one of *Observer*'s
      special lines': Horne, *Into the Open*, p. 25.

17   Donald Horne, 'Has Australia Got a Chance?', *Observer*, 31 May 1958, pp. 227–28.
      Mads Clausen calls this 'apocalyptic rhetoric': Mads Clausen, 'Donald Horne Finds
      Asia', in David Walker and Agnieszka Sobocinska (eds), *Australia's Asia: From Yellow
      Peril to Asian Century* (Crawley: UWA Publishing, 2012), p. 306. Peter Coleman also
      noted Horne's particular strain of early 1960s Australian 'catastrophism'. In Horne's
      eyes, Australians were 'eternal cricketers forever strolling out to the crease unaware
      that the game was over': Coleman, '*The Bulletin*, the Editor and *The Cherry Orchard*',
      p. 88.

18   Horne, 'Let Us Rejoice'.

19   Horne, *Into the Open*, pp. 25–26.

20   Donald Horne, 'Delegation', n.d., MLMSS 3525 MLK 2151: 'Mr P Coleman is to be
      fully responsible for the production of ideas and the quality of copy for all the general
      pages of the *Observer*, and the book review section'. Baume would be responsible for
      'The World, Arts, Finance, letters, Science and Mugga'. On 4 September 1958, Coleman
      wrote to Horne with a list of articles to be run on New Guinea, which suggests the
      change likely happened prior to this: Horne to Baume, Coleman, Jerrett, 19 December
      1958, MLMSS 3525 MLK 2151.

21   The mid-to-late 1950s were breakthrough years for small magazines in Australia:
      Voice (1952), *Overland* (1954), *Quadrant* (1956), *Outlook* (1957), *Observer* (1958),
      Nation (1958), *Prospect* (1958), *Dissent* (1961) and *Australian Book Review* (1961), along
      with the reinvigoration of existing magazines such as *Meanjin*, *Australian Quarterly*,
      Westerly, *Southerly* and *The Bulletin* (relaunched in 1960). See McLaren, *Writing in
      Hope and Fear*.

22   *Nation* even had a rival Kings Cross restaurant, Vadim's to *Observer*'s Ada: Ken Inglis,
      'Opening the Windows in a Stuffy Room', *Inside Story*, 26 September 2018. Horne
      asked Packer to declare Hughes 'persona non grata', because 'His sudden move has
      inconvenienced us a bit and hardly seems the right reply for what we have done for
      him': Horne to Packer, 1 December 1959.

23   *Observer* was thought to be tougher and more conservative than its left-liberal rival:
      Vincent Buckley, 'The Fortnightly Universe', *Prospect*, no. 2 (1960); 'Highwayman's
      Diary', *The Australian Highway* (March 1959). As one letter writer put it, both
      magazines were, 'by contrast with the much trodden, littered and familiar parks of our
      dailies and weeklies, quite new, unexpected and even exciting bits of forest country to
      roam in. But you don't enjoy the *Observer* forest quite so much – how can you when
      you know there's a fivepenny tiger always lurking there': Clement Semmler, letter to
      the editor, *The Australian Highway*, July 1959.

24   In his survey of the foreign policy perspectives of the two fortnightlies, Vincent
      Buckley deemed *Nation* 'dignified and perceptive', while *Observer* 'emerges with
      a "self-interest" line that nearly persuades but does not move': Buckley, 'The
      Fortnightly Universe'.

25   Donald Horne, 'Living with Asia', *Observer*, 7 March 1959.

26 Horne's experience in Kenya had left him with a deep moral ambivalence about the upending of settler regimes: Horne, 'A Liberal among the Mau Mau', *Observer*, 20 September 1958. Coleman had also been to Africa, working as a teacher in Sudan. Nicholas Brown argues *Observer*'s writers saw only two options for Asia: 'Western industrialism or chaos': Nicholas Brown, *Governing Prosperity: Social Change and Social Analysis in Australia in the 1950s* (Cambridge: Cambridge University Press, 1995), p. 48. For Horne's foreign affairs writing in early 1959, see the following *Observer* articles: Horne, 'Living with Asia'; 'Who's Afraid of Big Bad Asia?', 21 March 1959; 'How to Be Small', 4 April 1959; 'Putting Diplomats in Touch', 30 May 1959; 'Australia's China Lobby', 13 June 1959; 'Khrushchev: Disarming Diplomacy', 3 October 1959.

27 On oppositionism, see Stefan Collini, '"What, Ultimately, For?" The Elusive Goal of Cultural Criticism', *Raritan* 33, no. 2 (2013), p. 1.

28 Horne, 'Policy and Practice in the *Observer*'. Horne had used the 'gatecrashing' metaphor as early as 1946 when recalling his time as a Canberra public servant, writing 'It is almost as if you were trying to gatecrash an old established club': Horne, '20-Year-Old Rules and Prejudices'. He used it again in 1976: 'In trying to push a new subject on to the political agenda one may do so theatrically . . . Such actions help new issues to gatecrash our prejudices about what politics should be concerned with and it might often be only by such theatrical aids that we get new issues onto the political agenda': Donald Horne, 'The Cult of November 11', *Nation Review*, 5 November 1976. And again in 1986 in his book *The Public Culture: The Triumph of Industrialism* (London: Pluto, 1986, p. 178). Peter Coleman also used the metaphor to describe this period in *Memoirs of a Slow Learner* and in his book *Australian Civilization: A Symposium* (Melbourne: Cheshire, 1962), p. 147: 'Robert Hughes, for example, even pushed in, gatecrashing the party as it were'.

29 This is best evidenced by the structure of Horne's memoirs. *An Interrupted Life*, the amalgamation of his three early autobiographies, concludes in 1958 at the foundation of *Observer*. The book's subtitle is 'An Autobiographical Masterpiece About Growing Up'. In contrast, in *Into the Open* he describes the post-1958 period as 'a changeover time for ideas in Australia – perhaps its biggest' (p. ix). Horne's archive also noticeably swells at the beginning of *Observer*, and this weight of material itself seems significant. This periodisation is repeated by some of Horne's contemporaries – e.g. Vincent Buckley: 'If the fifties were a decade of radical learning, 1958 was for Australian intellectuals a crucial year: *Cutting Green Hay: Friendships, Movements and Cultural Conflicts in Australia's Great Decades* (Melbourne: Penguin, 1983), p. 193. Also Robert Hughes: 'Finally the cork came out of the bottle . . . In Australia in the late fifties and early sixties you felt a terrific *jouissance*, a sense – near orgasmic at times – of celebration and enjoyment': *Things I Didn't Know*, p. 216.

30 Horne and Baume, 'Oh Lucky Man?'.

31 Horne, *Into the Open*, p. 16, Myfanwy Horne, 'Requiem', in Horne and Horne, *Dying: A Memoir*, p. 109.

32 Myfanwy Gollan, 'Two Schools', *Quadrant* 13, no. 6 (1969). Ed Campion described first seeing her in 1951, aged eighteen, 'a dark-haired vivacious girl who seemed very self-assured': Edmund Campion, *Rockchoppers: Growing up Catholic in Australia* (Ringwood: Penguin, 1982), p. 1. Horne, *Into the Open*, p. 16; John Rickard, 'Sydney: The Class of 51', *Australian Historical Studies* 27 (1997); Julia Horne and Nick Horne, 'Myfanwy Horne: Writer, Editor, Helped Foster National Identity', *The Sydney Morning Herald*, 2 November 2013.

33 Horne, interview by Turner.

34 Spender cited in Coleman, *The Liberal Conspiracy*, p. 144.

35 Menzies had allegedly promised to fund *Quadrant*, but ultimately voted against it. Cassandra Pybus suggested that the reason for this about turn was that Menzies needed an excuse to deny funding to the recently launched *Overland*, edited by the ex-communist Stephen Murray-Smith: Pybus, *The Devil and James McAuley*, p. 174. See also Horne, 'Cost-Plus Culture', *Observer*, 29 November 1958.

36   Krygier, 'The Making of a Cold Warrior', pp. 38–43; Coleman, 'The Prodigal Sons'; Coleman, *The Liberal Conspiracy*; Horne, *Into the Open*, pp. 66–67; Peter Coleman, 'Henry Richard Krygier (1917–1986)', in Diane Langmore (ed.), *Australian Dictionary of Biography Volume 17, 1981–1990: A–K* (Carlton: Melbourne University Press, 2007).

37   Horne, *Into the Open*, pp. 66–67, 104; Coleman, *The Liberal Conspiracy*, p. 96. According to Krygier, Horne had allegedly declared that *Observer* would be an 'organ of the Association for Cultural Freedom' because he 'completely agreed' with its views. Krygier returned that he was 'very pleased' to have 'direct access to an intellectual fortnightly': Richard Krygier, interview by J.D.B. Miller, January 1984, audio recording, NLA.

38   The 'unseemly shouting match' quote appears in Coleman, *The Liberal Conspiracy*, p. 157. See also Coleman, 'The Prodigal Sons', p. 15.

39   Horne, *Into the Open*, p. 106. Krygier noted 'Our relationship with the *Observer* has become rather close': report by R Krygier to CCF, 8 March 1960, AACF papers, Box 9, file 3, cited in McLaren, *Writing in Hope and Fear*, p. 133. In 1994, Horne commented that for 'about three years … I had this enormous obsession with what was actually a dying organism [The Australian Communist Party] and it was in that stage that I became an enthusiastic member of the Australian Association for Cultural Freedom … I was beginning to abandon all of that anti-planning stuff … but I became too intensely concerned with the Australian Communist Party': Horne, interview by Turner.

40   John McLaren, 'Peace Wars: The 1959 ANZ Peace Congress', *Labour History* 82 (May 2002), pp. 97–108; Ralph Summy and Malcolm Saunders, 'The 1959 Melbourne Peace Congress: Culmination of Anti-Communism in Australian in the 1950s', in Curthoys and Merritt, *Better Dead than Red*, pp. 74–98. Pybus says the congress was in November: *The Devil and James McAuley*, pp. 174–76. See also Horne, *Into the Open*, p. 106; Frank Moorhouse, *Conference-ville* (North Sydney: Vintage, 2008 [1976]), pp. 27–28.

41   Horne, 'Khrushchev: Disarming Diplomacy'; Horne, 'Do-It-Yourself-Guide: How to hold a Congress', *Observer*, 14 November 1959; Horne, letters to the editor, *Observer*, 14 November 1959.

42   James McAuley, 'On Being an Intellectual', *Quadrant* 4, no. 1 (Summer 1959–1960), pp. 23–31. The published piece was actually an edited version of a speech McAuley had given at the 1959 Christian Social Week. Earlier that year, McAuley had published a collection of his essays under the title *The End of Modernity*. According to his biographer, Cassandra Pybus, it was intended as a riposte to the 'antimetaphysical, modern mentality' expressed in Lionel Trilling's 1950 collection *The Liberal Imagination*: see Pybus, *The Devil and James McAuley*, pp. 172–73. Peter Coleman later called McAuley's manifesto 'one of the basic texts of Australian conservatism': Coleman, 'The Prodigal Sons'.

43   Donald Horne, 'A Time of Sadness', *Observer*, 20 September 1958.

44   Donald Horne, 'A Plimsoll Line for Intellectuals', *Observer*, 9 January 1960.

45   Horne, *Into the Open*, p. 101. It was rumoured that Robert Menzies thought *Observer* was 'a magazine which Australia has been badly in need of for years': Robert Kennedy to Horne, 7 April 1958, MLMSS 3525 MLK 2151.

46   Donald Horne, 'Meeting Professor Manning Clark', *Observer*, 5 March 1960. The fact that Clark's book was published serially in *Nation* probably fanned the flames of Horne's outrage.

47   Horne, *Into the Open*, p. 107.

48   Manning Clark, 'Donald Horne: From Pub Wit to Prophet', *National Times*, 2 August 1976; Hugh Stretton, 'Persistent Preaching', *The Critic*, April 1976.

49   Coleman, 'The Prodigal Sons', p. 17. Other shouty Horne articles from this period include: Horne, 'The Organisation Don', *The Australian Highway*, December 1959, MLMSS 3525 MLK 2177 J-2; 'Cowatchers of Diplomacy', *Observer*, 23 January 1960; 'Getting Down to Business', *Observer*, 6 February 1960; 'Excerpts from Meeting American Man by Banning Mark', *Observer*, 30 April 1960; 'McCarthyism', *Observer*, 28 May 1960; 'The Big Crack-Up', *Observer*, 11 June 1960; 'The Press in Politics', *Observer*, 23 July 1960; 'The Weight of Rottenness', *Observer*, 20 August 1960.

50   Horne, 'How to Hoax the English (and the Australians)'. Horne also criticised Sayle's characterisation of Australian businessmen as ignorant and provincial (in *Encounter*) in his chapter on 'Businessmen' in Coleman's *Australian Civilization* (p. 180).

51   Horne, 'How to Hoax the English (and the Australians)'.

52   *Observer* argued that divorce should be granted for the breakdown in a marriage even if neither party has committed a matrimonial offence: 'The Divorce Bill', editorial, *Observer*, 16 May; Trevor Martin, 'Divorce: The Real Crisis', *Observer*, 30 May 1959, p. 325. See also Horne, *Into the Open*, pp. 16–17.

53   Griffen-Foley, *The House of Packer*, pp. 234–35; Patricia Rolfe, *The Journalistic Javelin: An Illustrated History of The Bulletin* (Sydney: Wildcat Press, 1979), p. 301; Horne, *Into the Open*, p. 36.

54   Rolfe, *The Journalistic Javelin*.

55   Horne, *Into the Open*, p. 42. Horne made much of the drama of his removal of *The Bulletin*'s slogan, recounting the story in memoirs and interviews – e.g. in a 1992 interview (*Australian Biography*): 'I went down to the composing room, and I said to the head compositor, "Would you take that off", and I can remember seeing it, you know. It was in metal. He puts his tweezers down and he pulls it out: "Australia for the White Man", and I said, "Would you melt it down."' Similarly, in *Into the Open*: 'The compositor pulled that line out with tweezers, held it up like an extracted tooth, and then threw it onto the waste metal box for remelting. Well, he said, that should have been done years ago' (p. 46).

56   Donald Horne, 'The Bulletin no. 3 – Prepared for the Advertising Department', n.d. [~late 1960], MLMSS 3525 MLK 2152.

57   Rolfe, *The Journalistic Javelin*, p. 302. 'One of the most extraordinary combinations in the history of editing': Horne, interview by De Berg.

58   Donald Horne, 'The Changes in the *Bulletin*', editorial, 18 January 1961; 'Dreaming of the Past', editorial, *The Bulletin*, 19 August 1961.

59   Donald Horne, 'Low Life in the Short Story', editorial, *The Bulletin*, 10 June 1961; Coleman, 'The Bulletin, the Editor and *The Cherry Orchid*', pp. 88–95 (Horne's brief was to 'revitalise the magazine while preserving its character as a literary-political review of strong Australian bias').

60   Horne, *Into the Open*, p. 49.

61   'The *Bulletin* Changes', letters, *The Bulletin*, 25 January 1961; 'For and Against the Changes', letters, *The Bulletin*, 1 February 1961.

62   The poems were not originally conceived to attack Horne but Leonie Kramer, and indeed Harwood's original conspirator, Vincent Buckley, had been a largely sympathetic acquaintance of Horne's since the Peace Congress in late 1959. See Griffen-Foley, *The House of Packer*, p. 236; Horne, *Into the Open*, pp. 56–57. The Bulletin published a reply in its editorial a week later: 'Sad Jest', *The Bulletin*, 19 August 1961.

63   Horne, 'The Changes in *The Bulletin*'. In a private memo, Horne described this as a 'hard-headed, sardonic Australian realism': Horne, 'The Bulletin, Stage Two Memo No. 1', 27 April 1961, Peter Hastings Papers, ADFA Library, MSS 374, Box 7, Folder 2.

64   For example, in his first *Bulletin* editorial, Horne declared that 'nothing better could have happened to Australian than to enjoy a long period of Conservative rule': Horne, 'Who's Afraid of Next Year', *The Bulletin*, 28 December 1960. Similarly: 'The Prime Minister [Menzies] has lent his great gifts to *not* governing the country as much as governing it and this is an attitude that now takes considerable nerve and principle to maintain': Donald Horne, 'Praising the PM', comment by Observer, *The Bulletin*, 22 March 1961.

65   'Australia Back in the Picture?', editorial, *The Bulletin*, 29 July 1961.

66   Donald Horne, 'Looking Behind Our Backs', editorial, *The Bulletin*, 18 January 1961; 'The Bulletin and Communism', Plain English, *The Bulletin*, 29 September 1961 ('the threat of Communism is so great in world affairs that in our view most international questions cannot be considered without considering their relation to Communism').

67 Horne, 'Praising the PM' ('Hard-headed'); 'The Great Debate: Russia and China', *The Bulletin*, 19 August 1961; 'Khrushchev Fights His War', 28 August 1961; 'A Muddled Australian Party', 2 September 1961. For examples of Horne's approach to Cold War diplomacy, see Donald Horne, 'Let Peter Have It, Dear', editorial, *The Bulletin*, 8 February 1961; 'Scaring the Neutrals', editorial, *The Bulletin*, 9 September 1961; 'Mr Khrushchev's Aching Heart', *The Bulletin*, 19 September 1961; 'Disposing of New Guinea', *The Bulletin*, 7 October 1961; How to Be Stubborn', *The Bulletin*, 21 October 1961; 'Screwing Up the Tension', *The Bulletin*, 29 October 1961; 'On Surviving', *The Bulletin*, 4 November 1961.

68 Horne, 'Still Living with Asia', *The Bulletin*, 17 March 1961: a restatement of his argument from 'Living with Asia' in March 1959. Robin Gerster and Jan Bassett have argued that by showing the idea of a monolithic 'Asia' to be a Western myth, Horne anticipated the more famous 'Orientalist' arguments of Edward Said: *Seizures of Youth: The Sixties and Australia* (Melbourne: Hyland House, 1991), p. 122.

69 Immigration Reform Group, 'Control or Colour Bar?' (Melbourne: Immigration Reform Group, 1960).

70 Donald Horne, 'Australia for the White Man', editorial, *The Bulletin*, 21 January 1961; 'Living with Asia' ('The kind of face you pull'); 'A Glimmering House of Cards', *The Bulletin*, 19 April 1961 ('The great purpose of any foreign policy is not primarily commercial … and certainly not cultural: it is to survive'). When South Africa was kicked out of the Commonwealth for its racist internal policies in March 1961, Horne pointed out that Australia was now open to a similar criticism:'Commonwealth Stones', Comment by Observer, *The Bulletin*, 15 March 1961.

71 R.M. Crawford, letter to the editor, *The Bulletin*, 12 April 1961; Horne, 'Thugs on the Waterfront', editorial, *The Bulletin*.

72 'Melbourne University Communists at Work', *The Bulletin*, 19 April 1961; 'Melbourne University Communists Again at Work', *The Bulletin*, 3 May 1961; 'The Smearing of Professor Crawford', *The Bulletin*, 26 April 1961; 'Inquiring Into Universities', *The Bulletin*, 3 May 1961; 'Melbourne University: The Central Issues', *The Bulletin*, 10 May 1961; 'A Long Campaign?', *The Bulletin*, 17 May 1961; 'Taking Stock', *The Bulletin*, 24 May 1961.

73 Fay Anderson, 'Into the Night: Max Crawford, the Labyrinth of the Social Studies Enquiry and ASIO's "Spoiling Operations"', *Australian Historical Studies* 125 (2005), pp. 60–80.

74 Stuart Macintyre and Simon Marginson, 'The University and Its Public', in Tony Coady (ed.), *Why Universities Matter* (Sydney: Allen & Unwin, 2000), pp. 49–71; Fiona Capp, *Writers Defiled* (Melbourne: McPhee Gribble, 1993); Cassandra Pybus, *Gross Moral Turpitude: The Orr Case Reconsidered* (Melbourne: William Heinemann, 1993); Brian Martin, *Intellectual Suppression: Australian Case Histories, Analysis and Responses* (Sydney: Angus and Robertson, 1986).

75 Horne cited in Anderson, 'Into the Night', pp. 60–80 ('As I saw it at the time (which for me was an 18-month or so period of excess), yes I believe there were issues of academic freedom – a line strongly supported, of course, by Knopfelmacher. Looking back, as I suggested … I can now see it as the recurrent feature of that intermittent feature of university life – a school dispute'); Horne, 'The Orr Case', 31 May 1961. Horne later switched sides: Horne, 'Why I Ratted on the Orr Supporters', *The Bulletin*, 23 September 1961.

76 Cited in Elisabeth Wynhausen, 'Death of the Lucky Country or Birth of Donald Horne, the Conservative Radical?', *National Times*, 8 March 1976; Horne, *Into the Open*, p. 112. Jake Kane, the Secretary of the NSW DLP, included Horne as a member of his 'brains trust' at this point in time.

77 Horne, *Into the Open*, p. 111.

78 Ibid., pp. 112–13. Horne confirmed this in an interview with Faye Anderson in 2002: Anderson, 'Into the Night', pp. 60–80.

79 Krygier thought Kerr had 'never had a meaningful fight about anything at all', cited in Pybus, *The Devil and James McAuley*, p. 188. See also Horne, *Into the Open*, p. 113.

80 Horne cited in Pybus, *The Devil and James McAuley*, p. 188.

81 After an article in *Nation* (leaked by Wootten) about the 'split' in the AACF between liberal and anti-communists, Paris wrote to express their concern. Horne responded on behalf of the AACF: It was a storm in a tea-cup – 'We are down a lawyer and up a journalist'. In the future, he wrote, the AACF was going to widen its membership and target younger intellectuals: Horne cited in Coleman, 'Prodigal Sons', p. 17. According to Elisabeth Wynhausen, 'When John Kerr stood for the Association's Presidency, Horne most actively opposed him on the grounds that among other things, Kerr was "too soft" on communism': Wynhausen, 'Death of the Lucky Country or Birth of Donald Horne'.

82 'The Gentle Fifties?', *Observer*, 26 December 1959.

83 Donald Horne, 'This Australia, 1961', editorial, *The Bulletin*, 30 December 1961.

84 Donald Horne 'In Times Like These: A Kaleidoscope of 1961', *The Bulletin*, 30 December 1961.

85 Donald Horne, 'A Need for Patriots', *The Bulletin*, 6 January 1962.

86 Griffen-Foley, *The House of Packer*, pp. 235, 260. In 1945, by contrast, *The Bulletin*'s circulation had been 58,000.

87 Horne suspected conspiracy, but Hastings was probably an unwilling conspirator. On 20 December 1961, Hastings – then the editor of *The Sunday Telegraph* – sent a memo to Packer protesting about rumours that he was being shifted to *The Bulletin*. In response, on 26 December, Packer poured water on the rumours, suggesting he was probably the chief conspirator: 'If nobody mentioned to you officially about the transfer to *The Bulletin* and you have not been transferred to *The Bulletin* how did you know about it?': Peter Hastings Papers, ADFA Library, MSS 374, Box 7, Folder 2. Michael Baume's theory was that Horne's sacking was the inevitable result of an irreconcilable rift with Packer that began with the 'beer on the head' incident a few years earlier: Horne and Baume, 'Oh Lucky Man?'. For Coleman it was simply a business decision: 'Sales remained low and Horne was sacked': Coleman, '*The Bulletin*, the Editor and *The Cherry Orchard*', p. 89. In 1973, Horne suggested he had had an 'argument with management in about March 1962', interview by De Berg.

6. OVERTHROWALS

1 Wynhausen, 'Death of the Lucky Country or Birth of Donald Horne'. In a letter to Peter Hastings in May 1964, John Pringle, editor of the British *Observer*, wrote of his 'distrust' of Donald Horne, while acknowledging his 'talent': Peter Hastings Papers, Box 7, Folder 2, ADFA Library.

2 'Bulletin no. 3', 'prepared for the advertising department', n.d. [~early 1961], MLMSS 3525 MLK 2152.

3 Donald Horne, 'Mr Menzies' Stops and Starts', *The Bulletin*, 1 March 1961.

4 Geoffrey Dutton, *Out in the Open: An Autobiography* (St Lucia, University of Queensland Press, 1994), p. 244: 'Donald was also sceptical about the trendy left when it was fashionable to be one-eyed about communism'.

5 According to Michael Baume, 'Packer's ... sacking of Horne as editor of *The Bulletin* provided the time and incentive to write the book that earned him the fame he craved': Horne and Baume, 'Oh Lucky Man?'. According to Peter Coleman, *The Lucky Country* was born of 'rage at his rivals who had masterminded his humiliating dismissal as editor of *The Bulletin*': Coleman, 'Don's Party Tricks', *Spectator Australia*, 8 November 2014.

6 Peter Coleman himself recalled the difficulty of overhauling *The Bulletin* in 'a confused, transitional period like the middle 1960s': Coleman, '*The Bulletin*, the Editor and *The Cherry Orchard*', p. 89.

7   Donald Horne, 'Life Without Migrants', *The Bulletin*, 12 August 1961. One External Affairs policy paper suggested that without British leadership, 'the Commonwealth would atrophy and in time cease to exist':Ward, *Australia and the British Embrace*, p. 75. Horne recalls 'I began shifting myself around in the early 1960s – at first mainly by reading': Moorhouse, *Days of Wine and Rage*, p. 415.

8   Donald Horne, 'The Perplexing Paradox of the DLP', *The Bulletin*, 22 July 1961.

9   Donald Horne, 'A Policy Without a Party', *The Bulletin*, 23 December 1961.

10   Horne, 'A Need for Patriots'.

11   Horne, 'Policy and Practice in the Observer'.

12   Horne, 'A Policy Without a Party'; Horne, 'In Times Like These'; Horne, 'A Need for Patriots'; Horne, 'What Is to Be Done?', *The Bulletin*, 11 November 1961 (on 'planned capitalism'): 'We have reached a stage when questions of detail, difference and quality are the main questions of social welfare and these would best be considered in a non-political approach . . . The main differences of opinion are on the kinds of State intervention and the degree with which they are used.'

13   See Bolton, *The Oxford History of Australia Volume 5*; Judt, *Postwar*.

14   Horne, 'Who's Afraid of Next Year'.

15   Edward Shils, 'Further Thoughts on the Congress in the '60s', 1961, cited in Coleman, *The Liberal Conspiracy*, p. 171.

16   Coleman, 'The Prodigal Sons', p. 16: 'some abandoned their anti-communism the way some had abandoned their Marxism ten years earlier … almost everyone everywhere joined the debate'.

17   C.A.R. Crosland, 'New Moods, Old Problems: On Politics in the Welfare State', *Encounter*, February 1961, pp. 3–6; 'Radical Reform and the Left', *Encounter* 15 (October 1960). See also Daniel Bell, *The End of Ideology* (Glencoe: The Free Press, 1960). Horne had an aborted meeting with Bell in London in 1963: Donald Horne to Myfanwy Horne, Collection 5, Box 68.

18   Horne, *Into the Open*, pp. 60, 61; Myfanwy Horne, 'Requiem', p. 122; Kathleen Dermody, 'Ross Francis Gollan (1902–1961), in Ritchie (ed.), *Australian Dictionary of Biography* Volume 14. Horne's father also died 1962: Donald Horne to Irene Morley, 12 February 1969, MLMSS 3525 MLK 2135: 'My father died seven years ago – of a heart condition he had been suffering for some years'.

19   Horne, *Into the Open*, p. 60.

20   Ibid., pp. 117–18.

21   Ibid, pp. 64–65; Horne (as 'Observer'), *The Bulletin*, 5 August 1961: 'It is fortunate for Australia that a band of Australian unionists distinguish themselves from the rest of the community by actively carrying on the fight for decency and democracy when the rest of us – politicians, businessmen, intellectuals – blather away without ever bothering to acquaint ourselves with the facts, or believe them when they are thrust under our noses. In some ways it is this kind of unionist who is doing the real fighting for democracy in Australia.'

22   James McClelland, *Stirring the Possum: A Political Autobiography* (Ringwood: Penguin, 1989), pp. 110–11.

23   'Report of Subcommittee on "Free Spirit" to the Management Committee', 23 November 1961, MLMSS 3525 MLK 2143 Q-1; Horne, *Into the Open*, pp. 67–68; Pybus, *The Devil and James McAuley*, pp. 188–91.

24   Donald Horne, 'Freedom in Australia', address to the Sydney Fabian Society, July 1962, Horne Papers, Add-on 1871, Box 2, G-23.

25   Donald Horne, 'Until You Go Pink in the Face', *The Bulletin*, 24 March 1962.

26   Donald Horne, 'The Metaphor of Leftness', *Quadrant*, no. 3 (Winter 1962), pp. 59–66. For 'butter bread', see Baker to Horne, 'Notes on the Observer II', 12 July 1957.

27   Coleman, *The Liberal Conspiracy*, pp. 178–81.

28   Programme, Seminar on Literary Journals and Journals of Opinion, 24–27 August 1962, MLMSS 3525 MLK 2144 Q-6; Donald Horne, 'Dysfunctional Exorcism', *The Australian's Review of Books* 4, no. 6, July 1999.

29   Donald Horne to Will Phillips, 11 May 1962; Pybus, *The Devil and James McAuley*, pp. 190–91: Paris were not happy with Krygier and Lloyd Ross's takeover of the organisation.

30   Horne to Phillips, 11 May 1962; Stephen Murray-Smith to Donald Horne, 1 May 1962, MLMSS 3525 MLK 2144 Q-6; Horne to Murray-Smith, 14 May 1962; Jim Davidson, *Emperors in Lilliput* (Melbourne: Melbourne University Press, 2022), p. 271: Clem Christesen, editor of *Meanjin*, allegedly treated Murray-Smith's attendance at the seminar as a personal betrayal.

31   Programme, Seminar on Literary Journals and Journals of Opinion.

32   Horne, 'Policy and Practice in the *Observer*'.

33   The original suggestion, according to Horne, occurred in his office at *The Bulletin* in 1961: Horne, *Into the Open*, p. 127. See also Dutton, *Out in the Open*, pp. 244; Horne, *The Lucky Country*, p. 293 ('Max's idea'); Harris to Horne, 29 January 1963, MLMSS 3525 MLK 2135 L-19: 'Glad to hear you are rising to my original bait'. 'Living with Asia' was published in *Observer* on 7 March 1959; the follow up, 'Still Living With Asia' was published in *The Bulletin* on 17 May 1961. See also Dutton, *A Rare Bird: Penguin Books in Australia, 1946–96* (Ringwood: Penguin, 1996).

34   Horne, 'Businessmen', pp. 176–90.

35   Frank Bongiorno, 'The Right Kind of Middle Class?', *Inside Story*, 19 December 2012; Coleman, *Australian Civilization*, pp. 1–11; John Curtain, 'Peter Coleman's *Australian Civilization* and Its Successors', *Publishing Studies* 4 (Autumn 1997), pp. 45–49; John Docker, *In a Critical Condition: Reading Australian Literature* (Ringwood: Penguin, 1984).

36   Donald Horne, 'Encounter at the Belvedere', *Free Spirit*, Sep/Oct 1962, pp. 4–6.

37   Donald Horne, 'Australia Obsolescent', *Spectator*, 28 December 1962, p. 9. On Krygier selling Horne to Hartley, see Horne, *Into the Open*, p. 71.

38   Horne, 'Australia Obsolescent', p. 9

39   Horne, *Into the Open*, pp. 76, 86. Horne's first contact with Jackson Wain had been during his editorship of *Weekend* in 1954: Horne, *Portrait of an Optimist*, p. 138. See also Robert Crawford, *But Wait, There's More . . . A History of Australian Advertising 1900–2000* (Carlton: Melbourne University Press, 2008), p. 126.

40   Horne, 'Policy and Practice in the *Observer*'.

41   Horne, 'Report on Free Spirit', AACF Executive Meeting, 1–2 December 1962, MLMSS 3525 MLK 2143 Q-1.

42   McAuley was not happy with the arrangement: Pybus, *The Devil and James McAuley*, p. 192. Unsigned to Richard Krygier, 21 December 1962, MLMSS 3525 MLK 2143 Q-1; McAuley, interview by Santamaria.

43   Edmund Campion, interview with author, 19 September 2018. For the story of the 1962 meeting at The Entrance, see Horne, *Into the Open*, pp. 71–72. On Catholics, see Horne, *The Next Australia* (Sydney: Angus and Robertson, 1970), pp. 124–25.

44   Donald Horne, 'Two Ends of Taiwan', *Spectator*, 19 April 1963; untitled and unpublished account of trip to Taiwan, 1963, Horne Papers, MLK2140 G-15.

45   Donald Horne, 'Strong for Malaysia', *Spectator*, 8 March 1963; 'Malaysia from Manila – As Big as Muddle as You Could Want . . .', *The Bulletin*, 13 April 1963; 'Two Ends of Taiwan'; 'Khrushchev and Cuba', *The Bulletin*, 3 November 1962.

46   Geoffrey Dutton to Donald Horne, 30 April 63, MLMSS 3525 MLK 2135 L-18; Brian Stonier to Geoffrey Dutton, 8 February 53, Geoffrey Dutton Papers, Box 24 Folder 6, NLA. Clausen, 'Donald Horne Finds Asia', p. 315: Clausen notes the issues on which Horne diverged from progressive orthodoxy included 'his somewhat belated conversion to immigration reform, fervent anti-communism and outspoken criticism of many radical imaginaries'.

47   'New Interpretations of Australian History', AACF Seminar, 25 August 1963, MLMSS
      3525 MLK 2144 Q-10.
48   Frank Bongiorno, 'The New Progressivism: Anthony Crosland and the Coming of
      the Australian Sixties', in Shirleene Robinson and Julie Ustinoff (eds), *The 1960s in
      Australia: People, Power and Politics* (Cambridge: Cambridge Scholars Publishing,
      2012), pp. 179–98.
49   Crosland papers cited in Bongiorno, 'The New Progressivism'. As Bongiorno
      notes, Crosland also possessed a copy of Horne's 'Australia Obsolescent' *Spectator*
      article from December 1962. The dates of Crosland's tour were 17–23 May: AACF
      Management Committee meeting, 7 March 1963, Peter Coleman Papers, MLMSS
      10399, Box 5, SLNSW. On dining in King's Cross, see McClelland's recollection in
      Gillian Appleton, *Diamond Cuts: An Affectionate Memoir of Jim McClelland* (Sydney:
      Pan Macmillan, 2000), p. 239; Horne, *Into the Open*, p. 109. McClelland himself
      remembered Horne in this period as 'on the turn to the enlightened radical which he
      ultimately became': McClelland, *Stirring the Possum*, p. 111.
50   Jack Mack to J.E. Kelso, 16 July 1963; R.S. Fountain to J.E. Kelso, 1 October 1963;
      Donald Horne to James Plimsoll, 27 August 1963; 'Proposed Itinerary'; 'Expenses
      Summary', MLMSS 3525 MLK 2153 JW-2. Horne's papers also include a detailed
      notebook from the Fiji leg of the trip, MLMSS 3525 MLK 2140 G-16.
51   For Donald's letters to Myfanwy, see Horne Papers, Collection 5, Box 68: 'Julia has
      been hellish. She woke up twice during the night'.
52   On meetings, see Donald's letters to Myfanwy in 1963, Collection 5, Box 68. Horne
      to Ethel Woolley, 27 August 1963, MLMSS 3525 MLK 2153 JW-2. Horne provided
      some scant details of his return to Bow Brickhill in 'Bingo for Britain: Make It New
      for You're on the Way Up', *The Bulletin*, 26 October 1963. See also Horne, *God Is an
      Englishman* (Sydney: Angus and Robertson, 1969), p. 88; Letters to Plimsoll, Pritchett
      and O'Grady in MLK 2153 JW-2.
53   See Stuart Ward, *Untied Kingdom: A Global History of the End of Britain* (Cambridge:
      Cambridge University Press, 2023), pp. 323–350. See also Bongiorno, 'The New
      Progressivism'. On 'What's wrong with Britain', see Christopher Booker, *The
      Neophiliacs* (London: Collins, 1969). A non-exhaustive summary of the What's
      Wrong authors includes: Anthony Sampson, *Anatomy of Britain* (London: Hodder &
      Stoughton, 1961); Anthony Hartley, *A State of England* (London: Hutchinson, 1963);
      Michael Shanks, *The Stagnant Society: A Warning* (Harmondsworth: Penguin, 1961);
      Paul Einzig, *Decline and Fall: Britain's Crisis in the Sixties* (London: Macmillan, 1969);
      Crosland, 'Radical Reform and the Left'; John Mander, *Great Britain or Little England*
      (London: Secker & Warburg, 1963). The *Encounter* issue was collected in Arthur
      Koestler (ed.), *Suicide of a Nation: An Enquiry into the State of Britain Today* (London:
      Hutchinson, 1963).
54   Dutton to Horne, 25 March 1963; Horne, 'Australia Obsolescent', p. 9; Horne, 'Bingo for
      Britain'; Stuart Ward, 'Backing Little Britain: Distempers', in Ward, *Untied Kingdom*.

7. THE LUCKY COUNTRY

1   Donald Horne, *The Lucky Country* drafts, MLMSS 3525 MLK 2158; Horne, interview
      by De Berg. In a series of letters between January and April 1963, Geoffrey Dutton
      approached Horne and encouraged him to write the book. Throughout 1963, Dutton
      and Brian Stonier, Penguin's managing director, were frequently frustrated by their
      inability to track down their globetrotting author, and their letters sometimes went
      unanswered for months. See also Horne, interview by Turner; Clausen, 'Donald
      Horne Finds Asia', p. 311; Clausen, 'The Vortex Is Here: Asia and Australian Post-
      Imperial Nationhood' (PhD thesis, University of Copenhagen, 2009).
2   Donald Horne, 'Sex Among the Conservatives', *The Bulletin*, 6 July 1963.
3   Donald Horne, 'Nation Without Ideas', *Der Monat*, n.d. [~August–October 1963],
      MLMSS 3525 MLK 2177 J-3.

4   Horne, 'Nation Without Ideas'. For *Observer* comment, see Horne, 'Policy and Practice in the *Observer*'.

5   Donald Horne, 'White Asians', *Spectator* (UK), 3 July 1964.

6   Donald Horne, 'Australia Goes East', *Spectator*, 24 January 1964; 'Bingo for Britain'; Horne, *The Lucky Country* drafts. In April 1963, Dutton himself had published an article in *Nation* that called for an Australian republic and declared the British connection an 'irrelevant anachronism': Geoffrey Dutton, 'British Subject', *Nation*, 6 April 1963, pp. 15–16. See also Donald Horne to Myfanwy Horne, n.d. [~late 1963], Collection 5, Box 86: 'Did I tell you that I became a republican today?'.

7   Brian Stonier to Donald Horne, 14 October 1963, MLMSS 3525 MLK 2135 L-18.

8   Donald Horne to Geoffrey Dutton, 23 October 1963, Dutton papers, Box 25, Folder 9, NLA.

9   Geoffrey Dutton to Donald Horne, 18 November 63, Dutton papers, Box 25, Folder 10, NLA.

10   Horne, *Into the Open*, p. 142; Horne, interview by De Berg; Horne, interview by Hughes; Horne, interview by Turner; Donald Horne, *On How I Came to Write 'The Lucky Country'* (Carlton: Melbourne University Publishing, 2006); Julia Horne, 'Donald Horne and the Lucky Country', ISAA Conference Proceedings; Julia Horne, 'An Armchair, a Desk, and 4000 Books: The Horne Family Study Gets a Second Life', *The Conversation*, 24 May 2018. On Nick's birth, see Nin Dutton to Horne, n.d. [~May/June 1964], MLMSS 3525 MLK 2135 L-18; Horne, *Into the Open*, p. 94.

11   Donald Horne to James McAuley, 8 December 1963, MLMSS 3525 MLK 2143 Q-3; Horne did find time to write an article on the most recent Australian federal election: 'Conservatives on Top Down Under', *Spectator*, 6 December 1963; Horne to Dutton, 8 December 1963, MLMSS 3525 MLK 2135 L-18; Horne, *Australian Biography*; Horne, interview by Turner.

12   Horne to Stonier, n.d. [~6 February 1964], MLMSS 3525 MLK 2135 L-18.

13   Ibid. See also Horne, interview by Turner: 'When I wrote that thing *The Lucky Country* I suddenly discovered that I had a range of belief much wider than I imagined I had, partly by the simple demands of the processes of composition.'

14   Horne to Dutton, July 1964; Dutton to Horne, 17 April 1964; Horne, *The Lucky Country* drafts; Stonier to Horne, 14 February 1964; Horne to Stonier, n.d. [~6 February 1964].

15   Early draft of *The Lucky Country* contents, MLMSS 3525 MLK2135 L-18, mid–late 1963.

16   Ibid. Reviewing John Douglas Pringle's *Australian Accent* in 1959, Horne judged it 'one of the few books on Australia that I have ever enjoyed reading'. It was a book that 'brings Australia to life by cutting it down to size, by universalising it': Donald Horne, *Quadrant* 3, no. 2 (Autumn 1959).

17   Geoffrey Dutton to Brian Stonier, 22 August 1964, Dutton papers, Box 25, Folder 12; Dutton to Horne, 24 July 1964; Dutton to Horne, 24 July 1964.

18   Donald Horne, 'Dissecting the Press: Professor Mayer's Nihilist Appraisal', *The Bulletin*, 20 June 1964.

19   Horne to Dutton, n.d. [~July 1964].

20   Dutton to Horne, 6 August 1964; Stonier to Horne, 3 August 1964, Dutton papers, Box 25, Folder 12. For an account of this episode, see Dutton, *Out into the Open*, pp. 293–95. They would eventually print 18,000 copies of the book.

21   Harris to Horne, n.d. [~April 1964], MLMSS 3525 MLK 2143 Q-3 *Quadrant* correspondence; Nin Dutton to Donald Horne, n.d. [~May-June 1964], MLMSS 3525 MLK 2135 L-18.

22   Dutton to Stonier, 17 April 1964, Dutton papers, Box 25, Folder 11. See also Dutton to Stonier, 6 May 64, Dutton papers, Box 25, Folder 12: 'We must get this one out as soon as possible'.

23   Horne to Dutton, n.d. [~July 1964]. See also Horne, interview by Turner: 'It's a truism of the advertising business that you have to appeal to something that's already in people'; Clausen, 'Donald Horne Finds Asia', p. 315: 'Horne must be credited for grasping and synthesising sentiments bubbling to the surface of public discourse, and for envisaging how Australia's nationhood and international relations could be reconstituted in a post-imperial age.'

24   Dutton to Myfanwy Horne, 22 September 1964; Stonier to Horne, 23 November 1964, MLMSS 3525 MLK 2135 L-18; Stoner to Dutton, 4 June 1964, Dutton papers, Box 25, Folder 12; Dutton to Stonier, 17 April 1964, Dutton papers, Box 25, Folder 11.

25   Dutton to Stonier, 20 November 1964, Dutton papers, Box 25, Folder 13. Carl Reinecke has written in great detail on the story of *The Lucky Country*'s conception, writing and publication. He argued that Horne went to great lengths to establish an 'agreed history' of the book's publication that painted him in a favourable light, citing the neatness of Horne's archive, as well as a document found in Dutton's papers that 'aimed to establish the story that would become commonplace in the years ahead'. This document, however, was probably composed decades later, and likely at Dutton's request. In the process of writing his memoirs, Dutton had probably asked Horne to consult his papers (already deposited in the State Library of New South Wales) and to summarise the story of the book's publication (a point made in response by Horne's son Nick). Horne was certainly conscious of his public image, but he did not construct an 'agreed history' in anticipation of the book's appeal forty years hence, nor can we assume he deliberately left it out of his archive. Absence of evidence is not evidence of absence. See Carl Reinecke, 'The Vanishing Point: The Story of the Publication of *The Lucky Country*', *Meanjin* 75, no. 2 (Winter 2016); Carl Reinecke, '*The Lucky Country* Turns Fifty', *Inside Story*, 14 December 2014; Nick Horne, 'Donald Horne and the Story of the Publication of *The Lucky Country*', *Meanjin* blog, 14 August 2017.

26   Stonier to Horne, 23 November 1964, MLMSS 3525 MLK 2135 L-18; Dutton to Horne, 20 November 1964, MLMSS 3525 MLK 2135 L-18; Horne to Dutton, 17 November 1964, Dutton papers, Box 25, Folder 13.

27   On *The Lucky Country* selling out, see Stonier to Kenneth Rivett, 22 December 1964, MLMSS 3525 MLK 2135 L-19. When the head of Penguin, Allen Lane, visited Australia in November, Dutton had personally convinced him to produce 10,000 copies in the United Kingdom, and after the book's successful Australian launch it was also decided to print '5–10,000' copies in the United States: Stonier to Horne, 21 January 1965, MLMSS 3525 MLK 2135 L-19. On 80,000 copies, see Michie to Horne, 3 May 1966, MLMSS 3525 MLK 2135 L-19; Harris wrote to Horne to congratulate him. 'The little project I suggested way back is going to bring you the royalties on some 40 000 copies', he wrote. 'You are morally obliged to write a free review for *Australian Book Review*', Harris to Horne, 21 December 1964, MLMSS 3525 MLK 2135 L-20; Stonier to Horne, 25 August 1964, MLMSS 3525 MLK 2135 L-18.

28   Horne to Stonier, 9 February 1965; John Michie to Horne, 29 April 1965; Horne to Michie, 17 May 1965, Michie to Horne, 21 May 1965, MLMSS 3525 MLK 2135 L-19.

29   Donald Horne, *The Lucky Country: Australia in the Sixties* (Ringwood: Penguin, 1964), p. 7.

30   Donald Horne, *The Lucky Country: Australia in the Sixties* [1st revised edition] (Ringwood, Penguin, 1965], p. 12. In 1970, he called the book 'a kind of album of snapshots of how things seemed in the last years of the Age of Menzies': Horne, *The Next Australia*, p. v. In 1995, he told an interviewer that the book 'didn't have any theme at all really, I invented one at the end. It was really just a series of fragments and in that sense highly post-modern, put together in different kinds of ways, just a bit of a carnival – to use a popular term – which people could read. It was intended to interest people in a few topics': Donald Horne, interview by Victoria Barker, 1995, UNSW Archives Oral History Project, OH 89.

31   Horne to Stonier, n.d. [~6 February 1964], MLMSS 3525 MLK 2135 L-18; Tom Fitzgerald, 'Breakthrough', *Nation*, 20 February 1965 ('tough, stylish wit').

32   Horne, *The Lucky Country* (1964 ed.), p. 22.

33   Ibid., p. 20.

34   Ibid., pp. 222–23.

35   Coleman, 'Introduction', *Australian Civilization*, p. 2; Horne, *The Lucky Country* (1964 ed.), pp. 16, 223.

36   Horne, *The Lucky Country* (1964 ed.), pp. 38–39. On Horne's ambivalence, see Rowse, *Australian Liberalism and the National Character*, p. 209; Coleman, 'Introduction', fn. 29.

37   Horne, *The Lucky Country* (1964 ed.), pp. 209, 215.

38   Curthoys and Merritt (eds), *Better Dead Than Red*; Lowe, *Menzies and the 'Great World Struggle'*; McLaren, *Writing in Hope and Fear*.

39   This is a view expounded by former prime minister John Howard in *The Menzies Era* (Sydney: HarperCollins, 2014); Judith Brett, *Relaxed and Comfortable: The Liberal Party's Australia*, Quarterly Essay 19 (Melbourne: Black Inc., 2005).

40   Manning Clark, 'The Years of Unleavened Bread: December 1949 – December 1972', *Meanjin* 32, no. 3 (September 1973). This was an interpretation popularised by Paul Keating, who said 'That was the golden age when Australia was injected with a near-lethal dose of fogeyism by the conservative parties opposite, when they put the country into neutral': Commonwealth, *Parliamentary Debates*, House of Representatives, 27 February 1992. For a critical account of this interpretation, see Brown, *Governing Prosperity*, pp. 4–5. Brown argues that the period was not one of rupture between reformers and reactionaries, but one of 'complexity, frustration and transition'. See also Murphy, *Imagining the Fifties*, pp. 8–9; Brett, *Robert Menzies' Forgotten People*; Brett, 'The Menzies Era, 1950–66', p. 126.

41   In 1966 – less than two years after *The Lucky Country* was first published – one critic called it 'epoch making': Derek Hartlock, 'Second Helping', review of 1966 hardback edition of *The Lucky Country*, publication unknown, MLMSS 3525 MLK 2135.

42   *The Lucky Country* (1964 ed.), pp. 87, 156, 183, 216. In a substantial 1970 revision of *The Lucky Country*, published as *The Next Australia*, Horne remembered 'hoping that the old man would stay in office until the book came out' (p. v).

43   *The Lucky Country* (1964 ed.), pp. 157–58.

44   Ibid., p. 113.

45   Ibid., pp. 91, 214.

46   Brown cited in Clausen, 'Donald Horne Finds Asia', p. 304; Gerald Mayhead, 'Jolts for Australia', *The Age*, 16 December 1964; Judah Waten, 'Literary Comment', *Guardian* (Melbourne), 10 December 1964; Malcolm Salmon, 'Donald Horne's Lucky Country – Another View', *Guardian* (Melbourne), MLMSS 3525 MLK 2135; Ian Turner: 'How Many Horns Has Donald: Is He a Bull or a Unicorn?', 'Swanning along on a Feather Bed', publication unknown, n.d. [~February 1965], MLMSS 3525 MLK 2135.

47   Reviewers were puzzled by the book's complicated brand of populism and leader-bashing. Both John Pringle and Desmond O'Grady thought it a paradox. In O'Grady's view, Horne had asked 'what is wrong with the country' and answered (unsatisfactorily) that it was 'those stupid politicians the intelligent voters elected'. For Pringle, Horne's polemical instincts exaggerated the problem. The truth, he wrote, was that 'the Australian people are not quite so tolerant, fraternal, just, courageous and stoical', and that their leaders 'are not quite so stupid, unimaginative, inefficient': Desmond O'Grady, '"The Lucky Country" Poses An Unlikely Paradox', *Catholic Weekly*, 18 March 1965; John Douglas Pringle, review, *Australian Journal of Politics and History*, 11 no. 2 (August 1965), pp 253–55, MLMSS 3525 MLK 2135.

48   Kippax, 'Australians'; Maurice Dunlevy, 'Well Said – But It's Been Said Before', *The Canberra Times*, 12 December 1964.

49   Horne included the quote from the first revised edition in 1965 ('Writing on the Run', p. 9). In the fifth edition, published in 1998, Horne wrote that 'one reviewer said it wouldn't outlast the season': 'Introduction to The Fifth Edition', *The Lucky Country* (Ringwood: Penguin, 1998), p. ix.

50   Horne, *The Lucky Country* [1964 ed.], p. 163. Frank Bongiorno, 'Whitlam, the 1960s and the Program', in Troy Bramston (ed.), *The Whitlam Legacy* (Annandale, Federation Press: 2015), pp. 34–41. Gerster and Bassett, *Seizures of Youth*; Tanja Luckins, 'Cosmopolitanism and the Cosmopolitans: Australia in the World, the World in Australia', in Robinson and Ustinoff, *The 1960s in Australia*, pp. 51–68.

51   Drafts and typescript of Donald's account of *The Education of Young Donald* for ABC broadcast, 5 April 1971, MLMSS 3525 MLK 2135 L-22, republished in *Quadrant*, Mar–April 1971, pp. 42–70; Horne, *Into the Open*, p. 132.

52   Donald Horne, 'Who Am I? Reviewing the Reviewers', *The Bulletin*, 13 February 1965, p 34. In February, Horne wrote to Dutton, 'Would I be right in assuming that [*Overland* editor] Stephen Murray-Smith was a little bemused that it was I who said all this?': Horne to Dutton, Dutton papers, Box 25, Folder 13

53   Donald Horne, *Quadrant* 9, no. 3 (May–June 1965), pp. 5–6.

54   The source of his disquiet, as he recalled rather dismissively in a radio broadcast several years later, was 'success, along with other reasons': drafts and typescript of Donald's account of *The Education of Young Donald* for ABC broadcast, 5 April 1971, MLMSS 3525 MLK 2135 L-22; Horne, *Into the Open*, p. 136; Horne to Stonier, 9 February 1965.

55   Dutton to Horne, 29 June 1965, MLMSS 3525 MLK 2135 L-21; Stonier to Horne, 30 July 1965, MLMSS 3525 MLK 2135 L-21: 'It is quite probable that we will build our whole opening promotion around this original novel, and so we certainly will do all we can to prevent the news of it leaking out too soon!'; Drafts and typescript of Donald's account of *The Education of Young Donald* for ABC broadcast, 5 April 1971, MLMSS 3525 MLK 2135 L-22.

56   Donald Horne, *The Permit* (Melbourne: Sun Books, 1965), pp. 37, 40, 45, 47. On Kafka, see Dutton to Horne, 29 June 1965; 16 July 1965; Stonier to Horne, 30 July 1965.

57   Geoffrey Hutton, review of *The Lucky Country*, *Walkabout*, June 1965.

8. AUSTRALIA LOOKS AROUND

1   Donald Horne to John Stephens, April 1966, MLMSS 3525 MLK 2135 L-19. See also Horne, *Into the Open*, p. 131 ('It took me five years to put together my full "lucky country" thesis'); Horne, interview by Turner.

2   Horne to Stephens, 10 October 1965; Stephens to Horne, 6 July 1965. Horne, 'Writing on the Run', *The Lucky Country* (1965 rev. ed.), p. 9. For Horne, ambivalence was its own kind of sociological truth – a point he made at this exact moment in defence of his own impressionistic approach in a review of Sol Encel and A.F. Davies' *Australian Society: A Sociological Introduction*: 'It is a feature of societies as of individuals that they are ambivalent. One may not be able to find a single word to describe their conduct. One simply records the differences in behaviour. One may never provide the explanation'. See Horne, 'Danger! Here Come the Sociologists', *The Bulletin*, 28 August 1965.

3   Horne, *The Lucky Country* (1965 rev. ed.), p. 9.

4   Ibid., pp. 12, 52, 110.

5   Ibid., pp. 106–07.

6   The book, said Horne in 2005, was a 'derivative society thesis . . . the essential thing in the writing of *The Lucky Country* was derivativeness': Horne quoted in Peter Hartcher, 'Are We There Yet?', *The Sydney Morning Herald*, 10 September 2005.

7   Dutton to Horne, 8 November 1965, telegram on publication of Horne's *The Permit*, MLMSS 3525 MLK 2135 L-21.

8   Horne commended Holt's 'contemporary style' and his 'recognition that he has to go on showing his face in the nations of Asia': 'The End of Do-It-Yourself', *The Bulletin*, 11 March 1967. See also Horne, 'The Passing of Sir Robert: Generational Changes in Australian Politics', *Parallel*, 1966, MLMSS 3525 MLK 2177 J-3.

9   The Australian group included Horne, Jim McAuley, Richard Krygier,
     Peter Coleman, Sabnarayan Ray, Bruce Grant, Doug McCallum, Brian
     Beddie, Owen Harries and Peter Samuel. See Horne, Diary of Journey to Kuala
     Lumpur for Seminar, MLMSS 3525 MLK 2140 G-16; Horne, *Into the Open*,
     pp. 122–24.

10   Horne, 'Giving In'. Australia's American obedience had its most (in)famous expression
     just four months later when Harold Holt visited Washington and declared that on the
     question of Vietnam, Australia would go 'all the way with LBJ'. Horne described the
     AACF disagreement as being about 'differences of emotional pitch': Horne, *Into the
     Open*, p. 120.

11   Horne, 'Reason – and the Murders and Miseries of Asia', in Sibnarayan Ray (ed.),
     Vietnam: Seen from East and West (Melbourne: Nelson, 1966).

12   Ibid.

13   Donald Horne, 'Australia Looks Around', *Foreign Affairs* 44, vol. 3 (April 1966),
     pp. 446–57.

14   Horne alleged that some people had stopped talking to him completely since he had
     started arguing for a republic and an end to Australia's 'royalist fundamentalism' – 'I
     always thought Horne was a Red anyway': Horne, 'Republican Australia' in Geoffrey
     Dutton (ed.), *Australia and the Monarchy: A Symposium* (Melbourne: Sun Books,
     1966). See also Mark McKenna, *The Captive Republic: A History of Republicanism
     in Australia 1988–1996* (Melbourne: Cambridge University Press, 1996), pp. 222–26.
     Frank Hardy was one of Horne's principal antagonists at the Peace Congress in 1959:
     Horne, *Into the Open*, pp. 121–22.

15   Letter sent to *The New York Times* on 4 May 1966 by Galbraith, George Kennan,
     J. Robert Oppenheimer and Arthur Schlesinger Jnr, MLMSS 3525 MLK 2143 Q-4;
     Letter from Spender, Kristol, Lasky, 10 May 1966, MLMSS 3525 MLK 2143 Q-4;
     Saunders, *Who Paid the Piper?*, p. 378.

16   Nicolas Nabokov to Donald Horne, 30 April 1966, MLMSS 3525 MLK 2143 Q-4.

17   Michael Josselson to Donald Horne, 7 October 1966, MLMSS 3525 MLK 2144 Q-6.

18   Epstein quoted in Saunders, *Who Paid the Piper?*, p. 377. See also Horne, *Into the
     Open*, p. 124.

19   Saunders, *Who Paid the Piper?*, p. 371. *The New York Review of Books*, launched in
     1963, gave a shape to this new spirit of intellectual independence and disillusionment
     with American foreign policy, as did Stanley Kubrick's 1964 film *Dr Strangelove* and
     John le Carré's 1963 novel, *The Spy Who Came in from the Cold*: Saunders, *Who Paid
     the Piper?*, p. 361.

20   Peter Coleman argued in his history of the CCF that the fault of the Congress's leaders
     may not have lain in their initial procurement of CIA funding, which might have
     been justifiable at an earlier time of political emergency and broad public support for
     US foreign policy, but in allowing it to continue until 1966, when attitudes towards
     America's foreign interventions had so radically changed: Coleman, *The Liberal
     Conspiracy*, p. 220.

21   Saunders, *Who Paid the Piper?*, pp. 391–406; Coleman, *The Liberal Conspiracy*, p. 220
     (the 'cockroaches' comment was Normal Mailer's, and 'spies' was Andrew Kopking,
     232–33: James McAuley was the sole Australian in attendance.

22   Horne to Krygier, 28 June 1964, MLMSS 3525 MLK 2143 Q-3; Pybus,
     The Devil and James McAuley, pp. 193–94: According to Cassandra Pybus,
     Horne's outburst was in response to the publication of an article in *Quadrant* by
     Bob Santamaria – he opposed publication, and McAuley supported it. Rumours
     continued to flood in that Paris was concerned the magazine was 'too right wing'.
     Krygier told Horne not to worry: he intended to 'ignore' their concerns. The
     McAuley story was confirmed by Peter Coleman when he took over as editor two
     years later.

23   Frank Packer to Donald Horne, 14 November 1966, MLMSS 3525 MLK 2152.

24 In early 1967, Horne travelled to Jakarta, Singapore, Saigon, Tokyo and Manila: MLMSS 3525 MLK 2175 R-12; Horne, *Into the Open*, pp. 154–55; Krygier, interview by Miller; Horne to Krygier, 30 December 1966. Horne also explained his defection to John Hunt a few months later, explaining that 'Over the last 12 months I . . . became increasingly irritated by the gap between [*Quadrant's*] potential and what was happening': Horne to Hunt, 10 February 1967, MLMSS 3525 MLK 2143 Q-4. Horne's new salary at *The Bulletin* was $12,000, versus the $400 yearly payment he had received for editing *Quadrant*: Packer to Horne, 14 November 1966.

25 McAuley, interview by Santamaria. 'The CIA made a well-intentioned blunder and places those whose independence they meant to respect in an embarrassing position. *Quadrant* will, however, continue to light its own path with such illumination as its joint editors and its contributors can supply': James McAuley, 'C.I.A.', *Quadrant*, May–June 1967.

26 See Krygier, interview by Miller. According to Krygier, AACF President Lloyd Ross wanted a 'tough line' on the CIA revelations and was 'very dissatisfied with Donald' because Horne thought the AACF should 'apologise' for the CIA funding.

27 Horne, *Into the Open*, p. 124.

28 Horne, interview by Turner.

29 Horne to Stephens, April 1966, MLMSS 3525 MLK 2135 L-19.

30 *The Lucky Country* had already had quite a good life: by mid-1966, Penguin had sold over 80,000 copies of the first two editions, with another 40,000 on the way in anticipation of its inclusion on mandatory reading lists in NSW and Victorian schools: John Michie to Donald Horne, 3 May 1966, MLMSS 3525 MLK 2135 L-19.

31 Horne to Stephens, April 1966; Horne to Michie, 6 May 1967.

32 Dutton to Horne, 9 February 1965: 'You mentioned a while back that you had ideas for another book. What are they? Have you had any more?'

33 Donald Horne, Drafts and typescript of Donald's account of *The Education of Young Donald* for ABC broadcast, 5 April 1971, republished in *Quadrant*, March–April 1971.

34 Horne to Stonier, 9 February 1965.

35 Horne, Drafts and typescript of Donald's account of *The Education of Young*, pp. 42–70; Horne, *Into the Open*, pp. 133–34.

36 Horne, Drafts and typescript of Donald's account of *The Education of Young Donald*.

37 He was borrowing from Henry Adams' 1918 autobiography, *The Education of Henry Adams*: ibid.

38 Horne, 'Life as a Waugh Novel – "You May as Well Laugh as Cry"', *The Bulletin*, 23 April 1966. See also Horne's review of *The Ordeal of Gilbert Pinfold* by Evelyn Waugh in *Quadrant* 2, no. 1, Summer 1957–58.

39 Horne, 'Life as a Waugh Novel'.

40 When *The Permit* was published in November 1965, one reviewer compared Horne favourably with Waugh, for the simple reason that – like the author of *Scoop* and *A Handful of Dust* – he had depicted the 'wild world' through the adventures of an 'innocent who has wandered into the jungle': Keith Thomas, 'The Permit', *The Bulletin*, 13 November 1965.

41 Waugh's was a fiction of externality. 'All we know of other people', Horne surmised, 'is what we see and hear them do': Horne, 'Life as a Waugh Novel'.

42 Horne, 'Foreword', *The Education of Young Donald* (1968 ed.).

43 See H.G. Kippax, 'An Australian Boyhood'.

44 Donald Horne to Frank Knopfelmacher, 12 December 1967, MLMSS 3525 MLK 2135 L-22.

45 See Horne, *The Education of Young Donald* drafts, MLMSS 3525 MLK 2160.

46 On style, see Horne, Drafts and typescript of Donald's account of *The Education of Young Donald*.

47 Horne, *The Education of Young Donald*, p. 64.

48 Horne to Knopfelmacher, 12 December 1967.

49   Horne, interview by Hughes.

50   Manning Clark, 'Young Donald', *Overland*, March 1968. Many years later, Horne suggested that after his decades of failure as a novelist, in autobiography he found 'a kind of fiction substitute': Horne, interview by Turner.

51   Vincent Buckley, 'Portrait of the Artist as a Young Shouter', *The Bulletin*, 2 December 1967.

52   Donald Horne to Vincent Buckley, 6 December 1967, MLMSS 3525 MLK 2135 L-22.

53   Horne made this argument to two separate correspondents: Horne to Dutton, 21 November 1967; Horne to Knopfelmacher, 12 December 1967.

54   Stendhal, *The Red and the Black* (Penguin: Harmondsworth, 1953); Horne, *Portrait of an Optimist*, p. 58.

55   Horne, 'Blind Man's Bluff'.

56   Ibid.

57   Horne to Dutton, 21 November 1967, MLMSS 3525 MLK 2135 L-22.

58   Horne, *The Education of Young Donald*, p. 1.

59   Knopfelmacher to Horne, 10 December 1967, MLMSS 3525 MLK 2135 L-22.

60   Max Harris, 'A Bush Candide Who Went Up in Flames', *The Australian*, 21 October 67. See also *Times Literary Supplement*, 22 February 1968: [the book is] 'likely to interest the social historian more than the general reader'; Clark, 'Young Donald': [the book is] 'a significant contribution to the discussion of the role of Australia and Australians in a world in which all the great ideologies of the past were losing their grip on men's minds'; *Grafton Examiner*, 27 November 1967: 'it is a study of a period and its people with the author's affairs offering a convenient peg on which to hang the tale'; H.G. Kippax, 'An Australian Boyhood: 'it will be read, for the light it casts on Australia in the reluctant years before "take-off", long after "The Lucky Country" is forgotten'; Desmond O'Grady, 'Horne Laughs at Young Donald': 'a precise social history of a slice of Australia in the years 1927–1941'; Alan Roberts, 'Growing Up in Australia': 'for my money it's worth all the social and political histories of this strange, wonderful and challenging land'.

61   Among them were Bruce McPherson, 'Horne Relives an Era', *The Canberra Times*, 20 January 68; Martha Lemming, 'Temps Not Quite Peru', *Australian Book Review*, November 1967; Harris, 'A Bush Candide Who Went Up in Flames'; Murray Sayle to Donald Horne, 24 December 1967, MLMSS 3525 MLK 2135 L-22.

62   Kippax, 'An Australian Boyhood in the Reluctant Years'. This idea was a central aspect of a more sustained critique of Horne made many years later by Tim Rowse in 'Culture as Myth, Criticism as Irony: The Middle-Class Patriotism of Donald Horne', *Island* 37 (Spring 1988).

63   The critic Mark Thomas compared Horne's characterisation of his younger self to D.H. Lawrence's summation of his protagonist in his Australian novel *Kangaroo*: 'he has wrestled with the problem of himself and called it Australia': Thomas, *Australian in Mind*, p. 121. Horne was not alone here. Mark McKenna has written about the relationship between autobiographical truth and Manning Clark's invention as a national figure. Clark's was a 'life story as an allegory of national awakening': Mark McKenna, '"National Awakening", Autobiography and the Invention of Manning Clark', *Life Writing* 13, no. 2 (2016), pp. 207–20.

64   Horne, 'Foreword', *The Education of Young Donald*, p. 1.

65   Among them were Manning Clark, Geoffrey Serle, Robin Boyd and Geoffrey Dutton:'The "Great Age of Confusion": Ideas', in James Curran and Stuart Ward, *The Unknown Nation: Australia After Empire* (Melbourne: Melbourne University Press, 2010), p. 58; Rollo Hesketh, '"In Search of a National Idea": Australian Intellectuals and the "Cultural Cringe", 1940–1972' (PhD thesis, University of Sydney, 2018).

66   See, for example, a review from 1968: 'The detachment he brings to his work is extraordinary, and contributes to a sense of the absolute authenticity of the narrative': Alan Hughes, 'Donald Blows His Horn', *Dissent* (Autumn 1968).

67   John Colmer, 'Autobiography or Sociography? Donald Horne', *Australian Autobiography: The Personal Quest* (Oxford University Press, 1989), p. 71.

68   Donald Horne, Drafts of *The Education of Young Donald*, MLMSS 3525 MLK 2160 PM-EYD4; *The Education of Young Donald*, pp. 88, 143. In response to a query from Murray Sayle in 1978, Horne insisted that the diaries were 'genuine': Horne to Sayle, n.d. [~ mid 1978], MLMSS 3525 Add on 1871, Box 1.

69   Horne, interview by Turner.

70   Nin Dutton to Horne, n.d. [~ late 1967], MLMSS 3525 MLK 2135 L-22.

71   Horne to Dutton, 21 November 1967, MLMSS 3525 MLK 2135 L-2.2

72   Horne, *The Education of Young Donald*, p. 308.

73   Horne, Drafts and typescript of Donald's account of *The Education of Young Donald*. The Young Donald–D.R. Horne sections, he told Buckley, were the hardest to write, 'perhaps because they were nearer the bone. One can cease resenting one's father: it is harder to cease resenting oneself, without engaging in self-justification': Horne to Buckley, 6 December 1967, MLMSS 3525 MLK 2135 L-22.

74   Clark, 'Young Donald'. Horne quoted Clark's review at length in his 1970 book, *The Next Australia*, as evidence of the way so many prewar Australians had 'learned' their ideas of what culture was from Europe.

75   Judah Waten, 'Young Donald Sowing His Oats', *The Age*, 4 November 1967.

76   Sayle to Horne, 24 December 1967.

77   Horne to Sayle, 5 March 1968.

78   Horne to Stonier, Draft blurb for new edition of *The Education of Young Donald*, 17 May 1968, MLMSS 3525 MLK 2135 L-22.

9. TIME OF HOPE

1   His subject, noted one Japanese newspaper, was 'Australia's role in South East Asia' (with some variations: in Korea it was 'Australia's Search for a New Identity'; in the Philippines, 'Australian Painting and Literature'), see 'Australian Writer-Editor', *Yomizu* (Japan), 4 February 1967; *Korea Times*, 20 January 1966; 'Australian Editor Talks on Country's Literary Movement', *Guidon* (Philippines), 8 February 1967, MLMSS 3525 MLK 2175 R-12. For letters and articles on Horne's 1967 trip see MLK 2175 R-12 and MLK 2143 Q-4. See also Horne, *Into the Open*, pp. 145–55.

2   Horne to Plimsoll, 10 February 1967, MLMSS 3525 MLK 2143 Q-4.

3   In Singapore he stayed with Bill Pritchett: Horne to Pritchett, 20 December 1966, MLMSS 3525 MLK 2175 R-12; Horne to Max Loveday (Australian Ambassador to Indonesia), 20 December 1966, MLMSS 3525 MLK 2175 R-12. He also received a foreign policy briefing from Gordon Jockel, highlighting the differences between Menzies' commitment to 'sticking by' the Americans and Holt's 'naïve' idea of Australia as an 'expeditionary power' in Asia: Gordon Jockel to Donald Horne, n.d., MLMSS 3525 MLK 2140 G-14.

4   For an account of Vietnam trip, see Donald Horne to John Hunt, 10 February 1967, MLMSS 3525 MLK 2143 Q-4; Horne, *Into the Open*, pp. 156–57. On his judgement that Vietnam was a 'controlled crisis', see Horne to Plimsoll, 10 February 1967. For brief mention of the village search, see Donald Horne, 'Australia and Indonesia: The Next 20 Years', *The Bulletin*, 11 March 1967. For some details of time spent with Australian troops, see Donald Horne to Myfanwy Horne, 20 January 1967, Collection 5, Box 86.

5   Horne, 'Australia and Indonesia'; Horne to Hunt, 10 February 1967. On meeting Lubis: Horne, *Into the Open*, pp. 154–55.

6   Horne, 'Australia and Indonesia'.

7   Horne, 'How East Is Our Middle North West?', *The Bulletin*, 24 June 1967.

8   Horne, 'Waiting for Trudeau', *The Bulletin*, 6 July 1968.

9   Horne, 'The End of Do-It-Yourself', *The Bulletin*, 11 March 1967.

10   Horne, 'The Australian Image'.

11   Bolton, *The Oxford History of Australia Volume 5*, pp. 165–70. See also Donald Horne, *Time of Hope, 1967–1972* (Sydney: Angus and Robertson, 1980), pp. 121–38.

12   Richard Nixon, 'Asia after Vietnam', *The Bulletin*, 14 October 1967. Not long later, Horne wrote a detailed country-by-country five-page feature on the possibility of a post-American Asia: 'If America Leaves?', *The Bulletin*, 25 May 1968. In August 1968, Horne quoted a US State Department representative: 'We do not intend to undertake any new commitments in regard to Malaysia or Singapore or replace the activities undertaken by the British . . . We have made it very clear that Australia and New Zealand must play the external role there, and that we do not propose to do so': Horne, 'How to Withdraw from the Future', *The Bulletin*, 3 August 1968.

13   A point made by Mark Thomas in a 1989 profile of Horne: 'At times this brand of writing has fed off itself; the result has been more repetition than refinement, more duplication than distillation' – see Thomas, *Australian in Mind*, p. 117.

14   Phillip Adams, 'Horne of Plenty', *The Sydney Morning Herald*, 13 December 1969, p. 20.

15   Geoffrey Jukes, 'So What Else Is New . . . ?', *The Australian*, 29 November 1969.

16   Max Harris, transcript, ABC Radio review, 18 November 1970, MLMSS 3525 MLK 2175 R-6.

17   Horne, 'Australia Looks Around' ('recognition' and 'new way of looking at things'); *The Lucky Country* [5th ed.], pp. 96, 106 ('reorientation'). Elsewhere, 'events are rapidly making nonsense of Australia's conventional wisdoms': Horne, 'Australia Obsolescent'; 'Australia, its conventional wisdoms exhausted and its antique leadership disenchanted, has let things drift so dangerously that it now needs sudden shocks of recognition': Horne, 'Republican Australia', in Dutton (ed.), *Australia and the Monarchy* (1966).

18   Alan Reid, *The Gorton Experiment: The Fall of John Grey Gorton* (Sydney: Shakespeare Press, 1971), p. 28.

19   Donald Horne, 'The New Nationalism?', *The Bulletin*, 5 October 1968.

20   Ibid.

21   Ibid.

22   Alan Roberts, 'Mystical Portrait of the Australian Common Man', *The Advertiser*, 12 August 1967. Horne admitted as much in an interview less than five years later, noting that throughout the '60s he had moved from 'a rather conservative frame of mind . . . back . . . or forward, whatever it might be – to something more closely approaching the kind of attitude I had had before my university education': Horne, interview by De Berg.

23   Margaret Jones, 'The Dining Out Boom', *The Sydney Morning Herald*, 5 September 1970, cited in Paul van Reyk, *True to the Land: A History of Food in Australia* (London: Reaktion Books, 2021), p. 192; Frank Moorhouse, 'How Australian Dining Began to Shift in the 1960s', *Gourmet Traveller*, 14 December 2016; Horne, *Into the Open*, p. 176.

24   Horne, *Time of Hope*, pp. 1–2.

25   Paul Strangio, 'Instability 1966–82', in Bashford and Macintyre, *The Cambridge History of Australia Volume 2*, pp. 135, 140 ('The conflict over Vietnam was the wellspring of an age of dissent'). The global literature on the 1960s is vast. For an Australian perspective, see Gerster and Bassett, *Seizures of Youth*; Horne, *Time of Hope*; Greg Langley, *A Decade of Dissent: Vietnam and the Conflict on the Australian Homefront* (Sydney: Allen & Unwin, 1992); Verity Burgmann, *Power and Protest: Movements for Change in Australian Society* (Sydney: Allen & Unwin, 1992); Meredith Burgmann and Nadia Wheatley, *Radicals: Remembering the Sixties* (Sydney: NewSouth, 2021); John Murphy, *Harvest of Fear: A History of Australia's Vietnam War* (Sydney: Allen & Unwin, 1993); Gregory Pemberton, *Vietnam Remembered* (Sydney: New Holland, 2002); Peter Edwards, *A Nation at War: Australian Politics, Society and Diplomacy During the Vietnam War 1965–1975*, (Sydney: Allen & Unwin, 1997).

26   Donald Horne, 'Anarchism – What Do the Students Want?', *The Bulletin*, 6 July 1968.

27   'Lunch is one of my principal forms of recreation': Horne quoted in Meg Stewart, 'My Sunday: Donald Horne', *The Canberra Times*, 11 August 1985. See also Horne quoted in Lenore Nicklin, 'Fanfare for the Public Nuisance', *The Bulletin*, 25 December 1990: 'I enjoy very much conversation with people and there are often things you can only discuss in a certain kind of depth and wisdom with people when you get them by themselves. Lunches are a part of my intellectual life.'

28   Sandra Hall, Marion Macdonald and Sandra Forbes, 'Charismatic Editor, Mentor and Master of the Long Lunch', *The Sydney Morning Herald*, 9 September 2005.

29   Meaghan Morris, quoted in Davis, 'The Endless Seminar' ('great, old-school Sydney lunchers'; ibid. ('great Sydney lunchers').

30   Coleman, *Memoirs of a Slow Learner*, p. 94.

31   Hall, Macdonald and Forbes, 'Charismatic Editor, Mentor and Master of the Long Lunch'.

32   For names, see 'A Mild, Suburban Kind of Apocalypse' in Horne, *Into the Open*; ibid. Walsh was the editor of *Nation Review*, a magazine that Donald admired as 'an idealisation of the conversation at an intellectuals' lunch': Horne, *Into the Open*, p. 171.

33   Patricia Rolfe quoted in Jennie Curtin, 'Journalist and Mentor to Many', *The Sydney Morning Herald*, 28 August 2008.

34   Richard Walsh, interview with author, 23 February 2022.

35   Peter Manning, 'Donald Horne', in Richard Walsh (ed.), *Great Australian Eulogies* (Sydney: Allen & Unwin, 2008), pp. 69–74.

36   Peter Manning, interview with author, 5 October 2018; Horne, *Into the Open*, p. 164.

37   Baume, interview with author. Baume also credits Horne with teaching him how to properly use semi-colons: 'I am now a semi-colonist', he quipped.

38   Hall, Macdonald and Forbes, 'Charismatic Editor, Mentor and Master of the Long Lunch'.

39   Horne, Bulletin on *The Bulletin*, no. 3, 5 October 1971, MLMSS 3525 MLK 2152 ACP-B5.

40   Ibid.

41   Manning, 'Donald Horne', pp. 69–74.

42   Hall, Macdonald and Forbes, 'Charismatic Editor, Mentor and Master of the Long Lunch'.

43   Moorhouse, *Days of Wine and Rage*, p. 109; Horne, *Into the Open*, p. 169.

44   Horne was also on speaking terms with several other newspaper editors, including Graham Perkin (*The Age*), John Douglas Pringle (*The Sydney Morning Herald*) and Vic Carroll (*Australian Financial Review*).

45   Horne, *Into the Open*, pp. 152–53.

46   Ibid., pp. 150–51. In his own papers, McMahon kept a copy of the October 1968 'New Nationalism' issue of *The Bulletin*: see AA1980/735 AA1980/735/1874, Department of Prime Minister and Cabinet – General correspondence.

47   Horne, *Into the Open*, p. 152.

48   Hall quoted in Moorhouse, 'How Australian Dining Began to Shift in the 1960s'.

49   Royalties by December 1966 were £8216. The Hornes purchased the Grosvenor Street house in 1966 for £7700.

50   Typically, only features were signed under his own name.

51   Frank Hardy, *The Unlucky Australians* (Melbourne: Nelson, 1968); Robert Ellis and Michael Boddy, *The Legend of King O'Malley* (Sydney: Angus and Robertson, 1974).

52   Horne, interview by Turner.

53   Horne quoted in Stewart, 'My Sunday'.

54   Horne, 'Requiem', p. 118.

55   Horne, interview by Turner.

56   Ibid.

57   Horne, 'Requiem', p. 126.

58   Ibid., p. 128.

59 For sales figures, see Horne, *Into the Open*, pp. 132–42.

60 Donald Horne to Andre Deutsch, 10 June 1968, MLMSS 3525 MLK 2135 L-23. Horne to McAuley, n.d. [likely 1967], MLMSS 3525 MLK 2135 L-23: 'Dear Jim, I have become very keen on the "God is an Englishman" idea and was wondering if you would be kind enough to give me the reference to it'; Horne, *Into the Open*, pp. 136–37. See also Donald Horne, 'Shocking the British Back Into Their Wits', *The Bulletin*, 25 Nov 1967.

61 Booker, *The Neophiliacs*.

62 Diana Athill (on behalf of Andre Deutsch) to Donald Horne, 13 August 1968, MLMSS 3525 MLK 2135 L-23. The book had a troubled publication. After cutting down his manuscript by nearly 50,000 words to satisfy Deutsch, Horne's potential American publisher pulled the plug, alleging that he had 'taken a lot of the fun out of the book: Angus Cameron to Donald Horne, 11 March 1969, MLMSS 3525 MLK 2135 L-23.

63 Donald Horne to Hillary Freeman (at Penguin), 12 January 1970, MLMSS 3525 MLK 2175 R-6.

64 According to Horne, *The Lucky Country* was still selling at a rate of 13,000 copies per year: Horne, *Into the Open*, p. 139.

65 John Abernathy (Angus & Robertson) to John Michie (Penguin), 19 June 1970, MLMSS 3525 MLK 2175 R-6. Horne later expressed regret at writing this book, which he called a 'waste of time': Horne, *Into the Open*, p. 139.

66 Horne, *God Is an Englishman*, p. 272.

67 Ibid., p. 61.

68 Ibid., p. 89.

69 George Orwell, 'Notes on Nationalism' (1945), in *George Orwell: Collected Essays* (Seeker & Warburg: London, 1961), p. 281.

70 As James Curran and Stuart Ward surmised of the broader 'new nationalist' phenomenon, Australians had 'embarked on a quest for a "national identity" at precisely the time when intense, absolute national allegiances were becoming outdated': *The Unknown Nation*, p. 256. See also Horne, 'Right! We're to Be a Multi-Racial Society. What Do We Do Now?', *The Bulletin*, 6 February 1971.

71 Horne, *The Next Australia*, p. 225.

72 Ibid., p. 8.

73 Horne, 'That's Not What They Do Overseas', *The Bulletin*, 27 July 1968.

74 Ibid.

75 Horne, *The Next Australia*, p. 225.

76 Ibid., pp. 76–77.

77 Adams, 'Horne of Plenty'. On Adams' departure from *The Bulletin*, see Nick Leys, 'Philip Adams', Australian Media Hall of Fame website, www.halloffame. melbournepressclub.com/article/phillipadams. Barry Jones, meanwhile, thought the book was 'indescribably tedious' and read like 'the unedited transcript of an interminable telephone monologue': Barry Jones, 'Not Much of a Giggle from Donald', *The Age*, 8 November 1969.

78 Max Harris, 'Sacred Cows and Blessed Hornes', *The Australian*, 21 November 1970; John Douglas Pringle, 'Father of the Year?', *The Sydney Morning Herald*, 14 November 1970.

79 Pringle, 'Father of the Year?'.

80 Trevor Kennedy, 'Donald Horne's England', *Nation*, 7 February 1970. See also Geoffrey Sawyer, 'Uninspiring Look at the British', *The Canberra Times*, 27 December 1969.

81 For details, see Horne, Journal of 1972 Eye Operation; Horne, *Into the Open*, pp. 184–87. For the date, see telegram from 'George and Ava', 24 February 1972, MLMSS 3525 Add on 1978, Box 1.

82 Horne quoted in 'Donald Horne: The Activist', *The Age*, 9 October 1976. See also Horne in an unpublished excerpt for book about the 1970s, 'The big "change" year for me ... was in 1972', Frank Moorhouse to Horne, MLMSS 3525 Add on 1871, Box 1.

83 Documents, Frank Moorhouse to Donald Horne, 24 January 1978, MLMSS 3525 Add on 1871, Box 1.

84 Jim Davidson, 'Notes on a Nationalist', *Meanjin* 30, no. 4 (December 1971), pp. 440–46. Horne mentioned Davidson's review several times in his own account of this period: Horne, *Into the Open*, pp. 144, 147, 162.

85 Barry Carman, BBC review discussion, 6 May 1970, MLMSS 3525 MLK 2175 R-5.

86 Ian Sainsbury, 'Aristocrats and Englishmen', *Morning Telegraph* (Sheffield), 2 May 1970.

87 John Mander, 'Death of a God', *Quadrant* (February 1970), pp. 13–19. Mander was the author of the 'What's Wrong' book *Great Britain or Little England* (1963).

88 'First thoughts', Horne Papers, Collection 5, Box 18.

89 Donald Horne to Max Harris, n.d., MLMSS 3525 MLK 2134, Letters 1959–77.

90 'New Interpretations of Australian History', AACF seminar.

91 Horne, *The Lucky Country* [5th ed.], p. 231.

92 Manning Clark, 'The Making of an Australian', *The Australian*, n.d. [~late 1971]; Russel Ward, n.d., n.p., – see *The Australian People* reviews, MLMSS 3525 MLK 2175 R-8.

93 Ian Turner, '"Cool", Angry and Fascinating', *The Bulletin*, 11 November 1972.

94 Blainey launched the book, and had read and commented on the manuscript: letters about *The Australian People*, MLMSS 3525 MLK 2136 L-24; Horne, *Into the Open*, pp. 142, 197.

95 Horne, interview by Barker; Horne, *Into the Open*, p. 197; Richard Walsh to Donald Horne, 3 January 1973; T.J. Daly to Donald Horne, 8 January 1973; MLMSS 3525 Add on 1871, Box 12.

10. SHOCK THERAPY

1 On the Blacktown speech, see Jenny Hocking, *Gough Whitlam: His Time, Volume 1* (Carlton, Miegunyah Press, 2012) pp. 395–96.

2 Donald Horne, 'The End of the Age of Menzies', *The Bulletin*, 9 December 1973; 'The New Politics', *The Bulletin*, 7 October 1972; *Into the Open*, pp. 146–47; 'A Hero Who Put Us Back on Course', publication unknown, n.d. [~1996].

3 Horne, *Into the Open* p. 146.

4 Gough Whitlam, Speech delivered at Blacktown, 13 November 1972.

5 Horne, 'The End of the Age of Menzies'; *Into the Open*, p. 146.

6 On Whitlam's leadership style, see Donald Horne, *Death of The Lucky Country* (Harmondsworth: Penguin, 1976), p. 75.

7 Donald Horne, 'Facing a Neutral Australia', *Nation Review*, 15 June 1973.

8 Ibid.

9 'I moved, I think, from the right of centre to the left of centre', Horne, interview by De Berg.

10 Moorhouse, 'Donald Horne', p. 111. Peter Coleman, more familiar than most with Horne's prior distaste for the Labor Party, saw it the latest amusing example of his unpredictability, see Coleman cited in Elisabeth Wynhausen, 'Death of the Lucky Country or Birth of Donald Horne, Conservative Radical?', *National Times*, 8 March 1976.

11 As Frank Bongiorno has noted, 'some of those whom Coleman identified as members of the [historiographical] "counter-revolution" found their hero in Gough Whitlam': Bongiorno, 'The Right Kind of Middle Class'.

12 Horne, *Into the Open*, p. 109.

13 Hocking, *Gough Whitlam*, p. 11.

14 Whitlam to Horne, 23 March 1967, MLMSS 3525 MLK 2134 Letters 1959–1977.

15 Horne, 'Those Easy Days Are Over for Mr Holt', *The Bulletin*, 2 December 1967.

16 Horne, 'What's Left of Whitlam', *The Bulletin*, 11 May 1968; Horne, 'How to Withdraw From the Future', 3 August 1968.

17 Horne, 'Who Speaks For Australia', *The Bulletin*, 8 November 1969.

18 On memories of Whitlam at Sydney University, see Horne, 'What's Left of Whitlam?', *The Bulletin*, 11 May 1968; Horne, 'A Hero Who Put Us Back on Course'.

19 Moorhouse, 'Donald Horne', p. 111.

20 Clark, 'The Years of Unleavened Bread 1949–1972'; Mungo MacCallum, *The Whitlam Mob* (Collingwood: Black Inc., 2014), p. 13; Russel Ward, 'The End of the Ice Age', *Meanjin* 32, no. 1 (March 1973).

21 On Vietnam and Whitlam, see Conal Condren, interview with author, 3 June 2019. Many viewed his republican agitation in the late 1970s with increasing disdain: Horne, *Into the Open*, pp. 207, 220.

22 Hannah Forsyth, *A History of the Modern Australian University* (Sydney: NewSouth, 2014), pp. 88–89. As Forsyth notes, however, this was only really true for 'white, male, middle-class graduates of a limited number of British and American institutions' (p. 89).

23 On John Paul, see Glyn Davis, interview with author, 9 December 2021.

24 Horne, *Into the Open*, pp. 198–99.

25 Daly to Horne, 8 January 1973.

26 Horne, *Into the Open*, pp. 197–98.

27 On Horne's appointment, see D.L. Moore to Donald Horne, 6 January 1975, MLMSS 3525 Add on 1871, Box 12;Horne, *Into the Open*, p. 208.

28 Donald Horne, 'A Return to Idealism', *Nation Review*, 25 May 1972; 'The New Nationalism', *Pacific*, 1974; 'Australia Counts Them In', *Newsweek*, 8 October 1972.

29 Donald Horne, 'Eye on the Calendar', *Newsweek*, 6 January 1975.

30 Donald Horne, 'Policies Above Politics', *Newsweek*, 3 June 1974.

31 The precise cast is unclear: Horne remembers lunching with Elaine Thompson, whereas Frank Moorhouse recalls being at lunch with Horne and Doug McCallum. Moorhouse thought that Owen Harries might also have been there, but Harries later insisted that he was not: Frank Moorhouse, 'The Professor's Lunch', in Sybil Nolan (ed.), *The Dismissal: Where Were You on November 11, 1975?* (Carlton: Melbourne University Press, 2015), p. 86; Horne, *Into the Open*, p. 303; Frank Moorhouse, 'The Budding Writer – The Dismissal 30 Years On', *The Australian*, 5 November 2005.

32 For first-person accounts, see Nolan, *The Dismissal*.

33 Gough Whitlam, Dismissal speech on the steps of Parliament House, 11 November 1975, PM Transcripts, Transcript ID: 31860.

34 David Marr, 'How People Got the News', *The Bulletin*, 22 November 1975.

35 Horne, *Death of the Lucky Country*, p. 17 ('assassination'). Horne also used this exact phrase in his *Newsweek* column: Horne, 'Fears of a Blind Optimist', *Newsweek*, 12 January 1976.

36 Horne, *Death of the Lucky Country*, p. 98.

37 Donald Horne to John Hooker, 20 November 1975, MLMSS 3525 MLK2136 L-26; ibid., p. 98; Horne, *Into the Open*, p. 304. For an account of the Liberal Party branch meeting, see Donald Horne, *Winner Take All* (Ringwood: Penguin, 1981), p. 43.

38 Donald Horne, Notes for Hyde Park speech, MLMSS 3525 Add on 1871, Box 17 CON-1. Newspaper accounts of the rally are scarce: 'Senator Was Dumped', *The Daily Telegraph*, 18 November 1975; 'Good Humour at Park Rally', *The Sydney Morning Herald*, 18 November 1975. See also Horne, *Into the Open*, pp. 251, 304; *Death of the Lucky Country*, p. 34 ('partisanship').

39 Horne, *Death of the Lucky Country*, p. 9; *Into the Open*, pp. 304–07.

40 Horne, *Death of the Lucky Country*, p. 9; *Into the Open*, pp. 304–07.

41 Horne, *Death of the Lucky Country*, p. 91.

42 MLMSS 3525 Add on 1871, Box 17. On *Money Made Us* changes, see John Hooker to Donald Horne, 2 December 1975, MLMSS 3525 MLK2136 L-26.

43 Horne, *Death of the Lucky Country*, p. 12; 'Why I Won't Vote for Fraser', *The Bulletin*, 29 November 1975; 'Coup d'etat in Canberra', *The Age*, 11 February 1976.

44 Strangio, 'Instability 1966–82', p. 150 ('vice-regal adventurism').

45 Horne, *Death of the Lucky Country*, p. 95.

46 Ibid., pp. 95–96.

47 Donald Horne, 'Interview Donald Horne', ABC Radio, n.d. [~1976], NAA C100, 1103882.

48   'A Message from Donald Horne', MLMSS 3525 Add on 1871, Box 17.

49   As Jenny Hocking has argued, the outrage over the dismissal was partly 'a lament for this thwarted agenda for reform': Jenny Hocking, 'Introduction: History by Numbers', in Nolan, *The Dismissal*, p. 6.

50   Horne, *Death of The Lucky Country*, pp. 91–93.

51   By April 1976, it had sold 53,264 copies: Anne Donovan to Donald Horne, 6 April 1976, MLMSS 3525 MLK2136 L-26.

52   John Douglas Pringle, 'A Royalist at Heart', n.d., n.p. – see MLMSS 3525 MLK 2175 R-9.

53   Douglas Brass, 'The Edification of Old Donald', n.d., n.p. – see MLMSS 3525 MLK 2175 R-9. For his part, Clark showered the book in praise, commending its 'genuine moral passion' and endorsing Whitlam's own judgement that it was 'the greatest philippic ever written in this country': Manning Clark, 'Are We a Nation of Bastards?', *Meanjin* 35, no. 2 (June 1976).

54   Imre Salusinszky, 'Leading the Blind', *Farrago*, 27 February 1976. Paul Reynolds, on the other hand, thought it was among the best passages in Horne's entire catalogue of books: Reynolds, 'Donald Horne', p. 8.

55   Horne, interview by Barker. See also Horne, *Winner Take All*, p. 94.

56   The party – a fundraiser – was $50 per head: Donald Horne to John Hooker, 20 November 1975, MLMSS 3525 MLK2136 L-26.

57   James McAuley, 'Culture and Counter-Culture', 1976 Latham Lecture, *Quadrant* 20, no, 9 (September 1976). See also Horne, 'Dysfunctional Exorcism'.

58   Ibid.

59   According to his biographer, McAuley had been cast into a 'deep depression' by the election of Whitlam in 1972: Pybus, *The Devil and James McAuley*, p. 245.

60   Donald Horne, 'Claudette Colbert Was Better', *Quadrant* 20, no. 9, September 1976.

61   Donald Horne, *His Excellency's Pleasure: A Satire* (Melbourne: Thomas Nelson, 1977); *Power from the People: A New Australian Constitution?* (Melbourne: Victorian Fabian Society, 1977); 'A Case for a Republic', in Geoffrey Dutton (ed.), *Republican Australia?* (Melbourne: Sun Books, 1977).

62   See, for example, 'We Accuse', pamphlet, December 1975, MLMSS 3525 Add on 1871, Box 17 CON-1.

63   Myfanwy Horne, 'Introduction', in Myfanwy Gollan (ed.), *Kerr and the Consequences: The Sydney Town Hall Meeting, 20 September 1976* (Camberwell: Widescope International Publishers, 1976); Horne, *Into the Open*; Jill Neville, 'Horne's Life After "Death"', *National Times*, 13 October 1979 (for recollections of Horne and Hardy); Franca Arena, *Franca: My Story* (Sydney: Simon and Schuster, 2002), p. 114: Arena thought that Horne and Hardy had founded Citizens for Democracy.

64   Details in Gollan, *Kerr and the Consequences*.

65   Donald Horne cited in ibid., pp. 34–41.

66   Ibid., pp. 38–39.

67   Though as Mark McKenna noted, Whitlam was still hamstrung in his public statements on republicanism by his role as Opposition leader: McKenna, *The Captive Republic*, pp. 232–33. For White, see ibid., p. 76.

68   Horne, *Into the Open*, p. 313; MLMSS 3525 Add on 1871, Box 18 CON-8.

69   MLMSS 3525 Add on 1871, Box 17, CON-7.

70   Donald Horne, Address at the National Press Club, 7 March 1977, NLA, ORAL TRC 505/1.

71   Horne, *Into the Open*, p. 321.

72   The officer reported Horne made a 'very poor speech' that was 'poorly received by the audience': NAA file, 16 March 1977. On abuse, seen McKenna, *The Captive Republic*, p. 234. On *Newsweek*'s discontinuation of his column, see Horne, *Winner Take All*, p. 94 and *Into the Open*, p. 198.

73   About a thousand people attended the Republic Day meeting at the Sydney Town Hall (down from three thousand three years earlier): 'Big Rallies Defend Rights', *Tribune*, 14 November 1979. For details of exhibition see MLMSS 3525 Add on 1871, Box 19. For details of conference see MLMSS 3525 Add on 1871, Box 18. See also McKenna, *The Captive Republic*, pp. 233, 238.

74   Horne withdrew from most commitments due to busyness: Donald Horne to Vic Baueris, 7 April 1978; Myfanwy Horne to Thelma Martel, 8 October 1978, MLMSS 3525 Add on 1871, Box 20, CON-30.

75   Horne, *Into the Open*, pp. 315–16.

76   On 'doom and gloom' and unemployment figures, see Frank Crowley, *Tough Times: Australia in the Seventies* (Melbourne: William Heinemann, 1986), pp. 410–11. See also Bob Hawke, 'The Resolution of Conflict', ABC Boyer Lectures, 1979, audio recording, NLA.

11. THE GREAT MUSEUM

1   Jim Davidson and Peter Spearritt, *Holiday Business: Tourism in Australia Since 1870* (Melbourne: Miegunyah Press, 2000), pp. 283, 298–99.

2   Prior to the 1970s, Horne had been to England, Africa, Germany, Finland, the United States, back to England in 1956, to New Caledonia in 1958, to over twenty countries as an advertising executive in 1963, to Taiwan and several other South-East Asian countries on AACF business and on a holiday to Fiji.

3   For accounts of these trips, see Horne, Journal of 1972 eye operation; *Right Way – Don't Go Back* (Melbourne: Sun Books, 1978); *The Intelligent Tourist* (Mahons Point: Margaret Gee Publishing, 1992), pp. 79–97; *Into the Open*, pp. 180–82, 234–35.

4   Horne, *Right Way*, p. 28: 'It is only later that one embroiders the themes: at the time things are more mixed up.' See also Horne, *The Intelligent Tourist*, p. 8: 'this book is not concerned with people who travel exclusively for one or more of the deadly sins of lust, avarice, gluttony or sloth . . . or, for that matter, shopping, sport or sociability.'

5   Horne, *Right Way*, pp. 27–28 (on family discussion), 29 (on planning and itineraries). For other accounts of family trips, see Horne, *Into the Open*, pp. 234–35; Julia Horne, *The Pursuit of Wonder: How Australia's Landscape Was Explored, Nature Discovered and Tourism Unleashed* (Carlton: Miegunyah Press, 2005), pp. 3–4; Edmund Campion, 'The Dishwasher Unstacker', *The Monthly*, October 2005. Most of the material from the driving trips was dropped into *Right Way – Don't Go Back*, which was published as a means of funding further travel. *Right Way – Don't Go Back* sold 16,000 copies: Horne, *Into the Open*, p. 235.

6   Horne, interview by Barker; interview by Turner: 'I sat down and read through an enormous amount of sociological and a little bit of anthropological stuff.' See Horne's discussion of Max Weber in two 1974 essays: 'Political Legitimacy in Australia' and 'Australian Nationalism', in Richard Lucy (ed.), *The Pieces of Politics* (North Sydney: Macmillan, 1975), pp. 132–38, 155–63. In 1973 and 1974, Horne presented sixteen different papers and public addresses: 'Recent Lectures, Public Address, Papers' in MLMSS 3525 Add on 1871, Box 12, UN-1. See also: Index cards in Horne Papers, Collection 5, Box 107; Horne, *Into the Open*, pp. 200–04.

7   Horne to Hooker, late 1975.

8   Horne, Application for Promotion to the Position of Associate Professor, n.d. [~1981], MLMSS 3525 Add on 1871, Box 12, UN-1: 'There has been an interplay between the courses I give and the writing I have done, or am doing. Some of the themes and general material in my books have been first worked out in teaching.'

9   Hooker to Horne, 23 July 1975.

10   See, for example, Horne, Application for Promotion: 'Power and policy in a society cannot be usefully studied merely within the ordinary confines of "government". They should be studied in the wider context of the collective habits of that society and its cultural repertoire of values, bodies of knowledge and ways of doing things.' For another example, see Horne, *Winner Take All*, p. 130: 'Government is only one part of politics. Other parts of politics belong to *us*.'

11   Donald Horne, 'A Social History of Mrs Edna Everage', in George Seddon and Mari Davis (eds), *Man and Landscape in Australia: Towards an Ecological Vision* (Canberra: Australian Government Publishing Service, 1976), pp. 281–88. See also Donald Horne, 'The Legend of the Legend', foreword to Boddy and Ellis, *The Legend of King O'Malley*; 'Keeping the Boys in Line: The Court as a Political Idea', paper presented to the Australasian Political Studies Association Annual Conference, 1973, MLMSS 3525 Add on 1871, Box 23 AD-1; 'The Queen as Queen of Australia' in *The Queen* (London: Allen Lane, 1977).

12   Stuart Sayers, 'Observer of a Changing Society', *The Age*, 7 December 1985: 'He is a noted catnapper, snatching moments of sleep as the chance persists'. Horne is quoted in Stewart, 'My Sunday'; Horne, interview by Turner; Horne, 'Donald Horne and the Lucky Country'.

13   His publishers included Penguin (*Money Made Us*), Macmillan (*Billy Hughes*) and Angus & Robertson (*Time of Hope*). See Brian Smith to Donald Horne, 22 October 1976, 26 October 1976, MLK2136 L-26. See also *Billy Hughes* letters and reviews, MLMSS 3525 Add on 1871, Box 37.

14   Diana Fisher, 'Walkabout', *The Sunday Telegraph*, 14 October 1979.

15   For example, Neville, 'Horne's Life after "Death"'; Stuart Sayers, 'Horne's Full Future', *The Age*, 14 February 1981.

16   Royalty statements, MLMSS 3525 Add on 1871, Box 37.

17   See Donovan to Horne, 6 April 1976.

18   John Ross to Donald Horne, 2 May 1977, MLMSS 3525 Add on 1871, Box 37; Royalty statements, MLMSS 3525 Add on 1871, Box 37. Only *Pelicans* was a serious flop: Horne, *Into the Open*, pp. 135–42.

19   See, for example, Horne's critique of academic specialisation in his 1974 paper 'The Art of Political Criticism'.

20   Horne, *Into the Open*, p. 205. On the *Australian Encyclopaedia*, see MLMSS 3525 Add on 1871, Box 15 AE-2 and AE-3.

21   These addresses were made in 1977 (on republicanism), 1980 (on *Time of Hope*), 1987 (on *The Lucky Country Revisited*) and 1989 (on *Ideas for a Nation*).

22   Meaghan Morris, interview with author, 16 August 2019. Horne tells the same story in *Into the Open*, p. 241. Morris published her paper as an essay in 1982: 'Sydney Tower', *Island* 9/10 (1982), pp. 53–61.

23   Helen Irving, interview with author, 27 September 2018.

24   Horne, interview by Barker; *Into the Open*, p. 209. Story also recounted in Elaine Thompson, 'A Celebration of a Life: Donald Horne', *Australian Parliamentary Review* 20 (Spring 2005), p. 12.

25   Owen Harries, Speech at Donald Horne's Memorial Service, September 2005, cited in Davis, 'The Endless Seminar'.

26   Brad Norrington, correspondence with author, 7 June 2019.

27   Neville, 'Horne's Life after "Death"'. Horne's short temper was also recounted in several obituaries: Appleton, 'Remembering Donald'; Stephen Garton, 'Private Life of a Public Man', Eulogy delivered at Donald Horne's funeral, 21 September 2005, republished in *Griffith Review*, December 2005.

28   By his own estimation, Horne's two objectives when teaching were 'clarity, and arousing enthusiasm for studying the subject. For this it is necessary to "put on a performance"': Horne, Application for Promotion.

29   Davis, interview with author.

30   Mark McKenna, 'Journey of a Lifetime', *The Australian*, 12 September 2005.

31   Donald Horne, National Press Club address, Canberra, 1 November 1989.

32   Dominant Culture in Australia – Course Outline, 1982, MLMSS 3525 Add on 1871, Box 13 UN-PS6.

33   Condren, interview with author.

34   McKenna, 'Journey of a Lifetime'.

35   Donald Horne to Rupert Myers, 18 July 1977, MLMSS 3525 Add on 1871, Box 24
      EXP-1. In the end, it took seven.
36   Donald Horne to Rex Vowels, 1 August 1977, MLMSS 3525 Add on 1871, Box 24 EXP-1.
37   Horne to Myers, 18 July 1977.
38   For a detailed itinerary, see MLMSS 3525 Add on 1971, Box 24.
39   These activities attracted the attention of ASIO: See Donald Horne ASIO file, NAA
      A6119 6696.
40   And the proceeds of selling papers to the Mitchell Library: Horne to Murray-Smith,
      29 November 1978. On the *Right Way – Don't Go Back* proceeds, see Horne, interview
      by Barker. For funding grants, see 'Report on Study Leave and Special Leave', MLMSS
      3525 Add on 1871, Box 24 EXP-2.
41   Donald Horne, 'Report on Study Leave and Special Leave', MLMSS 3525 Add on 1871,
      Box 24 EXP-2.
42   Application for overseas study leave, 28 June 1977, MLMSS 3525 Add on 1871, Box 24
      EXP-1.
43   Between 1976 and 1981, Horne literally ran a seminar at the University of New South
      Wales called 'Australian Political Culture'. The course, per the outline, was concerned
      with 'placing Australian politics in a wider cultural context than the narrowly
      "political"': MLMSS 3525 Add on 1871, Box 13 UN-PS6.
44   Donald Horne, interview, *Four Corners*, ABC television, aired 20 September 1980.
      In an address to the National Press Club on 13 October 1980, Horne described the
      election as 'devastatingly illusionist'.
45   Donald Horne, 'Hegemony: An Australian model', paper to the Australasian Political
      Studies Association Conference, ANU, 27 August 1980, MLMSS 3525 Add on 1871,
      Box 23. Horne envisioned a whole book on this subject with the title 'Power and
      Democracy in Australia': 'I have been thinking this book out for five years': Horne,
      Application for Promotion, p. 10, MLMSS 3525 Add on 1871, Box 12, UN-1.
46   Horne's book collection at the State Library of New South Wales includes *Selections
      from the Prison Notebooks of Antonio Gramsci*, edited by Quintin Hoare and Geoffrey
      Nowell-Smith (London: Lawrence and Wishart, 1971).
47   Though Horne put Gramsci's *Prison Notebooks* onto his 'Aspects of Australian Political
      Culture' course reading list in 1977, he took it off in 1978, instead directing students
      to more recent studies and applications of Gramsci's ideas. The most important was
      Raewyn Connell's *Ruling Class, Ruling Culture: Studies of Conflict, Power and Hegemony
      in Australian Life* (Cambridge: Cambridge University Press, 1977). Others included Carl
      Boggs' *Gramsci's Marxism* (London: Pluto Press, 1976) (mentioned by name in Horne's
      1981 book *Winner Take All*, p. 118); James Joll's *Antonio Gramsci* (New York: Viking,
      1977); and Anne Showstack Sassoon's *Gramsci's Politics* (London: 1980) and *Approaches
      to Gramsci* (London, 1982). See MLMSS 3525 Add on 1871, Box 13 UN-PS6.
48   Norrington, correspondence with author.
49   Horne, 'Hegemony: An Australian model', paper to the Australasian Political Studies
      Association Conference, ANU, 27 August 1980, MLMSS 3525 Add on 1871, Box 23.
      Horne also clarified this in *The Public Culture* (1986), pp. 52–53: '[Gramsci's] decision
      to call this process "hegemony" was unfortunate since in ordinary usage the word
      has the connotation of "dominance", while Gramsci was in fact using "hegemony" to
      distinguish it from "dominance"'.
50   Donald Horne claimed he was 'simply not equipped to handle some of the central
      technical problems of philosophy', in Robert Dessaix (ed.), *Speaking Their Minds:
      Intellectuals and the Public Culture in Australia* (Sydney: ABC Books, 1998),
      p. 219. A common criticism of *The Lucky Country* was that it was 'impressionistic'.
51   Horne, *Into the Open*, p. 237.
52   See, for example, Horne's bibliography in *The Public Culture* (1986). As Horne put
      it, 'There was almost nothing I wrote about the political life that wasn't touched by
      cultural perspectives': Horne, *Into the Open*, p. 218.

53   Dessaix, *Speaking Their Minds*, pp. 218–19.

54   Elaine Thompson, interview with author, 10 September 2018. In Horne's 1994 interview with Ann Turner, he said: 'I believe that I am, as it were, very widely read. But I believe you should carry your learning – wear your learning – lightly. I believe that you subsume what you've read.'

55   The title of *Winner Take All*, came, as so often happened, at the suggestion of Myfanwy: Horne, *Into the Open*, p. 236.

56   Horne, *Winner Take All*, p. 81.

57   For details of conference planning see MLMSS 3525 Add on 1871, Box 20 and 21. See also *Changing the System*, Pamphlet, Consultative Committee on Australian Constitutional Reform, 1981–83, organised by the Law Foundation of New South Wales, CON-35.

58   Donald Horne, Address to the National Press Club, 30 October 1980, NLA; Horne, *Winner Take All*, p. 94.

59   See course outlines, MLMSS 3525 Add on 1871, Box 13 UN-PS6, UN-PS7, UN-PS8; Horne, *Into the Open*, p. 215; 'Power and Democracy in Australia – 1982 Course Outline', MLMSS 3525 Add on 1871, Box 12 UN-PS4; Horne, *Into the Open*, p. 212. From 1980, he also ran another course called 'The Party System in Australia': MLMSS 3525 Add on 1871, Box 13. See also Horne, *Into the Open*, p. 219. Horne requested he take a back seat with the promotion of the Change the Rules conference pamphlet, *Changing the System*, in December 1981: 'Press Release', MLMSS 3525 Add on 1871, Box 20, CON-33. Press coverage still featured him prominently, however – e.g. 'Horne Argues for Simultaneous State and Federal Elections', *The Sydney Morning Herald*, 10 December 1981.

60   Donald Horne, 'The Two Half-Cultures', *Overland* 85 (October 1981); 'Myths and Rituals of the People's Choice', *Island*, Mythologies issue (1982); 'Agenda Setting in the Media', in Richard Lucy (ed.), *Pieces of Politics*, 3rd ed (South Melbourne; Macmillan, 1983).

61   Horne, interview by Barker.

62   Horne, *Into the Open*, p. 241. Campion later reviewed the book, rather negatively: 'Blinkered Insights into Europe', *The Bulletin*, 6 November 1984.

63   Horne, Application for Promotion. He also experimented with 'Power and Imagination in Europe': Donald Horne to Doug McCallum, n.d. [~1982], MLMSS 3525 Add on 1871, Box 12, UN-1.

64   MLMSS 3525 Add on 1872, Box 37, see individual letters.

65   Donald Horne to Brian Johns, n.d. [~1984], *Confessions of a New Boy* letters, MLMSS 3525 Add on 1871, Box 37: 'Because of not having an agent, I am in the unusual situation of giving a publisher rights.'

66   Donald Horne, 'Who Rules Australia?', in Stephen R. Graubard (ed.), *Australia: The Daedalus Symposium* (Sydney: Angus & Robertson, 1985).

67   Fulbright Fellowship application, 1984, MLMSS 3525 Add on 1871, Box 24. Glyn Davis described it as an 'optimistic' reading of Gramsci: Davis, 'The Young Educated by Donald', *Australian Parliamentary Review* 20 (Spring 2005), p. 4.

68   Horne, *Money Made Us*, p. 20.

69   Horne, 'Who Rules Australia?', p. 191.

70   His book-length account of this theory, *The Public Culture*, was subtitled *The Triumph of Industrialism*.

71   See MLMSS 3525 Add on 1871, Box 24 EXP-3.

72   The trip was partially funded by a Fulbright Fellowship: MLMSS 3525 Add on 1871, Box 24.

73   In France, for example, he and Myfanwy stayed with Gough and Margaret Whitlam: Donald Horne to Gough Whitlam, 18 June 1984, MLMSS 3525 Add on 1871, Box 24 EXP-3.

74   Peter Crawford, 'Middle-Class Radical or Progressive Conservative?', *Vanguard*, 24 February 1981.

75   Horne, *The Public Culture*, p. 24. See also Donald Horne, Graduation Address, West
      Australian Institute of Technology, 1985, MLMSS 3525 Add on 1871, Box 23, AD-3.
76   Timothy Pascoe to Donald Horne, 10 April 1984, MLMSS 3525 Add on 1871, Box 27, AC-1.
77   Jenny Orellana, 'The State of the Arts Is National', *The Herald*, 17 May 1984; Ellen
      Petersen, 'Donald Horne Appointed to Top Australia Council Job', *The Australian*,
      5 May 1984; Justin Macdonnell, *Arts, Minister?: Government Policy and the Arts*
      (Sydney: Currency Press, 1992), pp. 352–53.
78   *Newcastle Herald*, 28 January 1982.
79   Horne, *Into the Open*, p. 12; Order of Australia, Horne Papers, Collection 5, Box 91.
      The McClellands organised a party with the Whitlams and Patrick White and Manoly
      Lascaris, but the Hornes were disinvited because Donald had accepted his AO:
      Appleton, *Diamond Cuts*, p. 124. On receiving a Personal Chair, see Michael Birt to
      Donald Horne, 11 September 1984, MLMSS 3525 Add on 1871, Box 12, UN-1.
80   See Finding aid, Donald and Myfanwy Horne Papers, SLNSW. Another thirty-eight
      boxes were presented to the library in 1988, thirty-two in 1992, and 109 in 2015.
81   Paul White, 'Donald Horne: Towards an Intellectual Biography', Honours thesis, 1979,
      Donald Horne Papers, Mitchell Library, Sydney, MLMSS 352, Add-on 1871, Box 11;
      Judith A. Conacaud, 'Donald Horne: A Biographical Study', *Melbourne Journal of
      Politics* 11 (1979), pp. 34–44; Horne, *Into the Open*, p. 12.
82   Horne, *Time of Hope*, pp. 150–51; Stuart Ward, '"Culture Up to Our Arseholes":
      Projecting Post-Imperial Australia', *Australian Journal of Politics and History* 51, no. 1
      (2005), pp. 53–66.
83   Other administrative roles included Chair of the Faculty of Arts at the University
      of New South Wales, member of the Faculty Resources Allocation Committee, the
      Professorial Board and the University Council, adviser to the NSW government on
      arts subsidies, Advisory Board of the *Australian Encyclopaedia*.
84   The ALP's official arts policy was articulated by Susan Ryan in 1982: Di Yerbury, 'Arts
      Policy and Cultural Identity', in Susan Ryan and Troy Bramston (eds), *The Hawke
      Government: A Critical Retrospective* (Melbourne: Pluto Press, 2003), p. 255.
85   Justin Macdonnell called 1985 'the most destructive year in the career of any Arts
      Minister and probably in the history of the arts in this country': Macdonnell, *Arts,
      Minister?*, p. 363.
86   Turbocharged by the release of the McLeay Report in 1986, an inquiry into
      government arts assistance was commissioned by the Fraser government: Macdonnell,
      Arts, Minister?, pp. 340–43
87   Ibid., pp. 370-371.
88   Ibid., pp. 381–82, 356.
89   Horne, *Into the Open*. As Macdonnell put it, they 'could not and did not get along':
      Arts, Minister?, p. 354.
90   Horne quoted in Macdonnell, *Arts, Minister?*, p. 372.
91   Don Aitkin, correspondence with author, 31 July 2018.
92   Andrea Hull, interview with author, 7 February 2022.
93   See, for example, Peter Ward, 'The Smell of Something Fishy?', *Adelaide Review*, April
      1992: 'I had long heard of this endearing trait of Donald's, of his penchant for calling
      meetings for the purpose of consultation that then became lectures on a proper view
      of the world. I'm told when he was chairman of the Australia Council, many a pencil
      was broken in sheer frustration as officers discovered again and again that the best
      input they could give was to listen.'
94   Max Bourke, interview with author, 11 February 2022.
95   Michelle Field, 'Horne the Arts Tsar Plans a Return to Stir the Pot Gently', *National
      Times*, 16 November 1984.
96   He made similar arguments at his unveiling in May 1984: Andrew Fraser, 'Council to
      Promote Culture Outside Academia', *The Canberra Times*, n.d. [~May 1984]; Petersen,
      'Donald Horne Appointed to top Australia Council Job'.

97   Macdonnell, *Arts, Minister?*, p. 393.

98   Donald Horne, interview by Caroline Craig, ABC Books and Writing, 23 October 1985, National Archives of Australia. The images in *The Australian People*, said Horne, were 'a kind of museum'. On 'twelve months' see Horne, *Into the Open*, p. 258.

99   Donald Horne, 'Supporting the Arts in Australia', Inaugural Address, 16 January 1985, MLMSS 3525 Add on 1871, Box 27. Horne elaborated on this idea in *The Public Culture* (1986), pp. 232–36.

12. PUBLIC INTELLECTUAL

1   On public speaking, see 'Special Addresses', MLMSS 3525 Add on 1871, Box 23. Horne published the following books during this period: *The Great Museum* (1984), *The Story of the Australian People* (1985), *Confessions of a New Boy* (1985), *The Public Culture* (1986), *The Lucky Country Revisited* (1987), *Portrait of an Optimist* (1988) and *Ideas for a Nation* (1989).

2   Donald Horne, 'How to Be an Intellectual', Graduation Address, University of New South Wales, 1985, MLMSS 3525 Add on 1871, Box 23 AD-3.

3   See Russell Jacoby, *The Last Intellectuals: American Culture in the Age of Academe* (New York: Basic Books, 1987). For an Australian example, see Judith Brett's essay on Jacoby's book, 'The Bureaucratisation of Writing: Why So Few Academics Are Public Intellectuals', *Meanjin* 50, no. 4 (Summer 1991). For those on the right, meanwhile, these new 'tenured radicals' had ushered in a new age of conformity: Alan Bloom, *The Closing of the American Mind: How Higher Education Has Failed Democracy and Impoverished the Souls of Today's Students* (New York: Simon and Schuster, 1987); Roger Kimball, *Tenured Radicals: How Politics Has Corrupted Our Higher Education* (New York: Harper & Row, 1990).

4   Jacoby, *The Last Intellectuals,* p. 5. The term 'public intellectual' had been used cursorily before this point – e.g. in C. Wright Mills' 1958 book *The Causes of World War Three* – but Jacoby's book popularised it.

5   See, for example, Thomas, *Australia in Mind*; *The Public Intellectual, Meanjin* 50, no. 4 (Summer 1991); Robert Manne, 'Intellectuals: A Lament', *Quadrant* 36, no. 12 (1992), p. 2; Donald Horne, 'Public Intellectuals: A Symposium', *Australian Book Review* no. 182 (July 1996); Pierre Ryckmans, 'Aspects of Culture', ABC Boyer Lectures, 1996; Dessaix, *Speaking Their Minds*.

6   Richard A. Posner, *Public Intellectuals: A Study of Decline* (Cambridge: Harvard University Press, 2001); David Brooks, 'Notes From a Hanging Judge', The *New York Times*, 13 January 2002.

7   Edward Said, 'Representations of the Intellectual', BBC Reith Lectures, 1993.

8   David Carter, 'The Conscience Industry: The Rise and Rise of the Public Intellectual', in David Carter (ed.), *The Ideas Market: An Alternative Take on Australia's Intellectual Life* (Melbourne: Melbourne University Press, 2004), p. 21. Drusilla Modjeska called it an 'irredeemably pretentious' term: 'Our Future Thinkers', *The Monthly*, July 2006. Stefan Collini called it 'modish': 'Long Views: Specialization, Discontents', in Collini, *Absent Minds*, p. 470. For a number of similarly sceptical essays, see Carter, *The Ideas Market*.

9   In 1993, for example, Horne appeared on a list of seventeen prominent thinkers compiled by Labor MP Barry Jones, republished in *The Sydney Morning Herald*, 12 March 2005. See also Thomas, *Australia in Mind*; Dessaix, *Speaking Their Minds*.

10   'The Tally of Votes', *The Sydney Morning Herald*, 12 March 2005. In his own books, Horne did not refer to himself as a public intellectual until *10 Steps to a More Tolerant Australia* (Camberwell: Penguin Books, 2003). A collection of his writings published in 2017 described him as a 'leading public intellectual for nearly fifty years': Glyn Davis in Nick Horne (ed.), *Donald Horne: Selected Writings* (Carlton: La Trobe University Press, 2017).

11   Horne was a member of what Jacoby described as the 'transitional' generation, those – such as the Americans Irving Howe and Daniel Bell – who were born around 1920, who made their names in the little magazines of the 1940s and '50s and entered the academy in later life: Russell Jacoby, 'The Latest Intellectuals', *Chronicle of Higher Education*, 29 November 2015.

12   Horne in Dessaix, *Speaking Their Minds*, p. 218: 'The only way to be influential in this business . . . is to put into words for people something that's already floating around in their heads', p. 218. Horne, This was a point that Horne made over and over – for example, in his 1992 *Australian Biography* interview with Robin Hughes: 'In so far as writing is influential, it's always influential because it's telling people something they half knew or want to know . . . leading them on to a new kind of realisation'. Horne, interview by Turner: 'The way in which you influence people is that you say what they know.' Horne disliked the word 'stirrer': Nicklin, 'Fanfare for a Public Nuisance'.

13   'Magazine Proposal'.

14   Stretton, 'Persistent Preaching'.

15   Horne, *Ideas for a Nation*, p. 98; Australia Council, 'Unlocking the Academies', Clever Country Forum, August 1990, MLMSS 3525 Add on 1978, Box 28; Horne, interview by Barker.

16   Nicklin, 'Fanfare for a Public Nuisance'; Humphrey McQueen, 'The Wizard of the Oz Council', *24 Hours*, May 1991. For tributes, see MLMSS 3525 Add on 1978, Box 21.

17   Nicklin, 'Fanfare for a Public Nuisance'.

18   David Marr cited in Jonathan Chancellor, 'Revered Author Donald Horne's Longtime Woollahra Terrace Listing', Urban.com.au, 5 November 2014, www.urban.com.au/news/revered-author-donald-hornes-longtime-woollahra-terrace-listing.

19   'Australia Council Summons an Ideas Summit', draft memo, MLMSS 3525 Add on 1978, Box 27 ('intellectual infrastructure').

20   For details, see MLMSS 3525 Add on 1978, Box 27.

21   Horne, National Press Club address.

22   See Donald Horne, 'Serious Conversation', in Horne and Horne, *Dying: A Memoir*. On toughness and rational argument, see Condren, interview with author. Travel, too, remained central to Horne's existence: between 1990 and 1994, he and Myfanwy visited China, India, Iceland and Borneo.

23   Manning, 'Donald Horne', pp. 69–74. This habit was echoed by Campion, interview with author.

24   Elaine Thompson quoted in 'Face to Face', *Good Weekend*, n.d. [~1986]; Appleton, 'Remembering Donald'. See also Thompson, 'A Celebration of a Life', p. 12.

25   Bourke, interview with author. At *The Bulletin*, Horne could be 'quite difficult to work with if you didn't meet his standards'. Even during the Australia Council period, he was still known to throw the occasional book or kick the occasional chair: Hall, Macdonald and Forbes, 'Charismatic Editor, Mentor and Master of the Long Lunch'.

26   Horne, interview by Turner.

27   Horne, responding to a review of *The Next Australia* in *The Age*, n.d. [~ late 1970], MLMSS 3525 MLK 2175 R-6.

28   Donald Horne to Elaine Thompson, 21 December 1980.

29   Walsh, interview with author.

30   Appleton, 'Remembering Donald'. Horne's friend Meaghan Morris also acknowledged Horne's sensitivity, and added that he had a 'need for reassurance . . . if you slighted him he would remember forever': Morris, interview with author.

31   Tim Rowse, 'Culture as Myth, Criticism as Irony: The Middle-Class Patriotism of Donald Horne', *Island* 37 (Spring 1988). See also Boris Frankel, *From the Prophets Deserts Come* (Melbourne: Arena, 1992). 'If this was oppositional public intellectual life . . . then heaven help us': Boris Frankel, 'The Gentleman Is Not for Turning', *Modern Times* (April 1992).

32   Don Dunstan, 'What's Next?', *The Bulletin*, 21 November 1970.

33   Thomas, *Australia in Mind*, pp. 115–32.

34   Denis O'Brien, 'Donald Horne: The Maxi-Series – Volume Two', *The Weekend Australian Magazine*, n.d. [~1986]; Vincent Buckley, 'Donald Horne's Confession', *Quadrant* 76 (March 1986).

35   Thomas, *Australia in Mind*, p. 121.

36   McKenna, *The Captive Republic*, pp. 241–48.

37   Arena to Myfanwy Horne, 24 August 1990; Myfanwy Horne to Arena, 1 September 1990, MLMSS 3525 Add on 1978, Box 30.

38   On the 20 December meeting, see MLMSS 3525 Add on 1978, Box 30.

39   'Republicans Urge End to Dependence', *The Age*, 8 July 1991; Tony Stephens, 'With All Respect, Your Majesty, We Have Our Own Life to Live', *The Sydney Morning Herald*, 6 July 1991.

40   See Donald Horne, 'Dear Prime Minister', *The Age Saturday Extra*, March 1993; 'National Independence a Far Cry from Virulent Nationalism', *Australian Financial Review*, 14 June 1994; 'A Great Future, So Let's Believe in It', *Herald Sun*, 13 July 1994, Horne Papers, Collection 5, Box 23.

41   MLMSS 3525 Add on 1978, Boxes 27–30.

42   Thomas Keneally, 'Towards a More Democratic Australia', in Donald Horne (ed.), *The Coming Republic* (Sydney: Pan Macmillan, 1992), p. 194.

43   Horne, *Ideas for a Nation*, p. 26 ('imaginative constructs').

44   Donald Horne, 'Faint Stirrings of Change in the New Suburban Radicalism', *Financial Times*, 28 August 1973.

45   Donald Horne, 'A New Common Sense for Australia', in Horne, *The Coming Republic*, p. 26. Horne elaborated on this point in much greater detail in his 1989 book *Ideas for a Nation*, which he described, somewhat revealingly, as 'son of *The Public Culture* meets daughter of *Money Made Us*': Horne, National Press Club address.

46   See James Curran, *The Power of Speech: Australian Prime Ministers Defining the National Image* (Melbourne: Melbourne University Press, 2004), p. 191.

47   On the 'New Right', see Frank Bongiorno, *The Eighties: The Decade That Transformed Australia* (Melbourne: Black Inc., 2015), pp. 168–69. Their emergence in the mid-1980s, argues Bongiorno, was a revolt against the 'consensus politics' of the Hawke government. See also Dominic Kelly, *Economic Troglodytes and Political Lunatics: The Hard Right in Australia* (Melbourne: La Trobe University Press, 2019), pp. 3 (on the New Right), 105–07 (on the establishment of the Samuel Griffith Society on constitutional matters in 1992).

48   Patrick Cook, 'Cognito Egregious Sum', *The Bulletin*, 13 March 1990; Robert Manne, 'The Intellectuals Make Their Bid', *Quadrant*, April 1990. See also: 'Jungles Up the Summit', editorial, *The Advertiser*, 26 May 1990; Brian Buckley, 'No Flies on Donald', *Quadrant*, March 1990; Peter Coleman, 'On the Identity Bandwagon', review of *The Avenue of the Fair Go*, *The Australian*, n.d. [~1997]; Peter Ryan, 'A Self-Made Man', *Quadrant*, 1998; Nick Cater, 'Birth of the Sophisticates', *Spectator Australia*, 8 November 2014.

49   Frankel, 'The Gentleman Is Not for Turning'. See also Frankel, *From the Prophets Deserts Come*, pp. 99, 251.

50   On the Donald Horne Lecture, see 'Govt to Fund Lecture Tours by Whinging Aussies', *The Sydney Morning Herald*, 26 December 1990. The first Donald Horne Lecture, 'The Curse of the Lucky Country', was given by Ann Summers at the Sydney Opera House on 14 May 1991: MLMSS 3525 Add on 1978, Box 28.

51   Carter, 'The Conscience Industry', p 24.

52   NSW Liberal premier Nick Greiner launched 1989's *Ideas for a Nation*; however, see Elizabeth Swanson, 'Writers Do a Little Paperwork', *The Weekend Australian*, 18–19 November 1989.

53   Donald Horne, 'Foreword', in Hardy, *The Unlucky Australians*.

54   Bourke, interview with author; Horne, *Into the Open*, p. 298.

55   Horne quoted in Dessaix, *Speaking Their Minds*, p. 220; Horne, *Into the Open*, p. 323.
56   Donald Horne, 'The Medici Myth', *The Age Saturday Extra*, 5 May 1995; Paul Keating, 'The Council Was Stale – You Could Smell the Thing', *The Sydney Morning Herald*, 20 May 1995.
57   For the 'icons' story, see Horne, *Into the Open*, pp. 328–29. On the Republic Advisory Committee, see McKenna, *The Captive Republic*, p. 253.
58   Horne, *Into the Open*, pp. 332–35, 343–44 (on Horne's resignation). Horne did not make his resignation public.
59   Horne, interview by Turner. On *Sex and the City*, see Thompson, interview with author. On Iraq and watching strangers, see Helen Irving, 'On Donald Horne', *Australian Parliamentary Review* 20 (Spring 2005), p. 6. Iraq, Horne told Irving, had been 'fucked up'.
60   Kirsty Cameron, 'A Hard Act to Follow', *The Weekend Australian Review*, 29 December 1990.
61   Horne, interview by Turner; Thompson, interview with author.
62   He had a certificate to prove it: Collection 5, Box 61.
63   Horne, *Into the Open*, p. 337.
64   Matt Condon, 'Call Him Mr Lucky', *The Age*, 7 March 1998; Mark Thomas, *Gangland: Cultural Elites and the New Generationalism* (Sydney: Allen & Unwin, 1997).
65   Horne, *The Intelligent Tourist*.
66   Donald Horne, *The Avenue of the Fair Go: A Group Tour of Australian Political Thought* (Pymble: HarperCollins, 1997).
67   For Horne's correspondence with publishers and agent, see Horne Papers, Collection 5, Box 39.
68   John Button, 'Voices in the Park', *Australian Book Review*, October 1997; Murray Sayle, 'Fair Go, Unka Donald!', *The Age*, 13 September 1997; Ross Fitzgerald, 'The Road to Identity', *Spectrum*, September 1997. On sales, see Horne, *Into the Open*, p. 332.
69   Coleman, 'On the Identity Bandwagon'; Horne to Coleman, 21 October 1997; Horne, 'Letter to the Editor', *The Australian*, 23 October 1997; Horne to Coleman, 25 October 1997; Horne to Barry Oakley, 28 October 1997; Oakley to Horne, 29 October 1997; Horne to Oakley, 30 October 1997; see Horne Papers, Collection 5, Box 39.
70   On the New Zealand trip and breathlessness: Horne and Horne, *Dying*, p. 11; Horne, *Into the Open*, pp. 338–39.
71   Horne and Horne, *Dying*, pp. 8, 14; Horne, *Into the Open*, pp. 337–41.
72   Myfanwy Horne to Mr Bayliss, 11 December 1989, Collection 5, Box 86; Horne, interview by Barker: 'I've worked out that my life expectance would be about another five hundred weeks . . . So I've been uncommitting myself.'
73   In the early 2000s he attended the Byron Bay Writers Festival, Cooee Artists Festival in Rockhampton and the Cultural Vitality Seminar in 2003.
74   On the Barton Lectures and Centenary of Federation ,see Horne Papers, Collection 5, Box 23.
75   Horne, *10 Steps to a More Tolerant Australia*, p. 10.
76   Guy Rundle, Review of *Looking for Leadership*, *Australian Book Review*, September 2001.
77   John Howard is cited in Curran and Ward, *The Unknown Nation*, p. 16.
78   Nick Horne, 'Introduction' in Horne, *Donald Horne*, p. 7.
79   Horne, *The Avenue of the Fair Go* (1997), cited in Horne and Horne, *Dying*, p. 250.
80   Horne, *The Lucky Country* (5th ed.), p. 247.
81   Horne, 'Doing Things for Their Own Sake', Graduation Address, University of Sydney, 29 April 2005.

13. REQUIEM

1   Horne, 'Looking', in Horne and Horne, *Dying*, p. 232.
2   Horne, interview by Hughes.

3   Maurice Dunlevy, 'Making a Nation Out of a Limited Range of Myths', *The Canberra Times*, 11 November 1989.
4   Mungo MacCallum, 'Donald Horne, 1921–2005', *Overland*, April 2006.
5   Peter Coleman, 'When the Racket Had to Stop', *The Bulletin*, 5 December 1964, p. 53; Coleman, 'Don's Party Tricks'.
6   Campion, 'The Dishwasher Unstacker'.
7   Garton, 'Private Life of a Public Man'.
8   Horne is quoted in 'Son of the Lucky Country'.
9   On the 'noisy republic of ideas', see Garton, 'Private Life of a Public Man'.
10   Campion, 'The Dishwasher Unstacker'.
11   MacCallum, 'Donald Horne, 1921–2005'.
12   Horne, interview by Turner.
13   McKenna, 'Journey of a Lifetime'.
14   Horne, 'Serious Conversation', pp. 227–31.
15   On 'refresh[ing] the public discourse', see Appleton, 'Remembering Donald'.
16   Horne, *The Lucky Country* (5th ed.), p. 10.
17   Horne, 'Policy and Practice in the *Observer*'.

SELECT BIBLIOGRAPHY

I have not included specific references here to individual articles, letters and documents written by Donald Horne. All are referenced fully in the endnotes and can be found in his personal papers at the State Library of New South Wales.

MANUSCRIPT COLLECTIONS

Mitchell Library, Sydney
Donald and Myfanwy Horne Papers, MLMSS 3525.
James McAuley Papers, MLMSS 7920.
Lillian Roxon Papers, MLMSS 3086.
Peter Coleman Papers, MLMSS 10399.

National Library of Australia, Canberra
Geoffrey Dutton Papers, National Library of Australia, MS 7285.
James Plimsoll Papers, National Library of Australia, MS 8048.
Records of the Australian Association for Cultural Freedom, MS 2031.

SELECTED BOOKS BY DONALD HORNE
The Lucky Country: Australia in the Sixties (Ringwood: Penguin, 1964).
The Permit (Melbourne: Sun Books, 1965).
The Education of Young Donald (Sydney: Angus & Robertson, 1967).
God Is an Englishman (Sydney: Angus & Robertson, 1969).
The Next Australia (Sydney: Angus & Robertson, 1970).
But What If There Are No Pelicans? (Sydney: Angus & Robertson, 1971).
The Australian People: Biography of a Nation (Sydney: Angus & Robertson, 1972).
Death of the Lucky Country (Harmondsworth: Penguin, 1976).
Money Made Us (Ringwood: Penguin, 1976).
Right Way – Don't Go Back (South Melbourne: Sun Books, 1978).
In Search of Billy Hughes, 2nd ed. (Melbourne: Black Inc., 2000 [1979]).
Time of Hope: Australia 1966–72 (Sydney: Angus & Robertson, 1980).
The Great Museum: The Representation of History (Leichhardt: Pluto Press, 1984).
Confessions of a New Boy (Ringwood: Viking, 1985).
The Public Culture: The Triumph of Industrialism (Leichhardt: Pluto Press, 1986).
Portrait of an Optimist (Ringwood: Penguin, 1988).
Ideas for a Nation (Chippendale: Pan Books, 1989).
The Intelligent Tourist (Smithfield: Margaret Gee, 1992).

The Avenue of the Fair Go (Pymble: HarperCollins, 1997).

An Interrupted Life (Pymble: HarperCollins, 1998).

Into the Open (Pymble: HarperCollins, 2000).

Looking for Leadership: Australia in the Howard Years (Ringwood: Penguin, 2001).

Ten Steps to a More Tolerant Australia (Camberwell: Penguin, 2003).

Dying: A Memoir (Camberwell: Penguin, 2007).

DONALD HORNE INTERVIEWS

Horne, Donald, interview by Hazel de Berg, 24 January 1973, audio recording, National Library of Australia.

Horne, Donald, *Australian Biography: Donald Horne*, interview by Robin Hughes, 16 January 1992, Australian Biography Film Series, Canberra: Film Australia, 1993.

Horne, Donald, interview by Ann Turner, 24 May 1994, audio recording, National Library of Australia.

Horne, Donald, interview by Victoria Barker, UNSW Archives Oral History Project, 1995, OH 89.

ESSAYS, ARTICLES, AND CHAPTERS IN EDITED BOOKS

Anderson, Fay, 'Into the Night: Max Crawford, the Labyrinth of the Social Studies Enquiry and ASIO's "Spoiling Operations"', *Australian Historical Studies* 125 (2005), pp. 60–80.

Anderson, John, 'The Servile State', *The Australasian Journal of Psychology and Philosophy* 21, no. 2–3 (1943), pp. 115–32.

Appleton, Gillian, 'Remembering Donald', *New Matilda*, 20 September 2005.

Armstrong, David, 'John Anderson Remembered', Speech to the John Anderson Conference, 9 July 2005.

Beaumont, Joan, 'Creating an Elite? The Diplomatic Cadet Scheme, 1943–56', in Joan Beaumont, Christopher Waters, David Lowe and Woodward Garry (eds), *Ministers, Mandarins and Diplomats: Australian Foreign Policy Making 1941–69*, pp. 19–44, Carlton: Melbourne University Press, 2003.

Bongiorno, Frank, 'Whitlam, the 1960s and the Program', in Tony Bramston (ed.), *The Whitlam Legacy*, pp. 34–41, Annandale: Federation Press, 2015.

—— 'The New Progressivism: Anthony Crosland and the Coming of the Australian Sixties', in Shirleene Robinson and Julie Ustinoff (eds), *The 1960s in Australia: People, Power and Politics*, pp. 179–98, Cambridge: Cambridge Scholars Publishing, 2012.

—— 'The Right Kind of Middle-Class?', *Inside Story*, 19 December 2012.

Brett, Judith, *Relaxed and Comfortable: The Liberal Party's Australia*, Quarterly Essay 19 (Melbourne: Black Inc., 2005).

—— 'The Bureaucratisation of Writing: Why So Few Academics Are Public Intellectuals', *Meanjin* 50, no. 4 (Summer 1991).

Bridge, Carl, 'Look to America, Look to the Myth', *The Australian Special Edition*, 7 December 1991.

Buckley, Vincent, 'Unequal Twins: A Discontinuous Analysis', in Jim Davidson (ed.), *The Sydney-Melbourne Book*, pp. 148–58, Sydney: Allen & Unwin, 1986.

—— 'The Fortnightly Universe', *Prospect*, no. 2 (1960), pp. 2–3.

Buckridge, Patrick, 'Antagonism as an Art Form: Brian Penton and the Politics of Provocation', *Journal of Australian Studies* 21, no. 54–55 (1997), pp. 81–90.

Campion, Edmund, 'The Dishwasher Unstacker', *The Monthly*, October 2005.

Carruthers, Susan, 'Being Beastly to the Mau Mau', *Twentieth-Century British History* 16, no. 4 (2005), pp. 489–96.

Clausen, Mads, 'Donald Horne Finds Asia', in David Walker and Agnieszka Sobocinska (eds), *Australia's Asia: From Yellow Peril to Asian Century*, pp. 298–321, Crawley: UWA Publishing, 2012.

Cole, Creagh McLean, 'John Anderson's Political Thought Revisited', *Australian Journal of Political Science* 44, no. 2 (2009), pp. 229–43.

Coleman, Peter, 'Henry Richard Krygier (1917–1986), in Diane Langmore (ed.), *Australian Dictionary of Biography Volume 17, 1981–1990: A–K*, Carlton: Melbourne University Press, 2007.

—— 'Was Georges Sorel an Andersonian?', *Quadrant* 46, no. 9 (September 2002), pp. 54–57.

—— 'The Bulletin, the Editor and *The Cherry Orchid*', *Voices* 7, no. 1 (Autumn 1997), pp. 88–95.

—— 'The Prodigal Sons: The Unlikely Story of Richard Krygier and the Australian Association for Cultural Freedom', *Quadrant* 30, no. 11 (November 1986), pp. 10–21.

—— 'Don's Party Tricks', *Spectator Australia*, 8 November 2014.

Collini, Stefan, '"What, Ultimately, For?" The Elusive Goal of Cultural Criticism', *Raritan* 33, no. 2 (2013), pp. 4–26.

Colmer, John, 'Autobiography or Sociography?: Donald Horne', John Colmer, *Australian Autobiography: The Personal Quest*, pp. 71–85, Melbourne: Oxford University Press, 1989.

Conacaud, Judith, 'Donald Horne: A Biographical Study', *Melbourne Journal of Politics* 11 (1979), pp. 34–44.

Crawford, Robert, 'Supporting Banks, Liberals and the Australian Way: The Freelands and the 1949 Election', *History Australia* 2, no. 3 (2005), pp. 1–23.

Crosland, C.A.R., 'New Moods, Old Problems: On Politics in the Welfare State', *Encounter* 16, no. 2 (February 1961), pp. 3–6.

—— 'Radical Reform and the Left', *Encounter* 15 (October 1960).

Curran, James, '"Australia Should Be There": Expo 67 and the Search For a New National Image', *Australian Historical Studies* 39, no. 1 (2008), pp. 72–90.

Curtain, John, 'Peter Coleman's *Australian Civilization* and Its Successors', *Publishing Studies* 4 (Autumn 1997), pp. 45–49.

Darwin, John, 'Decolonization and the End of Empire', in Robin Winks (ed.), *The Oxford History of the British Empire, Volume V: Historiography*, pp. 541–57, Oxford: Oxford University Press, 1999.

Davidson, Jim, 'Notes on a Nationalist', *Meanjin* 30, no. 4 (December 1971), pp. 440–46.

Davis, Glyn, 'The Endless Seminar', *Griffith Review* 28 (2010), pp. 130–61.

—— 'A Public Intellectual: The Life and Times of Donald Horne', in Nick Horne (ed.), *Donald Horne: Selected Writings*, pp. ix–xlix, Carlton: La Trobe University Press, 2017.

Dermody, Kathleen, 'Ross Francis Gollan (1902–1961), in John Ritchie (ed.), *Australian Dictionary of Biography Volume 14, 1940–1980; Di–Kel*, Carlton South: Melbourne University Press, 1996.

Eather, Warwick and Cottle, Drew, 'The Mobilisation of Capital behind the "Battle for Freedom": The Sydney Banks, The Institute of Public Affairs (NSW) and Opposition to the Australian Labor Party 1944–49', *Labour History* 103 (2012), pp. 165–85.

Garton, Stephen, 'Private Life of a Public Man', Eulogy delivered at Donald Horne's funeral, 21 September 2005, republished in *Griffith Review*, December 2005.

Griffin-Foley, Bridget, '"The Crumbs Are Better than a Feast Elsewhere": Australian Journalists on Fleet Street', in Carl Bridge, Robert Crawford and David Dunstan (eds), *Australians in Britain: The Twentieth-Century Experience*, pp. 08.1–19, Clayton: Monash University ePress, 2009.

—— 'McNulty, Clarence Sydney (1903–1964)', *Australian Dictionary of Biography Volume 15 1940–1980: Kem–Pie*, Carlton South: Melbourne University Press, 2000.

—— 'Operating on "an Intelligent Level": Cadet Training at Consolidated Press in the 1940s', in Ann Curthoys and Julianne Schultz (eds), *Journalism: Print, Politics and Popular Culture*, pp. 142–54, St Lucia: University of Queensland Press, 1999.

Hall, Sandra, Marion Macdonald and Sandra Forbes, 'Charismatic Editor, Mentor and Master of the Long Lunch', *The Sydney Morning Herald*, 9 September 2005.

Hartcher, Peter, 'Are We There Yet?', *The Sydney Morning Herald*, 10 September 2005.

Hesketh, Rollo, 'A.A. Phillips and the "Cultural Cringe": Creating an "Australian Tradition"', *Meanjin* 72, no. 3 (2013), pp. 92–103.

Horne, Julia, 'Donald Horne and the Lucky Country', ISAA Conference Proceedings, Independent Scholars Association of Australia Inc., 2014, pp. 16–22.

—— 'An Armchair, a Desk, and 4000 Books: The Horne Family Study Gets a Second Life', *The Conversation*, 23 May 2018.

Horne, Nick, and Michel Baume, 'Oh Lucky Man?', *The Spectator* (Australia), 8 November 2014.

Inglis, Ken, 'Opening the Windows in a Stuffy Room', *Inside Story*, 26 September 2018.

Jacoby, Russell, 'The Latest Intellectuals', *Chronicle of Higher Education*, 29 November 2015.

James, Clive, 'Renegade at the Lectern', *The Monthly*, June 2005.

Kinnane, Garry, 'Johnston, George Henry (1912–1970)', in John Ritchie (ed.), *Australian Dictionary of Biography Volume 14, 1940–1980; Di–Kel*, Carlton South: Melbourne University Press, 1996.

Krygier, Richard, 'The Making of a Cold Warrior: The Prehistory of the Australian Association', *Quadrant* 30, no. 11 (November 1986), pp. 38–43.

Luckins, Tanja, 'Cosmopolitanism and the Cosmopolitans: Australia in the World, the World in Australia', in Shirleene Robinson and Julie Ustinoff (eds), *The 1960s in Australia: People, Power and Politics*, pp. 51–68, Cambridge: Cambridge Scholars Publishing, 2012.

Manne, Robert, 'The Whitlam Revolution', in Robert Manne (ed.), *The Australian Century: Political Struggle in the Building of a Nation*, pp. 179–223, Melbourne: Text, 1999.

Manning, Peter, 'Donald Horne', in Richard Walsh (ed.), *Great Australian Eulogies* (Sydney: Allen & Unwin, 2008), pp. 69–74.

McAuley, James, 'On Being an Intellectual', *Quadrant* 4, no. 1 (Summer 1959–1960), pp. 23–31.

—— 'Culture and Counter-Culture', 1976 Latham Lecture, *Quadrant* 20, no, 9 (September 1976).

McCarthy, John, 'The "Great Betrayal" Reconsidered: An Australian Perspective', *Australian Journal of International Affairs* 48, no. 1 (1994), pp. 59–66.

McDonald, James, 'A Good Sheep Station Ruined', *Australian Journal of Biography and History* no. 2 (2019), pp. 35–47.

McKenna, Mark, '"National Awakening", Autobiography and the Invention of Manning Clark', *Life Writing* 13, no. 2 (2016), pp. 207–20.

McLaren, John, 'Peace Wars: The 1959 ANZ Peace Congress', *Labour History* 82 (May 2002), pp. 97–108.

Meaney, Neville, 'Britishness and Australian Identity: The Problem of Nationalism in Australian History and Historiography', *Australian Historical Studies* 32, no. 116 (2001), pp. 76–90.

Melleuish, Greg, 'Donald Horne and the Idea of a Public Culture', *Quadrant* 36, no. 6 (June 1992), pp. 46–52.

Moorhouse, Frank, 'How Australian Dining Began to Shift in the 1960s', *Gourmet Traveller*, 14 December 2016.

O'Neil, W.M., 'Anderson, John (1893–1962)', *Australian Dictionary of Biography Volume 7, 1891–1939: A–Ch*, Canberra: Melbourne University Press, 1979.

Orwell, George, 'Notes on Nationalism' (1945), in *George Orwell: Collected Essays*, pp. 281–303, London: Seeker & Warburg, 1961.

Pemberton, Jo-Anne, '"O Brave New Social Order": The Controversy over Planning in Australia and Britain in the 1940s', *Journal of Australian Studies* 28, no. 83 (2004), pp. 35–47.

Pender, Anne, 'The Mythical Australian: Barry Humphries, Gough Whitlam and "New Nationalism"', *Australian Journal of Politics and History* 51, no. 1 (2005), pp. 67–78.

Phillips, A.A., 'The Cultural Cringe', *Meanjin* 9, no. 4 (Summer 1950), pp. 299–302.

Rees, Yves, 'The Pioneering Envoy Who "Waged War" on Canberra', *Inside Story*, 7 March 2019.

Reinecke, Carl, 'The Vanishing Point: The Story of the Publication of *The Lucky Country*', *Meanjin* 75, no. 2 (Winter 2016), pp. 42–52.

—— '*The Lucky Country* Turns Fifty', *Inside Story*, 1 December 2014.

Rickard, John, 'Sydney: The Class of '51', *Australian Historical Studies* 27 (1997), pp. 171–76.

Roe, Jill, 'Elliott, Sumner Locke (1917–91)', *Australian Dictionary of Biography Volume 19: 1991–1995, A–Z*, Acton: ANU Press, 2014.

Rowse, Tim, 'Coombs the Keynesian', in Samuel Furphy (ed.), *The Seven Dwarfs and the Age of the Mandarins: Government Administration in the Post-War Reconstruction Era*, pp. 143–67, Canberra: ANU Press, 2015.

—— 'Culture as Myth, Criticism as Irony: The Middle-Class Patriotism of Donald Horne', *Island* 37 (Spring 1988), pp. 12–22.

Ryan, Peter, 'Donald Horne: A Self-Made Man', *Quadrant* 42, no. 9 (August 1998), pp. 28–33.

Summy, Ralph and Malcolm Saunders, 'The 1959 Melbourne Peace Congress: Culmination of Anti-Communism in Australian in the 1950s', in Ann Curthoys and John Merritt (eds), *Better Dead Than Red: Australia's First Cold War: 1945–1959, Volume 2*, pp. 74–98, Sydney: Allen & Unwin, 1986.

Thomas, Mark, 'Donald Horne', in Mark Thomas, *Australia in Mind: Thirteen Influential Australian Thinkers*, pp. 115–32, Sydney: Hale & Iremonger, 1989.

Turner, Ian, 'Australian Nationalism and Australian History', *Journal of Australian Studies* 3, no. 4 (1979), pp. 1–11.

Ward, Stuart, 'The "New Nationalism" in Australia, Canada and New Zealand: Civic Culture in the Wake of the British World', in Kate Darian-Smith, Stuart Macintyre and Patricia Grimshaw (eds), *Britishness Abroad: Transnational Movements and Imperial Cultures*, pp. 231–63, Melbourne: Melbourne University Press, 2007.

—— '"Culture up to Our Arseholes": Projecting Post-Imperial Australia', *Australian Journal of Politics and History* 51, no. 1 (2005), pp. 53–66.

Wheatley, Nadia, 'Clift, Charmian (1923–1969)', *Australian Dictionary of Biography Volume 13 1940–1980: A–De*, Carlton: Melbourne University Press, 1993.

Wilson, Ian, 'Professor Brian Beddie, 1920–1994', *ANU Reporter*, 23 March 1994.

Wynhausen, Elisabeth, 'Death of the Lucky Country or Birth of Donald Horne, the Conservative Radical?', *National Times*, 8 March 1976.

BOOKS

Adams, Paul, *The Stranger from Melbourne: Frank Hardy, a Literary Biography 1944–1975*, Nedlands: UWA Press, 1999.

Alomes, Stephen, *A Nation at Last? The Changing Character of Australian Nationalism 1880–1988*, North Ryde: Angus & Robertson, 1988.

—— *When London Calls: The Expatriation of Australian Creative Artists to Britain*, Melbourne: Cambridge University Press, 1999.

Anderson, David, *Histories of the Hanged: Britain's Dirty War in Kenya and the End of Empire*, London: Weidenfeld and Nicolson, 2005.

Appleton, Gillian, *Diamond Cuts: An Affectionate Memoir of Jim McClelland*, Sydney: Pan Macmillan, 2000.

Arena, Franca, *Franca: My Story*, Sydney: Simon and Schuster, 2002.

Armstrong, Pauline, *Frank Hardy and the Making of 'Power Without Glory'*, Carlton South, Melbourne University Press, 2000.

Baker, A.J., *Australian Realism: The Systematic Philosophy of John Anderson*, Cambridge: Cambridge University Press, 1986.

Barcan, Alan, *Radical Students: The Old Left at Sydney University*, Carlton South: Melbourne University Press, 2002.

Bartlett, C.J., *A History of Postwar Britain 1945–1974*, London: Longman, 1977.

Bashford, Alison and Stuart Macintyre (eds), *The Cambridge History of Australia Volume 2: The Commonwealth of Australia*, Port Melbourne: Cambridge University Press, 2013.

Beaumont, Joan (ed.), *Australia's War, 1939–45*, St Leonards: Allen & Unwin, 1996.

Bennett, Bruce and Anne Pender, *From a Distant Shore: Australian Writers in Britain 1820–2012*, Clayton: Monash University Publishing, 2013.

Bennett, Huw, *Fighting the Mau Mau: The British Army and Counter-Insurgency in the Kenya Emergency*, Cambridge: Cambridge University Press, 2012.

Berman, Bruce and John Lonsdale, *Unhappy Valley: Conflict in Kenya and Africa*, London: J. Currey, 1992.

Bloom, Alan, *The Closing of the American Mind: How Higher Education Has Failed Democracy and Impoverished the Souls of Today's Students*, New York : Simon and Schuster, 1987.

Boggs, Carl, *Gramsci's Marxism*, London: Pluto Press, 1976.

Bolton, Geoffrey, *The Oxford History of Australia Volume 5, 1942–1988: The Middle Way*, Melbourne: Oxford University Press, 1993.

Booker, Christopher, *The Neophiliacs*, London: Collins, 1969.

Bongiorno, Frank, *The Eighties: The Decade That Transformed Australia*, Collingwood: Black Inc., 2015.

—— *Dreamers and Schemers: A Political History of Australia*, Collingwood: La Trobe University Press, 2022.

Boston, Ray, *The Essential Fleet Street: Its History and Influence*, London: Blandford, 1990.

Boyd, Robin, *The Australian Ugliness*, Melbourne: F.W. Cheshire, 1960.

Brett, Judith, *Australian Liberals and the Moral Middle Class*, Cambridge: Cambridge University Press, 2003.

—— *Robert Menzies' Forgotten People*, Chippendale: Macmillan, 1992.

Brown, Nicholas, *A History of Canberra*, Port Melbourne: Cambridge University Press, 2014.

—— *Governing Prosperity: Social Change and Social Analysis in Australia in the 1950s*, Cambridge: Cambridge University Press, 1995.

Buckley, Vincent, *Cutting Green Hay: Friendships, Movements and Cultural Conflicts in Australia's Great Decades*, Melbourne: Penguin, 1983.

Buckridge, Patrick, *The Scandalous Penton: A Biography of Brian Penton*, St Lucia: University of Queensland Press, 1994.

Burgmann, Verity, *Power and Protest: Movements for Change in Australian Society*, Sydney: Allen & Unwin, 1992.

Campion, Edmund, *Rockchoppers: Growing up Catholic in Australia*, Ringwood: Penguin, 1982.

Capp, Fiona, *Writers Defiled*, Melbourne: McPhee Gribble, 1993.

Carpenter, Humphrey, *The Angry Young Men: A Literary Comedy of the 1950s*, London: Penguin Books, 2002.

Carter, David (ed.), *The Ideas Market: An Alternative Take on Australia's Intellectual Life*, Carlton,: Melbourne University Press, 2004.

Childs, David, *Britain Since 1939: Progress and Decline*, 2nd ed., Hampshire: Palgrave, 2002.

Coleman, Peter, *Memoirs of a Slow Learner*, Pymble: Angus and Robertson, 1994.

—— *The Liberal Conspiracy: The Congress for Cultural Freedom and the Struggle for the Mind of Postwar Europe*, New York: Macmillan, 1989.

—— *The Heart of James McAuley: Life and Work of the Australian Poet*, Sydney: Wildcat Press, 1980.

—— (ed.), *Australian Civilization: A Symposium*, Melbourne: Cheshire, 1962.

Collini, Stefan, *Absent Minds: Intellectuals in Britain*, Oxford: Oxford University Press, 2006.

Connell, Raewyn, *Ruling Class, Ruling Culture: Studies of Conflict, Power and Hegemony in Australian Life*, Cambridge: Cambridge University Press, 1977.

Crawford, Robert, *But Wait, There's More … A History of Australian Advertising 1900–2000*, Carlton: Melbourne University Press, 2008.

Crowley, Frank, *Tough Times: Australian in the Seventies*, Melbourne: William Heinemann, 1986.

Curran, James and Stuart Ward, *The Unknown Nation: Australia After Empire*, Melbourne: Melbourne University Press, 2010.

Curran, James, *The Power of Speech: Australian Prime Ministers Defining the National Image*, Melbourne: Melbourne University Press, 2004.

—— *Curtin's Empire*, Melbourne: Cambridge University Press, 2011.

Curthoys, Ann, and John Merritt (eds), *Better Dead Than Red: Australia's First Cold War: 1945–1959*, Sydney: Allen & Unwin, 1986.

Darwin, John, *Britain and Decolonization: The Retreat from Empire in the Post-War World*, Basingstoke: Macmillan, 1988.

Davidson, Jim, *Emperors in Lilliput: Clem Christesen of Meanjin and Stephen Murray-Smith of Overland*, Melbourne: Melbourne University Press, 2022.

—— *A Three-Cornered Life: The Historian WK Hancock*, Sydney: UNSW Press, 2010.

Davidson, Jim, and Peter Spearritt, *Holiday Business: Tourism in Australia Since 1870*, Carlton: Miegunyah Press, 2000.

Day, David, *Chifley*, Sydney: HarperCollins, 2001.

—— *John Curtin: A Life*, Sydney: HarperCollins, 1999.

—— *Reluctant Nation: Australia and the Allied Defeat of Japan 1942–1945*, Melbourne: Oxford University Press, 1992.

—— *The Great Betrayal: Britain, Australia and the Onset of the Pacific War*, 1939–1942, Sydney: Angus & Robertson, 1986.

Dessaix, Robert (ed.), *Speaking Their Minds: Intellectuals and the Public Culture in Australia*, Sydney: ABC Books, 1998.

Docker, John, *Australian Cultural Elites: Intellectual Traditions in Sydney and Melbourne*, Sydney: Angus & Robertson, 1974.

—— *In a Critical Condition: Reading Australian Literature*, Ringwood: Penguin, 1984.

Dutton, Geoffrey, *A Rare Bird: Penguin Books in Australia, 1946–96*, Ringwood, Penguin, 1996.

—— *Out in the Open: An Autobiography*, St Lucia: University of Queensland Press, 1994.

—— (ed.), *Australia and the Monarchy*, Melbourne: Sun Books, 1966.

Edwards, Peter, *A Nation at War: Australian Politics, Society and Diplomacy During the Vietnam War 1965–1975*, Sydney: Allen & Unwin, 1997.

Einzig, Paul, *Decline and Fall: Britain's Crisis in the Sixties*, London: Macmillan, 1969.

Eliot, George, *Middlemarch*, London: Wordsworth Classics, 1994.

Elkins, Caroline, *Britain's Gulag: The Brutal End of Empire in Kenya*, London: Jonathan Cape, 2005.

Elliot, Brian (ed.), *The Jindyworobaks*, St Lucia: University of Queensland Press, 1979.

Ellis, Robert and Michael Boddy, *The Legend of King O'Malley*, Sydney: Angus & Robertson, 1974.

Forsyth, Hannah, *A History of the Modern Australian University*, Sydney: NewSouth, 2014.

Frankel, Boris, *From the Prophets Deserts Come*, Melbourne: Arena, 1992.

Franklin, James, *Corrupting the Youth: A History of Philosophy in Australia*, Sydney: Macleay Press, 2003.

Frame, Tom, *The Life and Death of Harold Holt*, Sydney: Allen & Unwin, 2005.

Gerster, Robin andJan Bassett, *Seizures of Youth: The Sixties and Australia*, Melbourne: Hyland House, 1991.

Gitlin, Todd, *The Sixties: Years of Hope, Days of Rage*, New York: Bantam Books, 1987.

Goldsworthy, David, *Losing the Blanket: Australia and the End of the British Empire*, Carlton South: Melbourne University Press, 2002.

Gollan, Robin, *Revolutionaries and Reformists: Communism and the Australian Labour Movement, 1920–50*, Sydney: Allen & Unwin, 1985.

Gollan, Myfanwy, *Kerr and the Consequences: The Sydney Town Hall Meeting, 20 September 1976*, Camberwell: Widescope International Publishers, 1976.

Griffen-Foley, Bridget, *The House of Packer: The Making of a Media Empire*, St Leonards: Allen & Unwin, 2000.

—— *Sir Frank Packer: The Young Master*, Sydney: HarperCollins, 2000.

Gyngell, Alan, *Fear of Abandonment: Australia and the World Since 1942*, Carlton: La Trobe University Press, 2017.

Haese, Richard, *Rebels and Precursors: The Revolutionary Years of Australian Art*, Ringwood: Penguin, 1988.

Hancock, Ian, *John Gorton: He Did It His Way*, Sydney: Hodder, 2002.

Hardy, Frank, *The Unlucky Australians*, Melbourne: Nelson, 1968.

Hartley, Anthony, *A State of England*, London: Hutchinson, 1963.

Hasluck, Paul, *Diplomatic Witness: Australian Foreign Affairs 1941–1947*, Carlton: Melbourne University Press, 1980.

Hocking, Jenny, *Gough Whitlam: His Time, Volume 1*, Carlton, Miegunyah Press, 2012.

—— *Frank Hardy: Politics, Literature, Life*, South Melbourne: Lothian Books, 2005.

Horne, Julia and Geoffrey Sherington, *Sydney: The Making of a Public University*, Carlton: Melbourne University Publishing, 2012.

Horne, Myfanwy (ed.), *Kerr and the Consequences: The Sydney Town Hall Meeting, 20 September 1976*, Camberwell: Widescope International Publishers, 1976.

Horne, Nick (ed.), *Donald Horne: Selected Writings*, Carlton: La Trobe University Press, 2017.

Horner, David, *The Spy Catchers: The Official History of ASIO, 1949–1963*, Crows Nest: Allen & Unwin, 2014.

—— *The Gunners: A History of Australian Artillery*, St Leonards: Allen & Unwin, 1995.

Howard, John, *The Menzies Era*, Sydney: HarperCollins, 2014.

Hughes, Robert, *Things I Didn't Know: A Memoir*, North Sydney: Vintage, 2007.

Jacoby, Russell, *The Last Intellectuals: American Culture in the Age of Academe*, New York: Basic Books, 1987.

Judt, Tony, *Postwar: A History of Europe Since 1945*, London: William Heinemann, 2005.

Kelly, Dominic, *Economic Troglodytes and Political Lunatics: The Hard Right in Australia*, Carlton: La Trobe University Press, 2019.

Kennedy, Brian, *A Passion to Oppose: John Anderson, Philosopher*, Carlton South: Melbourne University Press, 1995.

Kerr, John, *Matters for Judgement: An Autobiography*, Artarmon: Macmillan, 1978.

King, Peter (ed.), *Australia's Vietnam: Australia in the Second Indo-China War*, Sydney: Allen & Unwin, 1993.

Kinnane, Garry, *George Johnston*, Ringwood: Penguin, 1986.

Koestler, Arthur (ed.), *Suicide of a Nation: An Enquiry into the State of Britain Today*, London: Hutchinson, 1963.

Kynaston, David, *Austerity Britain 1945–51*, London: Bloomsbury, 2007.

Langley, Greg, *A Decade of Dissent: Vietnam and the Conflict on the Australian Homefront*, Sydney: Allen & Unwin, 1992.

Lowe, David, *Menzies and the 'Great World Struggle': 1949–1954*, Sydney: UNSW Press, 1999.

MacCallum, Mungo, *The Whitlam Mob*, Collingwood: Black Inc., 2014.

Macdonnell, Justin, *Arts, Minister?: Government Policy and the Arts*, Sydney: Currency Press, 1992.

Macintyre, Stuart, *Australia's Boldest Experiment: War and Reconstruction in the 1940s*, Sydney: NewSouth, 2015.

—— *A Concise History of Australia*, 3rd ed., Melbourne: Cambridge University Press, 2009.

—— *The Oxford History of Australia Volume 4, 1901–1942: The Succeeding Age*, Melbourne: Oxford University Press, 1993.

Mander, John, *Great Britain or Little England?*, Harmondsworth: Penguin, 1963.

Manne, Robert (ed.), *The Australian Century*, Melbourne: Text Publishing, 1999.

—— *The Shadow of 1917: Cold War Conflict in Australia*, Melbourne: Text Publishing, 1994.

—— *The Petrov Affair*, Sydney: Pergamon, 1987.

Marwick, Arthur, *The Sixties: Cultural Revolution in Britain, France, Italy and the United States, c.1958–c.1974*, Oxford: Oxford University Press, 1998.

McClelland, James, *Stirring the Possum: A Political Autobiography*, Ringwood: Penguin, 1989.

McGregor, Craig, *Profile of Australia*, London: Hodder & Stoughton, 1966.

McKenna, Mark, *The Captive Republic: A History of Republicanism in Australia 1988–1996*, Melbourne: Cambridge University Press, 1996.

—— *An Eye for Eternity: The Life of Manning Clark*, Carlton: Miegunyah Press, 2011.

McKernan, Susan, *A Question of Commitment: Australian Literature in the Twenty Years After the War*, Sydney: Allen & Unwin, 1995.

McLaren, John, *Writing in Hope and Fear: Literature as Politics in Postwar Australia*, Cambridge: Cambridge University Press, 1996.

McLaren, John, *Free Radicals of the Left in Postwar Melbourne*, Melbourne: Australian Scholarly Publishing, 2003.

Monk, L.A., *Britain 1945–1970*, London: G. Bell and Sons, 1976.

Moorhouse, Frank, *Conference-ville*, North Sydney: Vintage, 2008 [1976].

—— *Days of Wine and Rage*, Ringwood: Penguin, 1980.

Morrison, Blake, *The Movement: English Poetry and Fiction of the 1950s*, Oxford: Oxford University Press, 1980.

Morgan, Kenneth O., *Britain Since 1945: The People's Peace*, 3rd ed., Oxford: Oxford University Press, 2001.

Morton, Peter, *Lusting for London: Australian Expatriate Writers at the Hub of Empire, 1870–1950*, New York: Palgrave Connect, 2011.

Mullins, Patrick, *The Trials of Portnoy: How Penguin Brought Down Australia's Censorship System*, Melbourne: Scribe, 2020.

Murphy, John, *Imagining the Fifties: Private Sentiment and Political Culture in Menzies' Australia*, Sydney: UNSW Press, 2000.

—— *Harvest of Fear: A History of Australia's Vietnam War*, Sydney: Allen & Unwin, 1993.

Nolan, Sybil (ed.), *The Dismissal: Where Were You on November 11, 1975?* Carlton: Melbourne University Press, 2015.

Osmond, Warren, *The Dilemma of an Australian Sociology: An Analysis of 'Equality and Authority'*, Melbourne, Arena Publications, 1972.

Palmer, Vance and Nettie Palmer, *The Legend of the Nineties*, Melbourne: Melbourne University Press, 1954.

Passmore, John, *Memoirs of a Semi-Detached Australian*, Melbourne: Melbourne University Press, 1997.

Pemberton, Gregory (ed.), *Vietnam Remembered*, Sydney: New Holland, 2002.

Penton, Brian, *Censored! Being a True Account of a Noble Fight for Your Right to Read and Know, with Some Comment upon the Plague of Censorship in General*, Sydney: Shakespeare Head, 1947.

—— *Advance Australia – Where?*, London: Cassell, 1943.

—— *Think – or Be Damned: A Subversive Note on National Pride, Patriotism and other forms of Respectable Ostrichism Practices in Australia*, Sydney: Angus & Robertson, 1941.

Pesman, Ros, *Duty Free: Australian Women Abroad*, Melbourne: Oxford University Press, 1996.

Phillips, A.A., *The Australian Tradition: Studies in Colonial Culture*, Melbourne: F.W. Cheshire, 1958.

Posner, Richard A., *Public Intellectuals: A Study of Decline*, Cambridge: Harvard University Press, 2001.

Pringle, John Douglas, *Australian Accent*, London: Chatto and Windus, 1958.

Pybus, Cassandra, *The Devil and James McAuley*, St Lucia: University of Queensland Press, 1999.

—— *Gross Moral Turpitude: The Orr Case Revisited*, Sydney: William Heinemann Australia, 1993.

Ray, Sibnarayan, *Vietnam: Seen from East and West*, Melbourne: Nelson, 1966.

Reid, Alan, *The Gorton Experiment: The Fall of John Grey Gorton*, Sydney: Shakespeare Head Press, 1971.

Ritchie, Harry, *Success Stories: Literature and the Media in England 1950–59*, London: Faber & Faber, 1989.

Rolfe, Patricia, *The Journalistic Javelin: An Illustrated History of The Bulletin*, Sydney: Wildcat Press, 1979.

—— *No Love Lost*, London: Macmillan, 1965.

Rowse, Tim, *Australian Liberalism and the National Character*, Melbourne: Kibble Books, 1978.

Ryan, Susan, and Troy Bramston (eds), *The Hawke Government: A Critical Retrospective*, Melbourne: Pluto Press, 2003.

Sampson, Anthony, *Anatomy of Britain*, London: Hodder & Stoughton, 1961.

Saunders, Frances Stonor, *Who Paid the Piper?: The CIA and the Cultural Cold War*, London: Granta, 1999.

Serle, Geoffrey, *From Deserts the Prophets Come: The Creative Spirit in Australia 1799–1972*, rev. ed., Melbourne: Heinemann, 1987.

Shanks, Michael, *The Stagnant Society: A Warning*, Harmondsworth: Penguin, 1961.

Sligo, Graham, *The Backroom Boys: Alfred Conlon and the Army's Directorate of Research and Civil Affairs 1942–46*, Newport: Big Sky Publishing, 2012.

Strahan, Lynne, *Just City and the Mirrors: Meanjin Quarterly and the Intellectual Front 1940–1965*, Melbourne: Oxford University Press, 1984.

Sutherland, John, *Stephen Spender: The Authorised Biography*, London: Viking, 2004.

Thomas, Mark, *Gangland: Cultural Elites and the New Generationalism*, Sydney: Allen & Unwin, 1997.

Tolstoy, Leo, *War and Peace*, Ringwood: Penguin, 1978.

Townsend, Helen, *The Baby Boomers: Growing Up in Australian in the 1940s, '50s and '60s*, Sydney: Simon & Schuster, 1988.

van Reyk, Paul, *True to the Land: A History of Food in Australia*, London: Reaktion Books, 2021.

Walker, David, *Stranded Nation: White Australia in an Asian Region*, Crawley: UWA Publishing, 2019.

Ward, Russel, *The Australian Legend*, Melbourne: Oxford University Press, 1958.

Ward, Stuart, *Untied Kingdom: A Global History of the End of Britain*, Cambridge: Cambridge University Press, 2023.

—— *Australia and the British Embrace: The Demise of the Imperial Ideal*, Carlton South: Melbourne University Press, 2001.

Waters, Christopher, *The Empire Fractures: Anglo-Australian Conflict in the 1940s*, Melbourne: Australian Scholarly Publishing, 1995.

Wheatley, Nadia, *The Life and Myth of Charmian Clift*, Pymble: HarperCollins, 2001.

White, Richard, *Inventing Australia*, Sydney: Allen & Unwin, 1981.

Whitlam, Nicholas and Stubbs, John, *Nest of Traitors: The Petrov Affair*, Milton: Jacaranda Press, 1974.

Williams, John, *The Quarantined Culture: Australian Reactions to Modernism 1913–1939*, New York: Cambridge University Press, 1995.

Woolcott, Richard, *The Hot Seat: Reflections on Diplomacy from Stalin's Death to the Bali Bombings*, Sydney: HarperCollins, 2003.

UNPUBLISHED THESES

Clausen, Mads, 'The Vortex Is Here: Asia and Australian Post-Imperial Nationhood', PhD thesis, University of Copenhagen, 2009.

Hesketh, Rollo, 'In Search of a National Idea': Australian Intellectuals and the Cultural Cringe, 1940–1972', PhD thesis, University of Sydney, 2018.

White, Paul, 'Donald Horne: Towards an Intellectual Biography', Honours thesis, 1979, Horne Papers, MLMSS 3525 Add on 1871, Box 11.

IMAGE CREDITS

Donald Horne as a schoolboy (p. 9): image courtesy of Charles Woolley.

John Anderson, c. 1926 (p. 13): photographer unknown; image courtesy of the National Library of Australia.

Brian Penton, c. 1931 (p. 20): photographer unknown; image courtesy of the National Library of Australia.

Donald Horne reading to a group of soldiers (p. 28): image courtesy of Charles Woolley.

Elisabeth Lambert, 20 November 1947 (p. 40): photograph by Frederick Stanley Grimes; image courtesy of Mitchell Library, State Library of New South Wales and ACP Magazines Ltd.

Donald and Ethel Horne with Janet, Donald's sister (p. 49): image courtesy of Charles Woolley.

Donald Horne [left] at Stonehenge (p. 62): image from the Horne family collection, courtesy of Julia and Nick Horne.

Donald Horne [right] in England (p. 71): image from the Horne family collection, courtesy of Julia and Nick Horne.

Ethel Horne (p. 78): image courtesy of Charles Woolley.

Donald Horne, early 1950s (p 90): image courtesy of Charles Woolley.

Donald and Myfanwy Horne on their wedding day (p. 118): image from the Horne family collection, courtesy of Julia and Nick Horne.

Donald and Myfanwy Horne at dinner (p. 134): image from the Horne family collection, courtesy of Julia and Nick Horne.

Donald Horne in front of the Taj Mahal, 1963 (p. 149): image from the Horne family collection, courtesy of Julia and Nick Horne.

Donald Horne having dinner with friends, c. 1965 (p. 172): photograph by Robert McFarlane, courtesy of Josef Lebovic Gallery and the National Library of Australia.

Donald Horne addressing a dinner in Tokyo, 1967 (p. 191): image from the Horne family collection, courtesy of Julia and Nick Horne.

Donald Horne [left] speaking with Peter Manning and Gough Whitlam (p. 200): image courtesy of Peter Manning.

Myfanwy Horne in the Hornes' study in 1973 (p. 202): image from the Horne family collection, courtesy of Julia and Nick Horne.

Donald Horne speaking at an anti-Kerr rally in November 1975 (p. 222): image courtesy of Mitchell Library, State Library of New South Wales, SEARCH Foundation.

1976 George Molnar cartoon depicting Gough Whitlam riding a chariot pulled by Donald Horne, Germaine Greer, Manning Clark and Patrick White (p. 227): cartoon by George Molnar, published in *Quadrant*, September 1976; image courtesy of Katie Molnar.

One of the index cards Donald Horne used for recording his research notes (p. 237): photograph by the author.

Donald and Myfanwy Horne in Europe in the late 1970s (p. 243): image from the Horne family collection, courtesy of Julia and Nick Horne.

Donald Horne and his fellow members of the Australian Republican Movement in 1991 (p. 267): photographer unknown: from Geoffrey Dutton, *Out Into the Open: An Autobiography*, University of Queensland Press, 1995.

INDEX

Page references in **bold** are to illustrations.